Adapting Chekhov

Routledge Advances in Theatre and Performance Studies

1 **Theatre and Postcolonial Desires**
Awam Amkpa

2 **Brecht and Critical Theory**
Dialectics and Contemporary
Aesthetics
Sean Carney

3 **Science and the Stanislavsky**
Tradition of Acting
Jonathan Pitches

4 **Performance and Cognition**
Theatre Studies and the Cognitive
Turn
Edited by Bruce McConachie and
F. Elizabeth Hart

5 **Theatre and Performance in**
Digital Culture
From Simulation to
Embeddedness
Matthew Causey

6 **The Politics of New Media**
Theatre
Life®™
Gabriella Giannachi

7 **Ritual and Event**
Interdisciplinary Perspectives
Edited by Mark Franko

8 **Memory, Allegory, and**
Testimony in South American
Theater
Upstaging Dictatorship
Ana Elena Puga

9 **Crossing Cultural Borders**
Through the Actor's Work
Foreign Bodies of Knowledge
Cláudia Tatinge Nascimento

10 **Movement Training for the**
Modern Actor
Mark Evans

11 **The Politics of American Actor**
Training
Edited by Ellen Margolis and
Lissa Tyler Renaud

12 **Performing Embodiment in**
Samuel Beckett's Drama
Anna McMullan

13 **The Provocation of the Senses in**
Contemporary Theatre
Stephen Di Benedetto

14 **Ecology and Environment in**
European Drama
Downing Cless

15 **Global Ibsen**
Performing Multiple Modernities
Edited by Erika Fischer-Lichte,
Barbara Gronau, and Christel
Weiler

16 **The Theatre of the Bauhaus**
The Modern and Postmodern
Stage of Oskar Schlemmer
Melissa Trimingham

Adapting Chekhov
The Text and its Mutations

**Edited by J. Douglas Clayton
and Yana Meerzon**

NEW YORK AND LONDON

First published 2013
by Routledge
711 Third Avenue, New York, NY 10017

Simultaneously published in the UK
by Routledge
2 Park Square, Milton Park, Abingdon, Oxfordshire OX14 4RN

First issued in paperback 2015

*Routledge is an imprint of the Taylor & Francis Group,
an informa business*

© 2013 Taylor & Francis

The right of the editor to be identified as the author of the editorial
material, and of the authors for their individual chapters, has been asserted
in accordance with sections 77 and 78 of the Copyright, Designs and
Patents Act 1988.

All rights reserved. No part of this book may be reprinted or reproduced or
utilised in any form or by any electronic, mechanical, or other means, now
known or hereafter invented, including photocopying and recording, or in
any information storage or retrieval system, without permission in writing
from the publishers.

Trademark Notice: Product or corporate names may be trademarks or
registered trademarks, and are used only for identification and explanation
without intent to infringe.

Library of Congress Cataloging-in-Publication Data
   Adapting Chekhov : the text and its mutations / edited by J. Douglas
Clayton & Yana Meerzon.
       p. cm. — (Routledge advances in theatre and performance studies ;
23)
   Includes bibliographical references and index.
   1.   Chekhov, Anton Pavlovich, 1860–1904—Criticism and
interpretation. 2.   Chekhov, Anton Pavlovich, 1860–1904—Adaptations.
   I. Clayton, J. Douglas.   II. Meerzon, Yana.
   PG3458.Z8A33 2012
   891.72'3—dc23
   2012003918

ISBN 13: 978-1-138-93767-3 (pbk)
ISBN 13: 978-0-415-50969-5 (hbk)

Typeset in Sabon
by IBT Global.

Contents

List of Figures	xi
Foreword	xv
CARYL EMERSON	
Acknowledgments	xvii
Introduction: The Text and its Mutations—On the Objectives of the Volume	1
J. DOUGLAS CLAYTON AND YANA MEERZON	

PART I
On Categories, Techniques, and Methodologies of Mutation

1 Diagnosis and Balagan: The Poetics of Chekhov's Drama 17
J. DOUGLAS CLAYTON

2 Rewriting Chekhov in Russia Today:
Questioning a Fragmented Society and
Finding New Aesthetic Reference Points 32
MARIE-CHRISTINE AUTANT-MATHIEU

3 The Flight of the Dead Bird: Chekhov's
The Seagull and Williams's *The Notebook of Trigorin* 57
MARIA IGNATIEVA

4 Talking and Walking Past Each Other:
Chekhovian "Echoes" in Czech Drama and Theatre 68
VERONIKA AMBROS

viii *Contents*

5   Howard Barker's *(Uncle) Vanya*:
    Chekhov Shaken, Not Stirred   87
    CHARLES LAMB

PART II
Chekhov in the Post[ist] Context

6   Transtextual Crossbreeds in Post-Communist Context:
    An Anthropological Analysis of Horia Gârbea's
    The Seagull from the Cherry Orchard   109
    DIANA MANOLE

7   Chekhov in the Age of Globalization:
    Janusz Glowacki's *The Fourth Sister*   128
    MAGDA ROMANSKA

8   Theatre and Subaltern Histories:
    Chekhov Adaptation in Post-Colonial India   145
    BISHNUPRIYA DUTT

9   What Comes "After Chekhov"? Mustapha Matura
    and West Indian Reiterations of *Three Sisters*   161
    VICTORIA PETTERSEN LANTZ

10 From Moscow to Ballybeg: Brian Friel's Richly
    Metabiotic Relationship with Anton Chekhov   180
    MARTINE PELLETIER

PART III
Performing Chekhov in Radical Mutations

11 Daniel Veronese's "Proyecto Chéjov":
    Translation in Performance as Radical Relationality   203
    JEAN GRAHAM-JONES

12 Canadian Chekhovs: Three Very Different Mutations   217
    JAMES MCKINNON

Contents ix

13 The Work of the Theatre: The Wooster Group
Adapts Chekhov's *Three Sisters* in *Fish Story*   238
SHEILA RABILLARD

14 The Japanization of Chekhov:
Contemporary Japanese Adaptations of *Three Sisters*   261
YASUSHI NAGATA

15 Interrogating the Real: Chekhov's Cinema of Verbatim.
"Ward Number Six" in Karen Shakhnazarov's
2009 Film Adaptation   274
YANA MEERZON

Afterword: On Chekhov, Adaptation, and
Wonders of Writing Plays: Dialogue with Patrice Pavis,
J. Douglas Clayton, and Yana Meerzon   295

Contributors   305
Index   309

Figures

0.1 A scene from *The Seagull from the Cherry Orchard* by
     Horia Gârbea at the V.I.Popa Theatre in Bârlad, Romania. xiii
7.1 A scene from Janusz Glowacki's *The Fourth Sister*, Polish
     Television Theatre (1999). 130

Figure 0.1 A scene from *The Seagull from the Cherry Orchard* by Horia Gârbea at the V.I.Popa Theatre in Bârlad, Romania (1992). With: Marcel Anghel (Nikolai), Virgil Leahu (Vanea), Lili Popa (Nora). Set and costume design by Rodica Arghir. Directed and Photo by Bogdan Ulmu.

Foreword

Caryl Emerson

Watson Armour III University Professor of
Slavic Languages and Literatures, Princeton University

This book appeals to the huge Chekhov market (grown even larger after this sesquicentennial year) as well as to the growing interest in "adaptation" as a permanent feature of globalized culture, even as a valuable communication channel when other forms of international relations fail. Collectively, contributors suggest reasons for the surprising transposability and malleability of this most enigmatic, nonideological, and refined of Russian playwrights.

Among the organizing ideas/schools drawn upon for this project, one finds Russian Formalism (especially its idea of creative estrangement, *ostranenie*), the Tartu-Moscow School of Cultural Semiotics (with its concept of the spatial event), and Linda Hutcheon's seminal *A Theory of Adaptation* (2006), with its understanding of "repetition that is not duplication." In her case studies, Hutcheon allots more space to opera and film adaptation than to spoken theatre. The present volume supplements that emphasis, building on her categories in ways crucial to the dramatic stage. It also targets genre rather than narrative per se, moving attention away from the ever-popular and accessible question of "changing the story" (invariably accompanied by "fidelity wars") to something more deep-wired and genetic.

The contributors to this volume claim that Chekhov—and perhaps by extension any classic author—functions as an "intricate mechanism" that produces two types of aesthetic estrangement. The first is the more familiar, an invitation to later authors to alter or vary a canonical text by reconfiguring its plot. This is first-degree parody or stylization, universally practiced on conventional or authoritative texts and effective to the extent that the primary work is well known. The second procedure is the focus of the Clayton/Meerzon collection, more ambitious and systemically interventionist, which resembles a laboratory experiment rather than an isolated act of parody per se. It concentrates less on the surface recombination of characters, events, locations, and eras (although such moves always play a role), aiming instead to define and then to remake the substratum, to address the canonical play not only as the carrier of a story, but as a dramatic organism whose story is itself conditioned by the rules it sets for itself. These rules are all the more exciting to discover in a mutated text that, like any loving offspring, both challenges and pays homage to its venerable parent.

Acknowledgments

The book *Adapting Chekhov: The Text and its Mutations* is a new step in the ongoing collaboration between Professor J. Douglas Clayton (Department of Modern Languages and Literatures, University of Ottawa, Canada) and Yana Meerzon (Department of Theatre, University of Ottawa, Canada). This collaboration started a number of years ago with the 2004 workshop "Anton Pavlovich Chekhov: Poetics, Hermeneutics, Thematics"; organized by Professor Clayton and the Department of Modern Languages and Literatures, University of Ottawa.

The current volume and the project itself have had some significant milestones. The project received its inspiration from the curated panel on dramatic adaptations of Chekhov's corpus today titled "Generative Chekhov" and organized by Karen Bamford (Mount Allison University, Canada) for the 2010 annual meeting and conference of the Canadian Association for Theatre Research (CATR) that took place at Concordia University in Montreal, as part of the Congress of the Humanities and Social Sciences, Canada. This seminar was important in establishing some leading themes and ideas discussed in the current book. Hence, the coeditors would like to thank James McKinnon (Victoria University of Wellington, New Zealand) and Sheila Rabillard (University of Victoria, Canada), who were able to share their views on contemporary Canadian and American performative adaptations of Chekhov's works back in 2010, and also contributed to this collection with the final versions of their chapters.

The coeditors would also like to pay a special tribute to Professor Elinor Fuchs (Yale University, United States) for supporting this project at its very early stages. A special "thank you" goes to Professor Caryl Emerson (Princeton University, United States) and Professor Patrice Pavis (University of Paris; School of Arts, the University of Kent in Canterbury; and Department of Theatre Studies of the Korea National University of the Arts in Seoul) for their deep insights and advice on the project.

Finally, but most significantly, we would like to express our gratitude to all those scholars who contributed to this volume for their generous ideas, stimulating collaboration, patience, and self-discipline.

xviii *Acknowledgments*

The editors at the Routledge Advances in Theatre & Performance Studies, Liz Levine and Catherine Tung, have been extremely kind in the process of taking this project further. Their constant attention, precise feedback, ongoing support, and encouragement have been invaluable throughout the course of development of the book.

We would also like to express our gratitude to Julia Hartviksen, who spent hours reading, editing, and correcting all the material.

Introduction
The Text and its Mutations:
On the Objectives of the Volume

J. Douglas Clayton and Yana Meerzon

Adapting Chekhov: The Text and its Mutations is a collection of articles dedicated to the hundred years of rewrites of Anton Chekhov's drama. It recognizes Chekhov's dramatic corpus as "a machine for eliciting interpretation," to quote Umberto Eco ("Author") and thus presents a wide geographical landscape of Chekhovian influences in today's drama. The book considers the elusive quality of the Chekhovian universe as an intricate mechanism, an engine in which his enigmatic characters exist as the dramatic and psychological ciphers we have been decoding for a century and continue to decode.

Although the Chekhovian dramatic canon is clearly still relevant in today's dramatic and theatrical practice, there is as yet no clear picture of the nature of its influence on the development of dramatic literature. The present volume aims to reveal texts and productions directly derived from Chekhov's work and to establish their relevance in today's dramatic canon. In this volume are analyses of a variety of recent plays and performance texts created under direct influence of the Chekhov canon, from the work of the Argentinian theatre director Daniel Veronese to Japanese theatre makers such as Tomomi Tsutsui and Minoru Betsuyaku, from Horia Gârbea in Romania to the Indian Koushik Sen, from the Chekhov texts "in exile," adapted by the Polish dramatist Janusz Glowacki living in America today, to the West Indian author Mustapha Matura writing about his native Trinidad while in the UK, to such theatre experiments of the New York–based The Wooster Group which use Chekhov's plays only as their own creative inspiration. From these studies there emerges a portrait of a post-Chekhovian dramatic canon analogous to the post-Shakespearean dramatic corpus found in the world drama today. Examining the plays and performance texts created "After the Chekhov" (to paraphrase Jason Sherman's Canadian adaptation of *The Cherry Orchard*) the authors of the studies presented here seek to answer a number of questions. What is there about Chekhov's drama that makes it relevant not only for the past hundred years of Russian theatre's development, but also worldwide? What sort of poetic, contextual, philosophical, and structural enigma of Chekhov's plays makes the writers and directors, in cultural contexts remote

2   *J. Douglas Clayton and Yana Meerzon*

from Russia and free of Russian economic or political influence, wrestle with Chekhov's characters, dilemmas, themes, and style? This objective explains the choice of the contributors and the geographical variety of the productions and traditions examined. It is because the volume aims to describe the wide panorama of Chekhovian inspirations that the authors represent a broad spectrum of theatre specialists, not necessarily scholars of Russian drama and theatre. The book is primarily aimed at researchers and students of theatre and performance studies, as well as specialists in Russian drama.

* * *

The title of this volume—*Adapting Chekhov: The Text and its Mutations*—echoes Julia Kristeva's observation that the experience of newness and the literary avant-garde by "virtue of its very characteristics, is slated to become the laboratory of a new discourse (and of a new subject), thus bringing about a mutation" (92–93). For that reason, this is a book less about Chekhov than about the modern age we live in: an age characterized by two related phenomena that are at once cultural and in a broad sense political and philosophical, namely, postmodernism and post-colonialism. The contributions to be found here largely divide into those two categories, depending on their context. The theatre productions and the texts they examine are reflective of a world where the older discourses have lost their force and older systems (imperialism, communism) have lost their coherence. The practice of dramatic adaptation—from page to page (textual, *intramedial* transposition) and from page to performance text (performative, *intermedial* transposition)—constitutes a practice of individual and collective concretization, as well as transformation. Adaptation today is thus a particular emerging genre of literature, theatre, and film, reflecting the performative practices of the new millennium. Modern-day practices of adaptation express the need to engage with history, especially the history of dramatic forms and their evolution. This collection demonstrates that adaptation as a practice of transformation and an example of today's rethinking of habitual dramatic norms and generic definitions leads to the rejuvenation of existing dramatic and performative standards. Adaptation pioneers the creation of new dramatic and performative traditions and expectations. It also brings the works of the canon closer to the needs and tastes of contemporary popular audiences, thus helping not only to integrate the artistic, moral, and ethical ideas of the past into the present, but also to facilitate larger audiences and thus to increase box-office receipts. Finally, adaptation, as Linda Hutcheon argues, constitutes the "major mode of the storytelling imagination" today ("The Art" 1) and thus it builds upon and expands the audience's horizons of expectations in theatre aesthetics. The current volume, in other words, investigates what sort of "original, mobile, and transformative knowledge" (Kristeva 92) the history of the past century,

Introduction 3

the story of Chekhov's drama in mutations, offers to scholars of drama and performance and to students of modern literatures and cultures.

WHY CHEKHOV?

Laurence Senelick opens his seminal book *The Chekhov Theatre: A Century of the Plays in Performance* with the following statement: "A funny thing has happened. Anton Chekhov, who was judged in his own time to be a playwright narrowly culture-bound, over-refined and obscure, whose drama was persistently characterized at home and abroad as 'depressing' and 'pessimistic' has become second only to Shakespeare in reputation and frequency of production" (*Chekhov Theatre* 1). Why Chekhov? The question is interesting. Why not Ibsen? Or Shaw? The answer surely lies in Chekhov's liminal position between realism and modernism, and in the hermeticism of his works, which does not allow the kind of easy interpretation that we can ascribe to, for example, *A Doll's House*. Chekhov offers us not an ideological take on reality, but an inscrutable array of carefully observed and delineated characters and images. Their very inscrutability invites different readings and attempts to exploit the energy they contain. Moreover, as Clayton shows, Chekhov's work served to shatter the standard forms and narratives that had dominated drama, arguably since the beginning of theatre. Twentieth-century playwrights rushed through the breach he created in the fortress of theatrical tradition. It is a remarkable fact that productions of Chekhov's plays appear on the stages throughout the world as often as those based on Shakespeare's plays (Sanders). Moreover, many established and emerging playwrights find it a pleasure and challenge to attempt to apply their dramaturgical skills to Chekhov's plays, either by producing new "translations" or by adapting or rewriting them. They include, to name only a few, Tennessee Williams, Howard Barker, David Mamet, Brian Friel, Tom Stoppard, David Hare, Vacláv Havel, and Arthur Miller. It is hoped, therefore, that the present volume will shed additional light on the enigma of Chekhov's influence. No doubt one of the reasons for choosing Chekhov is that he is a "playwright's playwright": the works of the Russian playwright have never been used as a weapon for ideological propaganda and colonial ideology. In this he is unlike Shakespeare, regarding whom Sanders writes: "Shakespeare was undoubtedly deployed as a tool of empire, taught in schools across the world as a means of promoting the English language and the British imperial agenda. As a result, post-colonial texts that 'talk back' to the colonizing culture frequently deploy Shakespeare as a means of achieving this" (52). Indeed, "a funny thing has happened," because Chekhov, the playwright of Russian language and culture, whose enigma—much like that of Pinter or Beckett—rests more in language than in plot or characters, has been holding his influence over many writers worldwide.

4   *J. Douglas Clayton and Yana Meerzon*

Like all great dramatists, as Martin Esslin notes, Chekhov presented us with an "infinitely ambiguous image of the human condition" (366), and thus this ambiguity continues to hold us in its thrall, as many of the texts chosen for this volume prove. Many playwrights of the mid-twentieth century, from Pirandello to Beckett, focused their artistic search on a "different kind of dramatic suspense"; they chose *not* to satisfy the question what is *going* to happen next, but rather "what *is* happening" (Esslin 366). In that quest, as this collection demonstrates, twentieth-century dramatists have realized that Chekhov's plays, replete with "indirect dialogue in situations where the characters [. . .] hide their emotions behind trivial subjects" (Esslin 88), have already prefigured many of their innovations. "We cannot live without recognition," Elinor Fuchs tells us, "and we must" (532–33). But does Chekhov, like Beckett, withhold recognition of the type found in classical Greek tragedy? And does this "revelation about the nature of human consciousness itself" exist as a *leitmotif* in Chekhov, as it does in Beckett? Might we find, in Fuchs's exploration of that "shadow fulfill-ment" of the Aristotelian pattern in Beckett's suffering, a similar haunting in Chekhov's universe, one that allows us to re-envision him as a sage of our modern era? With these musings in mind this volume considers the following questions:

- What particular qualities are there in Chekhov's dramaturgy (themes, dramatic structures, theatrical devices) that allow and invite other writers, including such great playwrights as Tennessee Williams or Brian Friel, to write their own versions of his stories?
- How should we categorize those "rewrites": as translations, adaptations, or in fact "mutations," as the title of this volume proposes? What theoretical studies on translation and adaptation (such as those by Jakobson, Eco, Hutcheon, and Sanders, to name a few) could further orient and guide us in this discussion?
- What do we mean by "Chekhovian": a lack of resolution; the absence of a definitive conclusion, event, or catharsis; a realization that events progress but do not resolve; or the presence of a continuum of human endeavor over which fate hovers infinitely? May we consider then Chekhov's drama is anti-Aristotelian but not Brechtian?

The book aims not only to respond to these questions when analyzing the chosen adaptations; it also examines how Chekhov's themes, characters, and structural innovations of his plays evolve when seen within the socio-political context of newly created texts, their linguistic novelties, and performative possibilities. As Senelick writes, "Chekhov's world contained in some half a dozen major plays and a like number of one-acts, seems to revolve around one historically, nationally determined social class, one narrow spectrum of concerns, feelings and ideas. [. . .] and yet, of all playwrights, Chekhov provokes the strongest sense of proprietorship.

'That's not Chekhovian' is a common cry of critics and spectators, precisely because a consensus of what is Chekhovian has congealed over the last century" (*Chekhov Theatre* 1–2). To understand what "specifically Chekhovian" is there and to question whether it is possible and indeed necessary to transmit this "specifically Chekhovian" into a new play, a new ideological and sociohistorical context, is another objective of this volume. This enigma of the Chekhovian lies in our view in the playwright's wish to reflect the "human desires [which] in very present instance are torn between the desire to return to the known pattern, and the desire to escape it by a new variation" (Hutcheon, *Theory* 173). Thus the contributions to this volume reveal Chekhov's texts in mutation as examples of dramatic and performative palimpsest. Many authors approximate their renderings of Chekhov's texts in mutation with the audiences' experience to feel, see, and hear "two things at once: that oscillation between the adapted text and the adaptation. Palimpsest is a good image that describes the text that gives you the doubled experience that adaptations give you." Palimpsest works as a metaphor for "hidden doubleness" (Hutcheon, "Art" 5). These contributions also ask what role Chekhov's rewrites play in the development of individual dramatists and whether we can distinguish Chekhov's influence over the development of the national dramaturgy in the countries and cultures from which the adaptations of the Chekhov's texts stem, for, as Linda Hutcheon reminds her readers, "either stories are considered forms of representation and thus vary with period and culture, or they are what theorists like Marie-Laure Ryan identify as timeless cognitive models by which we make sense of our world and of human action in it" (*Theory* 175).

ON ADAPTATION

In his article "Literary Transduction" Lubomir Doležel introduces the concept of *transduction*, which refers to the text's transmission in time, across cultures or media, a transmission with some necessary transformations. Doležel takes Felix Vodička's theory of reception, his concept of *historical concretization*, and Jiři Levý's views on translation as the methodological ground to discuss transduction as the process of literary evolution based on the instances of critical reception and adaptation. As Doležel demonstrates, Vodička's concretization as a type of transduction helps us understand the mechanisms of *literary adaptation*, which usually unfolds within several target-points, such as the original text, its concretization by the first reader, the adaptor's subjective interpretation of it, and the target-reader's reception of the adaptation proper (171). Similarly to translation, adaptation involves the in-depth analysis of the text. Unlike translation, however, it is free from the responsibility to meet the target audience's horizon of expectations; it is created to exhibit the personal and artistic concerns of the adaptor. As the theoretician of cinematic adaptation Robert Stam suggests,

6 J. Douglas Clayton and Yana Meerzon

adaptation is not necessarily marked by the need to "fit our present situation"; it serves the adaptor to express his/her stylistic and ideological concerns, whether adaptation keeps its fidelity to the original or not (73–75). This volume, therefore, analyzes the processes of adaptation focusing on the figure of the receiver as the reader of the original text and his/her functions as the adaptor/creator of a new one. It argues that Vodička's reception theory and its further incarnations in literary and theatre studies allow one to examine the significance of the receiver/adaptor's subjectivity, the author's biographical and sociohistorical context as the major determining factors of the historical concretization, and the adaptation practices today. As Levý states, "the translator [. . .] is not influenced solely by the external cultural milieu, but also by his own personal biases" (223). Recognizing the subjectivity of the author/adaptor does not function as the "closing of the text gesture"; on the contrary, it allows the better understanding of the text's inner structure and its political and social functions, as well as its ideological intertextuality.

Patrice Pavis views theatre staging as a type of translation or adaptation that takes the form of multiple inter-semiotic transpositions and constitutes the primary historical and stylistic concretization of a dramatic text. Taking this proposition as its point of departure, this volume seeks to interrogate the text in theatrical translation from the position of "the final situation of reception, so that the translator would take into consideration the point of view of the target language and target audience" (138). This hermeneutic act of translation presupposes a number of concretizations, including the textual, the dramaturgical, the stage, and the audience's reception. Pavis's translator acts from "the position of a reader and a dramaturge [. . .]: he makes choices from among the potential and possible indications in the text-to-be-translated" (139). However, Pavis's focus remains the series of concretizations that define the journey of the dramatic text across cultures, languages, and semiotic systems, from page to stage. The major participant in this scheme is the foreign spectator at whom the translation is directed. In other words, this volume takes Pavis's scheme of translation in theatre one step further by emphasizing the active position of the adaptor as the receiver of the original text and the maker of the adaptation. It also advocates the need to study the participatory role of the audience members as the cocreators of the new artistic product. Searching for methodological tools to study adaptation, this volume proposes to exchange the Original Text versus Adaptation Text binary, with a more dynamic formula *original = adaptor/receiver activity = adaptation*. It questions how and to what degree a particular adaptation reveals the subjectivity of its author/adaptor as the filtrating, selecting, and communicating agent of the target text; how and to what degree it speaks to its target audience; and, finally, how and to what degree adaptation embodies the aesthetic norms of a particular epoch that the adaptor chooses to engage with in his/her work. Taking Jan Mukařovský's figure of the author as a dual entity comprised of (a) one's biography as it is informed and influenced by the author's historical, social, cultural, and linguistic context (161–80); and (b) the figure of the author as a literary fact, a sum of literary devices, and "a dynamically organized system" (Vodička 124), this study argues that today adaptation serves not only as the marker of the stylistic and genre shifts in literature, theatre, and film; it also declares the return and rebirth of the author. Adaptation often includes the figure of the author/adaptor both as the work's semantic concern and as its structural device, and it can be shaped on a wide scale of textual and performative transformations, which can vary from adaptations as calques of the original on one side of the spectrum to adaptations as fully independent artworks. Hence, adaptation today—the process of historical and artistic concretization—is conditioned not only by the obvious formal differences between media, but most importantly by the subjectivity of a particular adaptor, his/her own view of the material.

Secondly, as this volume argues, a dramatic adaptation rests somewhere between the actual translation of the play from one language into another (in the case of cultural adaptation) and creating a new work inspired by the original (Carnicke; Senelick "Seeing"). Unlike most of the current volumes of adaptation that engage with the processes and outcomes of moving one text, from one media, into another text, another media; this volume is specifically concerned with the process of *adaptation as analogy*, to use Geoffery Wagner's term, that takes place within intermedial and intramedial adaptations. This collection is equally concerned with the sociopolitical context, which ignites the wish of adaptation, and with the artistic enigma of Chekhov's poetics, as well as philosophical dilemmas that his plays embrace. Thus, it also utilizes the adaptation typology as devised by Julie Sanders, ranging from the texts with high degree of intertextuality, almost imitations of the originals, to texts vaguely corresponding to their source texts. Sanders writes:

> Studies of adaptation and appropriation intersect in this way not only with the scientific idiom [. . .] but also with the critical and cultural movements of postmodernism and post-colonialism [. . .] As well as throwing up potent theoretical intertexts of their own, adaptation studies mobilize a wide vocabulary of active terms: version, variation, interrelation, continuation, transformation, imitation, pastiche, parody, forgery, travesty, transposition, revaluation, revision, rewriting, echo. [. . .]To this end, sequels, prequels, compression, and amplification all have a role to play at different times in the adaptive mode. (18)

However, as this collection demonstrates, it is impossible to arrive at one single methodology of dramatic analysis of the Chekhov's texts in mutations: since it is the material of each single adaptation, each new target play, the play written with the Chekhov's text(s) in mind, which dictates new theoretical lenses to explain and theorize the relationships between

8   J. Douglas Clayton and Yana Meerzon

the source text and its adaptation. What the chapters of this volume demonstrate is that no matter how close/far the target text deviates from its source, adaptation takes pleasure in masking and unmasking the presence of the original in the target text. This process is inevitably based on the techniques of dialogue, polyphony, transmutation, and metamorphosis (among many) as described by Genette, Kristeva, Hutcheon, and Sanders. In its scope the volume reflects, however, both the concerns with "open structuralism," focusing in Part I on the dramatic methodologies of adaptation and looking at the normative elements of the original dramatic text and how they mutate in the later contexts, and the sociopolitical concerns as the inspiration to adapt.

TWO TYPES OF MUTATION: ON THE DRAMATURGY OF THE PRESENT VOLUME

A dramatic adaptation is located somewhere between the actual translation of the play from one language into another (in the case of cultural adaptation) and the creation of a new work inspired by the original. The studies presented here focus on two types of mutation widely practiced in today's theatre. One has to do with the techniques and methodologies of textual mutation or the evolution of the dramatic form as such. One might call this form of adaptation *intramedial transposition*; that is to say, as something that takes place within one medium—the dramatic text. Intramedial transposition, as this volume demonstrates, uses as its starting point the dramatic structures developed by Chekhov as well as performative forms and styles as he knew them at the intersection of nineteenth-century dramatic trends. These forms and styles include vaudeville and melodrama (the types of commercial theatre of the time), the newly emerging theatre of naturalism, and its counterpart the theatre of symbolism, which could be looked at as the period's avant-garde and the precursor of such twentieth-century theatrical movements as Futurism and Theatre of the Absurd.

Accordingly, Part I of the proposed volume, titled "On Categories, Techniques, and Methodologies of Mutation," focuses on these methodological and theoretical issues of textual mutation. It goes on to examine how these historical forms of dramatic writing and theatre performance as Chekhov knew them have mutated into something else, the post-narrative or rather post-dramatic modes of today's drama and performance. The collection opens with Douglas Clayton's chapter "Diagnosis and Balagan: The Poetics of Chekhov's Drama," in which the author addresses the questions of Chekhov's dramatic poetics, challenging the widely accepted notion of "Chekhovian realism." By investigating the synchronic connections between Chekhov's dramatic oeuvre and the literary and philosophical tendencies of his time, Clayton shows the impressionistic nature of Chekhov's dramatic poetics, a poetics that unfolds somewhere between

Introduction 9

the existential anxieties of his time, positivist ideas, the works of the great Russian realistic authors (such as Leo Tolstoy), and the technological experiments of the theatre innovators Appia or Craig, who were contemporaries of Chekhov. At the same time, the chapter, like the volume in general, reminds its readers that the most innovative artistic experiments are often rooted in the author's personal history. In Chekhov's case, Clayton writes, one should always remember that Chekhov was a student of natural science, a doctor, and thus possessed a very special view of the absurdity of the world. Aging, mortality, loneliness, and the travesty of the human desires, the routine character—the *man who wanted (chelovek kotoryi khotel)*, of Chekhov's dramatic universe—are the patterns of the particular Chekhovian worldview, something that will find its further manifestations in the style and morals of the works of futurists, existentialists, and even in-yer-face theatre.

This discussion of Chekhovian poetics and its various stylistic and structural echoing in today's drama, theatre, and even film is continued in many chapters of this collection, specifically in those by Autant-Mathieu, Ignatieva, Ambros, Lamb, Pelletier, and Meerzon. The volume therefore creates its own inner dramaturgy: by opening the discussion of Chekhovian mutations with the questions of style and artistry characteristic of the original, it goes on to look at the issues of dramatic character, action, space, language, and irony found in the Chekhov canon and dealt with in the works of such important dramatists of contemporary Western drama as Tennessee Williams, Brian Friel, Howard Barker, Vacláv Havel, Jason Sherman, and Ludmila Petrushevskaya, to name a few.

Part II of this book—"Chekhov in the Post[ist] Context"—illustrates this idea further. It addresses the issues of intramedial transposition from the perspectives of cultural transfer and post-colonial context. The part engages with the concept of adaptation as translation and cultural appropriation as outlined by Umberto Eco and Julie Sanders. To translate or to adapt, as Eco suggests, is "to lead beyond" (*Experience* 74). To adapt is to take a text out of its original context and graft additional meaning onto the original root. The chapters by Manole, Dutt, Lantz, Pelletier, and Romanska discuss the multiple mutations of Chekhov's texts (in Romanian, Indian, Trinidadian, Irish, and American-Polish contexts) that today, among others, constitute the "palimpsestuous" canon of "the cultural capital" of Western drama. These chapters collectively suggest that such new works are able to aid in the construction of a new "post[ist]" dramatic canon or the counter-discourse (Tiffin) emerging in post-colonial and post-communist dramatic and performative contexts. To use Hutcheon's terms, these new texts become "multilaminated works" born of a "transaction between texts and between languages," or a "re-mediation" where "as audience members, we need memory in order to experience difference as well as similarity" (*Theory* 16). Looking at a number of textual and performative mutations of Chekhov's canonical texts within the post-colonial and post-communist contexts, this

10   *J. Douglas Clayton and Yana Meerzon*

part shows that adaptation as an example of dramatic and cultural avant-garde can also "stimulate [. . .] and reveal [. . .] deep ideological changes that are currently searching for their own accurate political formulation, as opposed to the breakdown of a bourgeois 'liberalism' that never ceases to exploit and dominate" (Kristeva 92–93).

Part III, titled "Performing Chekhov in Radical Mutations," studies adaptation as the process of *intermedial transposition* or performative mutation, when an original dramatic text is transformed into the performance text of a theatrical event, or even a film. As Linda Hutcheon writes, intermedial adaptations are marked by the process of "re-mediation," that is, they act as the "intersemiotic transpositions from one sign system (for example, words) to another (for example, images). This is translation but in a very specific sense: as transmutation or transcoding, that is, as necessarily a recoding into a new set of conventions as well as signs" (*Theory* 16). Accordingly, this part features a number of chapters that analyze performance as a means of adaptation. Specifically, the contributions by Sheila Rabillard, James McKinnon, Jean Graham-Jones, and Yasushi Nagata examine how Chekhov's original texts mutate into performance texts in the work of a number of theatre companies that employ adaptation as the primary means of creating theatre. The chapters collectively address the major question presented by Chekhov's drama today, namely, what lessons in dramatic structure and composition Chekhov has taught us that we still try to understand, adapt, and apply to the much changed social, political, cultural, and aesthetic circumstances in which today's drama and performance are produced. They also examine how categories of translation, textual adaptation, and performative mutation can be constructive and useful in studying the post-Chekhovian dramatic and theatrical canon. Approaches examined include Walter Benjamin's concept of a literary translation as "unavoidable relationality" (Graham-Jones); Gérard Genette's view of "architextuality" as the relation of one text to another, as well as how the new text, the text of adaptation, meets the needs of its new target audiences (McKinnon); and Hutcheon's view of adaptation as the indigenization of the original, i.e., localizing, transposing, modifying, and adjusting the source text to the cultural, political and social context of the adapting theatre organism, as well as to the personal artistic and autobiographical needs of each of the members of a theatre company involved in the processes of collective creation and performance making (Rabillard).

In her contribution, "Interrogating the Real: Chekhov's Cinema of Verbatim," Meerzon brings the discussion back to the question of what constitutes "Chekhovian realism." In her analysis of Karen Shakhnazarov's 2009 film *Ward No. 6*, based on Chekhov's short story "Ward Number Six," Meerzon suggests that in today's world of interdisciplinary mutations, multimedia presentations, and digital technology the search for the Chekhovian effect of the real resumes. Although using an example of a cinematic, not dramatic or performative, adaptation, the author argues that the riddle of Chekhovian

Introduction   11

esthetics is transposed, preserved, echoed, and challenged once again. As Meerzon writes, today the Chekhovian effect of the real can be attained through the devices of dramatic, theatrical, or, in the chosen case, cinematic *paratext*. Adaptation as analogy (Wagner) allows a contemporary theatre or filmmaker to convey the atmosphere and stylistics of Chekhov's inbetweenness, something that Radislav Lapushin sees as "a permanent dynamic vacillation between opposite textual poles (semantic, thematic, and metaphysical)" (3). This chapter, in other words, returns the volume to its point of departure: it reminds the reader that the Chekhovian enigma rests with the quality of *stylistic liminality,* something that not only characterizes the Chekhov's own texts but is also sought, sometimes in vain and sometimes very successfully, by his further translators, adaptors, and scholars.

We close this volume with an unusual contribution: a dialogue between the editors of the book and Patrice Pavis, the widely known French scholar of theatre semiotics and contemporary dramaturgy. In this exposé, however, Patrice Pavis appears in an uncharacteristic role, as he shares with readers his personal experience and views as the translator and adaptor of Chekhov's dramatic texts. Known for his French translations of the Chekhov's "major four,"[1] Pavis recently started working on his own plays, heavily inspired by his personal reading of Chekhov's works. In his closing paragraph, Pavis writes: "Very quickly the inevitable drift of the writing gave me the illusory sensation of flying with my own wings rather than robbing a defenseless author" (p. 303 in the present volume): a statement, as this collection demonstrates, that every adaptor or translator of Chekhov's drama can share.

NOTE ON TRANSLITERATION FROM RUSSIAN

In the body of the texts and in the notes the popular system of transliteration is used; in the Works Cited romanization follows the ALA-LC system. Thus the name "Yury," for example, will appear as Iurii in the Notes and Works Cited when transliterated from the Russian.

NOTES

   1. Chekhov's plays translated or cotranslated by Patrice Pavis from Russian to French: *La mouette* (1985); *Oncle Vania* (1986); *Les Trois soeurs* (1991); *La Cerisaie* (1988).

WORKS CITED

Benjamin, Walter. "The Task of the Translator." *Illuminations.* Trans. Harry Zohn. Ed. Hannah Arendt. New York: Harcourt, Brace and World, 1968. 69–82. Print. An "emended" version of the Zohn translation appears in Walter Benjamin,

12 J. Douglas Clayton and Yana Meerzon

Walter Benjamin: Selected Writings, 1: 1913–1926. Ed. Marcus Bulbock and Michael W. Jennings. Cambridge: Harvard UP, 1996. 253–263. Print.

Carnicke, Sharon. "Translating Chekhov's Plays without Russian, or the Nasty Habit of Adaptation." *Chekhov the Immigrant. Translating a Cultural Icon.* Ed. Michael C. Finke and Julie de Sherbinin. Bloomington: Slavica, 2007. 89–100. Print.

Doležel, Lubomir. "Literary Transduction." *The Prague School and Its Legacy in Linguistics, Literature, Semiotics, Folklore and the* Arts. Ed. Yishai Tobin. Amsterdam: John Benjamins, 1988. 165–76. Print.

Eco, Umberto. "The Author and His Interpreters. 1996 Lecture at the Italian Academy for Advanced Studies in America." *TheModernWord.com.* Web. 1 Jan. 2012.

———. *Experience in Translation.* Trans. Alastair McEwen. Toronto: U of Toronto P, 2001. Print.

Esslin, Martin. *The Theatre of the Absurd.* New York: Anchor Books, 1969. Print.

Fuchs, Elinor. "Waiting for Recognition: An Aristotle for 'Non-Aristotelian' Drama." *Modern Drama* 5.4 (2007): 532–45. Print.

Genette, Gérard. *Palimpsests: Literature in the Second Degree.* Trans. Channa Newman and Claude Doubinski. Lincoln: U of Nebraska P, 1997. Print.

Hutcheon, Linda. "The Art of Repeating Stories. An Interview with Linda Hutcheon with Keren Zaiontz." *Performing Adaptations: Essays and Conversations on the Theory and Practice of Adaptation.* Ed. Michelle MacArthur, Lydia Wilkinson, and Keren Zaiontz. Newcastle upon Tyne: Cambridge Scholars, 2009. 1–9. Print.

———. *A Theory of Adaptation.* New York: Routledge, 2006. Print.

Kristeva, Julia. "How Does One Speak to Literature?" *Desire in Language. A Semiotic Approach to Literature and Art.* Trans. Thomas Gora, Alice Jardine, and Leon S. Roudiez. Ed. Leon S. Roudiez. New York: Columbia UP, 1980. 92–123. Print.

Lapushin, Radislav. *"Dew on the Grass": The Poetics of Inbetweenness in Chekhov.* New York: Peter Lang, 2010. Print.

Levý, Jiři. "The Translation of Verbal Art." *Semiotics of Art.* Ed. Ladislav Matejka and Irwin Titunik. Cambridge: MIT, 1977. 218–27. Print.

Mukařovský, Jan. "The Individual and Literary Development." *The Word and Verbal Art. Selected Essays by Jan Mukařovský.* Trans. and ed. John Burbank and Peter Steiner; foreword by Rene Wellek. New Haven: Yale UP, 1977. 161–80. Print.

Pavis, Patrice. *La Cerisaie.* Paris: Le Livre de Poche, 1988. Print.

———. *La Mouette.* Paris: Le Livre de Poche, 1985. Print.

———. *Oncle Vania.* Paris: Le Livre de Poche, 1986. Print.

———. "Toward Specifying Theatre Translation." *Theatre at the Crossroads of Culture.* Trans. Loren Kruger. London: Routledge, 1992. 136–59. Print.

———. *Les Trois soeurs.* Paris: Le Livre de Poche, 1991. Print.

Ryan, Marie-Laure. *Narrative as Virtual Reality: Immersion and Interactivity in Literature and Electronic Media.* Baltimore: Johns Hopkins UP, 2001. Print.

Sanders, Julie. *Adaptation and Appropriation.* London: Routledge, 2006. Print.

Senelick, Laurence. *The Chekhov Theatre: A Century of the Plays in Performance.* Cambridge: Cambridge UP, 1997. Print.

———. "Seeing Chekhov Whole." *Chekhov the Immigrant. Translating a Cultural Icon.* Ed. Michael C. Finke and Julie de Sherbinin. Bloomington: Slavica, 2007. 69–83. Print.

Stam, Robert. "Beyond Fidelity: The Dialogics of Adaptation." *Film Adaptation.* Ed. James Naremore. New Brunswick: Rutgers UP, 2000. 54–79. Print.

Tiffin, Helen. "Post-Colonial Literatures and Counter-Discourse." *The Post-Colonial Studies Reader*. 2nd ed. Eds. Bill Ashcroft, Gareth Griffiths, and Helen Tiffin. London: Routledge, 2006. 99–101. Print.

Vodička, Felix. "The Concretization of the Literary Work." *The Prague School Selected Writings 1929–1946*. Trans. John Burbank. Ed. Peter Steiner. Austin: U of Texas P, 1975. 103–33. Print.

Wagner, Geoffrey. *The Novel and the Cinema*. Rutherford: Fairleigh Dickinson UP, 1975. Print.

Part I

On Categories, Techniques, and Methodologies of Mutation

1 Diagnosis and Balagan
The Poetics of Chekhov's Drama[1]

J. Douglas Clayton

A reading of the numerous studies of Chekhov's plays reveals how much is left to be said about their poetics; indeed, one has the impression that an analysis of their poetics on the level on which Aleksandr Chudakov analyzed the poetics of the prose fiction has yet to be started.[2] Discussion of the plays has tended to be deeply influenced by classical productions of the works and to offer impressionistic discussions of the different characters' motivations or various motifs, such as the famous breaking string.[3] Even careful reading of the texts of the plays is hard to find, so that the implications of, for example, the ending of *The Cherry Orchard* remain unexamined. Moreover, less consideration is generally given to the vaudevilles and monologues, which are considered to be less important and substantial than the four final plays. Further, writing on Chekhov's dramaturgy has historically tended to separate it from the larger context of his work. The organic relationship between the short stories and the plays has tended to be neglected. This is surprising, since the dramatic principle is deeply engrained in the prose works, so that it would be appropriate to say that in Chekhov the writer the dramatic principle has precedence over the prosaic. If some works, such as the early story "On the Road," could be easily translated into a short play with a description of the decorations, stage directions, and dialogue, then others, like "Lady with Little Dog," are film scenarios waiting for a director, as Iosif Kheifits demonstrated in his 1960 film version. Chekhov's search for new dramatic forms thus has its origins in his prose fiction. This quest begins as early as his first short stories, many of which read as miniature scenarios that evoke either a comic scene or a parodistic monologue, e.g., "An Unsuccessful Visit" (1882); in it a visitor to a genteel house pats the rump of the hostess's daughter, thinking she is the maid. These brief mises en scène grew into the vaudevilles that Chekhov subsequently began to write and that constituted an important part of his dramatic output.

The following does not pretend to be an exhaustive examination of the question, but is intended to "reset" the discussion and offer a new perspective. What then are the questions that one should ask when attempting to define the poetics of Chekhov's plays? First, it should be asked how they

18 *J. Douglas Clayton*

are structured and how this structure relates to the traditional structure of the genres of comedy and tragedy. By structure we cannot mean simply the division into acts, although this is important in defining the shape of the spectacle, nor is it the way dialogue and episodes are constructed and coordinated with each other in the play, although that is important and also needs attention. A related, extremely important question is the nature of the ending of the play, a question that by all accounts Chekhov pondered at great length. We need to begin by asking the nature of the material that Chekhov chose to fashion into his plays. Where does it come from? As is generally known, playwrights up to the time of Chekhov tended to choose mythical or historical subjects. These are almost totally absent in Chekhov, except perhaps in vestigial, parodic form (Voynitsky as a Don Juan manqué in *Uncle Vanya*).

The general term that has typically been used to characterize Chekhov's plays is "psychological realism." It has its roots in the Stanislavskian interpretation of Chekhov's plays that has dominated their presentation in production after production. There are a number of reasons to reject this term as either inadequate or misleading. "Realism" in the general sense is a quality of convincing verisimilitude that can apply to works of art in different genres and of different eras. The case of Chekhov is, however, quite specific: he was writing in the shadow of the great realist writers of the mid-nineteenth century whose preferred genre was the prose novel and whose work is characterized in Russian as "Critical Realism." The work of the great critical realist novelists, especially Tolstoy, who left a huge impression on Chekhov, was grounded in the philosophical current known as Positivism. It assumed an all-encompassing worldview and an unambiguous relationship to the word. It also expressed an abiding belief in the perfectibility of the world—generally through scientific progress. In (Critical) Realism there is an unambiguous interpretation of existential problems with a prescriptive intent: what is to be done. By the time Chekhov began to write the philosophical underpinnings and the corresponding aesthetic and literary environment of the mid-nineteenth century had broken down. His inability to write a novel, for example, should therefore not be seen as a lack of talent, but rather a signal that the poetics of literature had changed along with the philosophical dominants. Chekhov's age was characterized by two contradictory tendencies. On the one hand, there was a commitment to technological change for its own sake and a concern with social issues without the optimism that characterized an earlier age; its literary and artistic equivalent was Naturalism. There was, at the same time, a realization that the older assumptions of Positivism about the nature of the world were excessively simplistic: the world is, in a word, more complex, and the need to capture that complexity presents undreamed-of challenges. The end of the nineteenth century therefore also saw a rejection of unambiguous prose and a new attention towards the ambiguity of the literary sign that we now call Symbolism, with its renewed interest in poetry and a growing hermeticism of the text. In their attention to the existential world, artists began to focus on the ever-changing flux of reality, which could not be perceived as a constant, but only captured at a given, unrepeatable moment in time: in a word, Impressionism. It is against the background of these philosophical and aesthetic tendencies that we need to situate Chekhov in order to begin to analyze the poetics of his plays.

According to accounts of his life, Chekhov's acquaintance with the theatrical world began early in the provincial theatre in his place of birth and home until eighteen years of age: Taganrog. This provincial southern town was quite prosperous and able to support a lively cultural program. The theatre in Taganrog (which was built in 1865 and is still standing today) alternated between opera and drama and also was a stopping point for many of the foreign theatrical celebrities that visited Russia. Chekhov began to visit the theatre regularly from a relatively early age, and there he was exposed to the principal theatrical genres as they then existed: tragedy, comedy, and vaudeville, both in theatre and in their operatic form (Rayfield, *Anton Chekhov* 27). The first performance he saw there was of Jacques Offenbach's *La belle Hélène*. Later Chekhov made the backstage of a production of this comic operetta the setting for his metatheatrical playlet *The Swansong* (written long before Stoppard thought of *Rosencrantz and Guildenstern Are Dead*). This prolonged exposure to the classical repertoire of the nineteenth-century theatre was formative, but in a negative sense: here was an object lesson in how not to write for his age, however moving he found *Hamlet* or *Othello*. By and large, drama until Chekhov had tended to imitate other drama, recycling subjects, themes, and dramatic forms. By the end of the nineteenth century there was a widespread belief that theatre was ripe for renewal; this led to the experiments of Gordon Craig, Georg Fuchs, and others. It also meant a renewal of dramaturgy. Chekhov was to radically disrupt traditional patterns by modeling his plays after clinically observed life, the touchstone being the play's faithful representation of chaotic, observed reality.

The importance of Chekhov's field of study when he moved to Moscow cannot be overemphasized: he chose medicine. In addition to lectures, his training consisted of the dissection of cadavers and writing diagnoses of sick patients, and his early practice comprised autopsies and social surveys of prostitutes (Rayfield, *Anton Chekhov* 108–9). In short, Chekhov was trained to examine and analyze: not only the physiology, but also the psychological makeup of the patient. The diagnoses he wrote (which have apparently survived, although they have not yet been published) comprise an important factor in his work, both as a doctor, a profession he was to exercise for most of his adult life, and also as a writer. Rayfield writes: "His bent—for diagnosis and forensics—was apt for a writer [. . .]. All his life his eye for a fatal disease and a victim's life expectancy was feared, and his autopsies admired. In psychiatry, then in its infancy, Anton also showed prowess" (74). Moreover, Chekhov was a keen student of natural

20   *J. Douglas Clayton*

history, the names of birds, trees, and animals figuring largely in his work. In a word, Chekhov was an observer: of nature and of human kind. It is precisely in Chekhov's powers of observation of humankind that we should seek the secret of the literary and intellectual content of Chekhov's writing, both prose and drama: in it he was constantly trying to reconcile his diagnostic presentation with the demands of art. There is a telling passage in a brief autobiographical note he wrote:

> The conventions of artistic creation do not always permit a complete agreement with scientific data: it is impossible to depict a death from poisoning on the stage as it happens in real life. But within this conventionality you have to feel an agreement with scientific data, i.e. the reader or audience must see that this is all convention and that one has to do with a knowledgeable writer. (*Polnoe sobranie sochinenii* [*PSS*] 16: 271–72)

Here, then, lies the fundamental explanation for Chekhov's innovative art: in it he seeks not to imitate inherited forms and subject matter, but to create a new art that is consonant with his dispassionate, one might say clinical, observation of humanity.

One of the features of Chekhov's mature plays that has generated a great deal of controversy or even bewilderment is his designation of two of them—*The Seagull* and *The Cherry Orchard*—as comedies. *Uncle Vanya* is designated not as a comedy (perhaps because it grew out of *The Wood Demon*, which *was* a comedy with the traditional happy end and united couples) but as "Scenes from Country Life in Four Acts," while *Three Sisters* is called a "drama." In fact, all four plays resemble each other in tone and outcome. Clearly, Chekhov was at a loss to describe the genre of the plays, hence the bewilderment that his various designations have evoked. The designation of two of them as "comedies" is particularly paradoxical, since the term evokes specific generic expectations. Northrop Frye summed up these expectations in his *Anatomy of Criticism*. He writes:

> Dramatic comedy [. . .] has been remarkably tenacious of its structural principles and character types. [. . .] The plot structure [. . .] in itself less a form than a formula, has become the basis for most comedy [. . .] What normally happens is that a young man wants a young woman, that his desire is resisted by some opposition, usually paternal, and that near the end of the play some twist in the plot enables the hero to have his will. In this simple pattern there are several complex elements. In the first place, the movement of comedy is usually a movement from one kind of society to another. At the beginning of the play, the obstructing characters are in charge of the play's society, and the audience recognizes that they are usurpers. At the end of the play the device in the plot that brings hero and heroine together causes

> a new society to crystallize around the hero, and the moment when this crystallization occurs is the point of resolution in the action, the comic discovery, *anagnoris* or *cognitio*. (163)

Such, in a nutshell, is the core myth of comedy as it existed for more than two thousand years. It is founded on a key notion: that love (usually love at first sight) is mutual, and that the wedding at the end celebrates the consummation of the desires of both the young man and the young woman.

Chekhov's plays constitute a radical break with this traditional comedic myth, which, as Frye points out, had shown extraordinary tenacity. He discards it for the simple reason that it does not correspond to his own observations of male–female behavior, and because he finds it impossible to accept the premises upon which the traditional myth was founded: that love can be mutual, that it can happen instantaneously, and that it leads to happiness. In his mature plays Chekhov discards the myth totally in favor of what might be called the Chekhovian plot structure, a complex of plot motifs that can be observed, mutatis mutandis, in all four of the major plays and that constitutes the framework around which the secondary plot elements are arranged.[4] In an early letter that Chekhov wrote his brother Aleksandr at the age of twenty-three, he outlined his project for a thesis on what he called sexual authority. This seems to have been an attempt to apply Darwinian theory to the evolution of difference between the sexes. Nothing came of the project, but the letter contains some interesting hints that are reflected in the plays and help to explain the origin of what might be called the Chekhovian myth. First, Chekhov points out that birds are physically differentiated because of the necessity for the female to sit on the eggs, while horses are much less differentiated physically because they are mammals. He tells his brother: "You are more like Anna Ivanovna [Aleksandr's common-law wife] and a male horse is more like a female horse than a male kangaroo is like a female" (*Polnoe sobranie sochinenii. Pis'ma* [*PSSP*] 1: 64). These tantalizing early comments about male–female sexuality and their inequality offer a glimpse of the thinking that went into the myth. They can also be traced in some of the imagery of the plays, especially the bird imagery.

The plot structure or Chekhovian myth can be summarized as follows. *A man is in love with a young woman of approximately eighteen years of age. She is seduced by his words and falls under their influence. Generally this happens in the presence of some natural stretch of water: a lake or a river. The moon rises. She experiences an intense moment of happiness and declares that she is happy. She is compared to a bird. The moment is over and the dullness of life begins. She becomes simply a drudge and a worker (a horse). The man is brought to desperate straits by the unrequited love of the object of his desire and commits, or attempts, suicide.* This is a generalized sketch of the complex of plot elements that can be derived from the four major plays. Not all the elements are present in all the plays; some

22 J. Douglas Clayton

of them are rearranged, so that, for example, in *Uncle Vanya* Voynitsky is in love with Yelena, but it is Sonya, seduced by Astrov's ecological rants, who declares that she is happy *even though her feelings for Astrov are not requited*. Indeed, in every play except one it is the young woman who declares she is happy (including, interestingly, the farce *The Wedding*, where it is practically the bride's only line). In *The Cherry Orchard*, which is in many ways a self-parody by Chekhov, instead of Anya declaring she is happy, Trofimov, her partner in a relationship that is "beyond love," declares, "we shall be happy."

What is striking about the Chekhovian myth is what is absent: love at first sight, requited love, lovers united, a new society coalescing around them. Instead of male and female hearts united, Chekhov sees disunity and inequality. His young women are self-contained; the adoration of the male and his declarations are, as it were, a catalyst, but her emotions are self-centered and there is no reciprocity to be found. If the young woman is surrounded with bird metaphors, most notably in *The Seagull*, then the male protagonist is generally depicted with a gun with which to shoot birds (for example, Konstantin shooting the seagull), that is, venting his frustration metaphorically on the object of his desire or turning the gun on himself. The suicide of the male character, the most problematic issue for Chekhov (see his comment in the preceding), is modulated in different ways in different plays. In *Uncle Vanya* the business of the fourth act is to stop Vanya from committing suicide: Astrov demands the return of the morphine, and the nurse hides the gun in the basement, while Sonya applies soothing words in her final speech. *The Seagull* has the classical suicide offstage at the end, whereas in the last act of *Three Sisters* Tuzenbakh chooses a suicidal duel with crack shot Solyony. In the parodistic *The Cherry Orchard*, at the end Lopakhin, who has desired Ranevskaya in vain, vents his frustration not on birds, but on the cherry trees. His instrument is the axe, not the gun (appropriately enough, considering his peasant origins). The gun, comically, ends up in the hands of Charlotta.

Regarding rewrites of Chekhov, it is remarkable how unproductive the Chekhovian myth has been: it had, so to speak, the effect of shattering the power of the New Comedy myth, a myth based on audience wish fulfillment that only lives on in mediocre Hollywood films, but it did not reproduce itself in the work of other playwrights. It did, however, convey one important meaning that was to resonate in twentieth-century dramaturgy. As Frye points out, the New Comedy plot encodes the transition from one society to another, or perhaps more accurately the passage of power from the older generation to the next. The Chekhovian myth does no such thing: there is no "party or festive ritual" (Frye 163) at the end to mark the orderly transition from one generation to another. On the contrary, the younger generation is frustrated or destroyed, and with it the dreams of a better future. Chekhov's clear-eyed analysis of life precludes any facile optimism or rose-tinted view that everything is as it should be. For this reason we

Diagnosis and Balagan   23

are perhaps justified in arguing that the Chekhovian myth was a productive source of twentieth-century absurdist theatre, with the difference that absurdist theatre not only abandoned the rosy optimism of New Comedy and its vision of societal coherence; it also gave up any pretence of coherence of plot. Chekhov, by contrast, understood the need for the formative power of plot: quite simply he invented his own on the basis of his observations of the reality of human sexuality and relationships.

In his discussion of New Comedy Frye comments that it was not only because of its plot structure that New Comedy was productive; it was also because of the wealth of stock characters. Here, too, we find Chekhov abandoning tradition. Instead of using the stock characters of comedy, Chekhov drew his characters based on clinical experience. His character portrayal might be transparent for a doctor who, out of experience with thousands of patients, is able to recognize in an instant the symptoms, the pathology of the character, whether it be physiological or psychological, and offers us in words and gestures the individual on a deep, holistic level. This requirement that the material of the play—character portrayal, relationships— be in agreement with scientific data actually makes the texts hermetic for the average audience (and even more so for the average director). Chekhov gives us the symptoms, but assumes we have the clairvoyance necessary to diagnose for ourselves the nature of the pathology out of the character's brief comments, verbal tics, and reactions to situations. We might say that Chekhov's problem, the reason so much ink has been spilled to so little result about his plays, is that his directors and audience are not doctors. There is in his writing a reticence, a characteristic unwillingness to impose his opinion: "Genuine talents always sit in the dark or take their place in a crowd far away from an exhibit" (qtd. in Bunin 127).

A case in point is the presentation of Nina at the end of *The Seagull.* Ignoring the evidence that Chekhov considered Treplev a secondary character, most focus on his suicide, reading it as an admission of his failure as a writer and contrasting it with Nina, who is seen as steadfast in her resolve to pursue her acting career. Such is the reading given by, for example, Richard Gilman: "Nina is 'more advanced' than Trigorin, we might say more 'positive'; but both are better equipped to go on, to survive, than Konstantin" (94). Magarshack writes in a similar vein: "All the hopes Konstantin had cherished about Nina's visit [. . .] were shattered by her refusal to stay or let him go with her, by the light-hearted way in which she invited him to come and see her when she became 'a famous actress'" (74). John McKellor Reid follows suit, writing: "Most modern actresses follow the lead of Komissarzhevskaya in showing Nina as someone who has won through, who has faith in her work, and who aspires to be a great actress" (58). Rayfield offers a slightly modulated version of the future: "Nina, abandoned by Trigorin, becomes an actress of the same kind as Arkadina. Full of stamina, intoxicated by the joy of acting, traveling third class from one provincial backwater to another, she is just as much a victim of the theatre as Katya in

24   *J. Douglas Clayton*

'A Dreary Story'" (*Understanding* 146). A comparison of these more or less upbeat descriptions of the Nina of act 4 and of her projected future with the information Chekhov gives us in the text is instructive.

Before Nina actually returns, Dorn questions Treplev about her. We learn that Treplev has followed her and observed her acting; not only that, they have maintained a correspondence. First Treplev comments: "As far as I can understand from what I know, Nina's personal life has been a complete failure" (*PSS* 13: 50).[5] He then goes on to describe her acting: "She took on all the big roles, but her acting was coarse, tasteless, with wailing and harsh gestures. There were moments when she cried out or died in a talented way, but these were only brief moments" (50). Treplev then talks about her letters: "In every line one senses a morbid, stressed nerve. And her imagination is somewhat disordered. She signs her letters 'The Seagull'" (50). This description coincides with her speech when she appears and talks to Treplev. The dominant note is exhaustion: "If only I could rest, just rest [. . .] I can hardly stand on my feet . . . I'm worn out" (58). These complaints about tiredness are interspersed with expressions of unjustified optimism: "I'm already a real actress, I enjoy acting, I'm ecstatic, I get intoxicated onstage and feel I'm beautiful." Or: "When I become a great actress, come and watch me." Treplev seems to be infected with this optimism: "You've found your path" (58–59). Or is he, given the description of her acting that he has given Dorn? Do we the audience have any basis to share her optimism?

What indeed might be Nina's future? This question is key in how we understand the ending of the play. Can we believe Treplev's words to her? Has she indeed "found her way" and will become a "great actress" (59)? Such an ending offers us a ray of hope, a counterpoint to the "wrong way" chosen by Treplev. His suicide might simply be seen to be the result of her telling him that she still loves Trigorin (and hence does not love Treplev). Or are his words insincere, just playing along with her "disordered imagination"? If indeed she is going to "bear her cross" (58) and achieve success, then we have a didactic ending, a sermon about how we should all live our lives: just suffer and believe and everything will be well, as the scholars quoted earlier seem to think. But is Chekhov really a didactic writer? What if Nina is not and never will be a "real actress," not even in that God-forsaken Yelets, where she is planning to go next and where "the merchants will pester" her (57)? What if everything she says is simply delirium? What then?

A careful reading of the hints Chekhov gives us in Nina's words and behavior and in the stage directions offers a different prognosis to that found in the writings of the scholars quoted in the preceding. When Treplev sees Nina enter in act 4 he remarks: "You have gotten thin, and your eyes have grown bigger" (56). Moreover, in the course of her speech she keeps mopping her brow. Why this stage direction? For a physician in the late nineteenth century, and especially for Chekhov, the symptoms are all too obvious: the thinness, the huge eyes, the sweating, the delirium, the

Diagnosis and Balagan 25

unfounded optimism—all point in one direction: *Nina is in the last stages of tuberculosis*. This realization changes everything. First, it focuses the attention where it belongs: on Nina. For Chekhov Treplev was a secondary figure. Moreover, we might infer that his suicide is motivated by more than self-pity at Nina's love for Trigorin: perhaps he sees the truth, that Nina might not even get as far as Yelets, that she has come back to the lake to die, like the seagull that Treplev shot. She is Treplev's muse—and without her there is nothing. Interestingly, both Nina and Treplev die offstage. If Treplev found that in the moments when she was dying onstage Nina showed some talent, then it is hardly likely that his creator shared that opinion. As we have seen in the autobiographical note quoted earlier, the representation of dying onstage was a challenge for Chekhov, since he who had witnessed so much death in his professional life knew that the reality of death and the conventions of the contemporary stage were at almost irreconcilable loggerheads.

Perhaps a more important change that this realization brings about is the insight that in Chekhov we should not trust appearances: Nina's optimism is not optimism at all, but *spes phthisica*, a symptom of morbidity. It might be argued that Chekhov is not playing fair: why did he not have her spew blood? Why was Doctor Dorn silent? Why did Chekhov not tell us openly what her symptoms mean? The answer is that, as far as Chekhov is concerned, he *does* tell us: the truth is hidden in plain view. Anything else would be vulgar—*poshlo*—as the Russians say. Especially since he was himself suffering from the same disease, a fact that he was fastidious in avoiding discussing. Of course, for today's audiences, the inference is lost: no one in our world, thanks to the progress in medicine, is subjected to seeing friends, relatives, and loved ones die of this disease. But that is our problem, not Chekhov's. His problem is an artistic one: to *not* have his heroine die onstage, but to point at the fatal outcome for those possessing the "scientific data."

Regarding the situation in dramaturgy before the renewal of the late nineteenth century, of which Chekhov was a part, Martin Esslin writes: "The idea that theatre ought to represent a picture of the world the way it is in reality did not enter the head of theoreticians and practitioners of 'premodern' theatre" (136). Chekhov's response was radical: to present characters exactly as they are in real life, as he observed them, and to sketch them through their random words, silences, and gestures. He knew from his observations that most of the time people do not talk about their emotions: they *lie*; they cover up. Their words and their internal emotional reality are at odds. That is to say, reality—the reality of people's words and actions— is by its very nature hermetic. Such a presentation of Chekhov's characters thus presents considerable challenges: exactly what is the particular pathology of each of the characters? How should this influence the way they are presented onstage? How do we cope with the fact that in Chekhov so often appearances are deceptive, the way they are in reality? By and large, it is

26   J. Douglas Clayton

fair to say that Chekhov's texts have remained largely misunderstood, as Aleksandr Minkin has recently pointed out with regard to the monetary question in *The Cherry Orchard*, overturning the belief that, as Polotskaya states, "the Gayev family was left without money—and without the house and orchard" (17). Such mistaken assumptions doubtless remain in the interpretation of Chekhov's plays. With certain exceptions, productions have tended to mimic previous productions in a daisy chain going back to Stanislavsky, and innovators have tended to focus on surface elements such as the image of the cherry orchard in Georgio Strehler's famous 1974 production. One might say that the symbolist and impressionist elements have won out over the naturalistic ones.

If what I have described as the Chekhov myth is the deep structure on which the four major plays are based, there is also the surface texture, the interplay of the various characters that fill the series of events that constitute the action. Here it is useful to quote Chekhov's comments as reported by D. P. Gorodetsky:

> The public demands a hero, a heroine and stage effects. But in life people do not shoot themselves, hang themselves, or make declarations of love to each other. They do not say intelligent things every minute. Rather they eat, drink, flirt, and say stupidities. So all that has to be apparent onstage. One has to create the kind of play in which people come and go, have lunch, talk about the weather, and play whist . . . not because the author needs to, but because that is the way it is in real life. [. . .] It should not be forced into some framework or other. Life should be shown the way it is, and people should be shown the way they are, not wooden and stilted. (qtd. in *PSS* 12: 315)

This did not mean, as Martin Esslin rightly insists, that the characters' remarks are meaningless: rather they are what people say to cover up their true emotions. As Esslin points out, "it was merely the *appearance* of randomness and triviality that had to be evoked by creating a structure of which every element contributed to the production of meaning" (139). That is to say, the apparently chance remarks and "stupidities" of even minor characters hide an iceberg of meaning. With every word they betray their innermost thoughts and travails, but only if one has the perspicacity to see the hidden turmoil.[6] For this reason Chekhov's dialogues sound as if someone had turned on a tape recorder and then transcribed the conversation verbatim.[7] Thus, when Astrov in act 4 remarks, upon looking at the map on the wall, that "in that there Africa it must be terribly hot" (*PSS* 13: 114), he is in fact talking not about Africa at all, but about his own muddled sense of loss and embarrassment at the preceding events and his realization that he cannot easily show his face on the estate again. His bridges with both Vanya and Sonya are burnt, and he is more alone than ever. Each character thus has his or her own history, a history that comes out in dribs and drabs.

Diagnosis and Balagan 27

This does not alter the fact that there is a central myth: simply the author chooses to focus on a given young woman and the man in her orbit at a crucial point in her life. The other characters have had their own trajectories, but are now in a different place in their evolution. The implication of this observation is very interesting: if in the *structure* of the play the heroine (Sonya, Nina, Irina, Anya) is central, in the life of which the play offers us a slice she is just one more individual. In fact, the Chekhov play is democratic in that no character is more important than any other, even if certain characters occupy the focus of the play.[8] This is not surprising: in the doctor's office all patients are equal, and the illness of some unprepossessing person might be of greater interest than people who are full of their own importance. The Chekhov play thus offers a vision of the *comédie humaine* seen through the dispassionate eye of the clinician, a vision that is ultimately comic, not naturalistic or realistic, since the characters are caught as it were unawares, with all their flaws and foibles.

Usually discussion of Chekhov the playwright centers on the four major plays, as has this study so far. Yet Chekhov was also the author of shorter "vaudeville" pieces, several of which have proved extremely successful on the stage. Among these we find two humorous sketches—*The Bear* (1888) and *The Marriage Proposal* (1889)—in which the comedic genre is gently parodied. Thus, *The Marriage Proposal* offers, ironically, the traditional happy ending:

> LOMOV. Eh? Who? (*Kisses Natalya Stepanovna.*) Very nice . . . Wait, what's going on? Ah yes, I understand . . . The heart . . . Sparks . . . I am happy, Natalya Stepanovna . . . (*Kisses her hand.*)
> NATALYA STEPANOVNA. I . . . I'm happy too! (*PSS* 11: 330)

Here it is as if Chekhov is gently teasing both his characters and the audience: you want a happy end with all the traditional trappings?—Here it is! Similarly, in the one-acter *The Wedding* (1890) Chekhov explores that final element in the New Comedy structure: the wedding or festival. The focus is not, however, on the "happy couple"—poor Dashenka and her husband-to-be, the self-important and grasping Yepaminond Maksimovich Aplombov—but on the grotesque gathering of petty-bourgeois characters attracted to the feast. The grotesqueness is hinted even in the list of dramatis personae, with their bizarre names. The "action" is a series of arguments and quarrels that have nothing to do with the marriage as such, but rather the greed and pretentiousness of the individuals. There is a great deal of linguistic comedy, with malapropisms and misused foreign words interspersed with mangled French. As one reads the text, one begins to realize that this vaudeville element is present in the major plays as well. One of the guests, Dymba, is Greek and asserts that in Greece there is everything. His blind assertiveness has more than a little of Solyony's clownish obstinacy. Moreover, the dancing going on in the next room is more than vaguely reminiscent of the ball in act 3 of *The Cherry Orchard*. In other words,

28   *J. Douglas Clayton*

while the structure and material of Chekhov's major plays is derived from his careful observations of humanity, they are suffused with an element of vaudeville that is inherent in life itself.[9]

It was Chekhov's fate to have his work popularized by the Moscow Art Theatre. As Ivo Kuyl points out (139), Stanislavsky's art had its roots deep in nineteenth-century romanticism, realism, and critical realism; this background led the director to slant his productions towards psychological realism and give them a melancholic tone. But Chekhov's art is not realistic, which would imply making judgments and moralistic statements, but comprised observations of psychological reality presented without judgment in such a way that they take on a comic tinge. In a seminal article in the early twentieth century the poet and playwright Mayakovsky rejected the Stanislavskyan approach to staging Chekhov. Mayakovsky's own plays occupy a special place in the history of Russian dramaturgy and, I would argue, develop precisely the vaudevillian aspect of Chekhov's work. As Angelo Maria Ripellino has pointed out, they were, like Mayakovsky's poetry and his general poetic persona, an emanation of the avant-garde movement in Russia immediately prior to and in the decade or so following the Bolshevik seizure of power. Avant-garde theatre had developed in the work of Meyerhold and others as a rejection of the principles of Stanislavsky's psychological-naturalist theatre, its postulates being set out in Meyerhold's essay "The Balagan" (1912).[10] The fundamentals of the "theatre of convention" (*uslovnyi teatr*), as scholars tend to call the genre of balagan, were: constructivist stage design; the actor as clown, acrobat, or marionette; transgression of the stage/audience boundary; and metatheatre. The effect sought was grotesque. The objective was not to lull the audience into a false sense of security, but to challenge and exasperate. For Meyerhold, balagan refers not only to the business onstage, but in its colloquial sense to the entire theatrical event, audience included. There was, moreover, a clear political objective: to shatter the old theatrical conventions and, by implication, the social order as well.

It is generally thought that Mayakovsky, as an avant-garde artist, was hostile to Chekhov's drama, an opinion based on Ivan Ivanovich's remarks in *The Bathhouse* (1930):

> Yes, yes, yes! Have you seen The Squaring of the Cherry? I was at Uncle of the Turbins. Astonishingly interesting! (11: 316)

It is indeed true that Mayakovsky, like Meyerhold, rejected the psychological realism of the Chekhovian repertoire of the Moscow Art Theatre, which by the middle of the 1920s, after a period of decline, had become successful not only with the plays of Chekhov himself, but with productions in the same vein of Mikhail Bulgakov's *Days of the Turbins* (1926) and Valentin Katayev's *The Squaring of the Circle* (1928).

Diagnosis and Balagan   29

There was, however, another side to Chekhov's dramaturgy and another side to the traditional view of Chekhov's works in general. It is this side of Chekhov that is evoked with enthusiasm by Mayakovsky in his 1912 article "The Two Chekhovs." In it Mayakovsky writes: "The dishevelled life of the growing cities, which had thrown up new energetic types, required adapting to the speed a rhythm that would renew the language. And so, instead of periods with tens of sentences we find phrases of a few words" (1: 301). One vaudeville in particular has a clear resonance in Mayakovsky, namely, *The Wedding*. In his play *The Bedbug* (1929), Mayakovsky inserts what is essentially a "rewrite" of Chekhov's playlet in the third scene (11: 236–41). As in Chekhov, the scene takes the form of a drunken scandal at a wedding—a *balagan*. There are similar elements that leave it in no doubt that Mayakovsky had Chekhov's text in mind: the linguistic satire of a pretentious petty-bourgeois social group, including the contrast of vulgar speech and fragments of French; the tradition of the invited ceremonial general or sponsor of the marriage; the promise of winning lottery tickets to the groom who is marrying not for love for the bride, but for social advancement; and even some comic business with a fork. For Mayakovsky the New Economic Policy (NEP) represents a revival of the bourgeois customs and pretensions found in Chekhov's playlet; his wedding is one element in a larger play and contrasts with the futuristic second half of *The Bedbug*. Thus the poet of revolution sought to develop both the generic innovations represented by *The Wedding* and Chekhov's renewal of language, emulating, not, in his words, the "singer of twilight," but the other Chekhov, the "powerful and merry artist of the word" (1: 301). It was this other Chekhov—arguably the real one—that Meyerhold was later to highlight by putting Chekhov's vaudevilles together in the production *Twenty-Two Swoons* (1934). The *balagannost'* of Chekhov found its continuation not only in Mayakovsky's *Bedbug*, but also in the brilliant *Yelizaveta Bam* (1927) by Daniil Kharms; unfortunately this strain in Russian dramaturgy was to be stillborn with the onset of Socialist Realism in the 1930s.

Chekhov's dramaturgical art was the result of the age in which he lived. He found unique ways to resolve the difficulties of rejecting theatrical tradition, being totally true to the reality of human nature as he observed it, and yet creating a satisfying theatrical experience. All rewrites of Chekhov seem to take only a part of the whole, often an impression or some thematic material wrested from the entire complex. Moreover, there is a danger in quoting a character's words as if they are the author's opinion. A good example is the statement "Life must be represented not as it is, or should be; but as it appears in dreams," quoted twice in the Company Finzi Pasca's performance *Donka: A Letter to Chekhov* presented at the Chekhov International Theatre Festival in Moscow in 2010 (Liber). This is, however, not Chekhov's statement, but Treplev's. Nina's retort: "There is so little action; it seems more like a recitation" (*PSS* 13: 11) is surely closer to Chekhov's

30   *J. Douglas Clayton*

opinion. Nina's remark is a critique of Maeterlinckian symbolist drama: in Treplev he shows us a playwright who believes that this is how art should be, not how Chekhov would want it. Chekhov's art is life not as it ought to be, but as it is, as the contradictory perception of different individuals, each one of whom is dreaming.

NOTES

1. The ideas presented in this study are based partly on two articles published by the author in Russian (Clayton, "'Ia chaika. Net, ne to'"; and "Zhenshchina kak ptitsa i loshad'").
2. This statement may be superseded by the projected appearance of Harai Golumb's *A New Poetics of Chekhov's Plays: Presence through Absence*, announced for 2012.
3. Harvey Pitcher has given a generalized description of the Chekhov play, but one strongly influenced by British productions, and thus focusing on the emotional interaction between characters. He writes: "Chekhov is the dramatist of the emotional side of man's nature" (12). I shall argue that the analysis of the personality goes deeper than that and that in Chekhov one cannot judge characters' emotions by their speeches.
4. What Zinovy Paperny called the "microsubjects."
5. In this chapter all translations from the Russian are by the author.
6. In describing the opening of *Uncle Vanya*, Eric Bentley notes: "Astrov is sitting with the Nurse. She offers him tea. She offers him vodka, but he is not a regular vodka-drinker" (177). Bentley takes literally Astrov's assertion that "I don't drink vodka every day." We learn later from Sonya, when he and Vanya get drunk together, that this is the declaration of someone who drinks too much, and who is here evidently trying not to give in. In act 4 the Nurse's offer is taken up: Astrov is back on the slippery slope.
7. Peter Brook uses precisely this metaphor (qtd. in Gottlieb 192).
8. As Pitcher rightly points out: "Even the obviously minor characters stand out as independent figures, and are never just an incidental part of someone else's world, as in conventional drama" (13).
9. On the mature plays as an extension of the one-acters, see Gottlieb 191.
10. For information on the *balagan* as a concept, see my book *Pierrot in Petrograd 54–55*.

WORKS CITED

Bentley, Eric. "Craftsmanship in *Uncle Vanya*." *Critical Essays on Anton Chekhov*. Ed. Thomas A. Eekman. Boston: G. K. Hall, 1989. 169–86. Print.

Bunin, Ivan. *About Chekhov: The Unfinished Symphony*. Ed. and trans. Thomas Gaiton Marullo. Evanston: Northwestern UP, 2007. Print.

Chekhov, Anton. *Polnoe sobranie sochinenii*. 18 vols. Moscow: Nauka, 1983–88. Print.

———. *Polnoe sobranie sochinenii. Pis'ma*. 12 vols. Moscow: Nauka, 1974–83. Print.

Chudakov, A. P. *Chekhov's Poetics*. Ann Arbor: Ardis Publishers, 1984. Print.

Clayton, J. Douglas. "'Ia chaika. Net, ne to': k istolkovaniiu obraza Niny Zarechnoi v p'ese A.P. Chekhova." *Drama i teatr 5* (Tver', 2005): 135–39. Print.

———. *Pierrot in Petrograd: Commedia dell'arte/Balagan in Twentieth-Century Russian Theatre and Drama.* Montreal: McGill-Queen's UP, 1994. Print.

———. "Zhenshchina kak ptitsa i loshad': k fenomenologii chelovecheskikh otnoshenii v khudozhestvennom mire Chekhova." *Filosofiia Chekhova: Mezhdunar. nauch. konf. (Irkutsk, 27 iiunia—2 iiulia 2006 g.): Materialy.* Ed. A. S. Sobennikov Irkutsk: Izd-vo Irkut. Gos. Un-ta, 2008. 75–86. Print.

Esslin, Martin. "Chekhov and the Modern Drama." *A Chekhov Companion.* Ed. Toby W. Clyman. Westport: Greenwood Press, 1985. 135–45. Print.

Frye, Northrop. *Anatomy of Criticism: Four Essays.* New York: Atheneum, 1970. Print.

Gilman, Richard. *Chekhov's Plays: An Opening into Eternity.* New Haven: Yale UP, 1995. Print.

Gottlieb, Vera. *Chekhov and the Vaudeville.* Cambridge: Cambridge UP, 1982. Print.

Kuyl, Ivo. "The Objectivity of Parody. Observations on Chekhov's Literary Aesthetics." *1894: European Theatre in Turmoil.* Ed. Hub. Hermanns, Wessel Krul, and Hans van Maanen. Amsterdam: Rodopi, 1996. 138–48. Print.

Liber, Vera. Review of *Donka, a Letter to Chekhov. British Theatre Guide.* Web. 12 Dec. 2011.

Magarshack, David. *The Real Chekhov: An Introduction to Chekhov's Last Plays.* New York: Barnes and Noble, 1973. Print.

Maiakovskii, Vladimir. *Polnoe sobranie sochinenii v trinadtsati tomakh.* Moscow: Gosud. izd-vo khudozh. lit-ry, 1955–1961. Print.

Minkin, Aleksandr. *Nezhnaia dusha.* Web. 9 Dec. 2011.

Papernyi, Zinovii. "Microsubjects in *The Seagull.*" *Critical Essays on Anton Chekhov.* Ed. Thomas A. Eekman. Boston: G. K. Hall, 1989. 160–69. Print.

Pitcher, Harvey. *The Chekhov Play: A New Interpretation.* London: Chatto and Windus, 1973. Print.

Polotskaia, Emma. *"Vishnevyi sad": Zhizn' vo vremeni.* Moscow: Nauka, 2003. Print.

Rayfield, Donald. *Anton Chekhov: A Life.* New York: Henry Holt, 1998. Print.

———. *Understanding Chekhov: A Critical Study of Chekhov's Prose and Drama.* Madison: U of Wisconsin P, 1999. Print.

Reid, John McKellor. *The Polemical Force of Chekhov's Comedies.* Lewiston: Edwin Mellen Press, 2007. Print.

Ripellino, Angelo Maria. *Maiakovski et le théâtre russe d'avant-garde.* Paris: l'Arche, 1965. Print.

2 Rewriting Chekhov in Russia Today
Questioning a Fragmented Society and Finding New Aesthetic Reference Points

Marie-Christine Autant-Mathieu

> In principle a work of art has always been reproducible. Man-made artifacts could always be imitated by men. Replicas were made by pupils in practice of their craft, by masters for diffusing their works, and, finally, by third parties in the pursuit of gain. (Benjamin 218)

The sesquicentenary of Chekhov's birth in January 2010 was marked by sumptuous celebrations, especially in Moscow and Yalta on the occasion of the Chekhov International Theatre Festival, which attracted participants from Canada, Germany, Chile, Spain, Argentina, France, Sweden, Switzerland, and Japan. The Russian contributions alone included productions of the plays (*Uncle Vanya, The Cherry Orchard, Ivanov*), a short story adaptation (*The Marriage* by Vladimir Pankov's SounDrama) and dramatic texts based on the writer's life and work (*Ta-ra-ra-boom-de-ay* by Dmitry Krymov and *The Ch. Brothers* by Yelena Gremina). Chekhov's fame remains undiminished. Before perestroika and since the breakup of the Soviet Union audiences have remained faithful to him and are little disturbed by the shock treatment that certain avant-garde artists have given his texts.[1]

This remarkable, constant, overwhelming omnipresence raises the hackles of new playwrights who have been trying since the end of the twentieth century to carve out a place in Russian repertoires and theatres. Yet by calling their first festival "New Drama," they invoked the renewal of dramatic writing that took place at the end of the nineteenth century in the works of Strindberg, Ibsen, Hauptmann, and Chekhov. They find themselves angry and frustrated at the domination of these classical writers, and especially Chekhov, and the way they monopolize the attention of directors and the theatregoing public to the detriment of contemporary dramatic works. Driven by their ambition to transform the writing for the theatre, they are nevertheless aware of the difficulty of competing with such an exemplary writer as Chekhov has become. Ivan Vyrypayev (b. 1974) expressed this dichotomy in an interview given in 2004: "I have not written a single play that could be compared, for its talent and professionalism, with the plays of Anton Chekhov. I have yet to produce a truly great work; no doubt it is because of the age we live in. I don't know how theatre ought to develop." The very fashionable director Kirill Serebrennikov has expressed a similar feeling of humility. While admiring the well-written literature of the nineteenth century, he observes that "these magnificent plays" have been followed by "texts for the stage" containing more rage than craftsmanship (qtd. in Zarkhi, Kutlovskaya, and Stishova).

The phenomenon of rewriting Chekhov's work takes place in this context of adulation and repulsion. Mikhail Ugarov, one of the initiators of the "Teatr.doc" movement and passionate promoter of new dramatic writing, calls for a break with traditional dramaturgy, arguing that it no longer corresponds to the expectations of post-Soviet society.[2] To get out of the rut of putting on the umpteenth version of *The Seagull*, certain proponents of renewal suggest putting Chekhov on the shelf and forgetting him for a few years, then giving his works to directors who have never read them or seen them put on, "because productions of Chekhov should reflect people of today and not a distant Russia that we have lost" (Serebrennikov 177). Less radical and more numerous are those who look for inspiration in his work. Incapable of "killing their father," they use it as a yardstick to measure the present. Both rewriting and adaptation are forms of writing for the theatre that have existed throughout history, from the very beginnings, and that arise for different reasons. In Russia, during the 1920s playwrights sought to fill the gap in the Soviet repertoire by rewriting works that corresponded to the transformations in society. Since perestroika, rewriting Chekhov has become part of a process of rereading the classics and of postmodernist play with mythologems. For Dmitry Prigov or Vladimir Sorokin the reference to Chekhov is a determining factor, since he was the only writer to have felt that the world is chaos overlaid and concealed beneath a veneer of culture. Chekhov's works, his representation of the world, the way his art reposes on the absurd, irony, playfulness, and the rejection of past forms of writing, all constitute a unique metadrama, a text of texts, a point of departure, a model that defines the parameters and an object of study, imitation, and rivalry.[3]

In the following study of a nonexhaustive series of dramatic texts written during the last thirty years, we shall use the categories proposed by Gérard Genette to show cases of intertextuality (Chekhovian fragments in plays by Viktor Slavkin, Nikolay Kolyada, Konstantin Kostenko, Nina Iskrenko, and in sequels); creation of paratexts (Yelena Gremina's use of biographical documents); metatextuality (most rewritings refer back without mentioning it to Chekhov's plays and adopt a critical stance towards them); and hypertext (in which text B is composed in relationship to a prior text A so that B cannot mention A, but would not exist without it) (*Palimpsestes*). We shall show the evolution in attitudes towards Chekhov over thirty years (1980–2010), beginning with works from the end of the Soviet period that comprise the antiestablishment movement of the "new wave" and ending with postmodernist and post-Soviet texts.[4] We can discern four paradigms:

34   *Marie-Christine Autant-Mathieu*

1. the deformed reference from the Soviet era to the Russian past (Lyudmila Petrushevskaya and Viktor Slavkin)
2. carnivalesque inversion (Nikolay Kolyada) and use of Chekhov as a yardstick to measure the present (Aleksey Slapovsky, Marina Gavrilova, Lyudmila Razumovskaya)
3. deconstruction (Vladimir Sorokin and Konstantin Kostenko) transforming Chekhov's characters into avatars of postmodernist popular culture (Oleg Bogayev and Nina Iskrenko) and blurring the dividing line between author and work (Yelena Gremina)
4. sequels (Boris Akunin, Aleksey Zenzinov, and Vladimir Zabaluyev and Lyudmila Ulitskaya)

THE DISTORTING MIRROR EFFECT

The more the Soviet Union eliminated traces of prerevolutionary life, the more intellectuals were affected by nostalgia for it. This is particularly true of the *shestidesyatniki*, i.e., the generation that came of age in the 1960s, who had believed that the death of Stalin would bring about a renaissance of socialist ideals. The artists of this generation were torn between indignation and resignation as they tried to make their dissonant voice heard against the homogenized mass of Socialist Realist art. To reveal the dysfunctions in present-day society (the period of stagnation at the end of the 1980s), they turned to Chekhov, using his drama as a subtext to bring out by implicit contrast the material and moral degradation that Soviet society of their age had undergone.

THE CHEKHOVIAN UNIVERSE AS A
BACKDROP FOR SOVIET REALITY

Lyudmila Petrushevskaya (b. 1938) was one of the most active, talented members of the "new wave" antiestablishment movement, which was strictly controlled. Her play *Three Girls in Blue* was written in 1980 but only put on five years later, thanks to the perseverance of Mark Zakharov, artistic director of the Lenkom Theatre. It was the way the play showed the seamy underside of the rosy image of reality found in official art that shocked the censor and a segment of the audience. The defenders of Socialist Realism used the term *chernukha* (literally "black art," comparable to British "kitchen sink drama") as a derogatory label for this type of work. Petrushevskaya's play did not remain unscathed, since she turned on its head the idyllic vision of family life in the country. From the start the poetry of the play's title is deceptive, invoking Proust's girls surrounded by flowers or dreamy, elegant figures. The reality of the storyline is a different matter. The main characters are single mothers in their thirties just scraping by. Chekhov's *Three Sisters* serves as a remote reference, an archetype that contrasts jarringly with everyday Soviet life in the 1980s. Relations between the generations (three as in Chekhov: parents, children, and grandchildren) have changed radically. The war has decimated the men, so that the world presented by Petrushevskaya is almost exclusively feminine, comprising tyrannical, cantankerous, or absent grandmothers; combative daughters worn out by the vicissitudes of everyday life; and argumentative children who provoke the jealousy of the adults. There are two pathetic men who traverse the play: Tatyana's husband, a somewhat simpleminded alcoholic, and Ira's on-again, off-again boyfriend, a calculating, opportunistic coward. Being better-off and richer than the others (his dacha is in good shape and even has running water), he can get foreign drugs and uses his privileges to buy Ira's affections. He provides her with the medication she needs to treat her son and installs a toilet for her. The three women—Irina, Tatyana, and Svetlana—are related, being third cousins by virtue of having great-grandparents in common.[5] In act 1, Valera remarks: "We don't really know each other, but we are related. We are sort of from the same litter." Tatyana sniggers: "There's an expression for you . . ." Valera: "A litter" (*He raises his fist.*) "That's when a sow gives birth. That's called a litter. A litter of piglets" (Petrushevskaya 147).

The ties of affection are broken, except for omnipresent and obsessive maternal love. Talking about her seven-year-old son Anton, Tatyana says: "For him I'm capable of killing anyone!" (157). Ira echoes her sentiments: "For a woman having a child to love is everything: family, love, everything" (184). This exclusive love for the children turns into hatred when the children get older: "Ira: As for me, my mother hates me. She doesn't love me" (156). Chekhov's plays are full of generous feelings, and intergenerational and family relations are marked by tenderness. Not so for *Three Girls in Blue*, in which the characters have a glaring lack of empathy for one another: Old Fedorovna loudly proclaims her dislike of men and children; Svetlana declares, apropos of her mother-in-law, Leokadiya: "It's a good thing I don't love her, otherwise I would go mad when I bury her" (190). Petrushevskaya takes to an extreme the ambivalent relationship between Arkadina and Treplev, turning Ira's mother into a narcissistic egoist, capable of abandoning her grandson to go and get treatment herself. Relations between men and women are motivated by the desire for momentary physical pleasure, and are, most of the time, mercenary.[6] The first line of *Three Sisters* concerns the father's death, which is seen to be a rupture. Later, Andrey, under Natasha's thumb, will be ordered to take care of Bobik. In *Three Girls in Blue*, on the other hand, fathers are conspicuous by their absence on the levels of both affection and material support. They neither pay child support nor participate in the education of the children. The wretched material situation in which the characters find themselves occupies the center of attention in the play: in the shared dacha, which has become a source of income, the roof leaks, there is only one toilet, and there is no shower.[7] The conversations are far from being philosophical discourses, focusing instead on repairing the roof, paying for the work, and looking after the children, who are often sick and psychologically affected

36 *Marie-Christine Autant-Mathieu*

by their family situation. This harsh "comedy," interrupted only by lyrical passages (when a child's voice reads a fairy tale), concludes with a highly improbable happy ending that is so contrived that it serves to underline the fake naturalism of the work. The gloom is overcome; Petrushevskaya creates the conditions for a catharsis in the hope of raising the reader's (or audience's) consciousness. The three cousins agree to share the rent of the dacha and split the chores among them. Unlike in *The Cherry Orchard*, the property is not sold and the characters do not leave it, but the building will continue to deteriorate for lack of upkeep. Its nostalgic power and ancestral content seem to oblige the characters to stick together and make accommodations, at least temporarily (it is a summer residence). The dacha eventually turns out to be a home and a refuge—with no men. If in *Three Sisters* marriage offered Irina at least a glimmer of hope, for Petrushevskaya it is rather the Natasha type with her animal attachment to her offspring that has triumphed in the twentieth century.

THE IMPOSSIBILITY OF COMMUNAL LIFE

In Petrushevskaya's work Chekhov's model was implicitly contrasted with the present-day, "bastardized" degradation of society. *The Hoop* (1982) by Victor Slavkin (b. 1935), another notorious representative of the new wave, expresses in a very different way the dream of living in harmony in a dacha, that archetype of the home inhabited by a united family. The title sounds strange in Russian, referring back as it does to a toy that is as obsolete as the world of Chekhov's characters. Slavkin's starting point is a sense of nostalgia for a harmonious family life in a home of one's own, which he presents as an experiment, not as an observed reality. The proposition expressed in the following quotation is the expression of a desire, not the result of necessity or limitations:

> I have brought you all together because you have something in common. You are all, each and every one of you, and me as well, alone. [. . .] we are a group of free adults who don't depend on each other but are interested in being together. [. . .] what could be more beautiful than to live together and to see each other every day? (Slavkin 188)

Thus Slavkin presents a story that ends badly of a voluntary exile to a dacha, that symbol of the past and of life in the country surrounded by nature. The play opens with a situation opposite to that in *Three Sisters*: a group of Muscovites leave the city for the family home belonging to the grandmother of one of them. Unfortunately, in the 1980s communal life away from the world of politics and society proves impossible. No sooner does it happen than this dream of the "sixties," rooted in the utopias of the end of the nineteenth century (there is mention of the Barbizon painters), is destroyed almost without reason, "by the force of things," simply because it is incongruous.

Rewriting Chekhov in Russia Today 37

It is as if *The Hoop* is a sequel to *The Cherry Orchard*: two generations later the dacha is opened up, its doors and windows are repaired, and it is reoccupied. The new inhabitants take possession of the dishes, the clothing, and the letters they find there; dress up; soak up the atmosphere by dining by candlelight; play with hoops; and adopt the language of another era to read out loud the poems and love letters they discover. Then the house is closed up again like a tomb. The impossibility of going back in time marks the definitive end of the values the group had cultivated out of nostalgia: any collective understanding and belief in an ideal are dead. It has proved impossible to build on that past that has just been evoked and literally reread. It is useless to try to revive the values of an earlier time, since people have profoundly changed. The planned commune fails because it is not based on any ideal other than spending a nice weekend in the fresh air with one's significant other. The past provides nothing that can be useful to the present. Chekhov's characters have been condemned by the revolution and have only engendered a deceptive nostalgia. Yet Slavkin does not end on a tragic note. The mocking tone and ironic distance impart a playful lightness to this collage of quotations, one of the first Soviet postmodern plays, and to the disconcerting contradictoriness of the characters. The characters refer back to Chekhov: Vladimir Ivanovich, like Lopakhin, talks about his peasant origins. Koka, like Gayev, did not know what to do when he returned from Sevastopol in 1916: he has worked in a bank, then in Siberia as director of a home, and then on the construction of a railroad. Pasha, like Lopakhin, announces, "The house has been sold." (It is Koka who has sold it, instead of leaving it to his grandson.) Apart from these echoes of the source text, the characters have a blurred identity: they imitate each other, which in itself demonstrates their interchangeability and banality.

The Hoop should be read against the backdrop of *The Cherry Orchard*,[8] but with ironic twists: there are apple trees, not cherry trees, growing in the garden, and the fruit they produce is of no interest: "LARS. The main thing about fruit trees is not the fruit, but the leaves. One can live without fruit, but not without oxygen!" (182). Old Koka, who faints at the end of act 1, is reminiscent of Firs, but is a cruder, almost farcical version: at the end, in a final spurt of energy, he goes back into the house that is being pulled down in order to get some baby-bottle nipples for his pretend grandson (actually the child of his adopted daughter). These nipples exemplify the triumph of materialism even in the old man who had been so full of sentimental memories at the beginning.

CARNIVALESQUE INVERSIONS

At the very end of the 1980s the rejection of Socialist Realist dogma opened up a breach in the system of values and respect for conventions. One of the first to break the rules was Nikolay Kolyada (b. 1957), especially with regard to the hierarchy of genres and speech norms. This very prolific author went

38 *Marie-Christine Autant-Mathieu*

on to use Chekhov's works as a counterpoint for a grotesque representation of the present. Thanks to the shock effect caused by the contrast between the noble and the vulgar, the beautiful and the ugly, the quotations from classical, canonical works seem discordant and evoke laughter. This is the beginning of the reworking of the classics in the mass media, their retrieval, adaptation, vulgarization, and carnivalesque inversion.[9]

A POST-SOVIET CHERRY ORCHARD

Nikolay Kolyada created several debased versions of texts by Gogol and especially Chekhov. In *Oginski's Polonaise* (1993) he offered a carnivalesque transposition of *The Cherry Orchard* into post-Soviet Russia.[10] The text itself is sufficient and does not require any identification of the source text in order to function. No decoding is necessary, but if the reader or spectator makes the connection with Chekhov's work, his reading of this secondary level will enrich the reception of the play (Genette, *Palimpsestes* 11–12). Kolyada inverts everything: as one might expect after the revolution, the servants have become the masters. Lyudmila, an ex-cleaning woman, and her husband, Sergey, the former chauffeur, having first stripped Tanya, the daughter of their former masters, of all her possessions—both her apartment and its contents—go on to terrorize her and reduce her to washing the floors. Instead of the birdsongs, the barking of dogs, the croaking of frogs, the tinkling of bells, and the ticking of clocks made famous by the productions of the Moscow Art Theatre we hear the jarring yelps of a goose, the cries of a Swiss cuckoo clock, the wailing of police and ambulance sirens, and the honking of automobiles. There is no orchard, no countryside, no province. The action takes place in a Moscow apartment, as if the realization of the three sisters' hopes had led only to a disaster. Tanya returns to Moscow from the United States, where she had taken refuge after the assassination of her father, the ambassador in Afghanistan. She then tries to leave again (Oginski's polonaise is titled *Farewell to the Homeland*) after all her hopes of building a new life there have come to naught.

All the characters are of limited intelligence, immature, vulgar, of dubious integrity, and abnormal, as if they came out of a freak show. Tanya's one-eyed ex-fiancé, Dima, busks in the metro, playing a few bars of "Oginski's polonaise" on the violin. He lives with a goose, a vulgar substitute for his ex, Tanya, who is no more realized than Nina is, and whom life has shot down in full flight. Ivan is a version of Ivan the Simpleton, the fool in Christ of Russian folklore. Tanya, a mixture of Anya and Lyubov, has fled the USSR after being traumatized by the death of her parents. Abandoned by her lover, she took refuge in New York,[11] where she became a prostitute and drug addict and has turned into a paranoid wreck, aged beyond her years (126). Lyudmila and Sergey are a Russian version of Hugo's Ténardiers in *Les Misérables*, robbing and humiliating Tanya before chasing her into exile in order to continue to use her property. David, Tanya's American friend, is a transvestite and a drug addict. Instead of idealistic aspirations we find sordidness, stupidity, cunning servility, and self-abasement. The characters have no humanistic plans or generous impulses, seeking only to survive. Their dreams, like their memories, remain those of their childhood. Tanya would have liked to become a ballerina dancing *Swan Lake* in a white tutu (a new variation on the seagull) with Dima on the violin, accompanying her in the orchestra. In her hallucination Tanya imagines herself as a princess of a thousand and one nights on a magic carpet decorated with birds of paradise and accompanied by a one-eyed monster who metamorphoses into a prince charming. The prose of life takes care of this dream: Dima has sold the carpet of her childhood to buy booze.

At the end of the first scene several sentences heisted from Chekhov are drowned in the hysterical disjointed dialogue of the denizens of this madhouse. Tanya opens the door of her childhood room, closes it, and says, parodying Nina in her last tirade in *The Seagull*, "That's wrong, that's all wrong" (103). When a little later she greets David, she exclaims: "David! Kind David! Look! I am at home! A new life! I am at home! We're beginning a new life! There's no danger here. We're among our own, with no KGB! This is my house, David, there are no microphones, no hidden cameras, there can't be! Everything is clean!" (103). Her exaltation has Chekhovian overtones: "I think that in something like three hundred years people will celebrate their birthday and New Year's day every day and will always be happy. [. . .] I believe it. All Russia will become a garden. A cherry orchard. An apple orchard. And all the Russians in the world will go home, will return to their homeland because the best life and the best people are here in Russia" (132). But these effusions are out of kilter with reality and contrast with fragments of various Soviet discourses: the mechanically repeated slogans, poems, and songs that she has also been fed in childhood. Tanya's culture is made up of this mishmash. But whereas she still has in her traces of Chekhovian poetry, the other characters have broken with the Russian past. They bear the stigmata of Soviet civilization: the passion for spying, including between husband and wife, making demands based on class discrimination for material gain, bigotry disguised as patriotism, fear of others. . . . At the end the Soviet discourse—the song of the pioneers, a poem about Lenin—take over in Tanya's ravings. The servants have definitely triumphed: "We shall survive! We are unsinkable!" (139).

CHEKHOV'S WORKS AS A SPACE FOR EXPERIMENTATION

With the end of the USSR and the removal of taboos, Chekhov's works became the most popular choice for all kinds of experimental rewrites, derivations, and remakes. The loss of all landmarks, disruption of accepted lifestyles, and emergence of new classes of poor and rich drove many artists to see in the classics inexhaustible material for responses, lessons, and perhaps consolation. In his play *My Little Cherry Orchard* (1993), Aleksey

40   Marie-Christine Autant-Mathieu

Slapovsky (b. 1957) shows the conflict between the indomitable idealism of the older generation and the destructive radicalism of the young who reap the fruits left by their parents without planting anything themselves. The discovery of cherry stones attracts this disillusioned remark from the main character: "That's the way it is. You plant a tree, your own little cherry orchard, and someone comes and picks all the cherries and doesn't leave a single one" (13).

What will happen when the older generation disappears and with it the cherry trees, symbolic of the transmission of a beautiful and fruitful heritage? In *Three Sisters and Uncle Vanya* (1993) Marina Gavrilova (b. 1949) transposes Chekhov's texts to the twentieth century with abasement and variations. Chekhov's archetypal characters have become ordinary citizens whose life is completely devoid of poetry. *French Passions in a Dacha near Moscow* (1999)[12] by Lyudmila Razumovskaya (b. 1949) is a comedy of manners couched in the same vein, with plot elements from *The Cherry Orchard*, *The Seagull*, and *Uncle Vanya* spiced up with a detective story and focused on the inheritance of a dacha, which, with the fall of communism, had become a cherished sign of wealth for newly rich Russians.

These carnivalizations, vulgarizations, and reductions beg the question of what has survived and floated to the surface after the shipwreck that Chekhov has suffered at the hands of contemporary authors. The characters that emerge from these rewrites are essentially Vanya or Ivanov, superfluous men who have made a mess of their lives; Lopakhin, the Johnny-come-lately entrepreneur who has suddenly, at the beginning of the twenty-first century, become a topical figure; and to a certain extent Firs, who represents the forgotten world of long ago. As for the symbolic images, they boil down to the country estate or dacha and the cherry orchard, the first being the victim of the depredations of time or the greed of the newly rich and the second referring back to a lost paradise. These texts also question the role of art and writing: it is not the subject matter that makes the work, but the way it is treated. Few authors use Chekhov to create something new as Brecht did by using John Gay's *The Beggar's Opera* to found a new type of theatre, being content rather to invite the reader or audience to discover the resonances between their work and that of Chekhov. Kolyada is an exception, creating a language rich in sound inventions, pulsating rhythms, internalized refrains, neologisms, and idiosyncratic speech patterns.

DECONSTRUCTION

In the 1990s a certain number of Russian artists adopted Postmodernism, but the lateness of their adhesion leads some to question their attribution as postmodernists.[13] Their goal is not to break with Soviet norms or make them an object of play, but rather to join the international art scene and work in an interactive manner with all available sources.

RECYCLING

Vladimir Sorokin (b. 1955) is a famous conceptual artist with ties to Erik Bulatov, Dmitry Prigov, and other representatives of the neo-avant-garde. In *The Jubilee* (1993) he resorts to his usual technique of defamiliarization through collage. His work combines series, repetition, overabundance of variations, composition with constant intertextuality, and speech stereotypes. The play in question is a perfect example of the postmodern strain in the theatre, comprising as it does the classics in three parts. Part 1 is a parody of the official Soviet speeches that took place on anniversaries and were filled with statistics about factory production, the drive for socialist emulation, and an obsessive emphasis on over-fulfilling the plan. Part 2 is a parody of propagandistic Soviet documentaries with enthusiastic commentaries describing production processes (in this case the development of proteins). Both parts are in the Sots-Art vein. Part 3 shows a theatre production with stage decorations from *The Cherry Orchard* performed by actors from Kaluga who are coated with Chekhov proteins. This part references the absurdist experiments of the *oberiuty* or neo-futurists, as well as trash performances.

In this play the Chekhov cult is taken to absurd lengths. The writer has become so famous that his name has become a cliché. It has gotten to the point that the name can be suggested simply by the acronym ChPK, like other acronyms such as KPSS (Communist Party of the Soviet Union) and ChP (emergency situation): "Onstage a green dais with a silvered emblem bearing the letters ChPK. Behind the dais there is a giant white bust of Chekhov decorated with flowers; at the right-hand corner of the backdrop, the figure 10 is picked out in gold, and above it, on a blue background: 'In a man everything should be beautiful. A. P. Chekhov.'" The writer has been turned into a statue and honored on special days with great pomp, even giving his name to a unit of mass production, a "Chekhov Protein Works [*kombinat*]." The craving for spiritual nourishment has mutated into the masses' need for strength and energy. Like Chekhov, literary classics such as Pushkin, Lermontov, Turgenev, Gogol, Tolstoy, and Dostoyevsky have become raw material for the production of "class proteins" in a Russia that has shaken off communism but retained its modus operandi. The director is proud of the performance of his factory, announcing proudly that the initial production of 917 clones of Chekhov between the ages of eight and eighty-two has grown spectacularly regarding both the ages of the clones and the quantity: "In six years we have produced 17,612 Chekhovs aged between seven and eighty-six with a total weight of 881 tons." This is followed by the inevitable enumeration of the varieties of Chekhovian proteins, whether liquid, concentrate, in powder form, in strips, spirals, pipes, rings, coils, patches, extensions, or strings. The speech is illustrated with a documentary film showing the slaughter of eight clones of nine, twelve, sixteen, twenty-two, thirty-five, thirty-seven, forty-three, and seventy-two years of age; their being skinned;

cut into pieces with an electric saw; and gutted. The eight naked corpses are hung by the feet above eight vats, which catch the guts and the blood. Body parts are then hung on a chain, washed, and placed in autoclaves. Bones, fat, and flesh are then separated out to make flour, liquid concentrate, and powder. The film then shows the transformation of this raw material into derivatives (patches, strips, implants, etc.), which are then treated and shipped out. The objectification of art is thus taken to the extreme. The "immaterial" work, a production of the spirit that has been "assimilated" by every Russian, with which he has been impregnated, is confused with the man who has produced it and who, by transubstantiation, must contaminate the masses, galvanize them, and stimulate their energy. Thus a material Chekhov "in the flesh" is used in a procedure opposite to the mummification of communist leaders who are permanently preserved in their physical form to feed Soviet propaganda and illustrate posters.

The last part of the film resembles body art performances. The actress who is to play the role of Nina, instead of learning the text, dressing for the part, and putting on makeup, inscribes Chekhov on her body. She "incorporates" him in twelve stages, applying concentrated ChP protein on her body, ChP powder on her joints, ChP strips around the joints, rings on her wrists, a bandage on her head, blobs in her ears, and a diaphragm in her uterus; implants are sewn under her skin, tubes in the muscles of her legs, and spirals in her dorsal muscles. She uses straps to support her dress made of fresh Chekhov skin and filled with liquid protein. Then Ivanov, Astrov, the three sisters, Vanya, and Firs, who are all to accompany Nina in this performance, spend twenty-four hours in an incubator, the interior of which is smeared with Chekhov guts crushed with a hammer. Finally, the "Chekhovized" actors gather on a terrace looking out onto a cherry orchard in flower. Fragments of *The Seagull*, *Uncle Vanya*, *The Cherry Orchard*, and *Three Sisters* are put together and combined in an absurd montage, creating a round of recognizable elements (characters, lines, situations, and style) that are displaced and disjointed. Sorokin parodies Stanislavsky's "interior" acting: "all the set, including the slightest details such as the apples on the table, the leaves, etc., has been made from Chekhov's entrails." The expression "to speak from the bottom of one's heart" is taken literally, giving rise to passages that, like refrains, are chanted in the characters' dialogue of the deaf:

> A VOICE. Attention! The moment has come for Chekhov's internal organs to cry out. *Nina approaches the table, takes the heart, gets down on her knees, and shouts at it*: Votrobo! Votrobo! Votrobo! *Ivanov approaches the table, takes the liver, gets down on his knees and shouts at it*: Pasho! (Five times.) *Then they place the heart and the liver back on the table.*[14]

This parody of a ritual resembles a barbarous Eucharist in which the body of the god before which one must kneel is not symbolized, but literally cut

Rewriting Chekhov in Russia Today 43

in pieces. This inability to transcend, i.e., to make the transition from the material to a sign, is a characteristic of uncivilized man, which reminds one of Astrov's remark: "Those who will live one or two hundred years after us and who will despise us for our so stupid and untalented life—maybe they will find the means to be happy, but we . . ."

The ritual is orchestrated by the offstage voice of the organizer of the performance who repeats ten times the same expression: "Attention! The moment has come for Chekhov's internal organs to cry out." The cries themselves in neo-*zaum* (avant-garde "transrational" language) sometimes seem to relate to a bizarre reality.[15] In the course of this radical deconstruction famous lines from Chekhov can be heard: "The music is playing so gaily, so joyfully" (Olga); "They have forgotten me" (Firs); and "Men, lions, partridges . . . I am a seagull. No, that's wrong" (Nina). This assemblage of phrases and words produces *nothing* (thus resembling the absence of action in Chekhov's plays) and concludes with a transformation of the sound of the breaking string into a monotonous ringing that lasts sixty-nine seconds (an ultimate way of debunking the mania for pauses in Chekhov and Stanislavsky).

THE POSTMODERN REMIX

Konstantin Kostenko (b. 1966) gave his play *The Seagull by A. P. Chekhov* (2004) the subtitle "a remix." This musical term refers to two types of interaction with an original work: either the composition by the author himself of a "long version" or the adaptation of the work to a different genre by another artist who gives it his personal touch. This is the type of remix referred to by Kostenko. He starts by taking two collective characters, Sorin and Treplev, accompanied by an animated portrait of Chekhov himself, and transforms the original work into an infernal machine. Chekhov's text is mixed with fragments of technical works and distributed in incoherent snatches on a random basis between two "spokespersons."[16] Kostenko reifies the author, who is reduced to a portrait with a moving jaw, and materializes the play in the form of an infinite number of cutout birds from a single original. He thus removes Chekhov's work from the domain of artistic authenticity to place it in the "era of technical reproduction" (Benjamin), submitting it to the industrial process of serial production.[17]

There is no story, no intrigue, no character. Kostenko "mixes" Arkadina's, Polina's, Nina's, Shamrayev's, and Trigorin's lines and distributes them between Sorin, Treplev, and Chekhov's Portrait, which talks and eats. The heterogeneity resulting from the collages creates surprises such as this "technical" passage inserted in Chekhov's text:

> SORIN (*pronouncing Nina's lines*). Add the tribulations of love, jealousy, the constant fear for heterogeneous elements, the color of magnolia mixed with a hot nut, delivery and assembly at Khabarovsk in three days . . . (*behind the wall hammer blows and a cough*) Forming

44   *Marie-Christine Autant-Mathieu*

a kitchen interior, I have become mediocre, I acted without any idea [. . .] I can hardly stand on my feet (*offstage a cough*). I am exhausted; I want to eat . . . Although all these problems will disappear if one chooses the kitchen furniture correctly, with the help of a designer. The Salon Kitchen 2000 can be found at the following address.

Sometimes the mechanism goes haywire and produces a defective text:

> SORIN. What is the matter?
> TREPLEV. I have had the baseness to kill Konstantin Gavrilovich today. I place him at your feet. (*He throws a seagull at Sorin's feet. To the seagull.*) Farewell, Konstantin Gavrilych. No one thought or guessed that you would become a real writer.[18]

The text- and image-producing machine *The Seagull* relies in act 2 on sound effects and onomatopoeia. Act 3 consists of a long monologue (a mixture of legal and social ruminations) by Chekhov's Portrait, which is to be reeled off like a slightly accelerated tape. After a parody of silent cinema in which Treplev tries in vain to commit suicide, the play concludes in a Zen mood. Sorin and Treplev busy themselves with a strange activity, cutting out paper seagulls that are strictly identical to an anatomical drawing of a bird. To the sound of a flute and a Japanese guitar (the sound of the breaking string being replaced by that of a shamisen) Sorin and Treplev work away slowly as if in a state of meditation.

Both Sorokin and Kostenko explode the work, stripping it of its mythical aspects, but at the same time paradoxically turning the author into a ritual object of veneration. On the other hand, the plays are now emptied of their content and stripped of their refined writing and composition, fragmented, hacked to pieces, shredded, and they require a reader/audience capable of comparing the result to the source text. If this recognition does not take place, then the game does not work.

CHEKHOV AND FOLKLORE: FAIRY TALES AND MARIONETTES

The approach of Nina Iskrenko and Oleg Bogayev (b. 1970) is quite different: they prefer to make the author and his characters, after three generations of assimilation by readers and audiences, into folklore. In *The Dead Ears or a Completely New History of Toilet Paper* (2000), Bogayev adopts a grotesque and fantastic manner to use the classics as a weapon against the growing lack of culture of the Russian provinces. Era Nikolayevna is a giant two or three meters tall with an appetite as excessive as her height. She is visited by Chekhov's frail silhouette, but does not recognize him. The writer has come to beg her to enroll at the library and become a reader. If it closes for lack of readers, some of the classics will be burned; others will be stored in the basement; and, finally, a certain number of works will be used

Rewriting Chekhov in Russia Today   45

as toilet paper. Era is more impressed by the writer's thinness than by the future of his works so that, after giving him some soup, she offers him "a man's work on a building site" (227) and then equips him with enormous felt boots to combat the rigors of winter. A hundred years after the appearance of *The Seagull*, intellectual sustenance has become devoid of interest.

The avant-garde of the 1920s used small forms such as commedia dell'arte masks, street theatre figures, or Russian Punch and Judy (Petrushka) to rework Ostrovsky and Gogol, but not Chekhov.[19] In her play *Has the Cherry Orchard Been Sold?* (1993), Nina Iskrenko (1951–1995) takes advantage of the distance of time and applies them to Chekhov, creating a patchwork of derisory remnants of a useless, outdated culture. The avatars of Chekhov's characters are out of sync with the plays they come from. They babble about this and that; ramble on about love or the weather; mix their lines up (for example, Ranevskaya says one of Charlotte's lines); and abandon the text (Firs uses an architect's jargon to evaluate the house or speaks in proverbs). Archetypal characters are placed in a story they either don't know or have half forgotten, and refer to the dictionary to discover the meaning of words:

> RANEVSKAYA. Ah, the orchard. I had completely forgotten. I guess it's some symbol of spirituality?
> ANYA. No, mama (*she reads*), in the encyclopedia the orchard is defined as a plot of land planted with trees and bushes, and gardening is a branch of horticulture that comprises planting fruit-bearing trees and decorative plants.[20]

Iskrenko's characters are devoid of psychology, values, or purpose, and at the same time victims of their outsized mythical dimension. They have become cartoon or serial characters, who feed on imaginary worlds like vampires and can be reproduced, twisted, manipulated, or shaken. Varya says to Anya: "Yes, you could be bashed on the head with an oar so hard that you would turn into your opposite, a replica, a negative, made of modeling clay. [. . .] It seems to me that she would start to bark, screech, make yellow bubbles, and that her teeth would close onto the throat of a victim." Their actions resemble gags. As in a puppet show, the characters are stereotypes that adopt primitive behavior. For example, Firs washes Ranevskaya's feet when she returns from Paris, just as the feet of a pilgrim in a folktale are washed when he returns from a long voyage, and Lopakhin nibbles Anya's leg. They whack each other and fall over. Anya whacks Petya with a dictionary. Dunyasha swoons onto Firs's shoulder. The latter perches on a wardrobe, kicks Lopakhin away, and yells insults at him like Captain Haddock. Lopakhin whacks him on the sides to calm him down. Firs collapses and is then put in a straightjacket.

Iskrenko's characters' extreme sexuality manifests itself frequently and at inopportune moments: Lopakhin falls on his knees in front of Ranevskaya, puts his head in her lap, and embraces her thighs. Firs makes eyes at her, approaches her from behind, takes her by the waist, and presses gently

46   *Marie-Christine Autant-Mathieu*

against her while talking about the quantity of cherries they used to dry and marinate. Petya hides under Anya's dress. Yepikhodov puts a revolver in his fly. Anya and Varya undress, kiss, get aroused, and make love. Lopakhin pushes Anya and then Varya against a tree and takes them, all the while continuing the dialogue: "My head is turning a little. ANYA. Faster please. LOPAKHIN. I'm asleep. I'm dreaming. It's as if . . . (*He cries out.*) It's the fruit of your imagination, covered with the darkness of the unknown." The obscenity and mechanical repetitions (Gayev keeps kissing Ranevskaya while she covers the wardrobe with kisses) and the bursts of anger or hysteria, which would be appropriate for street theatre or Punch and Judy, are mixed up with cases of mistaken identity, puns,[21] circus gags, transformations, and fairy-tale marvels. After a thunderclap, a flash of lightning illuminates Lopakhin's face: "It looks like a fearful vampire's mask with fangs and bloodstains, but then it returns to normal." The transformation is repeated three times; the last time Lopakhin becomes a Priapus-like vampire and the flash of lightning reveals "a fanged mask and a skeleton with three enormous members that attack the tree-cum-cupboard; then the vision disappears." The Chekhovian figures thus become part of folk imagery, Lopakhin rivaling with the witch Baba-Yaga, Anya with Red Riding Hood, Firs with Petrushka. Having descended from their pedestal, these "masks" have kept all their force of attraction. They represent types or combinatory elements capable of "becoming animated with a new mood, giving rise to new formulations" (Veselovsky qtd. in Propp 116).

THE VULGARIZATION OF GENIUS

One final category of deconstruction should be mentioned to complete this section. It is symptomatic of the approach to Chekhov on the part of the promoters of the new dramaturgy, the very ones who desired the banishment of the classics. The form is less aggressive, but the result is just as destructive. Yelena Gremina (b. 1956), the leading figure in documentary theatre, has written two plays based on the life of Chekhov. The first, *The Sakhalin Wife* (1996), is inspired by the writer's journey to the Sakhalin prison colony, while the second, *The Ch. Brothers: Scenes*, which was commissioned for the 2010 Chekhov Festival, is based on letters and eyewitness accounts of the writer. Natasha loves Anton the way Masha loves Treplev in *The Seagull*, and would like to "tear him out of her heart." The desperate, spineless, alcoholic Chekhov brothers are reminiscent of Ivanov, Vanya, or Astrov. Dunya, the Jewish fiancée, resembles Sara. Anton, the writer adored by his family, makes one think of Serebryakov. The way the writer criticizes himself echoes the words of Trigorin. Chekhov's brother Aleksandr is full of self-pity like Vanya ("My life is lost. I have talent. I could have been a Schopenhauer, a Dostoyevsky"). Aleksandr shoots at Anton the way Vanya does in *Uncle Vanya*, and so on.[22]

Gremina is less interested in the echo of certain biographical situations in the works, but rather seeks to vulgarize the genius, who is brought down off his pedestal and shown in everyday life, in the company of his alcoholic brothers, in a universe full of jealousy and pathological sordidness (in one mimed scene Chekhov's brother Aleksandr hangs up his children's nightshirts covered in yellow and brown stains, as well as a woman's slip full of holes). The writer's family is far from glorious, as Anton reminds his father:

> The Chekhovs are peasants. The masters would beat them. My grandfather was birched and he in turn beat his wife. They punched him in the face. Punched faces and thrashed backsides, that's us! There's your heritage, merchant of the second guild: slave's blood, rot. (*The Ch. Brothers: Scenes*)

Rejection of his heritage, crudeness in his relations with his family, unrefined behavior, utilitarianism over everything, thinly disguised anti-Semitism, misogyny: "Woman is never superior to man. She may make a good physician, lawyer, etc. But in the field of artistic creation she's a goose" (*The Ch. Brothers: Scenes*). One looks in vain in this portrait for the sensitive, delicate model of an intellectual who carefully measured his words and was attracted by spirituality and ideals and treated his fellow beings with dignity and nobility. "Chekhov has been put in his place," remarked the critic Marina Davydova concerning Aleksandr Galibin's production at the Stanislavsky Theatre in May 2010: in his place among everyday people. But will a diminished genius perhaps leave more room for today's young playwrights?

SEQUELS

Some authors have invented historical or thematic sequels to Chekhov's plays, either moving the characters to a different period or composing a different ending that brings with it dramaturgical and stylistic variations. Unlike "continuations" where authors continue the work to bring it to its end, these sequels seek to take the play, in Genette's words, "beyond what was initially considered to be its end" (*Palimpsestes* 229). Chekhov's works today give the feeling of being open, impossible to conclude because they take the reader into a miraculous time and space that transcends genres, eras, and sociopolitical divisions. Vadim Levanov is the author of a "Firsiada," comprising two sequels to *The Cherry Orchard* titled *The Death of Firs* (1997) and *The Apocalypse of Firs* (2000) in which Firs is the main character. He explained his fascination in the following way: "What I like in Chekhov is that in his plays time is mythological, completely unreal, like in a folktale. This gives a certain feeling of comfort. It resembles a beautiful, fixed image, like old photos into which I would like to project myself" (qtd. in Moguilevskaia 2). To write a sequel is to insert

48 Marie-Christine Autant-Mathieu

into reality and a concrete world a time that is felt to be mythological and test the impact and the effects of the events and characters of the original work in this new time-space continuum.

A DETECTIVE STORY

In his play *The Seagull* (2000) Boris Akunin invents a detective sequel to Chekhov's work to correspond to the tastes of the post-Soviet Russian public. Akunin (real name Grigory Chkhartishvili, b. 1956) is the acclaimed author of a series of novels involving the detective Erast Petrovich Fandorin.[23] He uses his insights into the detective novel to reveal its tricks, and at the same time amuses himself by caricaturing Chekhov's characters (Arkadina's egoism, Treplev's jealousy) and exploiting the potential of certain details or events (the vial of ether, the final thunderstorm, the wheelchair, and the rivalry between Trigorin and Treplev). The rewrite begins with the final scene of *The Seagull*. Akunin revisits the set, multiplying the presence of stuffed animals and birds (crows, badgers, hares, cats, dogs, and an enormous seagull with its wings outstretched). The sound effects (the wind in the trees, the storm, and the lightning) evoke both the Chekhovian atmosphere and that of a detective thriller. A comic transitional scene presents the initial reactions to Treplev's presumed suicide. Medvedenko runs in pushing Sorin's wheelchair. Dorn confirms that Treplev is truly dead: his brain has splashed onto the wall. Arkadina gives a colorful image of her dead son with red blood on a green carpet. Shamrayev makes some down-to-earth reflections on the fact that the Persian carpet is done for and that one should try to remove the stains with some starch. Suddenly Dorn returns and declares that it was no suicide and, being a forensic doctor, gives the details: "The bullet came out through the left eye. It was fired at close range into the ear" (27). The murderer is close by. Since he has no relationship with the dead man, he suggests that he lead the inquiry. Akunin then offers six versions of the solution of the mystery. One by one Nina, Medvedenko, Masha, Shamrayev, Polina, Sorin, Arkadina, Trigorin, and Dorn himself are shown to have a motive for killing Treplev. Akunin's rewrite is paradoxical, since his play, if staged after Chekhov's, places characters and situations in a context where the action and the dialogues work brilliantly. The characters, coincidences, and inventions (Sorin as the hypochondriac, Treplev as the psychopath, Trigorin as the homosexual) in Akunin's anti-Chekhov are amusing as gags, but quickly lose their effect.

PLAYFUL ENTERTAINMENTS MINUS THE HAPPY ENDING

The play by Vladimir Zabaluyev (b. 1961) and Aleksey Zenzinov (b. 1961) *The Cherries Have Ripened in Uncle Vanya's Garden. A Dispute between Intellectuals in the Russian Style* (1999) is a historical continuation or

Rewriting Chekhov in Russia Today 49

montage in the form of a play within a play.[24] The frame play situates the characters of *The Cherry Orchard* fourteen years later in 1918, each character having joined a political camp.[25] The interior play is an exercise in styles, a variation on *Uncle Vanya* as Theatre of the Absurd, marionette theatre, commedia dell'arte, and Brechtian epic theatre. One version is intended to take place at the end of each of the acts of the frame play in an order that is suggested but random. As in the first scene of Mikhail Bulgakov's *Flight*, the characters have been arrested and gathered together in the cellar of a provincial manor house. Ranevskaya, in a wheelchair; Gayev, who is inseparable from his billiard cue; Varya's widower Jean-Louis Chrétien [*sic*]; Yepikhodov, a model prisoner; and Pishchik, who is glad to be relieved of his debts thanks to the revolution, have all been arrested as "bourgeois" and without party affiliation.[26] Lopakhin, who had been a minister in the Menshevik government, has been captured while fleeing. Yasha and Solyony (who has come from *Three Sisters*) are officers in the White Army. Opposed to them are the Reds: Charlotta and Petya Trofimov (rebaptized Shtykov: "The Bayonet"), who are dressed in leather jackets and carry revolvers, speak in slogans, and want only to shoot the bourgeoisie without delay.[27] (The executions take place just above the cellar: gunshots can be heard from time to time.) Petya, however, intervenes to delay their execution. The prisoners exchange memories and chat with their jailers. Lopakhin tells how Firs's death had reduced the value of the property and nostalgically recalls the jam season. Yepikhodov plays the guitar. Charlotta performs tricks, making appear in turn a billiard cue, a set of keys, and a rifle, all the while chanting: "My mother is the class struggle. My homeland is the social revolution. My fiancé is the revolver" (133). Lopakhin has been taken out to be executed, but comes back soaking: he has escaped being killed by running away, but Pishchik and Dasha have been shot. While waiting for their fate to be decided, Ranevskaya dies in her wheelchair. The others will remain hidden in the cellar.

Four stylistic variations are inserted into this dramatic material and refer back to *Uncle Vanya*. First, brief lines in telegraphic style create a pointillistic, incoherent, absurdist effect. Then, there is a scene where the actors have their faces fully turned to the audience behind a curtain where disjointed shapes of faces, false legs, and arms appear. The alternation of darkness and light allows the exchange of marionettes.[28] After that, Chekhov's characters adopt equivalent commedia dell'arte masks: Voynitsky is Pierrot; Sonya is Columbine; Yelena is Malvina; and Astrov is Harlequin.[29] This exercise foregrounds the erotic relations and female rivalries. The scene where Astrov shows his maps to Yelena happens in the following way: "The map of our district the way it was fifty years ago. Here you see the flora (*he loosens her hair*) and fauna (*he pinches her ear*). Now look down here (*he runs his finger over her neck*). This is what there was twenty-five years ago (*he takes her by the waist*). Now only a third of the surface is covered with forests . . . (*he slips his hand along her thigh*). Let's move to the third part (*he drops to the ground*

50 Marie-Christine Autant-Mathieu

and with one eye looks up her dress). The picture of the district today" and so on (152–53). The characters react to each other crudely: Malvina/Yelena pushes Harlequin/Astrov onto the bed and sticks her tongue out at Pierrot/Vanya when he discovers them. Astrov kicks Vanya several times. The latter falls flat on his face; Malvina pinches him, scratches him, and sits on his back. Marina takes a snort, sneezes, and wipes her nose with her dress. The final, Brechtian stylistic exercise echoes more the constructivist, eccentric trend of the 1920s than epic theatre. The characters wear the *prozodezhda* (constructivist work clothing) of the end of the twentieth century—jeans and T-shirts—and gambol on a steel construction, on a trapeze, and in front of a screen. Distance is achieved in several ways: the commentator gives a simultaneous translation of the English into Russian (which is bizarre, since Brecht was German); the same commentator gives summaries at the beginning of each tableau; and there are four Brecht-style ballads. Fragments of Chekhov's original text alternate with acrobatic numbers: Voynitsky, Astrov, Sonya, and Serebryakov lower themselves on ropes and remain suspended while talking; Telegin and Marina crawl over the metallic constructions. The intrusions of the frame play are very marked: little by little boys in red shirts appear, handcuff the characters, and lead them away. During Sonya's monologue, Vanya slashes his wrists and dies, letting his arms and legs hang from the metallic construction. Sonya, left alone, gets down on her knees with her head bent and says in a tired voice: "We shall rest . . . ," etc.

If the first part, the frame play, shows, unsurprisingly, the historical condemnation of Chekhov's characters as representatives of social types that were rejected by the revolution, in the second part they are tested as figures of popular and political theatre. They can hope for a future as marionettes or commedia figures, but seem condemned in the framework of political, Soviet, or Brechtian theatre. These Russian-style intellectuals seem to bear no useful value in the post-communist period and are difficult to integrate precisely because they do not have clear-cut features. Charlotta the revolutionary and Sonya the stubborn optimist are like machines that have become blinded by faith; they make no one laugh and, for the audience, their attitudes do not lead to any praxis.

THE END OF THE INTELLIGENTSIA

In Lyudmila Ulitskaya's *Russian Jam* (2003) the characters are direct descendants of Anya three and four generations later. The action takes place a hundred years after *Three Sisters*, which is the core text, with additions from *The Cherry Orchard* and *Uncle Vanya*.[30] Ulitskaya (b. 1943) portrays the descendants of Chekhov's idealistic characters as maladjusted, futile, lazy, and ultimately cowardly intellectuals.[31] The dacha, which was half demolished during World War II, is located in a "village of academics," and the fact that Natalya's father received the Stalin Prize for having

Rewriting Chekhov in Russia Today   51

created a species of kiwi refers back to a better time, a privileged situation that was brutally curtailed by the end of the USSR. The family faces inextricable money problems and cannot get a handle on their expenses, which keep growing (they are calculated in dollars) because of waste and a general impracticality. Mariya Yakovlevna declares indignantly:

> MARIYA YAKOVLEVNA. Five hundred dollars for the entire family. And believe me, I cut back on everything. [. . .]
> NATALYA IVANOVNA. Oh, stop talking about that. I am absolutely not interested.
> MARIYA YAKOVLEVNA. Well I am. [. . .] no one in this house, not one of you, knows how much a kilo of coffee costs!

They live on the rent from their apartment in Moscow, which they have rented to an Englishman; from Natalya's work as a translator; and from the financial help of Natalya's son Rostislav, a very rich investor in real estate. Yet they lack the bare necessities. Kostya is scratched by a cat and gets blood poisoning for want of disinfectant. They need to sell the dilapidated dacha, but refuse to do so in the name of their ancestors. Natalya declares: "The estate where the house is situated now with the village of Pokrovsky was the dowry of one of our great-great-grandmothers in 1828, when Pushkin was alive; I wrote it all down somewhere." Although they have been reduced to indigence by the coming of capitalism, they rattle on about literature and philosophize about Russian history, the national idea, the Slavophiles, and the theories of the Eurasians, to the total despair of the only member of the family to earn any money:

> ROSTISLAV. This family of crackpots represents the Russian intelligentsia on the way to extinction. [. . .] the literary term is superfluous people. They don't make any more like that now. I tell you these are rare specimens!

The family situation becomes dire when their English tenant in Moscow leaves the apartment a mess and Rostislav cuts off his financial help. First the electricity is cut off and then the water. As in *Three Sisters*, a fire occurs because of the conditions and further reduces their living space. Little by little strange underground vibrations drive away all the inhabitants in the environs; they go off to America, Israel, or Turkey. Mariya Yakovlevna tries to ensure the survival of the family by selling cherry jam, but then Rostislav arrives and pleads with them to leave urgently. After they have left the house explodes and collapses. In its place there will be an amusement park on top of a new metro station.

> VARVARA. There used to be the most beautiful estate in the world here. And now it's a desert. There's no one left to work!

52   Marie-Christine Autant-Mathieu

Rostislav. [. . .] We've worked enough! It's time to take it easy! There's going to be a Disneyland here! You understand? And you will see the sky filled with diamonds!

So this is where the hopes expressed in *Uncle Vanya* have ended up.

* * *

The transformations to which contemporary Russian authors have subjected Chekhov's works often twist the original text but rarely represent a pastiche or an imitation of the writing and the style. It is as if the rewriters have not felt themselves to be on his level and have restricted themselves to a reappropriation of the text itself in montages that caricature Chekhov's manner (laconicism, sound effects, and pauses). Chekhov's simple style is a sort of degree zero of pure language and seems to remain "inimitable." Only the subject of the plays, the situation, and the characters are susceptible to transformation (Petrushevskaya and Slavkin), burlesque travesty (Kolyada and Iskrenko), transposition and demotivation (Ulitskaya), deconstruction (Sorokin), and variation (Zenzinov and Zabaluyev).

These plays have been little staged. Following Meyerhold, directors have preferred to interpret Chekhov's original texts, whether plays or stories, in an original and caustic fashion. Witness the work of Kama Ginkas, who in his productions of the trilogy *The Black Monk* (1999), *The Lady with the Little Dog* (2001), and *Rothschild's Violin* (2004), directly transposed the literary text into a rich and fluid theatrical language, bypassing the adaptation stage. These inventive and often provocative productions attracted a large audience. It should also be said that Andrey Zholdak's *Seagull* (2001), staged as a series of attractions in a lake-cum-swamp, Yury Pogrebnichko's remakes of *Three Sisters* (since 1981), or *The Cherry Orchard Sketches* put on by Boris Yukhananov's MIR group (1990–1993) have attracted more interest and discussion than Sorokin's *Jubilee* or Zabaluyev and Zenzinov's *The Cherries Have Ripened in Uncle Vanya's Orchard*. Can it be that these rewrites go beyond the level of an exercise? According to Genette, "[a] true creator cannot touch the work of another without leaving his mark on it. Continuation thus becomes a pretext for an oblique rewrite" (*Palimpsestes* 223). With the exception of *Three Girls in Blue*, *The Hoop*, and (to a certain extent) *Oginski's Polonaise*, none of these plays has reached the level of notoriety of the original works that they transpose and parody. Whether or not their authors are overtly postmodern like Sorokin, they have simply played around with the original texts, appropriating and deconstructing them. Yet, like a phoenix, Chekhov is always reborn, emerging unscathed by all these manipulations. Benjamin remarked that to destroy the "aura" of a work serves to sharpen the "sense of identity" and, through reproduction, succeed in "standardizing the unique" (221). The rewrites of Chekhov have fed an abundant second-degree literature, but this process

Rewriting Chekhov in Russia Today 53

of standardization and fabrication of what Genette calls "others of the same" ("L'autre du même") has not diminished interest in the original works, which have emerged enhanced from these iconoclastic enterprises and remain just as living, topical, and necessary more than a century after their conception.

Translated by J. Douglas Clayton

NOTES

1. This chapter addresses only original works inspired by Chekhov, not stage adaptations of his prose.
2. Mikhail Ugarov, in a polemical article of 2005, claims that Chekhov had nipped in the bud several generations of playwrights, so that, like Malevich's black square, he had blocked all evolution: "Nowadays we are interested in the text without a subtext" ("Chekhov i pustota").
3. V. Katayev 336–55. At a conference in 2010 marking the sesquicentenary of the writer's birth Anatoly Smelyansky observed: "Through Chekhov we began to understand each other and even to understand what was happening in Russia . . . In a purely metaphysical manner we began to use phrases from Chekhov in conversation instead of long discussions and explanations" (71).
4. I would like to thank Olga Kuptsova, professor at VGIK, for her suggestions for readings.
5. Ira is Sveta and Tanya's cousin through her aunt, who is the daughter of the common great-grandmother.
6. In order to fully abandon herself to her lover Nikolay, Ira is obliged to abandon her child, which will cost her dearly.
7. The part of the dacha that Ira rents is expensive: she pays 240 rubles in rent, although her salary is only 120 rubles. In her section the roof does not leak, but there is no toilet.
8. There are numerous direct allusions to *The Cherry Orchard*: the thuds of the ax at the beginning as the planks are removed that cover windows and doors, the garden with the fruit trees, and the passage of a mysterious bird. But there are also quotations from *Uncle Vanya*: "We shall work together; we shall rest together"; "A marvelous sky with shining stars"; as well as a parody of *Three Sisters*: "Some ten, twenty, or thirty years will go by, and where shall we go? . . . Who will receive us as brothers?" Lars parodies Charlotta by performing tricks and speaking English. Slavkin also imitates the Chekhovian style of conversation about this and that and talking trivia (*pustyaki*) and composes dialogues that are actually monologues where everyone expresses himself without listening to the other.
9. These works are a belated echo of the innumerable parodies of Chekhov that appeared during his lifetime and that underlined the astonishing originality of his writing by parodying the style, the pauses, the atmosphere, the noises, the gunshots, and the spinelessness of the characters. See Chudakov 209–38. In the post-Soviet period Chekhov's work, now part of the canon, has become an element of mass culture and these parodic games are not just for the literary elite, but rather addressed to all Russians.
10. Other debased versions of Chekhov by Kolyada include *The Hen* and *The Seagull Has Sung (without Hope)*. Among the numerous ironic variations on

The Seagull from the 1980s, Aksenov's play *The Heron* and Yury Kuvaldin's story *The Crow* deserve mention.

11. In the 1990s it was New York, a city where one could get rich, not Paris that attracted the Russians. See the monologue *The American Woman* by Kolyada (1991).

12. Like Petrushevskaya, Razumovskaya made her debut as part of the new wave in the wake of Aleksandr Vampilov. Leonid Borisovich, the wealthy bureaucrat in this play, is reminiscent of both Lopakhin and Mechetkin, the giver of lessons in Vampilov's *Last Summer in Chulimsk*.

13. See especially the debates between Boris Groys, Mark Lipovetsky, and Vyacheslav Kuritsyn on Modernism, Postmodernism, Post-Sots, Post-Sovietism, etc.

14. Nina declares: "Difficult to act in your play. It doesn't have living characters" (Chekhov 13: 11).

15. "Toboro! Stur! Uiato! Zache! Baro! Omon!" The term OMON (Otryad militsii osobogo naznacheniya) refers to the Special Operations Unit of the police.

16. Kostenko stated that apart from Chekhov's dramatic works he used "the magazine *Goods and Services.*"

17. Typical objects (a wing chair, wildflowers, a plaid, a book, a cane) and sounds off (coughing, hammer blows, a melancholic waltz, Chebutykin's famous "Ta-ra-ra Boom-de-ay," numerous gunshots) are clichés that situate the performance.

18. He repeats Polina's line to Treplev.

19. Meyerhold directed *Thirty-Three Swoons*, a montage of three Chekhovian one-acters, but only in 1935.

20. In Bulgakov's play *Adam and Eve*, one of the characters finds a half-burnt Bible from which he tries to comprehend the meaning of the catastrophe or apocalypse that has occurred.

21. Lopakhin tells Ranevskaya that he has read a book and didn't understand a thing: "Look, here. They mention here an orchard." RANEVSKAYA. "Orchard, what orchard?" GAYEV. "It's a surname." ("Sad"—the Russian for orchard—is placed in the dictionary next to Sade, the Marquis.)

22. I would like to thank Yelena Kovalskaya for obtaining for me the text of the play, which was unpublished at the time of writing this study.

23. Akunin is an expert on Japanese civilization, editor of the prestigious journal *Inostrannaya literatura*, essayist, literary translator, and novelist.

24. "The cherries have ripened" is the title of a gulag song composed in Magadan and very well known in popular culture. See Domansky 77–85.

25. Mention should be made here of a play by Viktor Merezhko, *If One Only Knew* (1992, unpublished), which also takes place during the civil war: Irina is a lesbian, Masha an alcoholic, Olga seduces her pupils in school, Tuzenbakh is a homosexual, and Chebutykin takes drugs.

26. As disasters accumulate, Yepikhodov's nickname changes to "seventy-seven misfortunes," then "1001."

27. The authors have added two new characters: David Nedobeyko, commissar of armored train 14–69 (an allusion to Vsevolod Ivanov's famous play, which was put on in the Moscow Art Theatre in 1928 and sealed the acceptance by this theatre of the values of the Bolshevik revolution), and Yaroslav, a "White Czech," which permits a pun when the noun is used in the genitive plural: *belochekhov.*

28. Chekhov's text remains unchanged: "ASTROV'S MARIONETTE. It has been a long time since I have loved anyone. / SONYA'S MARIONETTE. A long time? / ASTROV'S MARIONETTE. A long time. / ASTROV'S MARIONETTE. The only person for whom I feel a little affection is your old

Rewriting Chekhov in Russia Today   55

nurse, for old times' sake … […] What still moves me is beauty (*he wiggles his false right leg*). I am not indifferent to it (*he wiggles his false left leg*). It does seem to me that Yelena Andreevna could, if she wanted, turn my head in just one day" (150).
29. Malvina is the name of a pretty girl with blue hair in Aleksey Tolstoy's *The Little Golden Key or the Adventures of Buratino* (1936).
30. Anya was the grandmother of Natalya Ivanovna and Andrey.
31. Andrey and Natasha are brother and sister. Andrey is reminiscent of Vanya because of his financial and relational problems and Yepikhodov because of his awkwardness. He dresses in a robe, is a secret drinker, and plays the piano. Natalya has three daughters (Varvara, a religious fanatic; Yelena, an amateur painter who refuses to be a letter carrier because she speaks three languages; and Lisa, a punk rebel) and a son, Rostislav, the only one to have both feet on the ground and a remunerative profession. Rostislav is married to Alla, a successful novelist, who supports the family indirectly since it is her mother-in-law, Natalya, a graduate in English, who translates her novels for export. Yelena's husband, Kostya, is a complete good-for-nothing, a yoga adept whose passion is electronic music. Natalya's sister-in-law Mariya (or Makaniya), who devotes herself to the housework, also lives in the dacha. Last there is a handyman neighbor, Semen, who is permanently on call to repair the very dilapidated building with its dangerous flooring, its unusable inside toilette, and its frequent electrical cuts.

WORKS CITED

Aksenov, Vasilii. *Tsaplia*. N.d. modernlib.ru. Web. 16 Dec. 2011.

Akunin, Boris. *Chaika*. Saint Petersburg: Neva, 2001. Print.

Benjamin, Walter. "The Work of Art in the Age of Mechanical Reproduction." *Illuminations*. Trans. Harry Zohn. Ed. and introd. Hannah Arendt. New York: Schocken Books, 1969. 217–51. Print.

Bogayev, Oleg. *Mertvye ushi ili noveishaia istoriia tualetnoi bumagi. Arabeski. P'esy ural'skikh avtorov.* Ed. N. Kolyada. Ekaterinburg, 2000. 217–54. Print.

Bulgakov, Mikhail. *Adam and Eve. Six Plays*. London: Methuen Drama, 1991. Print.

———. *Flight & Bliss: Two Plays*. New York: New Directions Pub. Corp., 1985. Print.

Chekhov, Anton. *Polnoe sobranie sochinenii*. 18 vols. Moscow: Nauka, 1983–88. Print.

Chudakov, A. P. "Dramaturgiia Chekhova v krivom zerkale parodii." *Chekhovskii sbornik*. Ed. A.P. Chudakov. Moscow: Literaturnyi institut im. Gor'kogo, 1999. 209–38. Print.

Davydova, M. "M. Chekhova postavili na mesto." *Izvestiia*. 2 June 2010. Smotr. ru. Web. 16 Dec. 2011.

Domanskii, Iurii. *Stat'i o Chekhove*. Tver': Liliia Print, 2001. Print.

Gavrilova, Marina. *Tri sestry i Diadia Vania. Baltiiskie sezony*. Baltiiskie sezony: St. Petersburg, 2001. 4–20. Print.

Genette, Gérard. "L'autre du même." *Figures IV*, Paris: Seuil (Coll. Poétique), 1999. 101–107. Print.

———. *Palimpsestes: La Littérature au second degré*. Paris: Seuil; Coll. Poétique, 1982. Print.

Gremina, Elena. *Brat'ia Ch. Stseny*. Unpublished manuscript provided by Elena Kovalskaia. TS.

56 Marie-Christine Autant-Mathieu

———. *Sakhalinskaia zhena.* 1996. theatre.ru. N. pag. Web. 16 Dec. 2011.

Iskrenko, Nina. *Vishnevyi sad prodan?* 1993. vavilon.ru. N. pag. Web. 16 Dec. 2011.

Kataev, Vladimir. *Chekhov plius . . . Predshestvenniki, sovremenniki, preemniki.* Moscow: Iazyki slavianskoi kul'tury, 2004. Print.

Koliada, Nikolai. *Amerikanka.* 1993, pub. 2008. lib.rus.ec. Web. 16 Dec. 2011.

———. *"Chaika spela." (Beznadega). P'esy dlia liubimogo teatra.* Ekaterinburg: Bank kul'turnoi informatsii, 1994. 47–83. Print.

———. *Kuritsa* [*The Hen*]. *Persidskaia siren' i drugie p'esy.* Ekaterinburg: Kalan, 1997. 377–412. Print.

———. *Polonez Oginskogo. P'esy dlia liubimogo teatra.* Ekaterinburg: Bank kul'turnoi informatsii, 1994. 85–139. Print.

Kostenko, Konstantin. *Chaika A. P.Chekhova (remix).* N.d. theatre-library.ru. N. pag. Web. 16 Dec. 2011.

Kuvaldin, Iurii. *Vorona. Novyi mir.* 1995–1996. magazines.russ.ru. Web. 16 Dec. 2011.

Levanov, Vadim. *Apokalipsis ot Firsa ili vishnevyi son Firsa.* N.d. Theatre-library. ru. Web. 16 Dec. 2011.

———. *Smert' Firsa.* N.d. Theatre-library.ru. Web. 16 Dec. 2011.

Moguilevskaia, Tania. "À propos des tendances dans la dramaturgie russe actuelle." *Ubu. Scènes d'Europe.* 22–23 Oct. 2001. theatre-russe.info. Web. 16 Dec. 2011.

Petrushevskaia, Liudmila. *Tri devushki v golubom.* Moscow: Iskusstvo, 1989. Print.

Propp, Vladimir. *The Morphology of the Fairy Tale.* 2nd ed. Trans. Laurence Scott. Rev. and ed. Louis A Wagner. Austin: U of Texas P, 1971. Print.

Razumovskaia, Liudmila. "Frantsuzskie strasti na podmoskovnoi dache." *Sovremennaia dramaturgiia* 1 (1999): 31–55. Print.

Serebrennikov, Kirill. "Raz v mesiats publika khochet byt' razdrazhenna. Razgovor vedet Polina Bogdanova." *Sovremennaia dramaturgiia* 1 (2002): 174–78. Print.

Slapovskii, Aleksei. *Moi vishnevyi sadik.* 2004. theatre-library.ru. Web. 16 Dec. 2011.

Slavkin, Viktor. *Serso. Vzroslaia doch' molodogo cheloveka. P'esy.* Moscow: Sovetskii pisatel', 1990. Print.

Smelianskii, Anatolii. *Slovo o Chekhove. Teatral'nyi festival' im. A. P. Chekhova. K 150–letiiu so dnia rozhdeniia A. P. Chekhova.* Moscow: MTF A. P. Chekhova, 2010. Print.

Sorokin, Vladimir. *Iubilei.* 2007. <lib.rus.ec/b/53569/read>. N. pag. Web. 21 Mar. 2012.

Tolstoi, Aleksei. *Zolotoi kliuchik, ili Prikliucheniia Buratino.* Minsk: Universitetskoe, 1998. az.lib.ru. Web. 27 Mar. 2012.

Ugarov, Mikhail. "Chekhov i pustota." *Teatral,* 1 Sept. 2005. Web. 16 Dec. 2011.

Ulitskaia, Liudmila. *Russkoe varen'e. Luchshie p'esy 2006.* Moscow: Deistvuiushchie litsa, 2007. N. pag. <http://lib.aldebaran.ru>. Web. 16 Dec. 2011.

Vampilov, Akeksandr. *Duck-Hunting; Last Summer in Chulimsk.* Trans. Patrick Miles. Nottingham, England: Bramcote Press, 1994. Print.

Vyrypaev, Ivan. "Ia—konservator. Beseda vedet Elena Kutlovskaia." *Iskusstvo kino* 2 (2004). Web. 16 Dec. 2011.

Zabaluev, Vladimir, and Aleksei Zenzinov. *Pospeli vishni v sadu u Diadi Vani.* 2000. netslova.ru. Web. 16 Dec. 2011.

Zarkhi, N., E. Kutlovskaia, and E. Stishova. "'Otkazat'sia ot banana radi interestnoi igry.' 'Novaia drama': anketa IK." *Iskusstvo kino* 2 (2004). Web. 16 Dec. 2011.

3   The Flight of the Dead Bird
Chekhov's *The Seagull* and Williams's *The Notebook of Trigorin*

Maria Ignatieva

It is no secret that Tennessee Williams deeply loved Chekhov's prose and plays: he admitted it many times himself. But did Chekhov influence Williams's plays and creativity in general as much and as deeply—both in content and form—as the latter wanted us to believe? Williams's final play, *The Notebook of Trigorin*, was based upon Chekhov's play *The Seagull*, which had been his lifelong artistic and literary infatuation. A study and comparative analysis of these two plays allow us to observe an exciting process described by Yury Lotman as the development of a "meaning-space created by the text around itself [which] enters into relationship with the cultural memory (tradition) already formed in the consciousness of the audience" (18). On the one hand, Tennessee Williams is a perceiver of the play. On the other, while translating the play from one cultural mode into another, he gave the play new meanings, in which the themes, topics, and motifs have mutated. The text of Chekhov's play itself, if we use Lotman's image, is like a grain of wheat, which contains within itself a program for its own development, which "is not given once and for all [. . .] The inner and as yet unfinalized determinacy of its structure provides a reservoir of dynamism when influenced by contacts with new contexts" (18). Hence Williams, by giving his own interpretation of *The Seagull*, modified Chekhov's play: he decoded it from Russian culture and then re-encoded it in American culture, presenting it to American audiences in a way that he assumed would be better understood than in even the best literal and literary translation of the original. By doing so, Williams changed the play's capacity for cultural memory, which now included historical events and other interpretations that occurred outside the text and in the twentieth century in general, as well as in Williams's personal life. Thus, Williams's play becomes a most interesting example of Chekhov mutations, and it allows us to see how the Chekhovian modes—his style, themes, and characters—have been transformed in the laboratory of the world's most popular American playwright.

The Seagull was Williams's passion since he was in his early twenties. Throughout his life, he reinterpreted the play, each time according to his personal and professional development. As a young writer, he associated himself with Konstantin, who, like Williams himself, was unrecognized, was

58 *Maria Ignatieva*

dreaming about new forms in theatre, and was fighting the theatre routine. At that time, Williams's homosexuality often placed him in the position of a social outcast, which paralleled Konstantin's loneliness and his existence on the periphery of life. In middle age Williams, having established himself as a writer and a playwright, and open about his homosexuality, identified himself with Doctor Dorn: a wise and cynical worldly *bon vivant* who was detached from the realities of the lake and yet was fully enjoying life. At the end of his life, Williams reinterpreted *The Seagull* once again, and this time he was able to create his own play based on it: *The Notebook of Trigorin.* This time it was Trigorin who had become the central figure of the play. Williams perceived him as an individual torn between conflicting masculine and feminine forces similar to those that Williams had been fighting all his life. Although Trigorin bitterly complained about his writing, about not being as great a writer as Turgenev or Tolstoy, his creativity could not be called insignificant: in a sense, the whole play is being written by him, but at the same time he is a character in it as well. Perhaps, as a person, he is meek and gutless; however, Trigorin the writer is put on a par with both Williams and Chekhov.

While working on *The Seagull*, Chekhov infused the play with his own life experiences. The relationship between Chekhov's life and his work has been thoroughly studied by Chekhovian scholars (such as Magarshack and Golomb), who have revealed how much Chekhov's personal experiences contributed to the themes of the play (Mizinova's affair with Potapenko and the death of their illegitimate child is echoed in the story of Nina Zarechnaya and Trigorin; the attempted suicide of Isaac Levitan is mirrored in Treplev's attempted and actual suicide, etc.). In no other play written by Chekhov did life and art so counteract, echo, mirror, and parody each other as in *The Seagull*. It is all about art and the artists, either real or "wannabes," and their interference with real life. It is about creativity and fame: Arkadina is a famous actress, and Nina is a wannabe; Trigorin is a successful writer, and Konstantin is a wannabe. "Two hundred pounds" of love, as Chekhov wrote in a letter to Suvorin of 21 October 1895 (*PSS* 12: 357) filled the play with lyrical and farcical scenes: between Polina and Dorn, Konstantin and Nina, Nina and Trigorin, Arkadina and Trigorin. It therefore does not come as a surprise that Williams, whose personal life experiences had in general been a major ingredient in his plays, was so attracted to *The Seagull* in particular. It is quite revealing that Williams's personal approach to the play (which is a forte of American drama, in general) changed several times the sum of the play's context and reconstructed its integral meaning. In this context, it is useful to refer again to Lotman:

> If a text stayed in the consciousness of the perceiver only as itself, then the past would be represented to us as a mosaic of disconnected fragments. But for the perceiver, a text is always a metonymy of a reconstructed integral meaning, a discrete sign of the non-discrete essence.

The sum of the context in which a given text acquires interpretation and which are in a way incorporated in it may be termed the text's memory. (18)

Thus, *The Notebook of Trigorin* became an absolutely unique cultural document, which absorbed not only the interpretations of several generations of twentieth-century theatre, but also several layers of Williams's own interpretations of the play. These were accumulated during the playwright's life and became encoded in the text. Additionally, the fact that Williams was a playwright himself is exceptionally important, for a text "which is filtered through the code of tradition is a text filtered through other texts which serve as its interpreter" (Lotman 70). Thus, the text of *The Notebook of Trigorin* should be interpreted through the texts of Williams's plays, as well, just as Williams's plays should be analyzed in the context of Chekhov's plays.

Williams's early analysis of Chekhov strikes readers as thoughtful and rather mature, and the playwright would remain faithful to some of his thoughts and impressions for the rest of his life. In his first essay, Williams defined all Chekhov's major plays, including *The Seagull*, as "tragedy of inaction" (*New Selected* 251). The dilemma of action versus inaction and external versus internal action in Chekhov's plays has been one of the most explored avenues in Chekhovian studies, from the first reviews of his plays and throughout a hundred years of semantic, semiotic, comparative, and other types of analysis. Recent scholars insist that Chekhov's plays are packed with action. However, Williams did not apply the same meaning as theatre and literary critics and Chekhovian scholars. The expression *tragedy of inaction* for Williams does not refer to the structure of the play, but describes a certain existentialism that he saw in Chekhov's plays: the characters, like seagulls, were "shot down by chance," and whatever they did, their fates would not change (*New Selected* 251). Critics often called Williams's plays "Chekhovian," referring to their mood, atmosphere, and the essence of the characters' connections, which are all based on misunderstanding and miscommunication. I would argue, however, that although Chekhov influenced Williams, the latter is the least Chekhovian playwright in the twentieth century, and his interpretation of *The Seagull* demonstrates this. If the outcome of events does not change the state of things in Chekhov's drama, action in Williams's plays, on the contrary, significantly changes the state of things. In all of his plays, on the other hand, tragic *inaction* is the condition in which characters exist. The *tragedy of inaction* is profoundly explored during the course of each play and contrasted with the *tragedy of action*. In *The Glass Menagerie*, the final action—the departure of Tom—is the only true action with consequences, which will presumably destroy the lives of the two women. A similar situation exists in *A Streetcar Named Desire* and in *Cat on a Hot Tin Roof*. This *inaction* is the essence of the unhappy balance of Williams's characters' worlds, its

60 *Maria Ignatieva*

solidifying ground: if the character(s) decided to act at the end of the play, this unhappy balance would be destroyed, and reality itself would be presented in its prosaic and merciless certainty. Although action for Williams is in the ability to change one's own world, and by doing so to change the worlds of others, both changes are often equally tragic. Thus, Tom's final action in *The Glass Menagerie* ruins the lives of his mother and sister and drastically changes the state of things; on the contrary, in *The Seagull*, although Konstantin kills himself, the state of things remains unchanged. Williams emphasized that the characters in *The Seagull* are captives of life, and whether they act or not, the results would be the same. The characters' fates are such that whether Konstantin failed or succeeded, Nina would not love him; whether Nina were a bad or a good actress, Trigorin would not love her; and whether Masha is married or not, Konstantin still would be annoyed with her. It is "a tangle in which all are helpless victims: no one is really to blame" (*New Selected* 251).

Williams's *The Notebook of Trigorin* is carefully wrapped in such legal terms as "a free adaptation," "based on a translation from the Russian," "edited, and with an introduction." At the time when Williams was *freely interpreting* the play, it was not a common practice, but, as we know, has become so ever since. There was nothing surprising about the adaptations based on Greek myths. Here, however, Williams was reinterpreting a revolutionary play that had remained popular in the twentieth century, which he called the "first and greatest of modern plays." So why reinterpret it? Williams explained: "I have an intense longing to somehow utilize my quite different qualities as a playwright to bring him [Chekhov] more closely, more audibly to you [the spectator] than I have seen him brought to you in any American production" (*Notebook* 33). In other words, although Williams called *The Seagull* a great play, he obviously did not believe in its ability to deliver itself to the American audience.

Thus, his "free adaptation" is more of a directorial plan of *The Seagull*. As Allean Hale wrote, "Early on, Williams thought of directing *The Seagull*, and over the years, often returned to the play" (Williams, *Notebook* 1). In order to understand the origins of Williams's intention to rewrite/reinterpret *The Seagull*, it is important to remember that his initial infatuation with the play was literary and not theatrical. The play that he envisioned after the first reading and his lifelong rereadings of it differed from the productions that he later saw in theatres. Thus, he decided that either the translation was bad or the creative team and the American audiences did not understand it. On the other hand, all that Williams read about the Moscow Art Theatre productions in historical retrospective convinced him that it was possible to stage the play ideally . . . in Russia. Thus, Williams's love for the text and his additional reading of the history of its interpretation and Chekhov's life created in his mind an ideal yet imaginary theatre production: he needed to be the director of this play and the cultural interpreter of the realities, which, he assumed, Americans would not understand

The Flight of the Dead Bird   61

unless they were translated by an American and for Americans. The kind of work that Williams had undertaken placed him in Stanislavsky's shoes when the latter was writing his mise-en-scènes for *The Seagull* in 1898, trying to make the play comprehensible for Russians.

The directorial plan or directorial explication was a new literary-theatrical genre created by Stanislavsky at the dawn of the Moscow Art Theatre. Stanislavsky's directorial plan of *The Seagull*, published in 1938 for the first time, was his detailed vision of the play, which was based upon Chekhov's play and yet seriously differed from it. Konstantin Rudnitsky writes: "Essentially, the idea of the creation (of such plan) transformed the director into a full author of the performance [. . .] demanding the complete subordination of all the theatrical means and determining [. . .] not only the general idea of the show, but all the details" (12). Stanislavsky divided the text of the play: Chekhov's text was on the left-hand pages of his notebook, and his directorial interpretation was on the right; this became an independent literary and theatrical document. The mutation of Chekhov's play began at this moment, when a director's vision was written as an independent text that nonetheless originated in the play. I believe that that was exactly Williams's method of interpreting the play: as coauthor and director, translating it into a new theatrical reality. Like many contemporary directors, Williams cut parts of the text, emphasized some characters' lines and eradicated others, changed the play's tempo-rhythm and replaced it with his own; he developed his own symbols and even reworked the ending. Every text mutates when a director models it according to his vision and interpretation; Williams, while working on his play/directorial plan, made the Chekhovian text undergo tremendous transformations. If we were to use contemporary medical terms, it might remind us of recent successful facial transplants, but however successful the medical procedure was, its theatrical counterpart did not reach the desired fruition.

Williams's changes to Chekhov's *The Seagull* are found in the changes of the characters, the motivations of their behavior, the events in their lives (for example, Nina's child does not die but is adopted by an American couple, which makes this branch of the play a true soap opera), and in the alteration of Chekhovian theatrical devices. The first change touched the seagull as a symbol: it lost the uniqueness of its image, as well as its complex connections to multiple references (meanings), together with its poetry and its magic. Lotman writes:

A symbol is bound to cultural memory, and an entire series of symbolic images runs vertically through the whole course of human history [. . .] But it is the system of relationships which the poet establishes between the fundamental image-symbol which is the crucial thing. Symbols are always polysemic, and only when they form themselves into the crystal grid of mutual connections do they create that "poetic world" which marks the individuality of each artist. (87)

62   Maria Ignatieva

In Chekhov's play, the "crystal grid" of a seagull is created, consisting of multilayered interrelations and interconnections between the story, the characters, and the seagull. As Nina makes her first entrance, she compares herself to a seagull (as noticed by many Chekhovian scholars, she had lived all her life by the same lake, only on the opposite side of it). However, as a seagull, she finds her true habitat only when she crosses the lake to the Sorins' estate. In the second act, Konstantin enters with the seagull that he has killed and puts the dead bird at Nina's feet. Then Nina (as if Chekhov were mocking the critics who would seek symbolism in the play through her words) refers to the dead seagull, saying, "And this seagull is a symbol of some kind, too, but forgive me, I don't understand" (*PSS* 13: 27). The third appearance of the seagull occurs in Nina and Trigorin's conversation: the writer calls it a beautiful bird and immediately compares the seagull to Nina. He composes a little plot for a short story about a happy girl who lives by the lake and whose life is accidentally destroyed, like that of the seagull. According to Trigorin's recollection on the following scene, his association of Nina with a seagull was inspired by color: the seagull was white and Nina was wearing a light-colored dress. The first round of multifaceted images of the seagull is complete. In act 4, the symbol of the seagull reaches its peak. Konstantin mentions that Nina signed her letters as "Seagull," as well as repeating in her letters that she was "a seagull." Shamrayev reminds Trigorin that the latter left something behind at the estate two years before and takes the stuffed seagull out of a cupboard. Trigorin claims that he does not have any memory of it. At the same time, Nina reappears in Treplev's study. She calls herself a seagull three times during her conversation with Konstantin, then insists that, no, she is not a seagull but an actress, and then leaves. As Vladimir Katayev writes, she gives Konstantin three blows, and the last one is lethal:

> But it is Nina who finally destroys him. At their last meeting, after they have summed up the consequences of their collisions with life [. . .] Nina inflicts three cruel and pitiless blows on Kostya: she again scorns his love, she acknowledges once more her desperate passion for Trigorin, and she reminds him of the play that was the beginning of all his subsequent misfortunes. (176–77)

In fact, if we compare this scene to the one when Konstantin throws the seagull at Nina's feet, we find that in this scene the hunter and the bird are completely reversed. Now it is the seagull that kills the hunter, which, although echoing the first act, has the completely opposite result. As Lotman writes, "symbols with elementary expression levels have greater cultural and semantic capacity than symbols that are more complex" (104). Chekhov's *Seagull* is proof of this postulate. We can ask ourselves whether Nina or Konstantin were seagulls; certainly, they were seagulls, too, but

The Flight of the Dead Bird 63

no one owns the symbol in particular, and yet both lives are reflected upon and are created through the seagull.

Tennessee Williams desymbolized the text, turning the symbol into a collection of comparisons and messages. Even as a young man, in the 1930s, Williams did not see the seagull as an exceptional representation of either Nina or Konstantin: for him, all the characters are "like seagulls shot down by chance. What happens to them is mainly outside their control" (*New Selected* 251). Williams never changed his belief that all of them (except Dorn, in the final version) deserve being "treated" like seagulls, including Trigorin, Masha, and Medvedenko, for the circumstances of their life and love "made them captive" (251–52). Trigorin is a prisoner of his sexual ambiguity; Masha is a prisoner of her love for Konstantin; Medvedenko of his love for Masha; Polina of her love for Dorn; and Arkadina is a prisoner of the stage and Trigorin. But, if everyone is a seagull, then no one is a seagull. Williams's play based on *The Seagull* could be called *A Seagull* or *The Seagulls*. But such an approach—that they all are seagulls—deprives the play of the necessary contrast of the seagull and the play's realities, the comparison of the infinite and the finite, as well as of comic characteristics that go side by side with the characters' hierarchical positioning in the play, especially that of Medvedenko and Shamrayev, the characters who are associated with the stuffed seagull rather than with the flying or the killed one. Williams eradicates the line in which Nina compares herself to a seagull in the first scene. In fact, there is only one mention of the bird in Williams's version: when Konstantin compares Nina's weight to that of his mother's. We can speculate that perhaps American culture does not carry an image of the seagull in the so-called symbolic nucleus of the culture that would be compatible with the Russian one. The image of the seagull in American culture finds itself between Richard Bach's *Jonathan Livingston Seagull*, which was written in 1970 and became a best seller for two years (the image of Christian stoicism and self-improvement) and Alfred Hitchcock's *The Birds* (1963), as well as seagull scavengers, associated with piles of trash rather than with the beauty of flight. Similar transformations happened in Williams's adaptation. In Chekhov, we read that Treplev enters with *the dead seagull*, lays *the seagull* at Nina's feet, tells Nina how ghastly it was of him to kill *that seagull*, then Nina picks up *the seagull* and looks at it. Comparing this scene to Williams's, we read that Konstantin abruptly drops *the dead bird* at Nina's feet, Konstantin picks up *the bird* and holds it towards her, then Nina, after mentioning that the bird was a seagull, asks Konstantin whether presenting her with *this dead bird* was his new way to communicate through symbols. The dead bird (it just happens to be a seagull) is covered with blood. The multifaceted life of Chekhov's symbol (Nina as a seagull—the dead seagull—Nina and the seagull in Trigorin's story and his life—Nina's life as that of a seagull—the stuffed seagull—Nina's liberation from the symbol) is replaced by a singular object, which is mentioned for the first time in the play when Konstantin has killed it and

64 Maria Ignatieva

has no previous references. In Williams's last act, in the same nonpoetical manner, through comparisons and explanations, the seagull reenters. Nina calls herself a seagull, explaining that a seagull is free and does not belong to anyone. In response to Konstantin's comment about Trigorin, she denies that Trigorin owns her: "It must be a thing of the moment, then flight again and even when flying together they seem to be each alone" (88). Thus, Williams continues to explain the title of Chekhov's play, and, in doing so, he diminishes and desymbolizes it even further. Nina's comparison of herself and her child to seagulls—"the child of a seagull is a seagull too" (90)—sounds clichéd and further waters down the onetime symbol. At the same time, Trigorin explains to Shamrayev that he had never ordered a dead seagull to be mounted, for dead things were depressing. Having, however, explained (and thus destroyed) the Chekhovian primary symbol, Williams chose to develop another one, secondary in the play, but that had cast a spell on him: the mysterious, bewitching lake. In the original *Seagull*, Dorn comments on the enchanting lake at the end of act 1. In Williams's version, the lake as a symbol gains its multiple and interconnected meanings throughout the play. Thus, referring to it, Trigorin says, "what the lake tells us is what God tells us—we just don't know his language" (28). Swimming in the lake is a part of pagan ritual: it is sinful and associated with male homosexuality. Trigorin often goes swimming with Yakov, while obviously involved in homosexual games. In the very first scene, he invites Konstantin for a swim, too, but the latter refuses. Konstantin and Nina are described by Trigorin as *companions by the lake.* Nina talks about the lake as if it were her real pagan parent, "The lake must let me go and so must Kostya" (47). A storm accompanies the last act, with thunder and lightning. Konstantin kills himself by "the lakeshore which is lighted slowly in the background" (97). However, it would not have seemed strange if Konstantin, like Johannes in Hauptmann's *Lonely Lives*, walked into the water and was devoured by it.

One of the most important changes that Williams undertakes, which goes to the core of Chekhov's dramas in general, is the eradication of subtext. In *The Notebook of Trigorin* subtext (meaning the wealth of underlying feelings and unspoken thoughts) is not a means of communication between the characters and between the characters and the audience; it is replaced by hints of hidden secrets and by the gradual or not-so-gradual unearthing of them (for example, Trigorin's swimming with Yakov, Trigorin's invitation to Konstantin to swim with him, and then the discovery of Trigorin's sexual orientation in act 3). While Chekhov's Medvedenko does not even hint at his knowledge of Masha's love for Konstantin, Williams's Medvedenko, who is sexually obsessed with Masha, not only knows about it and discusses it with her, but also accuses her of giving herself to him. While Chekhov's Trigorin answered Shamrayev with one line ("I don't remember"), Williams's Trigorin talks about the dead bird; Arkadina then goes on to ask him about his love for fishing. Everything

The Flight of the Dead Bird   65

is said and explained sooner or later, and there could be no doubts about Dorn's past and present relationship with Polina or Masha's unchanged feelings for Konstantin after marriage (in fact, she says that she would have given herself to Konstantin at once if he were interested), etc. Williams had no interest in the hidden feelings of the characters, and he brought all the concealed emotions to the surface. From the start, Medvedenko knows about Masha's love for Konstantin, and he mockingly confronts her. Masha talks about Arkadina's love–hate relationship with Konstantin. In general, the love–hate relationship is the most significant aspect of all the characters' relationships: Konstantin and Arkadina, Arkadina and Trigorin, and Masha and Medvedenko after they marry. As much as Williams accentuates the physical nature of Medvedenko's love for Masha, the nature of the Arkadina–Trigorin relationship is also described in the very first scene. According to Masha's mother, Arkadina and Trigorin rarely share a bedroom, and most of the time they sleep separately. In Williams's interpretation of *The Seagull*, his characters have embarrassingly direct lines about the things they feel, did, or would do: everything becomes definite and nothing is left for any kind of ambivalent interpretation. It would seem, based on everything said in the preceding, that there is nothing in common between Chekhov and Williams, and that Chekhov's writing had become Williams's lifelong passion because "opposites attract." Nevertheless, however paradoxical it may sound, the reasons for and the results of Chekhov's use of subtext and Williams's eschewal of it are similar: whether emotions and thoughts are not expressed verbally (Chekhov) or said with absolute clarity (Williams), the state of the world does not change and can hardly be explained.

A child of Freudian, twentieth-century American society, Williams was liberated from the classical conventions and also brazenly modified sexual norms of life in his writing. His use of subtext was often an equivalent of *sub-sex* (and here I introduce a new term), motivating characters' behavior through powerful sexual drives. Human sexuality for Williams was eternal, bewitching, and beyond human control, as beguiling as the lake in *The Notebook of Trigorin*. Masha passionately desires Konstantin; Medvedenko is sexually obsessed with Masha, even more so after marrying her and being completely deprived of intimacy; Nina is sexually drawn to Trigorin and vice versa; Dorn tries to seduce both Masha and Nina; Nina is almost sexually assaulted by a stranger on the way to the Sorins' estate; Trigorin is involved with Yakov, is flirting with Konstantin, and, at the same time, is falling in love with Nina, while, needless to say, he continues to live with Arkadina as her companion. We also hear about Trigorin's young male lovers, and Arkadina even unfavorably compares him to Oscar Wilde.

As if he were a director, casting actors for the roles and adjusting their parts according to his vision, Williams's reinterpretation changed the characters' life stories significantly. The American audience that confronts Arkadina at the end of the play is the same group of people whose cultural

66 Maria Ignatieva

memory required Williams's changes in the play and demands explanations from Chekhov (from his point of view). Following his understanding of the audience's perception of "Russianness," Williams adds the conversation about the Tsarina who does not understand Russian and speaks only German; he makes the servants speak Russian as they bring a samovar onstage, together with red wine and beer. He also rethinks the reasons behind the characters' relationships, incorporating American pragmatism into them instead of Russian codes of behavior unknown to American audiences. According to Williams's interpretation, it was Arkadina who started Trigorin's literary career: she used her connections to introduce a young unknown writer, Trigorin, to the literary world, and thus has reminded him of the favor she did him ever since. Furthermore, she resorts to blackmailing him and threatens to disgrace him publicly for his homosexuality. Being drawn to Nina and being encouraged by her, the writer starts their relationship, openly admitting that he would not break up with Arkadina. He is thrilled with her understanding that the "world turns on—successfully practiced—duplicity" (68). So, unlike in Chekhov's play, Nina enters the relationship with Trigorin knowing about his commitment to Arkadina and not having any illusions about him. Williams also makes it clear that in her future Nina could become either a kept woman or a common prostitute. Before Nina leaves for Moscow, Trigorin thrusts "a number of bills lingeringly down the bodice of her white dress" (67). To no surprise, in the last act Nina and Dorn both refer to their child as a bastard. Thus we see how the great playwright consistently transforms *The Seagull* into America's most popular television genre: the soap opera. The body of Konstantin is brought onstage by servants at the end of the play "(*Slowly, from far upstage two male servants are bearing Constantine's body downstage*)" (98); the scene is reminiscent of the one that was eradicated by Chekhov in *The Three Sisters*, in which the body of Tuzenbakh is being carried in the distance. Thus, at the end of the play, Williams completely reverses the trajectory of development of the Chekhovian drama, in which more and more events occurred backstage, from *Ivanov* to *The Cherry Orchard*.

The play *The Notebook of Trigorin* suffers from the multiple objectives with which Williams loaded it. Besides being a directorial plan and containing Williams's practical directorial vision, it is also the summary of his favorite characters, themes, and motifs, as well as his attempt to infect American spectators with his love for and devotion to Chekhov and his fondness of Russian culture. In Chekhov's characters, Williams summarized some of his lifelong favorite characters from his own plays and reproduced them in Arkadina, Trigorin, and Treplev: his powerful, egoistic, and manipulative women, facing their aging with anguish, and torn men, both gifted artistically and weakened morally.

In Chekhov's writing style, Williams recognized features of his own, but adjusted them according to the cultural traditions of Americans, not Russians, thus changing the major symbol of the play from the seagull to the bewitching lake. Completely eradicating subtext as the principal Chekhovian dramatic communication device, Williams brought forward the characters' sexual drives and dissatisfaction as the reason for their dramas. Williams also revised the end of the play, saving Nina's "bastard child" and sending it to America, thereby connecting the two plays and two traditions with embarrassing straightforwardness. The deformation of the play *The Seagull* transforms it, and it becomes *The Notebook of Trigorin*. Though not a dramatic masterpiece, Williams's interpretation of *The Seagull* is a phenomenal cultural and theatrical document. It serves as both a source of insight into the plays of Tennessee Williams and a case study of Chekhov's mutations in American drama and theatre, illustrating how new theatrical meanings can be generated through the collision of nineteenth-century Russian and twentieth-century American cultures.

WORKS CITED

Chekhov, Anton. *The Cherry Orchard* [*Vishnevyi sad*]. *Polnoe sobranie sochinenii.* [*PSS*] 18 vols. Moscow: Nauka, 1983–88. 13: 195–254. Print.
———. *Ivanov. PSS,* 12: 5–76. Print.
———. *The Seagull* [*Chaika*]. *PSS,* 13: 3–60. Print.
Hitchcock, Alfred, dir. *The Birds.* Universal Pictures, 1963. Film.
Katayev, Vladimir. *If Only We Could Know!* Trans. and ed. Harvey Pitcher. Chicago: Ivan R. Dee, 2002. Print.
Lotman, Yuri. *Universe of the Mind: A Semiotic Theory of Culture.* Bloomington: Indiana UP, 1990. Print.
Rudnitskii, Konstantin. "Rezhisserskaia partitura K.S. Stanislavskogo i 'Chaika' na stsene MKhT v 1898 godu." *Rezhisserskie ekzempliary K.S.Stanislavskogo.* 6 vols. Moscow: Iskusstvo, 1980–1994. 2: 6–50. Print.
Williams, Tennessee. *Cat on a Hot Tin Roof. Plays.* 2 vols. New York: Library of America, 2000. 1: Print.
———. *Glass Menagerie. Plays.* New York: Library of America, 2000. 1: Print.
———. *New Selected Essays: Where I Live.* New York: New Directions, 2009. Print.
———. *The Notebook of Trigorin.* New York: New Directions, 1997. Print.
———. *Streetcar Named Desire. Plays.* New York: Library of America, 2000. 1: Print.

4 Talking and Walking Past Each Other
Chekhovian "Echoes" in Czech Drama and Theatre

Veronika Ambros

Dedicated to the memory of Václav Havel

This chapter was prompted by reviews of two Czech plays, František Hrubín's *A/The Sunday in August*, (1958)[1] and Josef Topol's *Their Day* (1959) performed in the late 1950s; the reviews characterized these dramatic texts as "Chekhovian," yet did not provide any explanation as to the meaning of this designation. Surprisingly, a recent history of Czech literature repeats this claim almost verbatim without a further analysis (Janoušek et al. 344). The authors speak about "Chekhovian inspiration connected with Brechtian techniques and songs, [and] authorial comments"; however, they do not specify what they mean by the alleged "inspiration," nor do they acknowledge the fact that at the time Chekhov was staged only rarely.[2] Hence, they begged the question of what can be considered Chekhovian when the author's work is barely known. The title of this volume led me to seek an answer regarding the "mutations" of the text. The editors of the present collection themselves suggest a possible list of topics related to this search such as the transformation of aesthetic norms and the de-automatization of perception due to the *actualization* of aesthetic devices. These are concepts discussed in the semiotic writings of the Prague School (see the following) on which this chapter is based. Although my contribution explores mostly what the Czech literary historian and reader's response theorist Felix Vodička calls *echo* and *concretization*, I will also address the topic of adaptation where appropriate.

Vodička's approach to literary history is rooted in the theoretical works of the so-called Prague School. This semiotically oriented group of linguists, aestheticians, and literary scholars was founded in 1926 as the Prague Linguistic Circle and dealt with several aspects of the work of art such as its functions, norm, value, intentionality, and reception as an element of what Vodička calls the work's "biography" (*Struktura* 284). These topics are also fruitful with regard to the investigation of the ways an author, his/her texts, and their mutations are perceived in a given epoch. This task further requires that "the work is understood as a sign whose meaning and esthetic value are comprehensible only on the basis of the literary conventions of a specific period" (Vodička, "Concretization" 110).

In Vodička's view, "a literary work of art is understood as an aesthetic sign designated for the public" (*Struktura* 50). Hence, instead of turning to its genesis he examines its reception, more specifically its "echo in the literary public which perceives the literary work of art as an aesthetic object" (*Struktura* 286).[3] The concept of "concretization," originally introduced by the Polish phenomenologist Roman Ingarden, described the individual response to a literary work, whereas Vodička expands the study of concretization into his approach to literary history. In his article "Dějiny ohlasu literárních děl" published in English as "Response to Verbal Art," Vodička lists among the tasks of literary history: "The study of the concretizations of literary works (both past and present) that is a study of that manifestation of a work, which we encounter in the conceptions [views—VA] of a given epoch (especially in the critical concretization [by critics—VA])" (*Struktura* 53).[4] New concretizations of a work of art are subject to constant changes due to new circumstances, in which the individual work of art or a particular genre appears. In Vodička's view, "the echo of a literary work is accompanied by its concretization and the change of norm requires also a new concretization of the work" ("Response" 206).[5]

The translator of Vodička's article, however, replaced the word *konkretizace* with another key term of the Prague Linguistic Circle, *aktualizace* (actualization) (199), which refers to the phenomenon of making things topical again. Although it was originally conceived as a linguistic phenomenon, prominent member of Prague Linguistic Circle Jan Mukařovský considered it as a distinctive feature of so-called poetic language as opposed to its practical variant[6]: "In poetic language foregrounding [i.e., aktualizace—VA] achieves maximum intensity to the extent of pushing communication into the background [. . .] it is not used in the service of communication, but in order to place into the foreground the act of expression, the act of speech itself" (Mukařovský, "Standard Language" 168). Here, too, the translation changes the meaning of the original *aktualizace* (making something topical again) to foregrounding, thus transforming the originally temporal metaphor into a spatial one. As a result, Keir Elam, concludes that "*foregrounding* is essentially a spatial metaphor, and thus well adapted to the theatrical text" (18).

By contrast, the linguist Havránek evokes the temporal connotation of *aktualizace*, when he refers to "the use of the devices of the language in such a way that this use itself attracts attention and is perceived as uncommon, as deprived of automatization, as deautomatized, such as live poetic metaphor (as opposed to a lexicalized one, which is automatized)" (10).[7] Furthermore, Vodička's notion of echo includes the unexpected connections that might arise from the transfer of a work of art from a foreign context into the indigenous one, which can be understood as "mutation" of a text in a foreign context. Mukařovský describes this process thus:

70   *Veronika Ambros*

> A phenomenon which, in one time period, country, etc., was the privileged bearer of the aesthetic function may be incapable of bearing this function in a different time, country. [. . .] As soon as we change our perspective in time, space, or even from one social grouping to another [. . .] we find a change in the distribution of the aesthetic function and of its boundaries. (*Aesthetic Function* 3–5)

Hence, based on the alleged lyrical quality of their dramatic texts, a parallel has been drawn between the Czech poet and playwright Fráňa Šrámek, an author of lyrical dramas, and Chekhov. Incidentally in Šrámek's play *The Summer* (1915) one of the characters declares himself not to be the hero of a Chekhov novel, thus exposing the ignorance of the speaker and indicating the then generally accepted notion of the novel as the dominant genre of Russian literature at the turn of the twentieth century. However, as will be discussed later, the supposedly lyrical quality of both writers informed the concretization of Chekhov in Czech context especially in the late 1950s. Vodička also examined the impact the collection by Jan Neruda had (at a time when no contemporary critic acknowledged its existence) on the author (who tried to adjust his subsequent work to more mainstream poetry) and on the development of Czech literature at the end of the nineteenth century. A variation of this mode of responses applies to Chekhov's reception in the 1950s, when the author was for a while mostly absent from the Czech stage, and appeared merely as the echo of his previous presence in Czech theatre. Hence, the section on "Chekhov's Presence in Absentia" explores the initial question by taking "the literary conventions of a specific period" (Vodička, "Response" 110) into account.

Another definition of the echo as "a wave that has been reflected by a discontinuity in the propagation medium,"[8] complements Vodička's understanding of the concept and suits the theatre especially with respect to *actualization* of older texts, staging methods, and traditions. The notion of discontinuity is also close to Vodička's description of literary history, which, depending on the historical conditions, oscillates between the tendency to expand the national literary tradition and open it to international trends or to narrow it to impulses coming from within the national conventions. In his view expressed in the mid-1960s, the "discontinuity is [. . .] either a way of finding a new continuity or a renewal of an interrupted continuity" (*Struktura* 164). This notion helps to understand especially the development of the initial postwar period, in which Chekhov's work was received in both ways (see the following).

Following Vodička's approach, which derives information about the *echo* and the *concretization* of a work of art from contemporary reactions, historical accounts, scholarly studies, and literary texts, the present study discusses three Chekhovian echoes in Czech theatre between the late 1950s and early 1970s, all connected with the director Otomar

Krejča: (a) Chekhov's presence in absentia—the lyrical mode; (b) Chekhov revealed—the dramatic mode; and (c) Chekhov variations, in Josef Topol's *The End of the Carnival* (1964), Milan Kundera's *The Owner of the Keys* (1962), and Václav Havel's *The Garden Party* (1963). Considered the most successful plays of the 1960s, these "echoes" or "responses" to Chekhov appear in the form of criticism and in indirect relations (allusions, character constellations, and settings in the selected works). Incidentally, *The Owner of the Keys* and *The End of the Carnival* serve Czech theatre scholar Eva Stehlíková as an example of the concretization of Greek drama in the Czech theatre of the 1960s. Stehlíková concludes her article by stating: "in contrast to the bloodless adaptations of Greek drama, both plays belong to the best Czech plays written in the last century and, through them, Czech audiences experienced the true meaning of the expressions such as 'classics' and 'tragedy'" (229). The present chapter draws a similar conclusion with respect to Chekhov, whose presence on the Czech stage revealed the dramatic conflict within the characters, the role of the atmosphere in a fictional world, and the function of space and language in expressing loneliness and lack of understanding of oneself and the others in modern society. Finally, I will review Havel's 1976 *The Mountain Hotel* and his most recent play *Leaving* (2007) as another mode of concretization. These plays denote two extremes with respect to their production and reception: *The Mountain Hotel* was written in a time when it was no longer permitted to perform Havel's texts in Czechoslovakia, while *Leaving* was created after his presidency (1990–2003). They no longer are connected directly with the Krejča era. In addition, both plays enter a different context, which is especially the case of *Leaving*, which is associated with a changed concretization of Chekhov.[9]

CHEKHOV'S PRESENCE IN ABSENTIA: THE LYRICAL MODE

> What is at issue is a speaking whose function is not so much that of having a meaning as of putting up a struggle [. . .] against silence, and leading back to it. (Beckett qtd. in Jenkins 3)

In the section of his book on the "crisis of modern drama," Peter Szondi considers talking past one another one of the key characteristics of Chekhov's dramatic texts; the Chekhovian technique of broken communication, however, that he mentions, which permeated modern drama[10] and is inherent in Beckett's struggle with silence, was excluded from the Czech stage for ideological reasons for a while. In the early 1950s the critics and literary scholars expected the artists to follow the principles of Socialist Realism, for which Stanislavsky served as a model of a realistic director. By contrast, Chekhov was all but excluded from the repertoire.

72   Veronika Ambros

Among the few exceptions was the stage performance of *The Cherry Orchard* in Brno in 1952, which elicited an analysis by Jan Grossman (244), who, a decade later as the director of the Theatre on the Balustrade, turned it into a stage synonymous with Czech productions of the so-called Theatre of the Absurd. But in 1952, Grossman's reading of the Russian classic seems to serve the unequivocal reading of the dramatic repertoire typical of the theatre productions at that time. Grossman considered the play "one of the most effective and masterful parodies of the old feudal world [. . .] that becomes a satirical image of the declining noble class, which squanders the property entrusted to it and then leaves history" (244).

Such a simplified reading shows the narrowing of the tradition Vodička speaks about, which adjusts a complex text to an ideological purpose. It is, however, difficult to perform the ambiguity inherent in Chekhov's texts in a simplified manner, a fact that might explain his absence from the stage as well as any echoes of this complex author, who is present in absentia toward the end of that decade. Thus the Chekhovian "echoes" or "responses" to Chekhov on the Czech stage in the 1950s reflect not only the changing critical and artistic attitude toward the author, but also issues of continuity and discontinuity in Czech theatre in general.

Soon, however, the normative aesthetics of Socialist Realism was subverted in several ways. Culture in general no longer complied with the demands expressed in the Statute of the Union of Soviet Writers in 1934, which included the official expectation of accessibility for the masses (*narodnost'*) and optimistic works promoting the ideals of the state and the party (*partiinost'*) presented by a positive hero as a model character to educate the audience. Paradoxically, such a hero appears in the first play that alludes to Chekhov directly, namely, Pavel Kohout's *The Third Sister* (1960) which, though still adhering to socialist ideology and the optimism of Socialist Realism, does not conform to its aesthetics. Kohout's choice of title points to the latent presence of the Russian playwright in that period, and is an attempt to *actualize*[11] him, to make him topical in a new context. In any case, Kohout's work is indicative of renewed interest in Chekhov (Janoušek et al. 344).

In fact, Chekhov was absent from the Czech stage in the late 1950s (among the exceptions was the one-act play *The Bear*, which was also made for Czechoslovak television in 1961, directed by Martin Frič, and followed by the film version of three short stories presented as *Tears the World Can't See*, directed also by Martin Frič in 1962). He was thus akin to an author whose "concretization," to use Vodička's term, was not "fixed" (*Struktura* 293). As a result, some contemporary critics (Vostrý, Lukeš, Kudělka) used the term "Chekhovian" to describe a variety of texts by Western authors such as Arthur Miller and Lillian Hellman as well as the Czech plays mentioned earlier, namely, Hrubín's *A/The Sunday in August* (1958[12]) and Topol's *Their Day* (1959). In fact, their vague designation as Chekhovian points to an attempt to expand the hitherto reduced selection of accepted works to those that do not adhere to the linearity and lack of ambiguity of Socialist Realism.

In addition, Chekhov appears as a substitute for the contemporary development of characters talking past each other represented by Beckett, Pinter, and Ionesco, whose works were not yet readily available to Czech audiences. As a result, the category of supposedly lyrical drama serves as a point of reference to replace ideological criteria with nonthematic, structural categories, such as those used by the contemporary theatre historian Jaroslav Vostrý. He claims that Chekhov actualizes (*zpřítomnit*) simultaneously two realities, and his dialogue "creates a space between the exchanges, which can include a large number of different meanings" (150). Based on this view of Chekhov, Vostrý criticizes the dialogue in works such as Hrubín's *The Sunday in August*, which he regards as mere conversations. The following quote from Hrubín's text confirms this statement and shows that these plays often foreshadow the so-called model dramas of the 1960s: "You don't listen to me, nor do you understand me. People speak with each other so that one does not listen to another. It is the time of monologues" (qtd in Janoušek et al. 344).

Although this exchange certainly points to the breakdown in communication typical of the Russian playwright, it is expressed explicitly, while the Chekhovian characters often articulate themselves in dialogues with a monological tendency (Mukařovský, "Two Studies"). That is the case of *Three Sisters* where the exchanges between Andrey and his servant Ferapont just emulate a dialogue motivated by the latter's being hard of hearing. In fact they are, as Szondi says, a "negation" of the dialogue, one that "calls the dramatic form into question" (208) and is rooted in the comic tradition. While Hrubín's characters address their inability to understand each other directly, Andrey's speech is an externalized interior monologue motivated by Ferapont's handicap that reveals an internal turmoil far removed from a comedy.

Hence, unlike the characters in Kohout's play, those presented in the texts that emerged in the initial stages of the so-called Krejča workshop lack the optimistic tendency and illuminate the mutation of the ideologically driven trend into a remote echo of Chekhovian characters talking past each other.

CHEKHOV REVEALED: THE DRAMATIC MODE

Since both Hrubín's and Topol's texts emerged from a workshop that initiated a number of modern Czech plays and was mostly connected with the director Otomar Krejča, both plays precede the second and most obvious mode of *concretization*, the staging of Chekhov's plays in a way that questioned what the theatre historian Jana Patočková calls the "lyrical, sentimental staging tradition" ("Otomar Krejča") of Chekhov and

74 Veronika Ambros

supposedly discovered Chekhov's "dramatic qualities" not in the action but within the characters (Kraus 212). Patočková sums up this mode as "Krejča's Chekhov."[13]

In fact, however, those internationally acclaimed productions were based on the extraordinary cooperation between a director (Otomar Krejča), a dramaturge (Karel Kraus), a translator (Josef Topol), and a set designer (Josef Svoboda). As Svoboda testifies, his collaboration with Krejča was successful because they were both precise in their thinking and in the way they expressed their ideas (Hrubín 20). These collaborators, working with a select group of actors, contributed greatly to the domestic and international acclaim of Divadlo za branou (The Theatre beyond the Gate, 1965–1972), which in 1968 at the Théâtre des Nations international festival Jean-Pierre Léonardini dubbed "a beacon of international theatre" (qtd. in Krejča et al., *Otomar Krejča* 62). The critic Claude Olivier summed up the actualization Krejča achieved, declaring that "Chekhov [was] revealed" and the theatre had accomplished "the miracle" of seeing the text and the future anew (qtd. in *Otomar Krejča* 69–73). Incidentally, the enthusiastic reactions in Paris merely confirmed the high esteem Krejča had already elicited abroad in 1964 when Peter Brook declared the performance of *Romeo and Juliet* "to be the best production of the tragedy he had ever seen" (J. Černý 5). In 1970 Olivier claimed that Krejča had provided *Ivanov* with topicality ("rend sensible l'actualité de la pièce"; qtd. in *Otomar Krejča* 72).

A brief analysis of this mode will serve to reveal the new concretization of Chekhov onstage, based on a new approach to text, actor, and space that showed a modern mutation of the Chekhovian disconnect in which the characters not only talk past each other but concurrently walk past each other, thus underlining the rift between verbal and physical action.

TEXT AND GESTURES

To Krejča "the world of the play" has to be in agreement with the "production world" ("From the Rehearsals" 57). That is to say, the fictional world presented onstage is "created by the imagination of [. . .] all those who [. . .] are participating in the 'mutual' reading of the drama" (55) and "build[ing] from the reading [. . .] a common fantasy experience" (56). He insists: "Everything in the actor's activity on the stage must be permeated by the matter, shape, spirit, color of the 'world of the play'" (56). His attitude towards the actors is based on his experience with the production of *The Seagull* (1972), which as Albertová notes, "did not follow the line of the story, but set the three acts into the context of the fourth. [. . .] the actors had to become real co-creators of the performance" (123). In fact, as Albertová says, "Krejča did not stage the linear story of Chekhov's play,

Talking and Walking Past Each Other 75

but examined the world of its characters by continuous illumination of their relationships." She even speaks about "a text collage [in which e]very character was on stage all the time" (123).

In an article about Krejča, Jiří Veltruský, a semiotician of drama and theatre and a spectator of several of the productions in Paris, emphasizes the role of gestures that concretized the text:

> In Krejča's productions, each stage figure is different, yet at the same time it is manifestly part of a complex cluster of figures. [. . .] In the production of *Three Sisters* the integration of individual stage figures into the whole [. . .] is brought about, for example, by different actors using the same object (chair, candle), occupying the same position or even making the same gesture. Each time this gesture perfectly fits in with the given actor's performance. [. . .] It becomes an integral part of a more general context within which each occurrence serves to some extent as an allusion to the previous ones and opens the perspective of further possible repetitions, while every time its meaning changes. (48–49)

Veltruský's account complements Karel Kraus's explanation of the intonation in *Three Sisters*. Kraus describes a tendency to divide the semantic line of the text and the intonation, which signifies different degrees of "self deception" (205). Kraus also confirms Veltruský's observation with regard to gestures, which, as Kraus maintains, serve for Krejča as a motif. In fact, however, they also seem to highlight the ambiguity evoked by the contradiction between words and action like that indicated in the closing lines of Beckett's *Waiting for Godot*: "Let's go," accompanied by the stage direction "they don't move." In Krejča's works such a disagreement between text and gestures points to what Kraus calls "Chekhov's ability of binary vision, which inspired modern drama and to which it keeps returning" (212). In Kraus's view the performance "draws the spectator in," so that he/she "not only follows the conversation and mood, but is curious how the story develops" (208).

In the transcripts of his notes for the rehearsals of *The Cherry Orchard* in 1990 following a period of eighteen years, after the Divadlo za branou was forced to close and the director himself had to work mostly abroad, Krejča condensed his experience of his imposed absence from Czech theatre ("From the Rehearsals" 55–61). These notes shed light on his reading of the dramatic text and on his artistic method with regard to the production process. He pays attention to every detail of the text and questions the meanings of the words, as well as that of the silences. To him the pause "is a period of intensive action [. . .] the result of [a] tension between the preceding and the following situation" (55–61). In addition, as he explained in Düsseldorf to the actors in *The Cherry Orchard*:

76 *Veronika Ambros*

> In the course of our work we shall put into the performance more and more details that will remain "invisible" [. . .]. Do not think that this procedure is useless. [. . .] [I]n this kind of production it is necessary to fill the time and space completely [. . .] the spectator takes it in—in his own way—and is affected even when he "does not see" it in detail. (Krejča qtd. in Veltruský 48)

Moreover, since he regarded the production as a collective work ("From the Rehearsals" 58), Krejča encouraged the actors to ask questions such as: "Why do Lopakhin's first words concern the train? What does it indicate?" (56).

Veltruský noted that he "had the impression of witnessing, perhaps for the first time since World War II, a genuinely avant-garde performance, instead of the usual eclectic imitation" (50). He further remarked that "the staging was in some way faithful to the play as written by Chekhov, although it handled the text with great freedom" (50). The explanation of this phenomenon he found in the analysis of Chekhov's plays by Herta Schmid, who pointed out that in them "speech often is not [. . .] a reaction to the speech that immediately precedes it." In addition, "the dialogue is interspersed with words, phrases and verbal motifs which keep returning as the play unfolds [. . .] and which take on a different sense every time the subject and situation of the dialogue changes" (Schmid 46).

SPACE

Krejča's interest in space and its role dates back to the time of his transition from an actor to the director of the National Theatre in Prague in the mid-1950s, when he and his colleagues focused on a collaboration with the actors (Svoboda, for instance, made models of his design and consulted the director and the actors about his ideas), for it is the actors "who are able to abolish the division between the stage and the auditorium and turn a non-committal spectacle into an artistic ritual." In order to make this possible they "moved away from decoration to a space which can be transformed in dramatic time" (Deweter 532).

Krejča's use of space was the result of a remarkable cooperation with Svoboda, a set designer who was active in the production process of the staging from the very beginning. The theatre historian Helena Albertová called the performance of *The Seagull* (1960) "a watershed in Czech theatre as far as stagings of this author are concerned," declaring that it "was a production which brought about a fundamental change in stage lighting" (95). Furthermore, "to convey distance Svoboda [. . .] used a moving walkway, installed into a footbridge" (95). This device implied a long run,[14] while "the flickering light on [Nina's] floating dress evoked the impression of a seagull in flight" (100). Albertová notes about the staging of *Ivanov* a decade later: "When Ivanov runs away from his wife to the home of his young bride he remains—symbolically—in the same place" (123). As a result the two worlds become intertwined; there is no *elsewhere*, and no confrontation of two "different worlds."[15] Their existence, however, is suggested by the motif of the window in *Ivanov* that has to be closed allegedly to protect his wife, Sara, but in fact to prevent Ivanov from being confronted with his role in her and his own ruin.

Krejča's attention to every detail comes to the fore in the question about the function of the window for Ranevskaya, asking, "Does the window have a function in the structure of the meanings of the play?" ("From the Rehearsals" 56). For Krejča, it suggests not only the spatial division of the fictional world, but a window, like a door, separating two different spheres. Incidentally, contemporary research shows with regard to the function of the door that: "entering or exiting through a doorway serves as an 'event boundary' in the mind, which separates episodes of activity and files them away" (Brenner and Zacks). A window, however, as Krejča suggests, might also link two temporally separated spaces, and evokes questions about the structure of the play:

> In the situation "at the window" in the first act Ranevskaya "sees" her deceased mother walking through the morning garden. [. . .] Why, as soon as she comes to the window, does she recall her childhood? Does the window have a function in the structure of the meanings of the play? Why does she address the orchard with such pathos, why does she talk to it [as] if it were a live being? ("From the Rehearsals" 57)

The film version of *Three Sisters* directed 1970 by Laurence Olivier, for which Svoboda created the set design, provides glimpses into Svoboda's spatial solutions and his metonymic use of objects, reminiscent of the way language and gestures were employed in Krejča's productions. For example, miniature models of the Kremlin conjure up repeatedly the characters' longing for Moscow, suggest the motivation for their mode of conduct, and serve as a constant reminder of their past. The relation to the past, however, is, as Schmid suggests, a dividing line between the characters depending how strongly connected to it they are.[16] For the Prozorov siblings the world of memory is connected with the city, as a concrete and an imagined place and simultaneously a force holding the family together and driving them apart, because the past is connected with unfulfilled expectations of oneself. Their "renunciation of the present" (Szondi 206) as the world of "collective and individual loneliness" (207) is in stark contrast to the vortex of their nostalgia.

The movements of the characters suggest their distance from each other, as do the spatial shifts inherent in the text but emphasized in this particular performance. In fact, by retaining the static mode of a stage performance, the film emphasizes the stasis of the fictional world, where characters not only talk, but also walk, past each other. Hence Olivier's film shows

78 *Veronika Ambros*

similarities with Krejča's staging, which, as Veltruský observed, has "the underlying general intention [. . .] to make the literary text theatrical by intertwining the dialogue with visual signs" (48).

In sum, this mode of concretization sets the ground for a complex understanding of the modern world, full of contradictions; clashes between the spoken word and the nonverbal means of communication; concealed loneliness that is expressed in dialogues, which are in fact monologues; fragmented reflections; exclamations; and questions about one's own identity. It shows the expanded continuity with the avant-garde, without imitating it, but, like its predecessors, by challenging the audience. The attention paid to space also exposes time as a category that contradicts linear continuity and shows the past as an integral part of the present.

CHEKHOV VARIATIONS

The dramatic texts by Topol, Havel, and Milan Kundera help illuminate the Czech concretization of Chekhov in the 1960s mainly with respect to their variations of Chekhovian use of space, time, and language. Incidentally, Stehlíková mentions two of these texts in her article on the reception of the Greek drama in plays, in which the connections are "not manifested by clear references" (229). Similarly, although Chekhov is not referenced in these texts, they show several points of contact with his works.

This third mode of the concretization of Chekhov, which is reminiscent of a musical composition, includes plays directed by Krejča and produced after his initial Chekhov production in 1960. As Helena Albertová states: "In many cases his interpretation influenced future productions of new Czech plays" (135). Kraus speaks about the fact that the acts in *Three Sisters* are very similar to the "function and connection of movements in a symphony" (210). This musical connotation applies also to dramatic texts in which the Chekhovian echo appears as a variation of the characters talking past each other, alluded to by the division of the space, by repetitions of phrases, motives, devices, and configurations. Rhythm and repetitions of verbal and nonverbal means, such as movements and visual techniques introduced by Svoboda, are other methods of evoking the musical bent of these texts, in which the authors de-automatized the thematic conventions of the previous era, such as the heroic discourse of the war experience, the positive interpretation of collectivization, or the mechanism of the bureaucratic system. Their aesthetic choices showed discontinuity with the poetics of Socialist Realism, stressed ambiguity, and foregrounded the aesthetic function in different ways.

In his third play, *The End of the Carnival*, Topol presented the allure of urban space for some characters and the desire for rural solace for others in a way that resembles the confrontation of different worlds of imagination, memory, and dreams present in the longing for Moscow in *Three*

Sisters. Another parallel between the two plays can be associated with the biblical connotations of the two young lovers Marie and Raphael, and the etymology of Ferapont's name, which means "servant" or "worshipper" in Greek. Suggesting the tradition of carnival and morality plays, Topol creates a fictional world in which characters are unable to find each other and even closed doors do not offer any privacy; where, as in *The Three Sisters*, people, characters with or without masks pass each other, remaining disenchanted, unrecognized, isolated, and desolate. The masks evoked by the title deprive the characters of their individual identity, while their refused entry in *Three Sisters* points to the changed circumstances in the Prozorov household.

Topol's urban lady character visiting the countryside to sell her house is reminiscent of Chekhovian landladies that are oblivious to the mayhem their arrivals and departures may cause. More importantly, however, the character of the "holy fool," Henry, the king of the carnival and the dim-witted son of the last farmer who does not want to join the cooperative, exposes the fictional world as an upside-down one. He fulfills a function similar to Ferapont's, by laying bare the lack of meaning in the talk around him, the deceit and the talking past each other that characterize the inhabitants of the seemingly idyllic village. The outsider character who visits the village claims it resembles pleasant rural pictures by Lada, the painter of idyllic country scenes, thus awakening corresponding expectations in the spectators. In addition, the carnival of the title evokes the connection to a nonspecific past, while many of the characters are tied to the recent history that has shaped their present views and attitudes.

In Milan Kundera's first dramatic text in one act and four visions, *The Owner of the Keys*, the motif of the keys and its association with closed, locked doors exposes the characters' talking past each other by the division of the space in the action proper. Hence, at times as Albertová notes, the exchanges, though "independent of each other, composed themselves into one dialogue" (105) to create a simultaneity that highlights either the divergent points of view of the interlocutors or their unexpected convergence. This technique is akin to Andrey's dialogues with the deaf servant Ferapont in *Three Sisters* and their monologic nature. Kundera also foregrounds the "negation" of dialogue in exchanges close to those described earlier by Szondi and Schmid. In addition, the process in which the imaginary future of the respective heroes Andrey and Jiří disintegrates is further highlighted by their marital situation. Both are characterized by being oblivious to the chatter of their wives, whose behavior marks the distance between the past dreams and present circumstances of their spouses. Kundera, however, creates in the parts called "visions" an imaginary space, which provides the play with a mythical dimension. This comes to the fore in Svoboda's set design, which presents a window placed up high and a very short ladder, stressing the insurmountable gap between the two, their absurdity as a means of bridging a distance. In that regard, *The Owner of the Keys*

80   Veronika Ambros

expands the hint of a supernatural intervention, which the final sound in *The Cherry Orchard* just insinuates.

Havel's first performed dramatic text, *The Garden Party*, shows many features of the specific Czech mode of absurdity that informed the *model drama*, i.e., a drama the revealed the absurdity of the social system rather than the absurdity of human existence typical, for instance, for Beckett. The protagonist, Hugo Pludek, follows the rules of a chess game that he plays with or against himself. The game itself frames Hugo's actions, punctuates the text, and appears as a motif throughout the play (Ambros, "Fictional World" 310–19). Like Andrey in *Three Sisters*, Havel's hero pursues the dreams of his parents who are, however, scenically present and not a figment of the past. Driven by their yearning for his public recognition, Hugo, unlike Chekhov's characters, uses the present moment to establish himself. Eventually, his endeavors are both satisfied and shattered at the same time. In fact, Hugo is somewhat akin to Ivanov, who commits suicide on the day of his long-awaited wedding.

In his insightful essay on Chekhov, James Wood notes a difference between Ibsen and Chekhov: "The secrets of his [Ibsen's] characters are knowable secrets not the true privacies of Chekhov's people" (64). Ivanov's final monologue expresses the latter: the character faces a conundrum of unanswered questions, unfulfilled expectations, and disillusionments, without being able to pinpoint a single cause of his despair. Hugo Pludek's final soliloquy is also full of rhetorical questions and exclamations, but it is not directed towards the past, nor does it relate any recognition of his own failings. Hugo's identity eludes even himself; moreover, when he eventually returns home to his starting point, his parents no longer recognize him, nor does he himself know who he is. His last move is a checkmate against himself, in which the device of talking past the other culminates; in fact, the verbal action no longer serves any communication:

> Me? You mean who am I? Now look here, I don't like this one-sided way of putting questions, I really don't! You think one can ask in this simplifying way? . . . Truth is just as complicated and multiform as everything else in the world . . . and we all are a little bit what we were yesterday and a little bit what we're today; and also a little bit we are not these things. Anyway, we are all a little bit all the time and all the time we are not a little bit . . . some only are, some are only, and some are only not so that none of us entirely is and at the same time each one of us is not entirely . . . Check-mate! (Havel, *Garden Party* 73–74)

Like Ivanov, Hugo Pludek also questions his own identity toward the end of the play, yet his suicide is verbal, his identity drowned in his discourse, "imprisoned" in a fictional world that seems to be governed by the rules of the chess game as performed by Hugo, who moves both colors on the chess board. Wood compares Chekhov with Flaubert and claims that

"Flaubert's characters are doomed while Chekhov's are only imprisoned" (49).[17] Incidentally, the dialogues in this play also resemble the exchanges in Chekhov's *Ivanov*, in which the replies do not appear as responses to previous utterances (Schmid 174). This type of talk mocks the kind of conversation in which the interlocutors often search for a topic they might share, and which, as a rule, avoids references to the imminent situation (Mukařovský, "Two Studies"). In this regard, the play is reminiscent of Chekhov's exchanges, which are missing a unifying subject and are imprisoned in a language bare of shared meaning.

Although directed by Krejča, *The Garden Party* is the only play in which Svoboda's set design was not used. Albertová comments that the author "had himself refused to use Svoboda's set design with mirrors. Havel required a realistic set, which would not distract attention from the text and the actors. Stage 'magic' would have been in conflict with the poetics of the small theatre" (134). This initial emphasis on the text exposed the characters talking past each other by using speech like a musical composition in which parts of the speech reappear in a new context, are repeated, and subsequently lose their semantic charge, thus setting the ground for Havel's further experiments. In spite of their differences, these plays show Chekhovian elements inherent also in Krejča's staging of the author: the monologic character of the dialogue, the role of the fictional and imaginary space, the dramatic features within the characters, and the role of the past.

HAVEL ADAPTING CHEKHOV

The Chekhovian traces in *The Garden Party* are mostly hidden; however they reveal themselves in Havel's later works. In *The Mountain Hotel* they are most palpable in the segmentation of the text through the whistle of a distant train, which makes the dialogues and actions stop. Reminiscent of the train whistle in *The Cherry Orchard*, it evokes imaginary space, the transitional stage of some characters, and foregrounds their coming and going. Their dialogues go beyond mere talking past each other: they show the interchangeability of the speakers. More than any of the Chekhovian characters, these "figures" and their exchanges transform a dramatic dialogue that "calls the dramatic form into question" (Szondi 208) into an almost musical piece, which seems to evoke the dance in *The Cherry Orchard*. Since their utterances as well as their movements keep shifting from one to another, their stability as characters relies solely on their names. Havel calls the play "a scenic poem about nothing," and admits that it is in fact a "scenic composition" consisting of utterances, movements and music. All these elements, as the author remarks, no longer serve to drive the "plot, but become the plot themselves" (*Spisy 4* 156).

Hence the dramatic text points to itself, showing the dominance of the aesthetic function and the culmination of both "unmotivated" (*Spisy 4*

82   *Veronika Ambros*

156) talking and walking past each other. This shift of focus from text to movements comes as a surprise in the context of Havel's reaction to Svoboda's set design mentioned in the preceding, which he rejected because it would allegedly occlude the emphasis on the text. Yet the semantic void of the exchanges with regard to the characters can be viewed as a continuation of Hugo's lost identity in *The Garden Party* and affects the dramatis personae, who react like puppets to the train signal by drawing their watches. Their movements are reminiscent of the repeated gestures and recurring use of objects in Krejča's concretization of Chekhov. Thus, the situations presented are reminiscent of a game of musical chairs, in which the characters and their speech reveal a grotesque universe marked by the fact that the characters appear to be interchangeable, showing only traces of individual identity and personal story. The setting (a hotel) motivates the constant coming and leaving typical of the Chekhovian fictional world.

The title of Havel's last play refers to the process of leaving, which ends with the departure of a former politician from a house that was tied to his previous political position. At the core of *Leaving* are several dramatic texts: *King Lear* and *The Cherry Orchard*, as well as Havel's own work. They are all either quoted directly or alluded to in configurations. Unlike Krejča's concretizations, however, this work presents a specific type of adaptation as the confrontation of texts by well-known playwrights, unified by one author, who invites the audience to a guessing game with regard to the origin of the characters, their utterances, and each sequence. By shifting their positions and functions, he foregrounds the device of selection and combination, and therefore their poetic function: as Roman Jakobson states, the poetic function "projects the principle of equivalence from the axis of selection into the axis of combination" (358). Havel presents a pastiche consisting of fragments of tragedy, comedy, and his own absurd texts enriched by references to his experience as a politician.[18] He actualizes the classical works; mixes period pieces with contemporary objects, such as a laptop on a Chekhovian swing; and includes anachronistic references to topical events.

The resulting fictional world is largely based on that of *The Cherry Orchard* presented as an absurd comedy or farce. Although the action is reminiscent of the fourth act in Chekhov's *The Cherry Orchard*, some of it evokes Ranevskaya's dance macabre in the preceding act. In fact, the protagonist, Vilem Rieger, appears to be a male version of Ranevskaya, as he too is oblivious of the consequences of his actions. His antagonist, Klein, has many features of Lopakhin, most prominently because he presents a new upcoming stratum of the society, with no scruples or sense of responsibility toward others, without any respect for tradition. His plans for the cherry orchard are as outrageous as Lopakhin's and symptomatic of the *nouveau riche.*

The list of mutated relationships between these texts could go on. Yet Havel also foregrounds such nonverbal elements in Chekhov as the sound of the trees being cut down. The mysterious thud, however, is replaced by the spoken comments of the author that mark the segmentation of the text

Talking and Walking Past Each Other   83

and are accompanied by characters freezing for a moment, hence fulfilling a similar function to that of the whistle in *The Mountain Hotel*.[19]

Havel's first experience as a film director was when he adapted *Leaving* for film, completing it in March 2011. Adjusting the story of the former chancellor to a new medium required several changes, which are significant because they turn the film into information about the authorial reading, i.e., concretization in Ingarden's sense. In the film version, the voice of the author is replaced visually by brief glimpses of a tempest that disrupts the action and evokes the tragedy of *King Lear*. In contrast to the Shakespearean allusions, and in addition to the dramatic irony derived from the confrontation between the fictional world and references to the actual world, there are many elements of comedy.

Rieger's female admirer, Bea, whose appearance evokes Alessandro Botticelli's *Birth of Venus*, is accompanied in the film by the musical motif of the famous aria from Antonín Dvořák's opera *Rusalka* that connotes the tragic story of a water nymph. This image is in counterpoint to a short appearance by Havel himself, who submerges and resurfaces from the pond as a water spirit to thank the audience for not using their cell phones. He mocks himself by announcing: "Truth and love must prevail over lies and hatred—." This famous adage refers back to 1989, when he became the leader of the Citizens' Forum, the loosely formed group consisting of former dissidents, students, and artists that initiated the so-called Velvet Revolution and made Havel president. And, typical of a comedy, the cast assembles for the last scene in which they all join in laughter about the water spirit. In fact, however, the end conjures up both the dance scene in Chekhov mentioned earlier, and the various types of leaving at the end of *The Cherry Orchard*, including Osvald, who is forgotten by his masters, as is his model Firs, and who repeats the final monologue of the servant in the house no longer belonging to Ranevskaya.

Although Havel's last play is a pastiche of different texts, it also evokes the preceding modes of concretization. Moreover, Havel's mode of adapting Chekhov foregrounds comedy as a genre, in which Gogolian laughter through tears belongs to the tradition conjured up by Havel as well. His last play presents a synthesis of the several approaches described here, showing continuity with Krejča's concretizations, in which verbal and nonverbal devices are intertwined and present the talking and walking past one another. Havel returned to his beginnings, using comedy and satire to mock present-day society. Moreover, his actualization of Chekhov's universe draws a parallel between the two fictional worlds and sheds light on the topicality of Havel's Chekhov in the Czech context.

NOTES

1. If not indicated otherwise all translations are mine (VA)

84 Veronika Ambros

2. F. Černý mentions in his *Kalendarium* Otomar Krejča's performance of *The Seagull* in 1960 as the first staging after 1945 (Černý 112). Vladimír Just's updated version of Černý's *Kalendarium* mentions a production of *The Cherry Orchard* in the National Theatre in Prague in 1951 as the only Chekhov performance that year (Just 231). There are remarkably few until 1960 and they often take place outside of Prague.

3. Paradoxically, although a large collection of essays honoring the author exists in English (see Works Cited), only a few articles allow the English-speaking reader to become acquainted with his work. In addition, as mentioned, the translation of one of them distorts the meaning of some key terms.

4. "Studium konkretizací děl literárních (současných a minulých), t.j. studium té podoby díla, s jakou se setkáváme v pojetí dané doby zejména v konkretizaci kritické" (Vodička, *Struktura* 53). Garvin and Elam translate the term as "foregrounding." See also Ambros, "Prague's Experimental Stage."

5. Translated as: "Response to a literary work is accompanied by its actualization, a change of norm necessitates a new actualization of the work" ("Response" 206).

6. This distinction was introduced by Yakubinsky.

7. More to this in Ambros, "Prague's Experimental Stage" 45–65.

8. See http://en.wikipedia.org/wiki/Echo_%28phenomenon%29 (accessed 26 Aug. 2011).

9. This applies most of all to Petr Lebl's staging of Chekhov on the same stage, which would deserve a separate study.

10. It is prevalent in the plays Martin Esslin included in his book on the Theatre of the Absurd. In the second edition of his book Esslin presented Havel and the Polish playwrights S. Mrożek and T. Różewicz in the section "Theatre of the Absurd in Eastern Europe." The influential British theatre critic Kenneth Tynan refers to the book, commenting: "Some critics have glibly assigned both writers to the grab bag marked Theatre of the Absurd" (Tynan 105).

11. This term was introduced by the members of the Prague Linguistic Circle in a series of polemic articles in Havránek and Weingart. For the English translation of Havránek's article "The Functional Differentiation of the Standard Language," see *Prague School Reader* 3–16. More to this in Ambros "Prague's Experimental Stage."

12. Dedicated to Otomar Krejča.

13. Patočková, "Krejčův český Čechov." Patočková has published several well-researched and comprehensive studies about the director in general and his staging of Chekhov in particular. Her monograph on Krejča is forthcoming. Two essays related to this topic were included in the initial issue of the journal *Czech Theatre/Théâtre tchèque* (1991): Jiří Veltruský about Otomar Krejča: "Krejča about Chekhov" and Otomar Krejča "From the Rehearsals on /sic!/ the Cherry Orchard."

14. Erwin Piscator achieved a similar effect by letting Švejk move on a conveyor belt in his staging of the novel by J. Hašek, *Fortunes of the Good Soldier Švejk during the World War*. See Ambros, "Great War."

15. Brenner and Zacks; see also Havel, "Kicking the Door"; and Trojanowska.

16. Schmid analyzes the different points (*Vergangenheitspunkt*) of the past used for each character (98).

17. I wish to thank Kate Caley for pointing me to this study.

18. The autobiographical nature of this play will be a subject of a separate study.

19. These, however, are missing in the English translation of the play.

WORKS CITED

Albertová, Helena. *Josef Svoboda: Scenographer*. Prague: Divadelní ústav, 2008. Print.

Ambros, Veronika. "Fictional World and Dramatic Text: Václav Havel's Descent and Ascent." *Style* 25 (Summer 1991): 310–19. Print.

———. "The Great War as a Monstrous Carnival: Jaroslav Hašek's Švejk." *History of the Literary Cultures in East-Central Europe*. Ed. Marcel Cornis-Pope and John Neubauer. Amsterdam: Benjamins, 2004. 28–36. Print.

———. "Prague's Experimental Stage: Laboratory of Theatre and Semiotics." *Semiotica* 168 (2008): 45–65. Print.

Beckett, Samuel. *Waiting for Godot: A Tragicomedy in Two Acts*. London : Faber and Faber, 1956. Print.

Brenner, Charles B., and Jeffrey M. Zacks. "Why Walking through a Doorway Makes You Forget." *Scientific American*, 13 Dec. 2011. Web. 21 Dec. 2011.

Chekhov, A.P. *Works*. Trans. and ed. Ronald Hingley. London; New York: Oxford U P, 1964. Print.

Černý, František. *Kalendárium dějin českého divadla*. Prague: SČDU, 1989. Print.

Černý, Jindřich. *Who Is Otomar Krejča?* Prague: Orbis, 1968. Print.

Deweter, J. "Nalezený zapalovač." *Divadlo* 11, (1960): 529–32. Print.

Elam, Keir. *Semiotics of Theatre and Drama*. 2nd ed. London: Routledge, 2002. Print.

Esslin, Martin. *The Theatre of the Absurd*. Harmondsworth: Penguin, 1968. Print.

Grossman, Jan. *Jan Grossman: texty o divadle. 2*. Prague: Pražská scéna, 2000. Print.

Havel, Václav. *The Garden Party and Other Plays*. New York: Grove Press, 1993. Print.

———. "Horský hotel" *Hry*. Praha, Lidové noviny 1991, 251–290. Print.

———. "Kicking the Door." Trans. Tamar Jacoby. *New York Review of Books*, 22 March 1979. Print.

———. Spisy 4. Eseje a jiné texty z let 1970–1989. Dálkový výslech. Prague: Torst, 1999. Print.

Havránek, Bohuslav. "The Functional Differentiation of the Standard Language." *A Prague School Reader on Esthetics, Literary Structure, and Style*. Ed. Paul L. Garvin. Georgetown: Georgetown UP, 1964. 3–16. Print.

Havránek, Bohuslav, and Miloš Weingart, eds. *Spisovná čeština a jazyková kultura*. Prague: Melantrich, 1932. Print.

Hrubín, František. *Srpnová neděle*. Prague: Československý spisovatel, 1958. Print.

Iakubinskii, Lev. "O zvukakh stikhotvornogo iazyka." *Sborniki po teorii poèticheskogo iazyka* 1 (1916): 37–49. Print.

Jakobson Roman. "Closing Statement: Linguistics and Poetics." *Style in Language*. Ed. Thomas Sebeok. New York: Wiley, 1960. 350–77. Print.

Janoušek, P. and Petr Čornej, Blahoslav Dokoupil, Pavel Janáček, Vladimír Křivánek, Jiřina Táborská. *Dějiny české literatury 1945–1989*. 4 vols. Prague: Academia, 2007. Print.

Jenkins, Alan. "Statement of Silences." *TLS* 4 (Nov. 2011): 3. Print.

Just, Vladimír. *Divadlo v totalitním system*. Prague: Academia, 2010. Print.

Kohout, Pavel. *Třetí sestra*. Praha: Orbis, 1961. Print.

Kraus, Karel. *Divadlo ve službách dramatu*. Prague: Divadelní ústav, 2002. Print.

Krejča, Otomar. "From the Rehearsals on /sic!/ the Cherry Orchard." *Czech & Slovak Theatre* 1 (1991): 55–61. Print.

86 Veronika Ambros

———, Josef Topol and Karel Kraus. *Otomar Krejča et le Théâtre Za Branou de Prague*. Paris: La Cité, 1972. Print.

Kudělka, Viktor. "Aby drama bylo dramatem." *Divadlo* 11 (1960): 166–67. Print.

Kundera, Milan. "Majitelé klíčů." *Divadlo* 12.9 (1961): 1–19. Print.

Lukeš, Milan. "Hledání ztraceného tvaru." *Literární noviny* 9 (1960): 5, 6. Print.

Matejka, Ladislav, and Titunik, Irwin R., eds. *Semiotics of Art*. Cambridge: MIT, 1976. Print.

Mukařovský, Jan. *Aesthetic Function, Norm and Value as Social Facts*. Trans. Mark E. Suino. Ann Arbor: U of Michigan P, 1970. Print.

———. "Standard Language and Poetic Language." *Praguiana. Some Basic and Less Known Aspects of the Prague Linguistic School*. Ed. J. Vachek and Libuše Dušková. Amsterdam: Benjamins, 1983. 165–85. Print.

———. "Two Studies of Dialogue." *The Word and Verbal Art*. Ed. John Burbank and Peter Steiner. New Haven: Yale UP, 1977. 81–115. Print.

Neruda, Jan. *Básně*. Ed. Felix Vodička. Praha: Československý spisovatel, 1951. Print.

Patočková, Jana. "Krejčův český Čechov (a jiní) na přelomu šedesátých a sedmdesátých let." *Divadelní revue* 18.3 (2007): 27–63. Print.

———. "Opožděná zpráva o likvidaci divadla." *Divadelní revue* 12.4 (2001): supplement, (documents). Print.

———. "Otomar Krejča: Divadlo a politika." *Divadelní revue* 12.4 (2001): 49. Print.

Schmid, Herta. *Strukturalistische Dramentheorie: Semantische Analyse von Čechows* Ivanov *und der* Kirschgarten. Kronberg/Taunus: Scriptor Verlag, 1973. Print.

Šrámek, Fráňa. *Léto*. Praha: B. Koči, 1915. Print.

Stehlíková, Eva. "The Encounter between Greek Tragedy and Two Czech Playwrights in the Sixties." *Eirene* 39 (2003): 229–33. Print.

Szondi, Peter. *Theory of the Modern Drama*. London: Polity Press, 1987. Print.

Topol, Josef. *Jejich den*. Praha: Orbis, 1962. Print.

———. "Konec masopustu." *Josef Topol a Divadlo za branou*. Ed. B. Mazáčová. Prague: Český spisovatel, 1993. 9–100. Print.

Trojanowska, Tamara. "Behind the Open Space." *Canadian Slavonic Papers* 38.3–4 (1996): 419–27. Print.

Tynan, Kenneth. *Show People: Profiles in Entertainment*. New York: Simon and Schuster, 1979. Print.

Veltruský, Jiří. "Notes Regarding Some Productions by Otomar Krejča." *Czech and Slovak Theatre/Théâtre tcheque et slovaque* 1 (1990): 46–55. Print.

Vodička, Felix. "The Concretization of the Literary Work: Problems of the Reception of Neruda's Works." Trans. John Burbank . *The Prague School: Selected Writings, 1929–1946*. Ed. Peter Steiner. Trans. John Burbank. Austin: U of Texas P, 1982. 103–34. Print.

———. "Response to Verbal Art." *Semiotics of Art: Prague School Contributions*. Ladislav Matejka and Irwin R. Titunik. Ed. and trans. Cambridge: MIT, 1976. 197–208. Print.

———. *Struktura vývoje: Studie literárněhistorické*. Prague: Dauphin, 1998. Print.

Vostrý, Jaroslav. "Od 'čechovování' k Čechovovi." *Divadlo* 11 (1960): 146–50. Print.

Wood, James. *The Broken Estate. Essays on Literature and Belief*. New York: Random House, 1999. Print.

5 Howard Barker's *(Uncle) Vanya*
Chekhov Shaken, Not Stirred

Charles Lamb

In *A Short Organum for the Theatre*, Bertolt Brecht was less than enthusiastic on the subject of programming theatre with a diet of "revived" and "reviving" classics. He wrote: "In establishing the extent to which we can be satisfied by representations from so many different periods [. . .] are we not at the same time creating the suspicion that we have failed to discover the special pleasures, the proper entertainment of our own time?" (505). Brecht argues the case in favor of this "proper entertainment," which, given his espousal of Marxism, could be taken to mean an entertainment appropriate to the current stage of human development, an entertainment that addresses issues that under previous epochs simply had not arisen. "Appropriate," "proper"—it is not easy in talking about this to escape from the semantic magnetism of the proprietorial with its connotations of ownership not only of property, but coincidentally of judgment and taste. In the field of literature, these attributes are reflected in the sign of the "author" with its cognates—"authority," "authorize." Indeed, the concept of a "proper entertainment" can seem somewhat paradoxical in that a strongly developed sense of propriety tends to detract from the seductive appeal characteristic of "entertainment." In this chapter, it is my intention to reflect on Howard Barker's play *(Uncle) Vanya*, to identify how it relates to Chekhov's "original," and to assess the extent to which it might offer the possibility of "special pleasures" and (timely) "proper entertainment."

According to Eduardo Houth, the idea of a "Barker version" of a Chekhov play seems to have surfaced initially in 1986, when Kenny Ireland and Hugh Fraser asked Barker for a script. They had just witnessed the success of a Barkerization of Middleton's *Women Beware Women* "and wanted a similar violation perpetrated on Chekhov [. . .] Barker felt an antipathy for Chekhov which later materialised in his *(Uncle) Vanya* but at this time he wanted only to write original plays" (Barker and Houth 20). In the case of *Women Beware Women*, Barker had edited and condensed the first half of Middleton's original; in terms of narrative, the second half was entirely his own, entailing a huge change of style—a transition effected not by subtle gradations but by a crashing of gears. It is worth noting that Barker has, throughout his career, written a significant number of plays that make

88   *Charles Lamb*

reference to works in the literary canon; thus, in *The Bite of the Night,* one encounters Helen of Troy against a catastrophic landscape of the destruction and sacking of that city. *Seven Lears* is set as a forerunner to Shakespeare's *King Lear* and focuses on the total erasure from Shakespeare's narrative of Lear's wife. In *Gertrude—The Cry* something similar happens when Barker, pursuant to this theme of historically silenced wives, takes the Gertrude/Claudius affair and places it center stage. This has the significant effect of reducing the dominance exercised over the play by Hamlet. In fact, it is no longer a drama rooted in the existential angst of a disinherited prince but rather a series of seductive duels ignited by Gertrude's sexuality. The advantage of this method of responding to classical texts is that, as a dramatist, one can count on the audience to arrive at the theatre already primed with certain knowledge and expectations.

In his remarkable essay, *Theory of the Modern Drama,* Peter Szondi argues—with a degree of plausibility—that the drama, from the Renaissance on, played a significant part in shaping the self-image of contemporary (Occidental) man:

> It (the drama) was the result of a bold intellectual effort made by a newly self-conscious being who, after the collapse of the medieval worldview, sought to create an artistic reality within which he could fix and mirror himself on the basis of interpersonal relationships alone. Man entered the drama only as a fellow human being, so to speak. (7)

This was a bold conjecture on Szondi's part, which provided him with the analytic tools to undertake a survey of the (Occidental) canon, including Chekhov, whose characters, according to Szondi, "live under the sign of renunciation—renunciation of the present and of communication before all else, renunciation of the happiness arising from real interaction. This resignation, in which passionate longing and irony mix to prevent any extreme, also determines the form of Chekhov's plays" (18). Because of this, the characters exist each in his/her personal solitude and, renouncing the present, express themselves in lengthy monologues concerned exclusively with memories of the past and dreams of the future: both categories easily idealized. The dialogue, in Szondi's opinion, "carries no weight" (20) and, theoretically, should be abandoned along with the action. In practice, however, Chekhov maintains the traditional elements of dramatic form "in a deemphasized incidental manner that allows the real subject negative expression as a deviation from traditional dramatic form" (20).

It was not until the early 1990s that Barker returned to the idea of a Chekhov project, fixing his attention on *Uncle Vanya*—a text that he believed exhibited the essence of Chekhovism. Barker's "version" received its premiere production in 1996 performed by The Wrestling School directed by Barker. His opinion that the piece showed typically Chekhovian characteristics would probably have been shared by Chekhov himself, who remarked in a letter to Stanislavsky dated 15 January 1901: "after all *Uncle Vanya* is my play, not anyone else's" (*A Life* 453). Chekhov was countering claims that his *Vanya* was essentially a revision of *The Wood Demon*, a play rejected by the Imperial Theatres in 1888, his point being that it was legitimate for a writer to plagiarize his own work. At the same time, he was asserting his rights and "authorizing" *Uncle Vanya*. For Barker, there was the challenge of examining more closely his feeling of antipathy for Chekhov, the results of which he set out in a short essay, "Disputing Vanya," included in *Arguments for a Theatre*. The article had first appeared in *The Guardian* on 17 April 1996 under the heading "Subverting Vanya," and it is interesting that Barker chose to make this alteration to the title, suggesting a more open debate than the political "hatchet job" implied by the original. He also reflected on the original Vanya (the character) in program notes for the premiere production. The argument here seeks to demonstrate "The Necessity for a Version of Chekhov's *Uncle Vanya*" (Notes). "Necessity" because of the all but universal veneration of him within the English stage tradition, a situation that would have been perfectly acceptable had its effects been benign. Barker believed emphatically they were not. His objections to Chekhov are summarized clearly: "Chekhov's *Uncle Vanya* is a danse macabre. Its charm lies in its appeal to the death wish in ourselves. In its melancholy celebration of paralysis and spiritual vacuity it makes theatre an art of consolation, a funerary chant for unlived life" (Notes).[1]

The clearest instance of this is Vanya himself: the life that he leads is a dull and monotonous treadmill without hope of any respite or recreation. He has sacrificed his own life chances in order to further the career of his brother-in-law, Aleksandr Serebryakov, a now retired professor of art history in Moscow. Along with his mother, Mariya, Vanya had revered Serebryakov as an academic genius. Now he has come to the realization that his idol has feet of clay and his personal sacrifices have been wasted. His sense of "unlived life" is acute: "If I had a normal life, I might have been a Schopenhauer, a Dostoyevsky" (*Plays* 231). When these claims are voiced in company, even Vanya himself is uncomfortably aware of how ridiculous they seem. There are several indications in the text that suggest his character could be based on a clown archetype: Pierrot in particular. Vanya's interruption of Astrov and Yelena's moment of passion brandishing a bunch of roses is a typical Pierrot gag: his hapless naivety contrasting with Astrov's cynical and brutal Harlequin. (It should not be forgotten that the classic Pierrot is also a murderer, as exemplified in the 1945 film, *Les Enfants du Paradis*, in which the actor Jean-Baptiste Deburau, who created the character, kills the clothes vendor.)

Chekhov provides stage directions that would enable a capable performer to strike a powerful note of pathos from Vanya's reaction. Typically, he falls back on ingrained habit and seeks to stifle his disappointment:

90   *Charles Lamb*

> VOYNITSKY (*lays the roses on a chair; in agitation wipes his face and neck with a handkerchief*). Never mind . . . no . . . Never mind. (*Plays* 225)

The face mopping provides the actor with a physical action that can be used expressively. Again, this could suggest itself as something of a mechanical reflex attesting to Vanya's painful confusion rather than a properly motivated action. At any rate, the moment serves to illustrate Barker's main criticism of the Chekhovian aesthetic: "We love Vanya, but it is a love born of contempt. It is Chekhov's bad faith to induce in his audience an adoration of the broken will. In this he invites us to collude in our own despair" (Notes). Vanya is "pathetic" in both senses of the word—stricto sensu and colloquial; Barker argues that the pathos of the clownish Vanya resonates with the audience's personal griefs, exalting them from the mundane into a species of poetry. The performance can then take on a social function, as Barker points out: "It is perhaps the function of the classic work to act precisely as this source of collective reassurance, moving from obscurity to prominence and back again as the state of society bestows significances never predicted or intended in the moment of its inception" ("Disputing Vanya" 169).

In acknowledging that Chekhov, or for that matter any playwright, must lose control of his creations, Barker tacitly admits that his polemic is aimed not so much ad hominem as at the niche Chekhov occupies in the pantheon of the contemporary British stage. Early attempts to introduce Chekhovian drama in England had met with limited success; compared with Ibsen, his plays lacked the overt sociopolitical content that might have appealed to typical theatre "progressives" of the time. From the outset, stagings were linked to the celebrity (or notoriety) of Stanislavsky, the Moscow Art Theatre, and the controversial Stanislavsky "Method." The end product of the latter was what appeared to early twentieth-century audiences as "slice of life" naturalism—though it is hard for us now to imagine passages such as Sonya's so-called "arias" just before the final curtain as anything other than wincingly melodramatic. In his essay on the English response to Chekhov's plays, Stephen Le Fleming argues that Anglo-Saxon regard was founded upon a view of the plays as the pink of civilization (54–64), a quality that would have recommended them to an English tradition of looking to theatre to provide reproducible models of social behavior. In particular, I am thinking here of the Comedy of Manners as exemplified from Congreve to Wilde. With this genre, costume assumed a special importance and we know that Chekhov was in the habit of specifying precise sartorial details to convey essential information—mainly concerning character. According to Stanislavsky, Chekhov insisted that Vanya should wear a silk tie:

> The costume and general appearance of a landed gentleman are well-known to all—high boots, a cap, sometimes a horsewhip, for it is taken

Howard Barker's (Uncle) Vanya   91

for granted that he rides horseback a great deal. But Chekhov was against all that.

"Listen, he has a wonderful tie; he is an elegant, cultured man. It is not true that our landed gentry walk about in tar-smeared boots. They are well-educated people. They dress well. They order their clothes in Paris." (272)

Clearly, what Chekhov was doing was to compel Stanislavsky to look beyond stage stereotypes in the process of creating the role. To confirm his argument, he appeals to the truth as it may be found not only in nature, but also in society. Chekhov had resorted to the same tactics with Stanislavsky when preparing *The Seagull*: while the actor poured his creative energies into the construction of a preening moustache-twirling seducer, Chekhov insisted that Trigorin must wear "torn shoes and checked trousers" (270).

Barker was not the first to characterize Chekhov's drama in melancholy musical terms: Desmond MacCarthy, a prominent theatre critic of the 1920s, wrote:

Chekhov is the dramatist of good-byes; good-byes to hopes and ambitions, good-byes between lovers. Yet out of this conception of life, which might be thought "depressing," Chekhov makes a work of art which moves us and exalts us like a beautiful piece of music. It is not in a mood of depression one leaves the theatre. (101)

Two points here elicit comment. First, the significance of what is variously referred to as mood, atmosphere, or "music," terms that crop up remarkably consistently with reference to the staging of Chekhov's plays. Indeed, Barker's words cited earlier ("danse macabre," etc.) reveal a response almost identical to MacCarthy's. The crucial difference is that whereas MacCarthy is concerned primarily with the experience, the emotions, Barker asserts an analysis that not only aims to lay bare how the plays operate emotionally, but seeks to draw out the implications of the end result. MacCarthy may leave the theatre "un-depressed" but this is a naive reaction because the "music," according to Barker, celebrates the essential failure of the characters' lives, thereby confirming that "it had to be thus" and endowing them with a spurious nobility as a reward for their stoicism. As audiences, the argument goes, we empathize with the characters and identify with Chekhov's aesthetic not least owing to the reality effects of the naturalism. This comforts and reassures audiences. Jean-François Lyotard makes this point with reference to more popular arts:

Industrial photography and cinema will be superior to painting and the novel whenever the object is to stabilize the referent, to arrange it according to a point of view which endows it with a recognisable meaning, to reproduce the syntax and vocabulary which enable the

92 *Charles Lamb*

addressee to decipher images and sequences quickly, and so to arrive easily at the consciousness of his own identity. (74)

I have cited Lyotard here because he emphasizes the significance of the "reassurance function" of art. It is a function that Barker explicitly rejects, preferring instead to have an anxious audience.

THE GUN

Barker creates his "version" of *Uncle Vanya* by dint of a startling reversal of the central action of the play: the rounds Vanya fires at Serebryakov find their target. This changes everything. With the Chekhov original, Vanya's bungled attempt at assassination leads back to the reestablishment of the status quo and reconciliation; after the killing of Serebryakov, the characters are left literally as well as figuratively in an entirely alien landscape. Before this, however, it is clear that for Vanya the revolver has become fetishized and possesses powers of transformation—powers that will drastically change his life:

I have a gun. For so long now I have had a gun. This gun I clean most nights. I clean it with oil in the light of the moon. This is certainly the habit of an assassin. (296)

In *The Wood Demon*, an earlier play that provided most of the materials for *Uncle Vanya*, the shooting incident bears a marked resemblance to the later version—apart from the actual killing itself: at the climax of the row concerning Serebryakov's plan to sell the estate, Vanya storms out. Shortly after a gunshot is heard from offstage and it is reported that Vanya has committed suicide. In both of the Chekhov plays then, the gun is relegated to the merely functional, making only a brief appearance in *Uncle Vanya*. In Barker's version, contrastingly, the gun is fêted and flaunted by Vanya, who describes it as "the lever of my life" (301) and "gun of ivory my doorway my birthplace" (305). Part of Vanya's glee with the gun is his awareness that Chekhov hated it; an opinion confirmed later by Chekhov himself: "The gun was always an error. The gun was always false" (332). False presumably because its use would not be Natural, would not seem Real, would appear artificial, a theatrical device bolted on to whip up vicarious excitement. And there is also the risk of characters seizing the weapon in order to use it in an unauthorized way—which is precisely what Vanya does. In contrast to Chekhov, he goes about reinforcing the reality of the gun, emphasizing its unique identity by reciting its serial number. Not only does this figure mark the revolver's place in the socioeconomic reality, but it has also taken on an initiatory quality with reference to the world of

Howard Barker's (Uncle) Vanya   93

the play—Vanya's world. Later, when he finds he can no longer recall the number he complains of a loss of substance:

> Perhaps I'm happy, is that it? Is this happiness? It doesn't feel like happiness, unless happiness is fog, perhaps it's fog, yes it must be . . .
> Who wants fog, not me! (337–38)

In the program notes of the premiere production, Barker says: "I remade Vanya because I loved his anger, which Chekhov allows to dissipate in toxic resentment. In doing this I denied the misery of the Chekhovian world, where love falters in self-loathing and desire is petulance." The first sections of both plays focus on this anger and it is clear that, in both cases, it emerges as the main driver of the action at this stage. Stylistically, the dramatists are very different, though Barker frequently integrates phrases and whole sentences from Chekhov's script. He is able to do this effectively because his own style is decidedly nonnaturalistic with a wide range of rhetorical, syntactical and figurative devices such as repetition, lengthy parentheses, and metaphor. The speech of Vanya is often saturated with irony. Barker's script starts thus:

> *A* Man *appears.*
> VANYA. Unc—le
> Van—ya *(Pause)*
> Unc—le
> Unc—le *(Pause)*
> Van—ya *(Pause. A guitar is strummed.)*
> Stop strumming stop that idle futile strumming you stop it.
> *(It ceases, then continues.)*
> I'll kill you
> *(It ceases.* ASTROV *enters)* (295)

Among the things that strike one here is the extent of Vanya's violent anger, which seems out of proportion to the offense caused by Telyeghin's musicianship; he scourges himself with the hated name in a paroxysm of self-loathing. It is possible to see in this brief conflict an outline of the material Barker has referred to in his comments. While Vanya is uniquely himself, Telyeghin, with his languid, improvisatory guitar meanderings, perfectly expresses the classic, Chekhovian melancholy. We learn later wherein lies his personal grief:

> MARINA. You couldn't keep your own wife, Waffles! *(Pause)*
> TELYEGHIN. So what? I loved her. Even when she abandoned me, I loved her. I still love her. That is love. Love and no returns . . . *(He smiles, shrugs.)* (328)

94   *Charles Lamb*

With this beatific posturing, "Waffles" tries to represent himself as a model of serenity, but there is plenty of evidence during the course of the action to suggest that he too suffers from "toxicity." This term is frequently applied by Barker to instances where characters repress powerful feelings and—over a period of time—become seriously embittered and incapable of action.

THE CHEKHOVIAN WORLD DISINTEGRATES

Regarding the dramatic structure of the plays, Chekhov follows the relatively conventional form of four acts with the main dramatic climax (the shooting incident) occurring towards the end of the third, followed by a "resolution" in the fourth. Such a scheme would have been entirely unsuitable for Barker's purposes. Being more concerned with what happens after rather than before the shooting, he compresses expository material so that Serebryakov is disposed of by page ten of the forty-six-page script. The immediate cause of the fracas is Serebryakov's announcement of his plan to sell the estate, invest the proceeds in stock, and live off the dividends. Thus far Barker sticks to Chekhov. However, while Chekhov's Vanya misses his potshot and is quickly overwhelmed by feelings of remorse, Barker's Vanya remorselessly turns an assassination into an atrocity by firing four rounds directly into Serebryakov's face. It is his intention to cast off the old, hated identity of "Uncle Vanya" and, on the basis of his crime, to establish a new personality to be known only as "Ivan"—for example, without the note of contempt-bred familiarity inherent in "Uncle Vanya."

Vanya kills/attempts to kill Serebryakov because he is outraged at the professor's proposal to sell up their home. Also, he has come to the conclusion that the academic genius he has lauded and supported for so many years isn't actually a genius at all. Furthermore, he has conceived a passion for Yelena, Serebryakov's stunningly beautiful young wife—a circumstance that compounds his jealous loathing of the older man. In Chekhov, Yelena is presented in the fairly conventional terms of the classic mismatch—old husband/young wife. He shows her doggedly clinging to the role of dutiful spouse while unremittingly besieged by would-be lovers. With Barker, things are very different. Firstly, his Helena admits to an active sexual relationship with her husband:

And he was potent God he was for all his sixty-seven . . . (306)

And I wanted him, am I lucid enough? I did. It made me shudder when he walked into my room naked and vaguely ugly yet he—(ASTROV *impetuously kisses* HELENA *on the mouth*) (307)

Astrov's action here is typically coercive and demonstrates a serious lack of control. When he proposes a rendezvous at the plantation, Serebryakov urges his wife to go:

Howard Barker's (Uncle) Vanya   95

Meet him. See what he can do for you. And then tell me. (301)

Serebryakov's behavior here brings to mind the relationship of Tortmann and Turner in *He Stumbled* as well as the King and Queen in *Knowledge and a Girl: The Snow White Case*. Concerning the latter, David Ian Rabey comments: "Thus—not without a frequently refined erotic anguish (comparable to Tortman's in *He Stumbled*)—the King maintains a distance that permits the Queen's (barely) controlled play within his own strategic display and control of patriarchal leadership" (126). Helena herself admits to having a passion for old men:

> I loved old men. Old men excited me. I wanted them to handle me intimately in public places. Doorways, for example, in wet weather. Train corridors on sunny afternoons. Department stores among the furnishings. Say you understand me. (308)

Maryia (Vanya's mother) positively refuses to understand and the remainder of act 1 is concerned with the struggle between those who support Vanya and those who don't—those who envisage possibilities in this new world and those who long for the security of the old one—however mundane. Helena conceives a passion for Vanya (now "Ivan") as the murderer of her husband. This kind of reversal is a typical seductive process where desire is maximized according to the force of the prohibition. So the killing of Serebryakov marks a boundary where Chekhov's real world collapses to be replaced by a seductive order. The collapse of the Chekhovian set and its replacement with the sea is both literal and symbolic. Literal because there exists an ongoing controversy as to whether it is there or not, symbolic because the concepts involved are capable of generating a rich set of meanings; "the sea," for instance, frequently stands as a metaphor for life in general. But it can also be death. In this context, it serves to contrast, particularly in its spatial immensity, with what Barker refers to as "the Chekhovian Room"—"stale with frustrated decision and annihilated will" ("Disputing Vanya" 168) The appearance of the sea prompts a wild and childish excitement amongst the characters who paddle and throw stones at the floating samovar. They are haunted, however, by a fear of their author returning to punish them for their mutinous misbehavior. Vanya attempts—unconvincingly—to reassure them: "Chekhov won't come now" (314).

Returning to the first dramatic climax, (which is where Vanya shoots Serebryakov offstage), Barker employs a device familiar to students of his work: he creates a chorus that, like other Barker choruses, is composed of the dead or the nearly dead (e.g., The Voices in The Canvas in *Scenes from an Execution*, The Gaoled in *Seven Lears*, or The Hanged in *Minna*). In this case, it's the recently dispatched Serebryakov who returns to the stage, attired, according to the stage directions, either in a hood or a facial bandage; he sits in a chair and lights a cigarette. Initially at least, it would appear that this ghost of Serebryakov, in the absence of Chekhov, is there to represent his views:

96   *Charles Lamb*

>SEREBRYAKOV. Chekhov says put the gun away before it leads to
>. . .
>VANYA. No
>SEREBRYAKOV. More trouble and . . .
>VANYA. No
>SEREBRYAKOV. Disturbs the fragile . . .
>VANYA. No
>SEREBRYAKOV. Balance of characters. (308)

Not all of these views are expressed as statements; some take the form of questions:

>SEREBRYAKOV. We reverence him because
>We reverence Chekhov
>Because in such a confined space the melancholy of
>Not tragedy
>The melancholy of
>Our unlived life is exquisitely redeemed
>We are forgiven
>We are forgiven
>We
>Do
>So
>Need
>To
>Be
>Forgiven
>Why
>Is
>That?
>(*Pause. Suddenly, TELYEGHIN begins to stamp his guitar into fragments . . .*) (311)

Stylistically, Serebryakov's language here connotes the liturgical in terms of its vocabulary—"reverence," "redeemed"—and its form—the repetition of "We are forgiven" suggests the ritual interchange of celebrant and response. However, it is almost as if the repetition of the word "forgiven" has prompted Serebryakov to reflect on it—a process indicated by the slow release of a single word per line, with the final question left hanging unanswered in the silence. As noted already, the guitar is credited with the capacity to evoke this Chekhovian mood. Telyeghin, of all the characters, is the most skeptical and resistant to the revolution attendant upon the shooting. His gesture here amounts to a somewhat theatricalized "conversion."

Having dealt with Serebryakov, Vanya's first order as instigator of the new chaos is to demand Helena remove her clothes. This provokes an outburst of revulsion from Astrov, Maryia, and Sonya. Helena, on the other hand, proceeds to strip, remarking: "It's only nakedness" (305), and seems disappointed when Vanya orders her to stop. The reversal in her attitude emanates from Vanya's killing of her husband and her consciousness of having participated in the crime: she senses that Vanya was motivated by his infatuation with her and is eager to know the details—"Did you shoot him in the face?" (306). It is at this point, as she describes the physical relations with her now deceased husband, that she is seized by Astrov, who forces a long kiss on her mouth. This gesture seems to terminate any interest she may have had in the ecological doctor.

Chekhov presents Astrov—one senses—not in the manner of the impartial witness he, as dramatist, aspired to be, but with a broad approval. Chekhov himself was a planter of trees, a physician, and—perhaps most significantly—a holder of enlightened views. However, taking Serebryakov into account, it is easy to read this as an example of the familiar Russian metanarrative of talent mired in provincial ignorance and sloth while mediocrity is heaped with honors. Chekhov does not present a wholly positive view of Astrov—for instance, his sexist remarks on friendship with women elicit from Vanya the put-down: "That's a crude sort of philosophy" (*Plays* 236)—and his efforts to seduce Yelena look unpleasantly coercive. Barker's version of this character, as might be expected, shows him in a completely negative light. Vanya regularly comments pejoratively, e.g., "Astrov's shallowness is that of the idealist with whom it is impossible to disagree" (300). When a smitten Sonya describes him as beautiful:

> ASTROV. Am I? Am I beautiful? I think I could never love a human being. Though what does still affect me is beauty. I think if Helena wanted to, for example, she might turn my head . . .
> VANYA. Fancy! Fancy, for all his terrible decline which is our fault, for all his tragic loss of hope, which is our fault, he could just—he might just manage—
> To fuck Helena! (300–301)

Thus Vanya attempts to convince Sonya that Astrov is not worthy of her. Barker presents the doctor becoming increasingly demoralized until he reaches a nadir of abjection with his rape of Helena. This, Barker seems to be saying, is how the idealistic end up—the humanists, the liberals. Vanya, responding to Serebryakov, hammers home the message:

> VANYA. I don't require sympathy tell him. *(Pause)* It is possible that I'm not human. I was comic and now I am inhuman. The comic, the pathetic, the impotence made me lovable, but underneath I was not human. And nor is anyone. Underneath. Human. Tell Chekhov! (309)

In respect of the characters, the one who evidences the most striking alteration at Barker's hands is probably Sonya, who, in the dramatis personae, is described as "A Spinster with Powerful Arms"; in the Chekhov

98 Charles Lamb

play Sonya provided another link in the chain of unfulfilled lovers: she desires Astrov, who desires Yelena. She represents an opposite tendency to Yelena, who is idle, languid, cold, and very beautiful: Sonya is industrious, warmhearted, and "plain." It is she who emotionally sustains her uncle—particularly in the reconciliation—just as she, probably more than anyone else and in all innocence, is responsible for the hated "Uncle Vanya" identity. With Chekhov's version, in the drama surrounding the pistol shots, Sonya seems to regress into an infantile state, clinging and appealing desperately to "Nanny"; in the Barker text, however, she challenges immediately Vanya's prohibition on addressing him by any Christian names other than "Ivan"—and is brutally slapped for her temerity. Shortly after this she attempts to restore the rule of law by having her uncle arrested:

> SONYA. . . . We could have lived at such a low, slow pulse like toads in winter waiting for God to lift us off the landscape *(Pause)* I do want you to suffer. Telyeghin, get down to the police post, my uncle yearns for his first interrogation. *(Pause)* I haven't been so animated for years! *(Pause)* It's hatred, isn't it? Animates me so? (310)

Telyeghin refuses, not on ethical grounds, but because he's afraid Helena will beat him. Sonya then announces she will hand over Vanya to the authorities herself but desists the moment her uncle threatens to shoot her. Instead of showing frustration or resentment at being thwarted in this way, she laughs and embraces Vanya and Maryia in a dance that expresses their sense of liberation. In this mood, which is totally "un-Chekhovian," Sonya bluntly demands of Astrov that he give her a child. Having set aside his finer feelings, the doctor tentatively discovers some attractions in the proposal. This exchange, however, is dropped when there is another collapse of the set and the characters are distracted by a view of the sea. Sonya has been considering her muscular arms and has come to the conclusion that they have been given her for a purpose—they are destined to strangle Astrov. Chekhov's Sonya is essentially a passive creature, a captive of her plainness who is conventionally virtuous after the fashion of nineteenth-century literary heroines. She waxes most passionate on the subject of endurance, which she sees as being the only available strategy for them. Barker's Sonya, contrastingly, discovers her "proper" destiny as a murderess in the liberated body—her powerful arms.

This matches the pattern evident in the cases of the other "liberated" characters: their revolt is stimulated at the level of the body: Helena and her beauty; Vanya and the steadiness of his trigger hand. From the outset of the mutiny, the characters are all haunted by a pervasive anxiety—a fear that Chekhov will return and punish them not only for their insubordination, but for the crimes they may have committed. As previously remarked, Chekhov's views continue to be expressed by the onstage chorus of the dead—Serebryakov. Chekhov's personal appearance—complete

Howard Barker's (Uncle) Vanya 99

with ethical dilemma—creates an effective climax in act 1 and a striking start to act 2. Sonya and Maryia have spotted a sinking ship. The sole crew member appears to be drowning. The two women consult with Vanya, who advises them to let the man drown on the presumption that he could be their worst enemy. Maryia, however, asserts that Vanya is simply "wrong" and Sonya is hopeful that this might be a husband. The former's argument in favor of rescue is that such a course of action is instinctive—in our genes; Vanya claims that the programming is cultural. We can see that this position is consistent with the point he made earlier to Serebryakov concerning humanism—that "underneath" people are not human (309). Humanity is a veneer that helps to convince us that we are civilized. The rescue is successful amidst general rejoicing even though the final image depicting Maryia being slapped "brutally across the face" by her servant Marina serves to dampen the euphoria.

CHEKHOV DIES

In act 2 the characters line up drill-style while Chekhov paces up and down, toweling his hair. One presumes that his intention is to restore the play to its "proper" form and content, for example, the version he authorized and to which (translated) I have been making reference in this chapter. The stage direction "Their heads hang like penitents" suggests that they have already been subjected to lengthy scolding. At this point, having concluded that Vanya is the ringleader of the "mutiny," Barker's Chekhov focuses on undermining his authority by ridiculing him before the others. In this way he goads him into losing control of his emotions—a tactic Helena points out. Her own responses are masterpieces of objectivity and understatement that leave precious little opportunity for sneering. She declares her love for Vanya in unequivocal terms—a conjunction that is anathema to Chekhov, who considers him a buffoon—"a fumbler in women's wardrobes" (331)—and unworthy of a woman such as Helena. The vehemence of Chekhov's objection to the Helena–Vanya relationship suggests a Pygmalion-style link between the author and his creation: has Chekhov fallen in love with Helena? Vanya himself has suffered the potentially shameful misfortune of impotence on his keenly anticipated first sexual encounter with Helena; the account he gives of this failure envisages the episode as an attempt by Chekhov to undermine his new identity as Ivan—an attempt he defeats:

> VANYA (*Going to SONYA*). Sonya, I triumphed. I did not submit.
> I turned shame inside out and silenced his contempt. The laughter died in Chekhov's mouth . . .
> SONYA. Yes . . .
> VANYA. I smothered him. (317)

100   *Charles Lamb*

When Chekhov appears in the flesh, however, this newly found confidence deserts him and he sobs uncontrollably. In his struggle with Chekhov, Barker's Vanya keeps asserting that he is a murderer. Presumably because the designated act is an experience outside Chekhov's ken and he will not be able to "see through" Vanya as he claims:

> (CHEKHOV *looks at him with contempt*)
> CHEKHOV. Vanya, I have such a withering knowledge of your soul. Its poverty. Its pitiful dimensions. It is smaller than an aspirin which fizzes in a glass . . .
> VANYA. What do you think murder is a hobby!
> HELENA. Shh!
> VANYA. He thinks it is a hobby!
> HELENA. Ivan—
> VANYA. It is an act of profound psychological and philosophical significance. *(Pause.* CHEKHOV *smiles)*
> HELENA. Ivan, he is making you infantile. Please don't go on. (330)

Maryia spends much of her time reading and annotating political pamphlets. Broadly, her views appear to be liberal humanist. In particular, she is enthusiastic about the works of Serebryakov, who is her son-in-law. She believed—contrary to her son—that her decision to rescue the man who turned out to be Chekhov was a moral imperative and she is finding the adulation lavished on Helena especially galling:

> MARYIA. What a magnificently fecund female and her depths are pure red and she never lifted her voice for the oppressed not one syllable or lost a second's sleep for another's pain. Magnificence! And yet she has a soul, she does, she has a soul you cannot diminish Helena, can you? Obviously I hate her but you cannot—*(Pause)* want to die I cannot tolerate another hour of myself this self squatting like a bear on my brain . . . (CHEKHOV *goes to her and unbuttons her dress at the breast. He exposes her breasts. Others watch . . .)* (330–31)

Exposing Maryia's breasts is a powerful dramatic effect that resonates both on and off the stage: just as outrage was produced when Vanya ordered Helena to remove her clothes, even greater revulsion is expressed regarding Maryia because Barker's Chekhov is using her to demonstrate and confirm his aesthetic—namely, that the beauty of his works is rooted in negation, the unlived life; thus, the beauty of Maryia's breasts comes from the awareness that they will never be touched; he shows little interest in her ethical confusion nor indeed any sensitivity to the humiliation his actions here might cause. I say "might" because Maryia seems to find the experience a

Howard Barker's (Uncle) Vanya   101

positive one. It is arguable that the demise of Serebryakov, among its other effects, involved the loss for her of a charismatic male "genius-figure"; Chekhov would probably have seemed an ideal "replacement": hence her acclamation of him as a god. On the other hand, Helena accuses him of being evil and he agrees that the word is appropriate, adding—"My crimes are, after all much worse than Ivan's, Ivan who thinks murder is serious, who sports his murder as a badge, who hangs his life from a hook, Ivan who is fundamentally inert" (331). He doesn't give any specific indication, however, as to what his own "crimes" might be.

The main dramatic event of act 2 is the death of Chekhov. Barker makes no attempt here to achieve even a semblance of biographical accuracy. His Chekhov's initial intervention would appear to be motivated by a desire to quell the "mutiny" and defend the integrity of his play—particularly as regards the characters. He focuses his efforts on cutting Vanya down to size but encounters unexpected opposition from other characters—especially Helena. Throughout this he seems lively and combative—"I do love a mutiny!" (329)—but there is a definite alteration in his tone when he finally reveals his other purpose:

> There are things even I do not understand and impotent at that really it is so unclean I could laugh, I do laugh, I resort to laughter when I am in deepest offence, listen, I am dying I have come here to die . . . *(Pause)* (331)

Chekhov is referring here to the liaison between Vanya and Helena. His admission concerning laughter—that he resorts to it in order to conceal actual feelings of offense—might prompt some reconsideration of his performance hitherto—particularly with regard to his feelings for Vanya about which there was much talk of laughter. The laughter, it appears, could well have been "toxic," and when Chekhov asks for a volunteer to sit with him, there is an embarrassed pause. He specifies Vanya, taking care to address him as Ivan, who demurs, "But you hate me" (332). And Chekhov agrees. Does he agree because—true or untrue—he knows the admission will humor Vanya, who positively revels in the thought that he is infuriating his author?

According to Baudrillard, "we seduce with our death, our vulnerability, and with the void that haunts us" (83). The dying Chekhov's request for someone to sit with him takes on the status of a seductive challenge, which Vanya, as a character open to seduction, would find hard to refuse. In spite of Helena's objections, he agrees and listens for the most part in silence while Chekhov expatiates on a fable of Borgesian ambition. His speech, however, is replete with crude manipulative devices—mainly attributing opinions and motives to his addressees that, given the opportunity, they would dissent from. His "last words" relate to the Chekhovian aesthetic:

102   *Charles Lamb*

> CHEKHOV. One day I hoped I would reach out and tell myself, pour myself like a liquid from a jug into the void of another, all, entire, to the last drop, how I struggled with this dream to pour myself into another man! A woman! To be drained . . . *(Pause. There are sounds on the beach of voices.)* And in abandoning that dream, I found something like freedom. In discarding all that was arguably the best in me, I found a peace of sorts. We are entirely untransferable. So hold my hand . . . Ivan . . . *(VANYA extends a hand to CHEKHOV, who holds it. CHEKHOV dies. TELYEGHIN hurries in.)*
> TELYEGHIN. The Sea's gone! (333–34)

Chekhov appears to be claiming here that, at some juncture, he gave up the search for a "soul mate" to whom he could "bare his soul" and thereby discovered a degree of happiness. He takes the argument further and asserts the impossibility of his previous ideal ("we are entirely untransferable"). It is probably relevant at this point to remind ourselves of a question from Barker's *Death, The One and the Art of Theatre*:

> Is dying immune to the liar? Have we not known those who even dying put on an act? (95)

Chekhov's performance here flatly contradicts the passionate rhetoric of the Helena/Vanya connection ("His hand in the very heart of me / His hand / In / My / Heart!" etc.), at which we know he took the deepest offense. Referring back to Szondi, it can be seen that his vision of Chekhov's theatre as a collection of individual solitudes is consistent with and supportive of Barker's account of his (the fictional Chekhov's) struggle to pour himself into another.

> What the Occidental most probably experiences only while intoxicated—participation in the loneliness of the other, the inclusion of individual loneliness in a growing collective loneliness—seems to be a possibility inherent in the Russian: the person and the language. (Szondi 21)

SOME CONCLUSIONS

Vanya responded to his author's request to hold his hand so that when the others enter trumpeting the disappearance of the sea, Vanya announces the death of Chekhov while holding his hand. There was previously much mention of Chekhov's "disease"—though he himself never actually specifies precisely what this is. It seems, however, to have a psychological as well as a physical dimension: Serebryakov and Astrov, in chorus mode,

Howard Barker's (Uncle) Vanya   103

suggest "self-murder," "self-betrayal," and "self-disgust." Helena, who was opposed to leaving Vanya with Chekhov, senses immediately that something is wrong:

> HELENA. I said we are not the same as we were . . . *(VANYA does not look at her.)* If you betray me I will kill you. I have the right to kill you. You don't dispute that right, do you? (335)

Helena is also angry that her relationship with Vanya is changing her personality: she is having to be more assertive and coercive because Vanya isn't . . . the inevitable termination of her reflections is that she will cease to be desirable. The shift into act 3 is signaled with the flying in of a massive mirror, on which Helena becomes fixated. Apparently she has escaped the prospect of having to play a coercive role and has reverted to being beautiful:

> Beauty does upset you beauty does irritate your nerves it is so very undemocratic beauty it is an unforgivable thing I have it however so and all things lead to my body what else is there but my body all things lead to it . . . I am the point and purpose of the world. (336)

She claims that she still loves Vanya even though it is clear to her that he is deteriorating. I have argued elsewhere (Lamb 180–87) that Barker's characters inhabit a universe that functions in ways that differ from what we call reality. Baudrillard describes it thus:

> A universe that can no longer be interpreted in terms of psychic or psychological relations, nor those of repression and the subconscious, but must be interpreted in the terms of play, challenges, duels, the strategy of appearances—that is, the terms of seduction. (7)

The relationship of Helena and Vanya is grounded in seduction—specifically the dual/duel. It is initiated with a challenge and proceeds by way of escalating counter-challenges; one of the outcomes here is death. So, for example, Vanya's ordering Helena to "get undressed" is a challenge to which she responds with insouciance and without protest—an attitude that, in itself, constitutes a counterchallenge. A little later her taunt "How long before you turn yourself in?" is really another challenge. In the final scene the duel becomes lethal in the shape of a suicide pact. The challenge here is conveyed by a look: "*Pause. They look at one another*" (338). While Vanya shoots Helena successfully, his nerve fails him when it comes to doing the same for himself. Disposing of the single remaining round by firing it into the ground suggests that he is far from suicidal and, as he strides out the door, has no idea of where he's going or even where he is. According to Barker himself, as cited in Rabey:

104 *Charles Lamb*

> Vanya's "Damn, missed . . ." is a failure, a cowardice, not matched to Helena's bravery. He has backslid. But the option of backsliding to chess or guitar playing is to repudiate all he has achieved. Thus he departs into the night with absolutely no destination. (67)

I read this as a victory for Chekhov, who successfully infects Vanya with his dying performance. Helena tries, unsuccessfully, to warn him off. She notices at the time that their relationship has changed and confirms this later in act 3, where she challenges Vanya with the accusation that he is "deteriorating."

Even though it includes the drama of Vanya and Helena, the final scene of Barker's *Uncle Vanya* shows the other characters peaceably occupied with routine domesticity. Both plays in the end feature reconciliation, though it is clear that Barker does not endorse this. Both reflect an acceptance of banality, banality being a price worth paying for the quiet life described by Sonya earlier. No grand passions. No ecstasies. No pain. Both writers present us with worlds that are essentially products of their imagination. (This is the case even with Chekhovian naturalism.) These worlds are represented not merely through background scenery, but via foregrounded characters as portrayed by the actors. In the end, the focus of the drama charts the challenge posed by the ecstatic love affair between Helena and Vanya to the banality of the mundane in its Chekhovian exaltation.

Chekhov's intention was to entertain his audiences by holding the mirror up to them, and he engaged them through a mixture of conventional and unconventional techniques. Taking the former first, the characters all appear as a balanced and integral group: so we have Astrov as hero—flawed hero, but hero nonetheless. In the opposite corner, the much reviled Serebryakov—tyrannical, selfish, snobbish, cowardly, and querulous. Sonya—sympathetic, virtuous—is, as is ever the case with virtue, plain. Yelena, as her name suggests, represents the dangerous erotic charge of a femme fatale. All this combines to form a familiar enough landscape for the audiences of Chekhov's day. Indeed, in its geographic essentials it's still familiar today. And insofar as this is the case, its effect can be pleasantly reassuring. We have considered briefly the suggestion that Vanya can be seen as a version of the commedia type, Pierrot. In the context of the original Chekhov play that boasts his name as its title, Vanya is presented as a clown. He seems to get away with outrageous behavior because the other characters don't generally take him seriously. There is, however, another side to Vanya, just as there is to Pierrot, which is not in the least comic: they are both capable of murder. As we have already seen, Barker seizes upon this potential turn of events and his Vanya engineers a process of self-transformation that rejects kindly Uncle Vanya in favor of the ruthless assassin, Ivan. The latter identity is put to the test not only with the killing of Serebryakov, but in the scenes that follow. Ivan successfully convinces the others that he would have no compunctions about shooting them should the need arise.

In rewriting Chekhov, Barker takes as his starting point an apparently chance-based incident that nevertheless has enormous consequences—the shooting. The rounds are fired accurately; Serebryakov is dead, and it rapidly becomes clear that Barker has rewritten the characters and the narrative. The killing causes a breakdown in authorial control that, in spite of the suggestion of some string-pulling, allows the characters to "make it up as they go along." The dramatic arrival of Chekhov on a mission to restore his authority leads to complications that expose his diverse relationships with the characters he has created. Barker's *(Uncle) Vanya* is not a play that purports to convey "messages," or institute "celebrations," or even simply "tell the truth." What it does do is puncture—if only for a short time—the complacent atmosphere of the Chekhovian room with its deep-rooted humanist faith in endurance and ultimate reconciliation. Barker achieves this radical solicitation by introducing Chekhov's protégés to the void.

NOTES

1. The names of the characters in Howard Barker's play *(Uncle) Vanya* are similar to those of Chekhov's original, but sometimes they take different spellings. For example, Chekhov's Uncle Vanya (Voynitsky Ivan Petrovich) becomes Vanya in Barker's play; Yelena Andreyevna turns into Helena; and Uncle Vanya's mother, Mariya Vasilyevna of Chekhov's original, is renamed Maryia by Barker. The names of other characters in the Barker's text take the following spelling: Serebryakov, Astrov, Marina (nanny), and Telyeghin.

WORKS CITED

Barker, Howard, and Eduardo Houth. *A Style and Its Origins*. London: Oberon, 2007. Print.

Barker, Howard. *Death, The One and the Art of Theatre*. Oxford: Routledge, 2005. Print.

———. "Disputing Vanya." *Arguments for a Theatre*. 3rd ed. Manchester: Manchester UP, 1997. 168–70. Print.

———. "Notes on the Necessity for a Version of Chekhov's *(Uncle) Vanya*." Program Notes for The Wrestling School premiere of *(Uncle) Vanya*. 1996. Print.

———. *(Uncle Vanya)*. *Collected Plays*. 3 vols. London: Calder Publications, 1993. Print.

Baudrillard, Jean. *Seduction*. Trans. Brian Singer. London: Macmillan, 1990. Print.

Brecht, Bertolt. "A Short Organum for the Theatre." Trans. John Willett. *Avant Garde Drama: A Casebook*. Ed. B. F. Dukore and D. C. Gerould. New York: Crowell, 1976. 500–32. Print.

Chekhov, Anton. *A Life in Letters*. Trans. Anthony Phillips. Ed. Rosamund Bartlett. London: Penguin Classics, 2004. Print.

———. *Plays*. Trans. Elisaveta Fen. London: Penguin Classics, 1964. Print.

Lamb, Charles. *The Theatre of Howard Barker*. Oxford: Routledge, 2004. Print.

106 *Charles Lamb*

Le Fleming, Stephen. "Coping with the Outlandish: The English Response to Chekhov's Plays 1911–1926." *Chekhov on the British Stage.* Ed. Patrick Miles. Cambridge: Cambridge UP, 1993. 54–64. Print.

Lyotard, Jean-Francois. *The Postmodern Condition: A Report on Knowledge.* Trans. Geoff Bennington and Brian Massumi. Manchester: Manchester UP, 1986. Print.

MacCarthy, Desmond. *Theatre.* London: MacGibbon and Kee, 1954. Print.

Rabey, David Ian. *Howard Barker: Ecstasy and Death. An Expository Study of His Drama, Theory and Production Work, 1988–2008.* Basingstoke: Palgrave Macmillan, 2009. Print.

Stanislavsky, Konstantin. *My Life in Art.* Trans. G. Ivanov-Mumjiev. Moscow: Foreign Languages Publishing House, 1925. Print.

Szondi, Peter. *Theory of the Modern Drama.* Ed. and trans. Michael Hays. Cambridge: Polity Press, 1987. Print.

Part II

Chekhov in the Post[ist] Context

6 Transtextual Crossbreeds in Post-Communist Context

An Anthropological Analysis of Horia Gârbea's *The Seagull from the Cherry Orchard*

Diana Manole

CHEKHOV IN ROMANIA: FROM PROPAGANDISTIC TOOLS TO TRANSCULTURAL MEDIATORS

Resignifying and/or rewriting Shakespeare's plays has become one of the means of establishing the imperial canon and subsequently "writing back" to the Empire in British colonies (Ashcroft, Griffiths, and Tiffin 189–91). A similar phenomenon has taken place with Anton Chekhov's works in the other countries formerly part of the Soviet bloc.[1] Until the fall of the pro-Soviet regimes in 1989, their stagings required a political statement, especially on the part of the director. This was the case not only because of the propagandist requirements imposed by the state censorship starting in 1971, but also because they belonged to what was perceived as the culture of the Russian colonizer (Verdery 96). Next to more recent Soviet plays, Chekhov's works were commonly used as propagandist tools in productions that embodied the communist agenda. Paradoxically, especially during Ceaușescu's dictatorship,[2] more daring directors began staging the same plays as anticommunist allegories, contesting the regime from within in complicity with the audiences and, sometimes, even the political censors.

Despite the absence of a Chekhovian tradition on the Romanian stage before the Second World War (Bratu 22),[3] during communist rule his plays were performed in Romanian theatres almost every season. In 1948 the communist government expropriated all private companies and opened several national and municipal theatres across the country, where Socialist Realism[4] and "propaganda replaced art" (Runcan 222).[5] Accordingly, the Chekhov productions emphasized social aspects and class consciousness of the new society (Fedorenco) and presented his characters as representatives of the flawed Russian aristocracy and intelligentsia and "part of a long and tense trail of inaction and lack of communication, in which they, more than society, bear the guilt" (Topologeanu), justifying the necessity of the communist revolution. For example, when *Three Sisters* was produced for the first time in Romania in 1950, at the Bucharest National Theatre, it was directed in a propagandistic manner by Moni Ghelerter, who

110 *Diana Manole*

"imprinted the entire production with a feeling of renewal that most of the characters share" (Massoff 8: 538). Taking advantage of the short period of relative freedom that followed Stalin's death in 1953, in the late 1950s and 1960s Socialist Realism slowly made room for some more experimental attempts and in-depth psychological analysis, often criticized by conventional and/or subservient theatre reviewers. In 1959, Marietta Sadova, the first female Romanian director, staged *The Seagull* at the National Theatre and *The Cherry Orchard* at Bulandra Theatre in Bucharest; sycophant critics responded to both productions with collective disapproval. Horia Bratu, the theatre critic for the theatre review *Revista Teatrul*, denounced the director's vision and "the melancholic and somber poetry of the disappearance of former aristocratic brightness" (27) in the name of "the ideological understanding of Chekhov's theatre" (23). He also emphasized the importance of Petya Trofimov and Anya in *The Cherry Orchard*, who supposedly represented "the poetry and joy of welcoming a new [communist] life [. . . t]he victory of detaching oneself from the [aristocratic] medium with no regrets" (26) and whom Sadova mistakenly ignored.

In 1968 *The Cherry Orchard*, directed by Lucian Pintilie at the Bulandra Theatre, challenged the usual politicized perspective of the play and subsequently changed the Romanian perception of Chekhov's works. According to Ileana Popovici, it was "the most 'cheerful' and 'lively' Chekhov show" (42) in the Romanian theatre to that date and "one of the most coherent and harmoniously constructed shows [. . .] orchestrated like a musical symphony" (44) of the time. Pintilie set his production in a sunny wheat field, the symbol of fruition and wealth, but also of death and the end of a cycle, when harvest-time arrives. The show did not mockingly reenact Chekhov's characters; instead it underlined "the real and bizarre, comical and unsettling dramas of some cheerful suicidal people, comfortably grounded in their incurable irresponsibility" (44). The social and political context was only treated as a necessary background, and the portrayal of Petya Trofimov, for example, did not render him as the herald of the future communist regime, but only exhibited his naiveté, kindness, and lack of practical skills (46).

This new approach generated several other experimental productions during the following decades. For example, Cătălina Buzoianu's 1970 production of *The Seagull* at the National Theatre in Iași focused on the power of art and love, Vlad Mugur's 1970 *Three Sisters* at the Hungarian Theatre in Cluj emphasized the aristocratic world's poetry and inability to survive, and György Harag's 1984 production of *The Cherry Orchard* at Târgu-Mureș State Theatre centered on a metaphor of time and death. Ceaușescu's 1971 July Theses had explicitly required all performance genres to promote exclusively works "with a militant, revolutionary character [. . .] with topics based on our people's fight for the triumph of socialism" according to the popular communist belief "You are either with us or against us!" (Popescu 122). Until the fall of the regime in 1989, most of the Romanian

Transtextual Crossbreeds in Post-Communist Context   111

theatre productions obediently expressed the official political agenda. In this context, the audiences perceived the Chekhov productions that managed to elude political censorship without fulfilling the ideological requirements as genuine acts of dissidence. At the same time, successfully directing and/or acting in Chekhov's plays was considered proof of talent and professionalism because of the commonly recognized challenge of embodying his complex characters and/or stage texts in which apparently "nothing happens." Next to Shakespeare, Chekhov became one of the core courses at the Institute of Theatrical and Cinematographic Arts (IATC) in Bucharest in the BA programs in acting and directing.

The number of productions of Chekhov's works further increased after 1989. During the first years of the post-communist transition, Romanian values were an odd and dysfunctional hybrid of Western and communist principles. Western, mostly American, media and film started having a strong effect on the national culture, with the sudden spread of digital forms of entertainment and communication heightening the collective alienation. In addition, the gradual adoption of the market economy unsettled most people after depending on the state for the fulfillment of their basic needs for fifty years (Verdery 50–53) and led to the gradual development of a "thriving black-market business" (Pralong 234) and the increased supremacy of material values. In this context, Chekhov's plays were often perceived as a prediction of the "degeneration of life into 'inauthenticity' and the transformation of the human personality into a simulacrum" (Fedorenco). The Chekhovian feeling of the end of a world and the beginning of another one reflected the audiences' sentiments. In other words, his depiction of the liminal state in which humanity found itself at the beginning of the twentieth century was found to be similar to that at the beginning of the twenty-first century. Younger directors did not usually choose Chekhov's works for their first productions, but many of the internationally renowned Romanian directors staged his plays, including Andrey Şerban (*The Cherry Orchard*, BNT 1992; *The Seagull*, "Radu Stanca" Sibiu National Theatre 2007; *Uncle Vanya*, Cluj Hungarian Theatre 2007; *Ivanov*, Bulandra Theatre 2011); Cătălina Buzoianu (*The Seagull*, Mic Theatre 1993); Alexa Visarion (*The Seagull*, Craiova National Theatre 1997; *The Cherry Orchard*, Craiova National Theatre 2006); Tompa Gabor (*Three Sisters*, Cluj Hungarian Theatre 2008); and Alexandru Darie (*Three Sisters*, Bulandra Theatre 1995).

After 1989, Chekhov's texts also generated postmodern transtextual adaptations. Matei Vişniec, a Romanian-born playwright living in Paris, believed in Chekhov's characters' ability to survive beyond their original texts, an attitude somewhat similar to Horia Gârbea's. His play, *The Chekhov Machinery* (2008), imagined the Russian playwright's last moments as a meeting with some of his major characters. Vişniec intentionally does not clarify if the scenes are memories, dreams, or delusions, but he offers interesting alternatives regarding what could have happened to the characters after the end of their original plays and/or if they encountered their

112   *Diana Manole*

author. In his version, Chekhov has tea with the three sisters, changes Treplev's bandage, and acts as a witness at Tuzenbakh's duel with Solyony, while Chebutykin, Astrov, and Lvov, three of his fictional doctors, take care of him when he is sick and perform the autopsy after his death.[6] Vişniec recycles Chekhovian characters once more in *Nina or the Fragility of Stuffed Seagulls* (2008), which depicts a meeting between Nina, Trigorin, and Treplev, who has survived his second suicide attempt. It takes place at Treplev's country estate fifteen years after the events that end *The Seagull*, during the First World War, and only a few months before the 1917 October Revolution. Vişniec is mainly faithful to Chekhov's characters, but the sociopolitical background simultaneously ridicules and heightens the poetry of their belief in love and art.

Despite the consistent interest in Chekhov, post-communist Romanian theatre professionals and critics did not instantly and/or completely free themselves from the politicized perspective of his works and the communist stereotypes, against which they still define their ideas, more than twenty years after the end of Ceauşescu's dictatorship. Thus, before the opening of *The Cherry Orchard* at the BNT in 2010, Gabriela Lupu asked director Felix Alexa if he approached the play "as a social drama like Stanislavsky or a comedy, like Chekhov wanted." In his answer, Felix Alexa stated that staging the play "only as a bourgeois drama would be a mistake" (Lupu), unintentionally defining the show in relation to one of the most common clichés of communist theatre criticism. In a similar vein, Buzoianu directed a controversial production of *Three Sisters* in Budapest in 2003, resetting the play closer to the 1917 October Revolution and ending the show with images of the three sisters in striped costumes, prisoners in a Soviet work camp, as members of "a social group swept off history's stage" (Buzoianu) and enemies of the people in the eyes of the communist power.

Chekhov's plays are still very popular in Romania, where "each generation finds in his texts strong characters, violent conflicts or a world that must be destroyed [. . .] Takes him as a witness, a relative, a friend" (Buzoianu). In this context, *The Seagull from the Cherry Orchard* by Horia Gârbea is an extreme example of a postmodern transtextual rewriting of Chekhov's plays and of how Romanians perceived and ironically reflected upon their post-communist transition. Although this is the playwright's first encounter with Chekhov, he is well known in Romania for his experimental and highly parodic works. In his preface to Gârbea's collection of texts *Who Killed Marx?* (2001), which includes *The Seagull from the Cherry Orchard*, but also *Madame Bovary Are the Others* and *Cleopatra the Seventh*, Mircea Ghiţulescu identifies this type of transtextualist plays as "comparative theatre" (7), alluding to the more established field of "comparative literature." Gârbea has had a rather unusual career, especially if one takes into consideration his rare mixture of accomplishments in both sciences and humanities. An engineer by training, he holds a PhD from the Bucharest Polytechnic Institute, has been a professor at the

University of Agronomic Sciences in Bucharest since 1987, and has published several works on engineering. At the same time, however, he is an award-winning and prolific writer, scriptwriter, journalist, translator, and adaptor. *The Seagull from the Cherry Orchard* was staged at the Victor Ion Popa Theatre in Bârlad in 1992, directed by Bogdan Ulmu, at the Alexandru Davila Theatre in Pitești in 1994, directed by Matei Varodi, and was also adapted and directed for Radio Romania by Gavriil Pinte in 2001. It is usually considered Gârbea's best intertextual play (Dumitrescu 368), ironically piecing together characters and elements from Anton Chekhov's plays and mixing them with others from some of the most famous works by Molière, Henrik Ibsen, and I. L. Caragiale.[7] The resulting text does not resemble the natural adaptations of living beings, which Linda Hutcheon mentions in her *A Theory of Adaptation* (31), but rather is similar to artificial crossbreeds people create by the "mating of individuals of different breeds, varieties, or species" ("Crossbreed"). In biology, the hybrids, such as the mule, are normally bred within the same genus, in order to combine the favorable characteristics of the both parents and obtain useful offspring. In visual arts, however, the mixed elements usually belong to very different species in order to create either fantastical animals, such as the nightmarish creatures in Hieronymus Bosch's *The Temptation of St. Anthony* (ca. 1505) and Salvador Dali's spider-legged horse and elephants, or ironic representations of a person's characteristics in caricatures. In both cases, the artistic effect depends on the fact that the parts are necessarily recognizable and clearly distinct from each other. Although he limits his borrowings to drama, Gârbea's strategy is similar because he relies on the audience's ability to identify the sources of the various elements and, thus, appreciate their ironic transformations. Furthermore, *The Seagull from the Cherry Orchard* is set in a rural community at the end of the nineteenth century, in a society and historical period familiar to Romanian audiences from Caragiale's comedies.

I will provide a brief synopsis of Gârbea's play *The Seagull from the Cherry Orchard*, since it is only available in Romanian. Uncle Vania, the middle-aged owner of a country estate and a widower, is in love with a niece of his dead wife, whom he has raised since she was five. The young girl's name is Nora, and she rejects a proposal of marriage to the Prefect's adoptive son, as she feels he would incarcerate her in a dollhouse. She also romantically identifies herself with a seagull and encourages Vania's courtship after he promises her they would leave the remote village and go to the sea together. However, when Nikolai Vasilievici, a marine officer, comes to the little village as a government representative in case of natural disasters, Nora falls in love with him and accepts his marriage proposal, to her uncle's chagrin. In addition to his failed romance, Vania is also trying to convince the Prefect to sell him a cherry orchard, not for financial gain, but for the sake of taking a peaceful walk among the trees. Eventually, he makes the purchase but his accomplishment comes too late, as seawater gradually submerges the place, ironically erupting from the depths of the

114 *Diana Manole*

earth. In the middle of a biblical flood, his house is mysteriously spared. As no news or help arrive from the government, Vania, converted to more parental feelings, invites Nora and Nikolai Vasilievici to live there together, awaiting either death or the natural end of the flood.

ONE PLAY, SEVERAL LITERARY GENRES
AND READING STRATEGIES

The Seagull from the Cherry Orchard combines literary strategies and attitudes towards reality that are characteristic of many genres and cultural movements. In the postmodern tradition, to which Gârbea is hurriedly catching up after the fall of the communism, the play expresses the need "to question, disturb and even subvert the dominance" of preestablished styles, codes, and forms of representation, which, according to Graham Allen, define postmodernism (190). As a parody, Gârbea's play also manifests most of the characteristics of the genre, which, in Hutcheon's words, simultaneously reinscribes and subverts the object of its irony (*A Theory of Parody* 101), while it "put[s] into question the usual hierarchy of what is being mocked" ("Literary Borrowing" 232). From a similar perspective, Romanian critic Octavian Soviany notes Gârbea's ironic engagement with literature: "The parodic here is given birth by the disabused conscience of a postmodern spirit, who knows that all books have been written and therefore only their 'rewriting' [. . .] is still possible."[8]

Consistent with the genre's more recent redefinitions, the target of Gârbea's irony expands, however, beyond the limits of literature, parody's traditional domain until postmodernism: "Parody includes *any cultural practice* which provides a relatively polemical allusive imitation of another cultural production" (Dentith 9; emphasis added). *The Seagull from the Cherry Orchard* alludes to Romania's history and post-communist transition while incorporating characters, situations, and lines from several canonical texts. Taking into account intertextualism and adaptation theories, it is easy to conclude that the play's relationship to other works asks its readers to become, in Hutcheon's words, "active co-creators of the text" ("Literary Borrowing" 232) and use what Marvin Carlson calls "binocular vision" (27). It is obvious that without previous knowledge of the source plays, the fact that a middle-aged man is desperately trying to purchase a cherry orchard or that a young woman claims to be a seagull would take on different meanings. From this point of view, I consider *The Seagull from the Cherry Orchard* an example of what Gérard Genette identifies as transtextuality: "all that sets the text in a relationship, whether obvious or concealed, with other texts" (1). Among the five aspects of transtextuality, which he distinguishes, intertextuality is the "relationship of copresence between two texts or among several texts [. . .] the actual presence of one text within another" (1–2),

Transtextual Crossbreeds in Post-Communist Context   115

including quotation and allusion, which is used extensively in Gârbea's play. At the macrolevel, Genette considers genres such as parody, travesty, and pastiche instances of hypertextuality, which refers to "any relation uniting a text B (. . . the hypertext) to an earlier text A (. . . the hypotext), upon which it is grafted in a manner that is not that of commentary" (5). Whereas an intertext may still be viable without quotations, the hypertext cannot exist without the hypotext, from which it originates through a transformative process and which "it consequently evokes more or less perceptibly without necessarily speaking of it or citing it" (5). As all its characters and some of its plot elements are borrowed from other authors, it is obvious that *The Seagull from the Cherry Orchard* cannot exist without its sources, which qualifies it as a hypertext.

Nevertheless, borrowing or, in Carlson's words, recycling characters, with or without the specific narrative they belong to, has been a common practice in world drama, from Roman comedy, commedia dell'arte, and Noh theatre to Falstaff, Figaro, and contemporary television sitcoms (16–51). Carlson argues that there has always been "a deeper connection of theatre as human activity with the dynamics of cultural memory" (166) because drama has been "associated in all cultures with the retelling again and again of stories that bear a particular religious, social, or political significance for their public" (8). He calls this specific type of recycling "ghosting" (7) and discusses theatre as "a site of memory, both personal and cultural" (4). Gârbea openly shares this perspective. In his short manifesto "A New-School Spectator," included in the same collection of texts as the play under discussion, he defines a play as "the parody of some existences, which in turn are parodies of some other plays. [. . .] A text for theatre is, because it operates with characters, a parody of the nth degree of the existence of the first troglodyte" (343).[9] Peter J. Rabinowitz makes a similar observation, but also notes that in the classical and neoclassical times "playwrights have retold familiar tales to permit their spectators knowledge denied to their characters" (258), completing but not fundamentally changing or contradicting them. Since romanticism and then realism's emphasis upon originality and uniqueness, ancient stories, legends, and myths were expected to be "ingeniously altered" (259) and/or express contemporary concerns when occasionally retold. This tendency culminated in postmodern theatre, which, according to Carlson, is defined by "the conscious reuse of material haunted by memory, but in an ironic and self-conscious manner quite different from classical usage" (14). In addition, some playwrights moved from rewriting one particular story to collating and retelling several, in works "haunted by a past surviving in sharp, disconnected fragments" (Carlson 25). This approach, which is easily recognizable in *The Seagull from the Cherry Orchard*, is also similar to Claude Lévi-Strauss's anthropological perspective of mythical thought, which he defines as "an intellectual form of 'bricolage' . . . [that] builds up structured sets, not directly with other structured sets but by using the remains and

116　*Diana Manole*

debris of events" (14). From this point of view, the traditional writer who creates original texts and may also implement new literary strategies can be compared to the engineer, who subordinates each task "to the availability of raw materials and tools conceived and procured for the purpose of the project" (11). In contrast, the author of a hypertext is similar to the bricoleur who is not interested in creating original works and/or developing new tools but always resumes "to make do 'with whatever is at hand', that is to say with a set of tools and materials which [. . .] is the contingent result of all the occasions there have been to renew or enrich the stock or to maintain it with the remains of previous constructions or deconstructions" (11). The bricoleur's ability to create myths using this strategy suggests the postmodern writers' similar desire to (re)create a mythology when using it in their transtextual works and even in parodies. Employing this anthropological reading strategy, *The Seagull from the Cherry Orchard* can be read as part of the larger post-communist project to de/reconstruct Romanian metanarratives. According to Richard Bauman, the "linked processes of decontextualizing and recontextualizing discourse—of extracting ready-made discourse from one context and fitting it to another—are ubiquitous in social life, essential mechanisms of social and cultural continuity" (8). After a drastic regime change, these processes are essential to a nation's adaptation to its new status.

Dudley Andrew notes in "The Sources of Film" that borrowing is also the "most frequently used mode of adaptation" (98) through which the adaptor is hoping to gain credibility for his/her creation by taking advantage of the prestige of a well-known title/work. From my perspective, Gârbea also uses the authority of the canonical characters he borrows to give more credibility to his post-communist satire. The way he treats them ranges from cultural worship to irony and auto-irony. On one hand, he transtextually crossbreeds Chekhov's characters among themselves and grafts elements from Shakespeare, Ibsen, and Caragiale's most famous works onto them. On the other hand, the playwright changes their ontological nature by treating them as raw materials instead of finished products. This transformation is similar to what is happening to the materials used in a bricolage, as Lévi-Strauss notes, because "in the continual reconstruction from the same material, it is always earlier ends which are called upon to play the part of means: the signified changes into the signifying and vice versa" (14). Although they do not have full autonomy like concepts, signs are "permutable, that is, capable of standing in successive relations with other entities" (13). Employing other authors' characters as signs, Gârbea acknowledges their ability to exist independently of the dramatic text they belong to and to interact with each other in a new work and cultural environment. In a postmodern context, his faith in characters recalls Luigi Pirandello's *Six Characters in Search of an Author* and contradicts the rather general tendency to dismiss them as obsolete. In her book, appropriately titled *The Death of Character*, Elinor Fuchs points to "the emergence of dramaturgical and performance strategies that deliberately undermined the illusion of autonomous character" (31), which started at the beginning of modernism and reached its peak with postmodern theatre.

The last genre I want to compare Gârbea's play to is what Hutcheon identifies as the transcultural adaptation, whose early beginnings Hutcheon traces to the Roman adaptations of Greek plays. Among several other theorists, she notes that "context conditions meaning" (*A Theory of Adaptation* 145). It is, thus, "logical that time and place shifts should bring alterations in cultural associations" (145), on the microlevel, in the case of adaptations within the same culture, and on the macrolevel, in the case of transcultural adaptations. To explain the latter, she uses a metaphor based on familiar objects from the international traveler's kit, "the adapter plug and the electrical converters [which] allow the transformation of power to a useable form for a particular place and context" (150), enabling us to use our personal devices across borders. In a similar manner, adapting across cultures makes works specific to a particular geographical and historical context comprehensible in other environments. To describe this special type of intercultural encounter and accommodation, Hutcheon borrows Susan Stanford Friedman's anthropological term "indigenization" (150). She also emphasizes that, the demands of the market and/or political leaders aside, the adaptors have the freedom and power, to "pick and choose what they want to transplant to their own soil" (150), according to their personal agendas. Therefore, adapting cannot be a neutral enterprise. For example, adaptations that engage the politics of the empire in a post-colonial culture are necessarily "wilful reinterpretations for a different context, even if the historical accuracy of the time and setting is retained" (153).

In post-communist Romania, Gârbea rewrites Chekhov's plays, challenging not only the Soviet/communist legacy, but also Western cultural symbols and theatrical traditions. Considering his attitude towards both his sources and the extratextual context, I identify *The Seagull from the Cherry Orchard* as a postmodern hypertext and a transcultural parody that uses collage as its main dramaturgical device. In the first part of this analysis, I will discuss the transtextual hybridization of characters as an ironic way to deconstruct some of the European cultural symbols and theatre traditions and to challenge the Soviet/communist legacy. After five decades of communist dictatorship, the playwright's resentments are consistent with Romanians' rejection of Russian domination and the feeling that the West abandoned them after the Second World War "in Stalin's hands" (Bulei 156). In addition, the auto-ironic recycling of Caragiale's characters makes evident the persistence of some of the nineteenth-century collective flaws and errors in Romania's post-communist social and political life. This idea is further emphasized through the gradual adaptation of the foreign character to the new environment and through a number of allegories of Romania's condition during the first post-communist years, which I will examine in the second part of my analysis.

118   *Diana Manole*

THE TRANSTEXTUAL RESURRECTION OF CHARACTER

A play called *The Seagull from the Cherry Orchard* may be expected to combine in an ironic manner characters from both texts quoted in its title. Gârbea not only fulfills this expectation; he exceeds it. Surprisingly, the man trying to buy a cherry orchard is called "Vania" instead of Lopakhin. The playwright presumably counts on the audience knowing not only who Vania [Vanya] is, but also making the connection to Lopakhin, who is not explicitly named, and recognizing both the similarities and the differences between the originals and the postmodern hybrid, appreciating the embedded irony. After being crossbred with Lopakhin and interacting with characters from other plays, Gârbea's character becomes a parody of the so-called Russian soul. Like his original namesake, he lives in the country, without many aspirations left (82) and without the ability to change his life. He is also hopelessly in love, but Gârbea adds immorality to his hybrid character. Somewhat similar to Arnolphe, who is in love with Agnes in Molière's *The School for Wives*, Vania is infatuated with a girl much younger than Chekhov's Yelena Serebryakova from *Uncle Vanya* and Lyubov Ranevskaya from *The Cherry Orchard*. He has raised her since she was five years old and she calls him "uncle" and even jokingly identifies him with her "mother" (81). Vania's feelings border incest, as the Prefect warns him: "You're her uncle, she calls you uncle, what can be between you?" (120). Instead of helping him gain some willpower and business instinct, as in the case of a biological hybrid, Uncle Vanya's crossbreeding with Lopakhin paradoxically aggravates his weaknesses. His ongoing dream of buying a cherry orchard emphasizes his lack of practical skills and failure as a farmer and landowner. He does not want the property to compensate for the family's past in serfdom and for the sake of financial profit, like Lopakhin, but only to have a chance to take a stroll among the trees in blossom (83). He eventually manages to buy the orchard, but the flood would most likely prevent the trees from ever blossoming again.

Gârbea also throws a bit of Shakespeare into the mix, as if intending to mock his hybrid character in comparison to its classical sources. In the very first scene of the play, Vania meets the village's Gravedigger, a ridiculous version of the Shakespearean original, who gives Vania a skull he found buried under the lawn. This short episode is a clear reference to Hamlet finding Yorick's skull, "Alas, poor Yorick! I knew him, / Horatio. A fellow of infinite jest, of most excellent fancy. He / hath borne me on his back a thousand times," and then meditating on the destiny of people such as Alexander and Caesar who, when "dead and turn'd to clay, / Might stop a hole to keep the wind away." In Gârbea's parodic version, the skull belongs to a dog and Vania holds the skull in a Shakespearean pose, meditating on the meaning of life and death inspired by his dead pet: "Oh, what a dog he was! First in the chase. English greyhound, Nora. A rare breed! I buried him in the garden and now look what he's become.

Ah, we're all headed that way" (80). As a last resort to save face, Vania challenges Nikolai to a duel for Nora's love but the Prefect and the flood prevent the fight from taking place. Like his Chekhovian namesake, at the end of the play Gârbea's character is resigned to losing everything he cared for and decides to bless Nora's union with Nikolai and even invites the young couple to live in his home.

The hybridization of the Chekhovian characters goes beyond their author's universe. The young woman who feels like a seagull is called Nora instead of Nina and borrows traits from the main character in Ibsen's *A Doll's House* and from several of Chekhov's characters. In addition to collating some of their most famous lines, the Romanian playwright also embodies in his dramatic hybrid ridiculous versions of their dramas and obsessions. From Nina Zarechnaya, he takes the love for water, "something seems to lure me to this lake like a seagull" (Chekhov 71) and the character's landmark line "I'm a seagull" (Chekhov 114; Gârbea 81, 118). In Gârbea's version, however, Vania pragmatically dismisses Nora's dream as unrealistic given their financial state, "I'm afraid we'll never see the sea" (82). From Ibsen's Nora, Gârbea borrows the famous expression of her disappointment with the way her husband has treated her: "I was . . . your little lark, your doll" (Ibsen 195). Although sharing her name with Ibsen's character, and claiming at one point that she does not want to marry Zoe's adoptive son because he would trap her in a dollhouse (91), Gârbea's Nora is a rather immoral young girl. Like Chekhov's three sisters, Nora longs to leave the remote village where she was raised, but what she imagines is something closer to a leisure trip then to a liberating departure. She makes a pass at her much older uncle and promises to become his wife if they travel to the seaside and he allows her "to remain a seagull" (92). When Nikolai, a younger man and a marine officer, arrives, she instantly abandons Vania, lured by the promise of a honeymoon on a ship (102). At the end of *A Doll's House*, Nora liberates herself and leaves her husband's house, while Chekhov's Nina Zarechnaya remains trapped in her illusion of being a seagull and an actress. In contrast, Gârbea ridicules the romantic illusions of his crossbred character. Surrounded by the waters, Nora ends up hating the sea (Gârbea 128), while her romantic vision of the seagull is definitively shattered. As a marine officer, Nikolai is the first to tell Nora the truth: "The seagull is a rapacious bird. It throws itself upon the fish and slashes it" (99). Towards the end of the play, Nora sees an actual seagull and is disgusted by what she believes to be "a fat duck" (130). Like Sonya from Chekhov's *Uncle Vanya*, she resigns to stay and spend the rest of her life on her uncle's estate. The source characters of Nikolai Vasilievici are less precisely identified. As an officer and a stranger, he recalls the fascination of Lieutenant-Colonel Aleksandr Vershinin from *Three Sisters*, who also comes from afar and makes Masha fall in love with him, whereas Gârbea's character sweeps Nora off her feet immediately after they meet for the first time (102). As his first and middle names are the same as Gogol's, Nikolai Vasilievici can also

120 *Diana Manole*

be read in connection to *The Government Inspector* as an actual representative of the central authority. He stirs up chaos in the sleepy village where he is deployed but eventually gives up, admits he is powerless in the face of the natural disaster, and agrees to wait for the end with Nora and Vania.

In addition to mocking Russian and Western characters, Gârbea revives Caragiale's canonical creations from his comedies, which parodied the emerging middle class and its lack of morality and education, as well as its pretentiousness. Exacerbating and mixing the flaws and mannerisms of several characters in each of his crossbred individuals, the post-communist playwright implicitly suggests the validity of the nineteenth-century social and political satire and ironically proves that nothing has changed for the better in Romanian politics and social life. The owners of the cherry orchard, the Prefect and his wife, do not share any features with Lyuba Ranevskaya. The Prefect borrows the administrative position and main traits of one of the main characters of Caragiale's *The Lost Letter*, a virulent satire of political corruption and falsified elections at the end of the nineteenth century. In the original text, he was in love with Zoe, who was married to the local leader of the party in power. In Gârbea's version, he has lost any romantic enthusiasm and has become an apathetic landowner and public servant. Although intelligent and able to talk about Pushkin and Machiavelli (117), he now prides himself in not having any more time to read books (86) and for always winning at cards (89). He is further crossbred with Catavencu from *The Lost Letter*, which has become the most common Romanian stereotype of the political opportunist, ready for any compromise to win elections, and Trahanache, from the same play, an apparently gullible party leader and cuckolded husband, citing some of their famous clichés, such as the latter's frequent request "Hey, there, just a grain of patience!" (Gârbea 116; Caragiale 77).

Zoe, his wife, also borrows the name, social position, and main traits from the female character in Caragiale's *The Lost Letter*. In Gârbea's version, she murdered her previous husband and became the wife of the Prefect, whom she now openly despises: "Figure it out, you're a man, not a pussy! When the old man was alive, you did the same shit. Oh, there's nothing I can do! Oh, what's going to happen! I had to do it for you! *(She mimes choking someone.)*" (18). When given the opportunity to hold a gun, Zoe shoots at the Prefect, openly trying to kill him. The character further combines stereotypes from other characters of Caragiale's and becomes a degraded version of her original namesake, losing any trace of the original's upper-class polish. She speaks with grammatical errors, craves entertainment, reads French pulp fiction, gets upset when the newest issue does not arrive on time, and complains of boredom (Gârbea 85–86), like Caragiale's quasi-illiterate but snobbish Zița from *A Stormy Night*, a comedy about a love triangle in a merchant's family. Gârbea's Zoe also makes jam, flatters her husband, and is excited by the prospect of a wedding, borrowing the suburban lifestyle of Efimița, the dumb but devoted housewife from *Mr. Leonidas and the Reactionaries* (1880): "You're so slick, people like you are few and far between!" (Gârbea 123). Zoe and the Prefect's flaws, value system, and lifestyle influence the foreign characters, who appear to adapt unconsciously to their new environment. This process makes it possible to read Gârbea's play as a transcultural adaptation and discuss its satirical reflection of the extra-textual post-communist context.

A TRANSCULTURAL REVENGE PARODY

Mircea A. Diaconu describes Gârbea's intertextual parodies as "a vengeance of the theatre" on the traditional historical record, which "emerges from the textual inconsistency of the world when faced with the consistency of history, or, better yet, from the inconsistency of history and the textual consistency of the world."[10] Reading *The Seagull from the Cherry Orchard* from a post-communist perspective, I would argue that, in this play, Gârbea is writing back to the former Soviet Union, but also mocking local mentalities and flaws. By showing what would have happened to Chekhov's Uncle Vanya, Ibsen's Nora, and the Shakespearian Gravedigger, if they had lived in Romania, Gârbea both accuses and excuses Romanians' historical evolution. On one hand, if foreigners gradually adopt some of the mentalities and habits common at the time, it should be obvious that anyone born there did not have any chance of resisting them. On the other hand, their actions imply choices for which they are entirely responsible. In this way, Gârbea mocks the so-called theories of the Romanian people as innocent victims of their geopolitical location at the crossroad of empires always striving to conquer them and of what Barbu calls "a history for which they are not responsible" (*Republica absentă* 115). From this perspective, Gârbea's transtextual collage and transcultural parody asserts itself as part of the complicated process of deconstructing and reconstructing Romanian value systems and metanarratives after the drastic changes determined by the fall of the communist dictatorship.

According to many historians, political and cultural theorists, and psychologists, Romanians' distorted perception of and relationship to the state is the most significant source of their collective flaws and historical misfortunes. Daniel Barbu, for example, notes that since medieval times for most Romanians the state and its institution have always been "embodied by individuals with whom you can reach an agreement through direct negotiation" (*Republica absentă* 147) and most often through corruption. Bacşişul (the bribe) and chilipirul (the bargain), presumably brought into the country by Greek merchants and Turkish invaders, have long appalled foreign travelers throughout the historical Romanian provinces, as some of the testimonies reproduced by Barbu demonstrate (*Firea românilor* 15–30). During the communist dictatorship, Romanians were unable to perceive

122   *Diana Manole*

their state as an abstract normative institution (*Republica absentă* 147); this problem was further exacerbated by what Katherine Verdery identifies as "socialist paternalism" (24). Treating the entire nation as an extended family, the Communist Party, which coincided with the state and the government, assumed the role of a patriarchal authority responsible for the welfare of all its children. Consequently, the party was the only one qualified to make political decisions, assign social functions, coordinate the distribution of the social product, reward, and punish (Verdery 25). In this context, a paradoxical "cult of nonwork" (23) gradually formed, while stealing from an abstract state, perceived as the collective enemy, evading taxes, and earning "extra pay, for example, by [store clerks'] saving scarce goods to sell to special customers, who tipped them or did some important favor in return" (27) were actually deemed acceptable.

In Gârbea's parody, corruption and the search for quick gain seem two of the most contagious flaws. As the cherry orchard does not belong to an empty-headed noble woman, but to the Prefect, who prides himself on buying it cheap and is not interested in selling it, Vania's only chance to achieve his dream is to compromise. He lets the Prefect win at cards, to make him feel better and also to bribe him. He is also willing to sacrifice his love for Nora, when the Prefect implies that he would sell him the orchard if the girl agreed to marry his adoptive son. In addition, the playwright gives Vania lines from Caragiale's plays, reinforcing the similarities between his landowner and the crooked politicians. Among many other popular clichés, Gârbea borrows a verbal tic, "Listen, honourable sir!" from Trahanache, the powerful local leader of the government party in *The Lost Letter* (Gârbea 84; Caragiale 23).

Another consequence of the communist dictatorship was a social and political collective paralysis that dominated the Romanian people with the exception of a small elite. Alina Mungiu-Pippidi explains that "the God of communist totalitarianism is the state" (140) and that Romanians expected it to take care of all aspects of economic, social, and political life. In the first years after communism was overthrown, "when chaos replaced dictatorship" (Betea 65), the immediate rise to power of the second tier of the communist ruling class and the persistent Leninist traditions determined the continuity of this type of relationships between the state and its citizens (Mungiu-Pippidi 103–66; Barbu, *Republica absentă* 143–59; Verdery 204–28). In *The Seagull from the Cherry Orchard*, the Prefect, the local representative of the government, acts as if he has unlimited power and "controls everything" (Gârbea 96). However, his authority is limited to automatically applying the law, as he naively admits: "as soon as an issue appears, I know the law and I immediately identify the applicable article" (110). As Vania ironically points out, he gets lost when an unscripted situation occurs: "Which article are you using for the seawater?" (110). The central political authority is depicted as an anonymous entity that is feared and obeyed. When a higher representative of the government is sent to the remote countryside where the

Transextual Crossbreeds in Post-Communist Context

play is set, presumably to override the Prefect, he is impersonally informed through a telegram. Despite his wife's pestering, he cannot conceive the idea of opposing orders coming from the government (91). This dramaturgical device is borrowed from Caragiale's *The Lost Letter*, where Dandanache, the candidate abusively installed in the local elections, is also announced through a telegram and comes from the Capital. However, when inserted into *The Seagull from the Cherry Orchard*, the significance of the powerful stranger multiplies. Consistent with Gârbea's anticommunist undertones, the government's representative bears the only undeniably Russian name in the play, Nikolai Vasilievici, and is a marine captain (94), a device that taps into Romanians' collective fear of the Red Army (Constantiniu 419–30). Like Vania and Nora, the character is also indigenized. He shows a lack of initiative like Chekhov's "Lovesick Major" but also speaks and acts like Caragiale's characters, using some of his popular clichés, "Don't say you can't, you have to can!" (115). His only actions in the face of the rising waters are to report on the situation to the central authorities and wait for orders (124, 131). When the telegraph system shuts down because of the flood, he decides that his mission has ended (131).

The flood determines some of Gârbea's most interesting transformations of the classic characters. Furthermore, the seawater emerging from the depth of the earth and flooding the land is an allegory of the "disaster" in which the Romanian society found itself in the early 1990s (Barbu, *Republica absentă* 110–12) and its "up-side down value system" (Slama-Cazacu). Consistent with the blind belief in authority that communism instilled in the masses, the Gravedigger awaits salvation from the government and Nikolai, its representative: "We're going to drown, sir! You can't leave things like this!" (Gârbea 124). Everyone else chooses to ignore the danger and continues to pay each other visits, drink tea, and play cards, even one week after the state of emergency has been officially declared (127). The collective inertia recalls Ranevskaya's lack of responsibility, as she refuses to do anything to save her property. In Chekhov's play, Lopakhin desperately tries to make her take action—"The cherry orchard and the rest of the land must be leased out for summer cottages. You must act at once" (Chekhov 262)—and eventually buys the orchard himself and cuts it down for business reasons.

In Gârbea's transcultural adaptation, Vania has become more inactive than everyone else, while the flood destroys the orchard. Whereas Patapievici violently condemns "the abysmal laziness of the stale Romanian soul" (49), the postmodern playwright mockingly presents inactivity as a consciously chosen and openly praised survival strategy. To Nora's amazement, Vania not only openly recognizes his fatalism, but also claims that his inertia is in fact the best and the only course of action: "Stop the water? Run through the mud? I might be a fatalist, but I'm not crazy!" (Gârbea 128). He also convinces Nora and Nikolai to do the same: "That's great, Uncle Vania! We'll stay here and rest!" (Gârbea 138).

124 *Diana Manole*

After fighting for one last chance at happiness, Chekhov's Uncle Vanya eventually gives up any hopes, resigned to a sad but altruistic existence, working for the others, with the only hope at rest and happiness for Sonya and him after death, when "God will have pity on us . . . and we shall find peace" (Chekhov 167). In contrast, Gârbea's characters resolve to hope for God's mercy on earth, waiting for the disaster to go away by itself (Gârbea 131). Their tragicomic isolation amidst the seawater becomes an ironic allegory of the more general state of "Romanians isolated not only from the West, but also from their own past" shortly after the fall of communism (Mărcuş 50). Patapievici bluntly stated that in the early 1990s Romania was "a brain-washed society that enjoyed being like that" (25). Gârbea embodies a similar disappointment, while renegotiating theatre's role as a site of cultural memory and social reflection.

From an anthropological perspective, Gârbea employs strategies similar to those of a bricoleur, rewriting and crossbreeding some of Chekhov's landmark characters in order to challenge the propagandistic perspective of his work and also the Western culture from which Romania was excluded during communism. In addition, his revenge tragicomedy ironically dismantles the popular excuse that Romanians are under the curse of their history and geographical location, which make them what they are. As its characters combine features of several canonical models with some of the local flaws and mentalities, *The Seagull from the Cherry Orchard* ironically emphasizes their freedom of choice and, thus, their personal weaknesses. In this way, it opens the genre of parody, which traditionally only ridiculed literary productions, to the extraliterary context, according to its postmodern redefinition.

From a dramaturgical perspective, however, Gârbea's ironic adaptation paradoxically reasserts the value of text in a time when the death of character and even of drama is consistently reiterated. Furthermore, *The Seagull from the Cherry Orchard* reclaims the place of Romanian theatre within the Western tradition. As a parody that depends on its sources, it implicitly reaffirms the existence of a theatrical tradition and of an audience able to enjoy a postmodern hypertext and a transcultural parody in a period when all of the Romanian value systems are being questioned. At the same time, it indirectly renegotiates the international status of Romanian theatre, taking advantage of the authority of its canonical source texts and mediating a dialogic relationship between their cultures of origin. In other words, if Romanian characters can prove their dramaturgical strength in the play's international makeup, then Romanian theatre itself can reassert its artistic value on the international stage, eventually overcoming the phase when it mostly fulfilled a political function as a tool of both the communist regime and its opponents. The subsequent development of Romanian drama and theatre has confirmed Gârbea's prediction.

NOTES

1. As Lyudmila Parts explains in *The Chekhovian Intertext*, an analogous process took place in post-perestroika Russia, where writers reappropriated the works of Pushkin, Gogol, Dostoyevsky, Tolstoy, and Chekhov, "as cult figures . . . symbolic entities by and through which [Russian] culture identifies itself and on which it relies to assure its identity and continuity [. . .] allowing for interaction among writers of different epochs" (7).

2. Nicolae Ceauşescu (1918–1989) was secretary general of the Romanian Communist Party from 1965 to 1989, and Romania's president from 1967 to 1989. Thanks to his opposition to the Soviet Union, starting with his public protest against the 1968 invasion of Czechoslovakia by Warsaw Pact forces, Ceauşescu was revered in Western countries as a reformer and defender of human rights. In reality, Romania was under an increasingly brutal and oppressive regime, which began in 1971 and ended after the popular uprising in 1989, when Ceauşescu and his wife, Elena Ceauşescu, were hastily tried by an improvised tribunal, condemned, and executed.

3. Before the Second World War, very few of Chekhov's plays were staged in Romania. *A Marriage Proposal* was produced at the Bucharest National Theatre (BNT) in 1910 to good box-office success but mixed reviews. *The Seagull* was also staged at BNT in 1923 and *The Cherry Orchard* at the Regina Maria Theatre also in Bucharest, but the shows did not have a significant impact.

4. First defined in the Soviet Union in the early 1930s, Socialist Realism was an artistic style and ideology whose initial purpose was to represent reality truthfully, with an emphasis on the lives of lower classes. As censorship and oppression gradually increased and the cult of the communist dictators became stronger, Socialist Realism was gradually enforced as the official artistic style in all the countries under Soviet control and/or influence. It came to mean presenting reality in an idealized manner with the explicit purpose of glorifying socialism and educating the people in its spirit.

5. In this chapter, translations from the Romanian are by the author unless otherwise specified.

6. In *Afterplay*, Irish playwright Brian Friel also imagined a meeting of characters from different plays that takes place long after Chekhov's death: Andrey Prozorov, from *Three Sisters*, and Sonya Serebryakova, from *Uncle Vanya*.

7. I. L. Caragiale (1852–1912) was a writer, theatre manager, political commentator, and journalist and was commonly praised as Romania's national playwright, not only for his plays' literary value and social satire, but also for his contribution to the creation of a national dramatic canon. *A Lost Letter* (1884), his best-known play, mocks politicians' corruption and immorality during provincial elections, whereas the comedies, *Carnival Scenes* (*D'ale carnavalului*, 1885) and *A Stormy Night* (*O noapte furtunoasă*, 1889), and the tragedy, *The Curse* (*Năpasta*, 1890), focus on love triangles and their consequences for urban and rural families, respectively.

8. The translation from the Romanian is taken from Gârbea's biography posted on Wikipedia.

9. To Romanian audiences, the title of Gârbea's manifesto recalls Caragiale's famous short story "A New-School Teacher," a parody of the nineteenth-century Romanian school system.

10. This translation from the Romanian is taken from Gârbea's biography posted on *Wikipedia*.

126 *Diana Manole*

WORKS CITED

Allen, Graham. *Intertextuality*. London: Routledge, 2000. Print.

Andrew, Dudley. *Concepts in Film Theory*. Oxford; New York: Oxford UP, 1984. Print.

Ashcroft, Bill, Gareth Griffiths, and Helen Tiffin, eds. *The Empire Writes Back: Theory and Practice in Post-Colonial Literatures*. London: Routledge, 1989. Print.

Barbu, Daniel. *Firea românilor*. Bucharest: Nemira, 2004. Print.

———. *Republica absentă*. Bucharest: Nemira, 2004. Print.

Bauman, Richard. *A World of Others' Words: Cross-Cultural Perspectives on Intertextuality*. Malden: Blackwell Publishing, 2004. Print.

Betea, Lavinia. *Mentalități și remanențe comuniste*. Bucharest: Nemira, 2005. Print.

Bratu, Horia. "Cehov și cehovismul." *Revista Teatrul. Institutul de Memorie Culturală* Feb. 1959: 22–34. Web. 30 Dec. 2010.

Bulei, Ioan. *O istorie a românilor*. 2nd ed. Bucharest: Meronia, 2004. Print.

Buzoianu, Cătălina. "Cehov a presimțit toate atrocitățile." *Yorik* 64 (2010). Web. 25 Jan. 2011.

Caragiale, I. L. *The Lost Letter and Other Plays*. Trans. Frida Knight. London: Lawrence and Wishart, 1956. Print.

Carlson, Marvin. *The Haunted Stage*. Ann Arbor: U of Michigan P, 2003. Print.

Chekhov, Anton. *Five Plays*. Trans. Ronald Hingley. Oxford: Oxford UP, 1998. Print.

Constantiniu, Florin. *O istorie sinceră a poporului român*. Bucharest: Univers Enciclopedic, 2002. Print.

"Crossbreed." *The American Heritage Dictionary of the English Language*, 4th ed. Houghton Mifflin Company, 2004. Answers.com. Web. 29 Aug. 2011.

Dentith, Simon. *Parody*. London: Routledge, 2000. Print.

Diaconu, Mircea A. "Horia Gârbea. Răzbunarea teatrului." *Ziua* 10 Feb. 2003. Web. 22 May 2011.

Dumitrescu, Bogdan. "Varianta Gârbea." *România literară*, Oct. 1993. *Cine l-a ucis pe Marx: Texte pentru teatru*. By Horia Gârbea. Bucharest: Vinea, 2001. 367–68. Print

Fedorenco, Victoria. "Jucăm Cehov, jucăm cu Cehov." *Sud-Est* Jan. 2005. Web. 25 Jan. 2011.

Friel, Brian. *Three Plays After: The Yalta Game, The Bear, Afterplay*. Oldcastle, County Meath: Gallery Press, 2002.

Fuchs, Elinor. *The Death of Character*. Bloomington: Indiana UP, 1996. Print.

Gârbea, Horia. *Pescărușul din livada de vișini. Cine l-a ucis pe Marx: Texte pentru teatru*. Bucharest: Vinea, 2001. 77–140. Print.

Genette, Gérard. *Palimpsests: Literature in the Second Degree*. Lincoln: U of Nebraska P, 1997. Print.

Ghițulescu, Mircea. Prefață. "'Teatrul comparat' al lui Horia Gârbea." *Cine l-a ucis pe Marx: Texte pentru teatru*. By Horia Gârbea. Bucharest: Vinea, 2001. 5–9. Print.

"Horia Gârbea." Wikipedia, the Free Encyclopedia. Wikimedia Foundation. 15 May 2011. Web. 22 May 2011.

Hutcheon, Linda. *A Theory of Adaptation*. New York: Routledge, 2006. Print.

———. *A Theory of Parody*. Urbana: U of Illinois P, 2000. Print.

———. "Literary Borrowing . . . and Stealing: Plagiarism, Sources, Influences, and Intertexts." *English Studies in Canada* 19.2 (1986): 229–39. Print.

Ibsen, Henrik. *The Complete Major Prose Plays*. Trans. Rolf Fjelde. New York: Plume, Penguin Books USA, 1978. Print.

Transtextual Crossbreeds in Post-Communist Context   127

Lévi-Strauss, Claude. *The Savage Mind*. Trans. George Weidenfield and Nicholson Ltd. Chicago: U of Chicago P, 1966. Print.

Lupu, Gabriela. "Cehov, fără clişee." *România liberă* 29 April 2010. Web. 25 Jan. 2011.

Mărcuş, Carmen. "Identitate naţională in societatea românească de tranziţie." *Studii* 11–12 (1995): 49–55. Erdélyi Magyar Adatbank 1999–2009. Web. 17 Aug. 2009.

Massoff, Ioan. *Teatrul românesc*. 8 vols. Bucharest: Minerva, 1981. Print.

Mungiu-Pippidi, Alina. *Românii după 1989. Istoria unei neînţelegeri*. Bucharest: Humanitas, 1995. Print.

Parts, Lyudmila. *The Chekhovian Intertext*. Columbus: Ohio State UP, 2008. Print.

Patapievici, H. R. *Politice*. Bucharest: Humanitas, 1996. Print.

Popescu, Marian. *Scenele teatrului românesc 1945–2004. De la cenzură la libertate*. Bucharest: Unitext, 2004. Print.

Popovici, Ileana. "Acest surâzător şi crud amurg . . ." *Revista Teatrul* Jan. 1968: 40–46. Web. 18 June 2011.

Pralong, Sandra. "NGOs and the Development of Civil Society." *Romania since 1989: Politics, Economics, and Society*. Ed. Henry F. Carey. Oxford: Lexington Books, 2004. 229–46. Print.

Rabinowitz, Peter J. "'What's Hecuba to Us?' The Audience's Experience of Literary Borrowing." *The Reader in the Text*. Ed. Susan R. Suleiman and Inge Crosman. Princeton: Princeton UP, 1980. 241–63. Print.

Runcan, Miruna. *Teatralizarea şi reteatralizarea în România: 1920–1960*. Cluj Napoca: Eikon, 2003. Print.

Shakespeare, William. *Hamlet*. George Mason U. OpenSourceShakespeare: An Experiment in Literary Technology. 2003–2010. Web. 30 Oct. 2010.

Slama-Cazacu, Tatiana. "O mentalitate dezorientată, un sistem de valori răsturnat pot prăbuşi o ţară." Larisa şi Constantin Iftime, Interview. *Lumina* 9 Sept. 2009. Web. 31 Oct. 2010.

Soviany, Octavian. "Potopul şi parodia." *Ziua* 11 Nov. 2002. Web. 22 May 2011.

Topologeanu, Ileana. "Dramaturgia lui A. P. Cehov în receptare românească." Diss. Bucharest U, 2011. Print.

Verdery, Katherine. *What Was Socialism, and What Comes Next?* Princeton: Princeton UP, 1996. Print.

Vişniec, Matei. *Maşinăria Cehov. Nina sau despre fragilitatea pescăruşilor împăiaţi*. Bucharest: Humanitas, 2008. Print.

7 Chekhov in the Age of Globalization
Janusz Glowacki's *The Fourth Sister*

Magda Romanska

In her latest book, *A Theory of Adaptation*, Linda Hutcheon points out that when discussing any adaptation, one should foremost ask oneself "what, who, why, how, when, and where" (xiv). As in his previous plays, in *The Fourth Sister*, Glowacki uses Chekhov's classic text as a springboard from which he weaves a modern story, with a characteristic sense of ironic inversion. Glowacki's *Antigone in New York* (1993) was a retelling of Sophocles's tragedy with a twist: the characters are not nobles caught up in the fickleness of fate and their own hubris, but homeless bums, desperately clinging to the remains of their senses of dignity. *Fortinbras Gets Drunk* (1990) was a retelling of the story of Hamlet from the point of view of Norwegians, a comic and macabre treatise on the ends of politics and its moral dimension. Even *Hunting Cockroaches* (1987) was a nod to *Hunting Flies*, the 1969 film directed by Andrzej Wajda, for which Glowacki himself wrote the script. Glowacki's form of adaptation is what Hutcheon calls "transcoding," changing medium, the frame of reference, cultural and historical context, or a point of view. It means "using the source as a raw material" on which one mounts an autonomous work of art (6–7). Transcoding brings forth its own sets of questions: "what can happen when stories 'travel'—when an adapted text migrates from its context of creation to the adaptation's context of reception" (xvi). In the case of *The Fourth Sister*, considering Glowacki's own Polish origins and biography (being an émigré writer in America), what does the play set in Russia with characters dreaming of life in America tell us about the global dimension of Chekhov's text? Where, geographically or psycho-geographically, is *The Fourth Sister* located, and in what way does that matter? For which audience was it written—Polish, Russian, American, émigré? Glowacki tries to capture the liminal quality of Eastern European life at the turn of the century: the world in transition from communism to capitalism, like all liminal spaces, is a universe characterized by the "dislocation of established structures, the reversal of hierarchies, and uncertainty regarding the continuity of tradition and future outcomes" (Horvath, Thomassen, and Wydra). If Chekhov's world was waiting for revolution, Glowacki's world is fractured by globalization and shifting political and economic circumstances, unable to grasp itself vis-à-vis its all-consuming transiency, and desperately trying to find grounding in a stable system of values, whatever they might be. As Glowacki put it: "I think that Russians, even the richest ones, have a sense of transiency. They remember their past and are afraid of the future" ("Rozmowa").[1] But that mode of adaptation—because it enters in a dialogue with Chekhov through the prism of broader historical, social, and cultural themes—heavily relies on audience's familiarity with Chekhov's play and its position in Russian and European culture. Hutcheon notes that "when we call a work an adaptation, we openly announce its overt relationship to another work or works" (6). But, we can reverse her statement, asking: what kind of covert, intertextual, and transpositional relationship does the work have to have to the original text, in order for it to even be considered an adaptation? In that sense, to what degree is Glowacki's *Fourth Sister*—and is not—an adaptation of Chekhov? Is it possible to make this judgment unequivocally, and what does each answer imply for both Glowacki and Chekhov?

Responding to raised issues of adaptation, Glowacki said: "I like writing on the other side of an already written text. The world is one giant library. I like to relate to what has already been written: myths, archetypes, fairy tales" (Baniewicz 101). In another interview, given specifically on account of *The Fourth Sister*, Glowacki added the following:

> *The Fourth Sister* was inspired by Chekhov's *Three Sisters*, but it is neither a fictional continuation, nor a new version, nor a pastiche of Chekhov. It's merely an ironic allusion to his play and points out a few depressing steps the world has made since Chekhov gazed upon it. [. . .] The underlying conviction of Chekhov's characters was that, although their own world was filled with trials and suffering, their children's would be a better one. It was easier for Chekhov to have some hope for the future at the end of the 19th century, when the concepts of truth, honor, commitment and love were seriously embraced. ("Tale of Two Moscows")

Classic texts provide a springboard for Glowacki's writing because they come with an already well-known metaphorical and symbolic framework. The well-known text can enrich but can also get in the way of the new play, putting it in the epistemologically constraining jacket of easy reference points and associations. Each classic comes with its own baggage that can also be misunderstood. Chekhov's text offers Glowacki, as Elżbieta Baniewicz argues, "the world of values," but because of its ironic treatment, the new text can often fall prey to a number of misinterpretations:

> *The Fourth Sister* is not "a variation on Anton Chekhov's well-known play about the Prozorov sisters," nor is it an "intelligent pastiche," nor "a travesty of Chekhov's world illustrating the post-communist melancholy," as some Polish reviewers persist in declaring. Writing *Antigone in New York* or *Fortinbras Gets Drunk*, was Glowacki travestying or

making a pastiche of Sophocles or Shakespeare, or showing the Greek or British reality? That's pure nonsense. Chekhov exists in this play, indeed, but as a point of reference, an allusion or an ironic quote—not in relation to the story line but the world of values. (100)

Written almost one hundred years after Chekhov's *Three Sisters* (written in 1900 and produced in 1901), Janusz Glowacki's *The Fourth Sister* opened on 10 December 1999 at Scena Kameralna in Wroclaw, Poland. It was the directorial debut of Agnieszka Glińska, with a set designed by Barbara Hanicka. A week later, on 18 December, the show had its official premiere in Warsaw at the Zygmunt Hübner Powszechny Theatre. Władysław Kowalski was the director, and Andrzej Witkowski designed the set. The Warsaw opening was greeted as a cultural and social event, and was attended by the Polish president and his wife. In 2002, the Polish Television Theatre broadcast Glińska's televised version of *The Fourth Sister*, with Janusz Gajos and Bogusław Linda, Poland's two leading actors, in the main roles. The film version won a number of awards at the National Festival of Film, Radio and Theatre (Krajowy Festiwal Teatru Polskiego Radia i Teatru TV "Dwa Teatry"). Following its Polish premier, *The Fourth Sister* was produced in several theatres in Europe, including the National Theatre in Athens, the National Theatre Novi

Figure 7.1 A scene from Janusz Glowacki's *The Fourth Sister*, Polish Television Theatre (1999). With: Jan Urbanski, Monika Krzywkowski, Agnieszka Pilaszewska, Patrycja Durska. Set and costume design by Barbara Hanicka. Directed by Agnieszka Glińska. Photo by Ireneusz Sobieszczuk/TVP.

Chekhov in the Age of Globalization 131

Sad in Serbia, the National Theatre in Bratislava, and Le Théâtre Silvia Montfort in Paris. It also played in Budapest, Sofia, and in Germany and Slovenia. In 2001, it won the grand prize at the International Theatre Festival in Dubrovnik. The American opening was scheduled for 2001, but was postponed for a year after the events of 9/11. Eventually the play opened, on November 2002, at the Vineyard Theatre, directed by Lisa Peterson, with Jessica Hecht, Marin Hinkle, and Alicia Goranson playing the three sisters.

The Fourth Sister is set in contemporary Moscow. The fantasy Moscow from Chekhov's *Three Sisters* is replaced by America, the Promised Land about which the sisters dream but which they never reach. Steeped in modern Russian political and economic circumstances, the play is an absurd retelling of a familiar storyline. In Glowacki's play, unlike in Chekhov's, the father is not dead but belongs to the lost generation, a former general and the product of a communist system unable to adapt to the new capitalist Russian reality. At the end of the show we see him drowning in vodka and childhood memories, unable to move forward in any direction. Wiera, who best resembles Chekhov's Masha with a subtle blend of hope and disappointment, has an affair with a corrupt married politician, Yuri. He promises her he most certainly will divorce his wife—right after the elections. Wiera becomes pregnant, and although the pregnancy thrills Yuri, it's not for the reasons Wiera initially hopes for. Raised in a culture of misguided Russian machismo, Yuri finally has proof he's not sterile ("a man who's sterile is like . . . a cripple, a reject" [25]), and that revelation spares him the shame of getting tested for infertility. Regardless, without batting an eye he asks Wiera to have an abortion. Wiera refuses his money and goes to a free state clinic to undergo the procedure, but even though she's without prospects or Yuri's support, she eventually decides to keep the baby.

Tania, the youngest of the three sisters, shares both the innocence and the youthful, self-centered hunger of Chekhov's Irina, together with a grand romantic vision of herself as self-sacrificing; she embodies Irina's unspoiled, vivacious naivety. She pretends to be a prostitute and sleeps with her childhood friend and upstairs neighbor, Kostia, "sacrificing" her virginity to obtain the money for Wiera's abortion. Kostia, a modern, Russian version of Hamlet, is a mafioso who as a younger man read a lot, a cause of grave concern to his mother, Babushka. As she puts it, "he would only sit in the library and read, read, read. I almost cried my eyes out" (10). Kostia once wrote a dissertation on Hamlet, a man who "talked too much and did too little," but eventually decided that being nice didn't pay well enough, so he joined the Mafia (32). Nonetheless, Kostia doesn't want to be like "all those other assholes out there who only dream of buying a Rolls-Royce"; he has ambitions to "protest" something, anything that would put him on CNN (37). Eventually, like Chekhov's Tuzenbakh, Kostia dies, accidently killed by the Mafia, who mistake him for someone else. As reparation, the Mafia

132   *Magda Romanska*

promise Babushka a crystal coffin and a life-size monument of Kostia, sculpted by an artist whose work was once exhibited in New York City.

The third sister, Katia, has a law degree, but she works at the circus, feeding a tiger named Pepsi, from whom she regularly steals meat. Like Chekhov's Olga, Katia can't find herself in the vulgar, brutal world that surrounds her. Rather than help her, her education and refinement stand in her way, and she has long ago given up on becoming a lawyer. Katia is in love with an American film director, John Freeman, who comes to Moscow to make a documentary film about underage Russian prostitutes. Although John meets many of them, they're not sufficiently touching for his film, and he desperately "needs one who will talk beautifully and tear-jerky for 600 dollars a day so that even New Yorkers will cry" (48). To make these six hundred dollars, the sisters decide to dress a young boy, Kolia, an orphan once adopted by the father, as a thirteen-year-old girl. The proverbial fourth sister, Kolia, acts out his part so well that his fake story wins John an Oscar for documentary film. Watching the ceremony on TV, the heart-broken Katia learns that John has a wife; the news devastates her because John was her last chance to escape from her life of misery and disappoint-ment. Kolia returns from America with the Donna Karan dress he wore at the Oscars, but nothing else. By now, however, the sisters' lives in Moscow have unraveled, and they send Kolia back to America to lay the founda-tions for their new life because, as Wiera puts it, "to change your address is to change your destiny" (73). Kolia intends to reconnect with their uncle Vania, who emigrated to America way back during the communist era, and "who's got three houses in Brooklyn," but Kolia loses Uncle Vania's address and ends up in a Russian brothel. He escapes the brothel intact and returns to Russia with a suitcase full of money, stolen from another gang-ster. But it no longer matters: "Just a few years earlier, [the sisters] knew what to expect from life. Now, they are at a loss" (Glowacki, "Tale of Two Moscows"). In the last scene, the most surreal of all, both John and Yuri, like two Prince Charmings, return to declare their undying love for the two previously abandoned sisters; Babushka wheels in the finished statue of Kolia, who holds a cell phone in one hand and keys to a Mercedes in the other. In the grand finale, Wiera's child, Hope, is born. It is a "grotesque happy ending," except that Wiera's child kills everyone with a Kalashnikov (Duniec and Krakowska-Narożniak 123). Only old Babushka stays alive, thanks to the bulletproof vest she is now advertising. The play ends with a metatheatrical twist: as Babushka endorses the bulletproof fashion, a voice from a loudspeaker announces: "Cut! Okay, thank you very much Akulina Ivanovna [Babushka]. That's a wrap" (73). In this world of vacuous emo-tions and values, everything and everyone is for sale.

In its structure, the play balances between realism and surrealism. As Glowacki put it, "In *The Fourth Sister*, naturalism blends with surrealism, and here too, the difference between them has become rather impossible

Chekhov in the Age of Globalization 133

to define" ("Tale of Two Moscows"). In one of the scenes, the walls move and shake; in another a newborn baby shoots everyone with a Kalashnikov. The play is also steeped in the absurdist sense of the grotesque, intertwining laughter with moments of clichéd sadness, melancholia, and pity. "Tears turn into maddening laughter within the framework of changing conventions: melodrama, documentary, TV reportage" (Wojciechowska). Glowacki said that the play shares Beckett's macabre sense of humor: "One of the fathers of the theater of the absurd, Samuel Beckett, after surviving both wars, decided that Godot will never come and that nothing is funnier than misfortune. Though Chekhov lived in the 19th century, this sentiment wasn't foreign to him, either, except his laughter has always been filled with compassion" ("Tale of Two Moscows"). As many theatre critics and directors have noted, there is a sense of the absurd in Chekhov's dramas. In his 1967 staging of Chekhov's *Three Sisters*, for example, Anatoly Efros, the Russian director, inspired by the absurdist interpretation of Chekhov's work, placed "the characters into a Beckettian limbo on a stage dominated by a tree with iron leaves" (Jestrović). *The Fourth Sister* is Chekhov on steroids, more in line with Christopher Durang's outrageous hyperabsurdism. Marin Hinkle, an American actress playing Katia in the Vineyard Theatre's American premier of the play, noted, "It's always that way with [Glowacki's] plays. When *The Fourth Sister* was done in Eastern Europe, it was greeted with uproarious laughter like it was an incredibly funny sitcom. American audiences take it quite seriously—there are a lot of times I feel like I have such egg on my face. But it's a comedy of absurdity about these frustrating lives" (Ehren). Why the discrepancy in receptions poignantly noted by Hinkle?

Glowacki's own biography provides complex insight into the global context of his play. When martial law broke out in Poland in 1981, many Polish artists and intellectuals who were traveling abroad decided to stay and settle there, among them Glowacki, who was attending a premier of his play *Cinders* in London. Those who, like Glowacki, eventually decided to settle in the United States received political asylum and what followed, the privileges of citizenship. The result of the experiences was *Hunting Cockroaches*, originally produced at the River Arts Repertory Company in Woodstock, New York, and then at the Manhattan Theatre Club under the direction of Arthur Penn and with a cast headed by Dianne Wiest and Ron Silver. Polly Warfield wrote then about the play: "the rigors, injustices, brutalities, humiliations and insanities his play portrays are his own experience and, like his play's protagonists, he has survived them with grace, psychologically sound and in good humor" (Arkatov 62). Sylvia Drake noted that in *Hunting Cockroaches* Glowacki "is depicting a condition, a stuck state of being, rather than a way to move on" (Arkatov 62). For Drake, the lack of plot captured precisely the liminal condition of an émigré, a person stuck in between two languages, two moral codes, and two value systems. Tamara Trojanowska made a similar point:

134 *Magda Romanska*

> Glowacki's play explores the plight of intellectuals in exile. It presents the most important phenomena discussed by the intellectuals themselves: the loss of social status and economic security, sudden and painful insignificance, cultural shock, appetite for success, deepening self-awareness, new sense of humility, the loss of communicable experiences and observations, and the loss of language. (276)

The émigré writer, for whom writing is intimately connected to culture and to the political system he grew up with, experiences a severe social, political, and cultural disconnect in a new culture. Glowacki describes it in one of his interviews: "I was trying to show somebody who is paralyzed by fright, by everything new, by not knowing what to do. I wrote the play, so it isn't me. But it is my feeling of being unsure of my writing—if somebody will be really interested in it. It came out of a feeling of being a stranger" (Leverett 27). To what degree can the liminal experience of the exile be translated to the cultural sphere of either the new or the old country—to what degree is it possible to communicate such an experience to either audience? The second, more important question, however, is to what degree did Glowacki's liminal condition as an émigré writer become a foundation for *The Fourth Sister*, and the play's own attempt to capture the liminal experience of Eastern Europe at the turn of the century?

Placed in the unique position of playwright forced to negotiate between a number of drastically different audiences—the native audience, the new foreign audience, and the émigré audience—Glowacki was also forced to negotiate between the symbolic systems, myths, and poetic vocabularies of each culture, as framed by the shifting moral and social norms and values. One of them was the myth of America that has dominated Polish society for over a century. This was particularly true during the forty years of communist rule that followed World War II. Immigration, particularly to the United States, became at least symbolically a form of "return" to a paradise lost: one escaped the political confines of the actual Poland into a broader, abstract idea of Poland as a free and sovereign nation—an idea that has brewed and been cultivated outside of the Polish borderlines for over three centuries. The free "Poland" was as if only hosted temporarily in its new geographic location: the United States. The communist system imposed strict travel restrictions. Obtaining a passport and being able to travel abroad was a privilege often limited to diplomats, athletes, and, occasionally, artists. It was presumed that once someone crossed the borders of Poland, there was a chance that she or he would stay abroad. For that reason, Polish government officials tightly guarded the tours of artists and athletes. Urban legends circulated about those who outwitted the system, escaped the guards, and managed to eventually obtain political asylum in the United States. Correspondence between escapees and their families back in Poland was closely monitored, as was access to outside media. In such a culture of limited outside access and oppression, America,

Chekhov in the Age of Globalization 135

the forbidden land of freedom and opportunity, gained mythical status. The idealized view of America was ironically reinforced by the official, state-controlled image of America as a country of vast economic and social discrepancies. A documentary about the homeless living with rats in the sewers of New York City was one of the most frequently shown movies on the Polish state television network. In the early 1980s under martial law, at the height of communist propaganda, Jerzy Urban, a government spokesperson, called for a charity drive of sleeping bags and blankets for New York's homeless in response to care packages sent by the U.S. government for impoverished Poles. The call was meant as an ironic commentary on America's own problems. However, nobody believed Urban's image of America. On the contrary, the negative image of America propagated by the Polish government confirmed people's conviction that America was the ideal land of plenty that everyone imagined it to be.

Because of the mythical image of America as the Promised Land that persisted in Polish society, those who came to the United States brought unrealistic expectations and were generally unprepared to deal with its competitive capitalist market economy. Whatever the eventual fate of the immigrants, the shame and degradation they initially encountered would always remain a secret, a secret they never shared with those back at home because they were simply too ashamed and because those at home wouldn't believe it. This secret was knowledge about "how America works," knowledge that could be gained only through experience. Having gained that knowledge, Glowacki could no longer idealize the image of America. As Baniewicz writes: "Living under hypocritical communism we had the delusion that things were different in the world beyond the Iron Curtain, but Glowacki, who has been living in the United States for a long time, sees both worlds clearly and feels no admiration for either" (101). Regardless of the reality, however, Baniewicz notes: "that focal, indestructible myth of America has become a universal myth" (101). The myth, Wojciechowska adds, "has been a typical dream of the poor part of Europe." Or, as Magdalena Mateja put it: "America is the center of the world, run by mass media. Moscow and other capitals of the Eastern Europe are deep, god forsaken provinces" (35).

In *The Fourth Sister*, the sisters' imagination constructs America as a dreamscape: "in America, they drink whiskey, in Russia, only vodka. Russian men are chauvinist. American men all look like Richard Gere" (Wojciechowska). But, as Leszek Pułka points out, in Glowacki's play, there are two versions of America: "There is the mythic America, located somewhere in the Caribbean, and there is the cynical America, which gives out Oscars for fake documentaries and traps immigrant girls into brothels" ("Pulp Erection"). According to Christine Ehren, Tania embodies the ideal image of America; she "is happy enough to have the comforts provided by her mob lover (including a VCR and *Pretty Woman* on video), but would rather have the country than the man." Alicia Gorason, who played Tania in

136 *Magda Romanska*

the American production, noted that Tania "is in love with America. We can laugh at that now some, depending where your stance is now. But she talks about America the way other countries think about America. And I think Tania embodies the good aspects of America—to have dreams, to get out of your circumstances and to make money" (Ehren). But for Glowacki, Tania's vision of America is not just naive; it is no longer valid: America is not America anymore. As he put it in an interview for the *New York Times*: "Russia has been depressed for centuries; today, with terrorism, a sputtering economy and cultural anomie, America is catching up" ("Tale of Two Moscows").

In *The Fourth Sister*, Wiera embodies this other image of America, as she says: "America's the same bordello as here. It's not the same America as before. Everything's changed" (74). But perhaps even America was never America in the first place. Capitalism exported into Eastern Europe has not brought the life that most expected and knew only from Hollywood movies. To quote Glowacki again: "The fall of communism hasn't changed the world into paradise" (Cieślik and Glowacki A5). On the contrary, it exposed the myth of paradise: there is no wizard behind the curtain. And the promises of capitalism, which once sustained those behind the Iron Curtain, now turned into a grotesquely mad rush for the material tokens of the imaginary American high life, leaving the vulnerable and naive in the emotionally arid jungle of impersonal sex and gratuitous violence. To quote Glowacki again: "For Chekhov's *Three Sisters*, the magical place that gave them hope of a better life and happiness was Moscow. For me, when I lived in Warsaw during Communist times, the promised land was America. In *The Fourth Sister*, the characters don't know where to go" ("Tale of Two Moscows"). After the initial euphoria that followed the fall of communism, the evolving economic stratification, accompanied by increasing differences in wealth, led to disappointment within those groups unable to adapt to the new political and economic reality. But while the economic reality changed, everything else has stayed the same: Tania, the most idealistic of them all, hasn't given up on America yet, pointing out: "Here, in Russia, they also say everything's changed. And what's changed? Father stopped drinking? They stopped taking bribes? Yuri stopped lying? There're fewer criminals? Less fear?" (37). Living in a world that combines the worse of what's left over from communism with the worse that was imported from capitalist America, "Glowacki's sisters are the inheritors of [the] dream turned into nightmare" (Sommer).

The second myth that Glowacki's play ponders is that of Russia. Leszek Pułka notices that *The Fourth Sister* takes place on two planes: "The first one is America. Double fantasy. [. . .] The second one is 'Russia-not-Russia'" ("Pulp Erection"). Following Sławomir Mrożek's *Love in the Crimea*, Józef Hen's *Lovers' Afternoon*, Tadeusz Słobodzianek's *The Bedbug's Dream*, and Maciej Wojtyszko's *Semiramida*, Glowacki's *The Fourth Sister* was the fifth Polish play written in the 1990s about Russia.

Piotr Gruszczyński poignantly noted: "We can't seem to shake off our fascination with Russia. We want to understand what is going on there right now. Maybe that is why contemporary Polish playwrights are bent on capturing Russian reality" (14). Glowacki offered different explanations for why he set his play in Russia. In an interview printed in the program notes, he said: "Russia is an interesting place and what happens there is important not just for Europe" ("Rozmowa"). In another interview, for a Polish newspaper, he attributed his decision to criticism he faced when writing about Poles: "Since whatever I write about Poland, I always step on someone's toes, this time, I decided to place my new play in Russia" (Mateja 36). In yet another statement, Glowacki pointed out that the choice of Moscow as the setting for his play was irrelevant: "I wanted Russia and America to look at each other. The play takes place in Moscow, but also in Hollywood and New York. It also could have happened in Poland" (Marzec and Glowacki A15). Agnieszka Glińska, who directed the Polish premiere, said that although the play takes place in Moscow, "the issues it touches can also be found here, in Poland" (R. B.). Glińska added that Glowacki's play talks about the "American madness that dominates modern culture, about the dangers that come from uncritical acceptance of its models and ideals" (R. B.). In the global context of omnipresent and omnipotent American pop culture, CNN, and the Hollywood dream, Moscow is simply a place "somewhere else." Magdalena Wojciechowska pointed out that "Moscow is only a decoration, in which the characters interact." And referencing *Ubu Roi*, Magdalena Mateja asked: "In Moscow, that is to say everywhere?" (36). Glowacki's Moscow is a place that's always nowhere *vis-à-vis* the imaginary American TV paradise that's always already "elsewhere."

In Poland, the responses to Glowacki's play have been mixed. Many Polish critics praised Glowacki's portrayal of Russia, pointing out its complexity and accuracy. One of them, Janusz Kowalczyk, noted the universal quality of Glowacki's writing:

> *The Fourth Sister* is a bitterly ironic synthesis of the end of the twentieth century. Using the example of a typical Russian family, Glowacki asks the elementary questions about the meaning of our existence. The issues are universal, and the absurd vision of Moscow, obsessed with the myth of America as a paradise on earth, echoes with both very familiar and very global undertones. (A9)

Kowalczyk praised what he perceived to be the authenticity of Glowacki's world: "Like all of Glowacki's plays, *The Fourth Sister* is brutal, bitterly ironic. It shows the Russian reality in lurid detail" (A9). Similarly, Elżbieta Baniewicz wrote about the genuineness of the emotional framework that forms the play's structural foundation:

The unity of time and place of action is constantly disrupted, as theatrical conventions change rapidly in this scene. Everything develops in the open from authentic elements: from pain, sympathy, terror, violence, great disappointments and small dreams, thoughtless ranting that drowns out emotional suffering, and above all, from helplessness in the face of what life brings the characters. [. . .] The world has lost its bearings and refuses to be tamed by any human measure. (99–100)

Jacek Sieradzki suggested that the play has a broader political context, as it tries to capture not just the political situation of Russia at the turn of the century, but rather a more metaphorical vision of Russia as one of the great empires, "the melting of frames and pillars of the gigantic empire that Russia once was" (46). In a similar mode, Magdalena Mateja pointed out that *The Fourth Sister* illuminates the complexities of the transition from the communist to capitalist systems, particularly "the impoverished society, and the degradation of those groups that during communism used to be cherished, but now, they are considered merely shameful tokens of the past system. The current world is ruled by organized crime and corrupt politicians, while the frustrated and increasingly helpless underclass watches the dissolution of traditional values" (35–36).

The dissolution of traditional values, however, is not an entirely negative process, Glowacki seems to suggest, as some of the values, particularly those that used to define Eastern European gender relations, need to be reexamined and perhaps even abolished. Under the Soviet regime, the communists saw gender relations primarily through the prism of class struggle. An image of a socialist working woman was contrasted with the image of a "bourgeois" woman of leisure, who was portrayed as hysterical and weak, and in constant need of male support. The socialist working woman, on the contrary, was simple, healthy, and able to work alongside men, contributing equally to the common, brilliant socialist future. The image of a codependent "bourgeois" woman of leisure naturally became a form of subversive fantasy that eventually came to dominate the symbolic sphere of Russian gender relations. Following the fall of communism, the codependent "bourgeois" woman of leisure, supported by either a nouveau-riche husband or mafioso lover, became a new standard and a new indicator of wealth.[2] Consequently, in most Eastern European countries, "the gender politics of the [. . .] transformation [began] to be hostile to feminist issues" (Filipowicz 122).

In their essay on *The Fourth Sister*, Krystyna Duniec and Joanna Krakowska-Narożniak suggest that Glowacki based his play on the schema of traditional Russian gender dynamics that historically has been connected to the sense of national pride and identity. The suffering of women in Russia is a "central fiction," passed on from generation to generation under the guise of maternal love. Framed by the national myth of Mother Russia, the family matriarch (mother or stepmother) is often the one responsible for curbing a young woman's independence: "Young women grow up having as role models their mothers who cooperate with men in forcing the women into codependence, sacralizing their suffering and cultivating masochistic attitudes in gender relations" (110). In *The Fourth Sister*, the mother rules the lives of the three sisters, even from beyond the grave, and her advice, as they imagine and remember it, usually involves scolding them for any signs of rebellion, and coaching them into permanent victimhood, a glorified and romanticized fantasy of eternal martyrdom and codependence. In one of the scenes, Wiera cheers herself by recalling her mother's motto: "Suffer as much as you can while you're still young" (28). While Wiera embodies the victimized, masochistic Russian woman, Tania symbolizes a break with that tradition. Although she constantly prays to her mother, asking for her advice and forgiveness, Tania eventually breaks down and shoots Kostia's killer, who suddenly becomes, in her eyes, the embodiment of all the men who wronged them: "Mommy, forgive me. Forgive me, sisters. *(Throws the Kalashnikov on the ground.)* That was for Kostia, for me, for Katia, for Wiera" (68), she says as she shoots him. Thus, Tania appears to break with the fantasy of female martyrology, even though it is Kostia's death (and thus, the loss of her last opportunity at happy codependence) that triggers her vengeance.

Despite the number of positive reviews the play received, many Polish critics also accused Glowacki of operating predominantly with clichés and stereotypes, without adding anything insightful to the discussion about Russia or politics at the end of the century. Roman Pawłowski, for example, noted that Glowacki's "image of Russia is too simplistic: a country of whores, gangsters and moronic politicians" (15). Mateja pointed out that Glowacki's language of stereotypes is not limited to Russians: "the Pole is a Catholic, the Russian is an alcoholic and the American is a drug addict" (36). Leszek Pułka accused Glowacki of basically writing the pastiche of a bad sitcom:

> These characters are caricatures. [. . .] We are not laughing at ourselves here. No sitcom is ever original. Sitcoms are based on stereotypes and "strong" jokes—about Jews, policemen, thieves, people from Wąchock [the Polish equivalent of Jersey City], or as in Glowacki's play—from Moscow. [. . .] But in theatre, the sitcom is always anachronistic. ("Barchantki")

Piotr Gruszczyński went even further, accusing Glowacki of mean-spirited snobbery and backward ignorance. Gruszczyński wrote that Glowacki "has nothing interesting to say about modern Russia. He operates with stereotypes, composing one big joke about Russia. That joke, of course, is Russophobic, chauvinistic, told by someone who feels superior to his

140 *Magda Romanska*

characters. To balance it out, there are also a few anti-American jokes in the play as well" (14). But, generally, *The Fourth Sister* "mocks not the system, but people who live there, and who deserve better than to be portrayed as midgets in Glowacki's big circus" (14).

Anticipating such criticism, in an interview printed in the program notes for the show's premiere, Glowacki said that the play was meant rather to be a caricature of the American lifestyle, and not a satire on Moscow ("Rozmowa"). Glowacki's explanation, however, didn't quell the criticism. On the contrary, it further instigated discussion about who was meant to be his audience. Gruszczyński authoritatively declared: "*The Fourth Sister* might be well received in America, but it won't have a long life. Soon, everyone will forget about it, the same way they forget about yesterday's news" (14). Others accused Glowacki of "selling out" by writing a play that would be easily digested by American audiences, catering to their tastes and prejudices. Joanna Godlewska wrote:

> [Glowacki's play] was written specifically for Americans, who, as is known, are obsessed with everything Russian, but who also like to feel superior towards everything Russian. Glowacki delivered a play that was as if written exactly according to those guidelines, and it is really surprising that it hasn't been a bigger success in the U.S. We have the array of Russian "souls" here: Russian mafiosos, tragic unfulfilled love, and to make the Yankees' satisfaction complete, there is also the Russian fascination with America. There is, of course, Russian song (too bad it's not the *kazachok*), tons of jokes about vodka and the essence of being Russian, and of course, a chauvinistic, idiot politician. Though, to be honest, all of the characters in this play are idiotic, more caricatures than complete human beings. In fact, in Polish, the language sounds as if it were a bad translation of a Russian play. (378–79)

Following Godlewska, Wojciech Majcherek made a similar observation:

> Glowacki wrote his play for Americans, who are most certainly interested in Russia with its problems following the fall of communism. Though beaten, Russia still appears dangerous, unpredictable, enigmatic, and exotic. In many ways, it is more interesting than any of the other countries in Eastern Europe from where folks escape en masse to the West. In America Glowacki became a professional playwright who knows that whatever he writes needs to find its customers, so he needs to provide what the customers demand. (42–43)

Defending Glowacki, however, Jacek Sieradzki pointed out that "*The Fourth Sister* is a conscious play with literary and cultural stereotypes. [. . .] Conventions get mixed up and Russian satire becomes global satire"

Chekhov in the Age of Globalization   141

(47). Łukasz Drewniak noted that the play was meant to be an exaggerated vision of Russia, never a realistic portrayal. Regarding the image of Russia in the play, Drewniak wrote: "[It] is purposely and consciously false and deformed (like John Freeman's fake documentary). Moscow becomes a formal construction" (14). The play is written like Kantor's adaptations of Witkiewicz: actors pick up the roles but without much conviction, acting "as if." In this world, everything is make-believe: some people walk around the stage, pretending to be women, artistic, and mafiosos, but they don't even know how to wear their costumes properly. In this world, "real suffering is impossible, truth is impossible, seriousness is impossible" (14). Drewniak blamed Agnieszka Glińska's direction for the overly realistic and hence melodramatic slant on a text that should have been "acted out like a crazy vaudeville, monstrous farce, Slavic Grand Guignol" (14.) Magdalena Wojciechowska offered a similar assessment of Kowalski's Warsaw version, writing that "the play was meant to be a tragifarce, but unfortunately, it was transformed into a comedy about naïve dreams. What was intended as a caricature and grotesque turned into handful of cheesy clichés."

The U.S. reception of *The Fourth Sister* was similarly lukewarm, and, as Piotr Gruszczyński unfortunately predicted, the play didn't have a long life. Christine Ehren called it a "black comedy" in which "the political, social and cultural life of current day Russia gets a brutal and funny theatrical airing." Elyse Sommer called it "a surrealist comedy with the comic and surreal elements used to enable viewers to take in the horror and absurdity of this collapsed society." But Sommer warned, "Not everyone will relate to this stylistic mix." Ben Brantley considered the play "a long and winding tragicomedy," one that "portrays contemporary Moscow as a place of such ragged sensibility, random violence and confused emotions that any form of action, reaction and inaction seems possible" (E4). Brantley, however, did appreciate the "moments of irresistible, go-for-broke absurdity in which the point is that nothing onstage can match the conjunctions of sorrow and silliness that real life dishes out these days." He concluded, "*The Fourth Sister* never quite achieves the mad momentum required to keep you unconditionally engaged" (E4). Marilyn Stasio pointed out that "despite the comic inventions of a dream cast [. . .], the savage bite of Janusz Glowacki's humor loses something in translation. There is bleak irony, for sure, [but there is also a] disconnect between Glowacki's seriocomic intention and the reaction of his audience" (31). Glowacki's transposition operates with globally recognizable tropes and cultural reference points. Using Chekhov's text as what Hutcheon calls a palimpsest through which the memory of the work can be intersected with contemporary semiotic codes, Glowacki was hoping to write a universal play that would transcend cultural differences and speak to all of his audiences, American, Polish, and Russian. He hoped that Chekhov's text, framed by the global language of American pop

142 *Magda Romanska*

culture, would provide the cultural springboard from which he could construct the "ironic inversion" of a classic with a modern, globally accessible twist. However, this time around, his attempt at universalism was too broad, and *The Fourth Sister* ripped at the seams, suspended, like its characters, in a vacuum of emotions and values. Perhaps it was because Chekhov's text is too embedded in its own contextual framework and to displace it means having to construct an equally dense structure—something that cannot be done if one is to operate with the superficial signpost of a globalized semiotic field. Perhaps, to use Hutcheon's phrasing again, to adapt Chekhov requires "an extended intertextual engagement with the adapted work" (8). Or perhaps it was a simple case of bad timing. By the time the play was produced in the United States in 2001, Russia, the Cold War, and its leftover Eastern European problematic were no longer interesting, replaced now by 9/11, and a new set of political and social issues and a brand new global framework.

NOTES

1. In this chapter the translations from the Polish are by the author.
2. In 1899, T. Veblen argued that the rise of capitalism required a well-defined system of economic indicators that would, on the one hand, differentiate the newly emerging bourgeois class from the rest of the society but that would also, on the other hand, provide a measuring system to allow males to recognize among themselves the most successful of the herd: "In order to gain and to hold the esteem of men it was not sufficient merely to possess wealth and power. The wealth and power must be put in evidence, for esteem is awarded only in evidence" (36). Veblen writes: "Women and other slaves are highly valued, both as an evidence of wealth and as a means of accumulating wealth" (53). Thus, the display of wives and hunting trophies became a new survival strategy: it allowed for a self-recognition of the leaders whom others could profit from, flatter, and emulate. A homebound wife, like other commodities, became a symbol of a male's *status quo*: he could afford to pay for her leisure.

WORKS CITED

Arkatov, Janice. "Seymour: Enjoying His Case of the 'Jitters.'" *Los Angeles Times* 6 Dec. 1987: 62. Print.

Baniewicz, Eżbieta. "Too Bad To Be True." Trans. Joanna Dutkiewicz. *PAJ. A Journal of Performance and Art* 67 (2001): 99–104. Print.

Brantley, Ben. "A Shaggy People Story about a Chaotic Moscow." Rev. of *The Fourth Sister*, by Janusz Glowacki. *New York Times* 22 Nov. 2002: E4. Print.

Cieślik, Jacek, and Janusz Glowacki. "Błazeństwa końca wieku." *Rzeczpospolita* 189 (1999): A1, A5. Print.

Drewniak, Łukasz. "W Rosji jak zawsze." *Tygodnik Powszechny* 4 (2000): 14. Print.

Duniec, Krystyna, and Joanna Krakowska-Narożniak. "Siostra, siostry, siostrzeństwo." *Dialog* 10 (1999): 108–23. Print.

Ehren, Christine. "Sisterly Love." Rev. of Glowacki's Black Comedy *Fourth Sister* at the Vineyard Theatre, New York. 21 Nov. 2002. Playbill.com. Web. 16 Dec. 2011.

Filipowicz, Halina. "Demythologizing Polish Theatre." *TDR: The Drama Review* 39.1 (Spring 1995): 122–29. Print.

Glowacki, Janusz. *Antigone in New York*. Trans. Joan Torres. New York: Samuel French, Inc., 2010. Print.

———. *The Fourth Sister*. Trans. Eva Nagorski and Janusz Glowacki. New York: Samuel French, 2003. Print.

———. *Hunting Cockroaches, and Other Plays*. Evanston, Il.: Northwestern U P, 1990. Print.

———. "Rozmowa o 'Czwartej siostrze'." Program notes, Scena Kameralna, Wroclaw, Poland, 1999. Print.

———. "Tale of Two Moscows." *New York Times*. nytimes.com. 17 Nov. 2002. Web.Godlewska, Joanna. "Zażenowanie." Rev. of *Czwarta siostra* [*The Fourth Sister*], by Janusz Glowacki. *Przegląd Powszechny* 9 (2003): 378–79. Print.

Gruszczyński, Piotr. "Ruski cyrk." *Tygodnik Powszechny* 4 (2000): 14. Print.

Hen, Józef. *Popołudnie kochanków*. Teatr Polski, Warszawa. 1994. Performance.

Horvath, Agnes, Bjørn Thomassen, and Harald Wydra. "Introduction: Liminality and Cultures of Change." *International Political Anthropology* (Special Issue) 2.1 (2009). politicalanthropology.org. Web. 16 Dec. 2011.

Hutcheon, Linda. *A Theory of Adaptation*. New York: Routledge, 2006. Print.

Jestrović, Silvija. "*Uncle Vania* after the Theatre of the Absurd: Or Shifting the Boundaries of Interpretation." *Toronto Slavic Quarterly* 34 (Fall 2010). utoronto.ca/tsq. Web. 16 Dec. 2011.

Kowalczyk, Janusz R. "Piąty żywioł." *Rzeczpospolita* 291 (1999): A9. Print.

———."Z obstawą do teatru." *Rzeczpospolita* 296. (1998): A8. Print.

Leverett, James. "From Killing Flies to Hunting Cockroaches." *Village Voice* 3 (1987): 27. Print.

Majcherek, Wojciech. "Russian Joke." *Teatr* 1.3 (18 Dec. 1999): 42–43. Print.

Marzec, Bartosz, and Janusz Glowacki. "Prawda mi się wydaje." *Rzeczpospolita* 9 (2003): A15.

Mateja, Magdalena. "Słowiańska depresja." *Akant* 4 (2001): 35–36. Print.

Mrożek, Sławomir. *Miłość na Krymie* ["Love in the Crimea"] Dir. Erwin Axer. Polish Television Theatre. 2010. Performance.

Pawłowski, Roman."Rosja z drugiej ręki." *Gazeta Wyborcza* 21 Dec. 1999: 15. Print.

Pułka, Leszek. "Barchantki." Rev. of *Czwarta siostra*, by Janusz Glowacki. *Gazeta Dolnośląska* 13 Dec. 1999. e-teatr.pl. Web. 16 Dec. 2011.

———. "Pulp Erection." Rev. of *Czwarta siostra*, by Janusz Glowacki. *Gazeta Dolnośląska* 10 Dec. 1999. e-teatr.pl. Web. 16 Dec. 2011.

R. B. "Ironiczna aluzja do Czechowa." *Rzeczpospolita* 10 Dec. 1999. archiwum. rp. Web. 16 Dec. 2011.

Sieradzki, Jacek. "Dwa razy cztery siostry." *Polityka* 8 Jan. 2000: 46–47. Print.

Słobodzianek, Tadeusz. *Sen pluskwy, czyli towarzysz Chrystus*. Teatr Nowy, Łódź. 2001. Performance.

Sommer, Elyse. Rev. of *The Fourth Sister* at the Vineyard Theatre, New York. Curtainup.com. 18 Nov. 2002. Web. 16 Dec. 2011.

Stasio, Marilyn. Rev. of *The Fourth Sister*, by Janusz Glowacki. *Variety* 25 Nov. 2002: 31. Print.

Trojanowska, Tamara. "Many Happy Returns: Janusz Glowacki and His Exilic Experience." *Living in Translation: Polish Writers in America*. Ed. Halina Stephan. New York: Radopi, 2003. 259–88. Print.

144 Magda Romanska

Veblen, Thorstein. *The Theory of the Leisure Class: An Economic Study in the Evolution of Institutions.* New York: Macmillan, 1899. Print.

Wojciechowska, Magdalena. "W poszukiwaniu Arkadii." *Przekrój* 13 (Feb. 2000). e-teatr.pl. Web. 15 Dec. 2011.

Wojtyszko, Maciej. *Semiramida.* Teatr Współczesny, Warszawa. 1996. Performance.

8 Theatre and Subaltern Histories
Chekhov Adaptation in Post-Colonial India

Bishnupriya Dutt

The notion of post-colonial studies has rarely managed to include theatre in the scope of its disciplinary paradigm. Being oriented towards literary criticism, in effect it marginalizes theatre and to a lesser extent drama. Theatre, moreover, needs tools of analysis, which would allow the critique to find its way back into the analysis of practice. True, the dramatic text has in recent times been an object of interest for post-colonial scholars, but it is deliberately examined outside the realms of practice. This dichotomy of text and performance has its historical roots in colonial tradition. The application of post-colonial critical theories to mere dramatic texts has its problems. What is interesting, however, is that subaltern studies, the predecessor of post-colonial studies in Indian academia, had very strong parallel ties with the theatre of its time. This allowed a strong critical dialogue between the academic domain and the progressive theatre movement of the 1960s–1980s in which Chekhov was featured for the first time as a popular post-colonial text.

LOCATING CHEKHOV IN POST-INDEPENDENCE INDIA

Chekhov is not given much prominence in the chronological history of post-independence Indian theatre, though translations and adaptations occupied a major part of its activities, particularly in Bengal. The colonial system of education and the importation of theatre culture through colonial routes are often held responsible for the dependence on Western texts. More often than not, translations and adaptations were the norm and Indian theatregoers were familiar with the European canon and dramatic texts through both the education system as well as theatre practice. The post-independence situation saw a mere continuation of the trend, although anti-British sentiments and the new nationalist euphoria led them to seek out alternate texts to the Anglo-American paradigm. These found their way into India through English translations, which the director/author adapted and translated into Bengali. Chekhov was inevitably coupled with

146 *Bishnupriya Dutt*

Ibsen and the new genre of psychological realism. They were the two textual sources that allowed the implementation of the Stanislavskian system, which was capturing the popular mind-set of the Indian audience. Texts in translation or adaptations are never a key area of interest in either theatre history or literary circles, which tend to concentrate on the small exclusively original repertoire. Thus the large body of translated or reworked texts is often ignored or underplayed, though it is absolutely impossible to construct and study post-colonial theatre history without taking them into account. These were the texts that helped to create a post-colonial modernity in parallel and contrast to a colonial modernity.

Colonial theatre came into existence around 1872 in Calcutta and emulated contemporary British theatre. Victorian melodrama formed the core structure of this genre. I have elsewhere emphasized how Shakespeare and other English classics too were molded in the style of Victorian melodrama, with an underlying influence of the burlesque, a feature that colonial history very carefully conceals in its "civilization" discourses (Dutt and Sarkar). Using this fact as a reference point of precolonial modernity, one of the most important characteristics of post-colonial modernity was a new and innovative reading of Western texts, including Chekhov, and liberation from the bonds of the canons of Victorian melodrama. The focus in the post-independence phase was on European naturalism, expressed in the form of relocalized Indian-language adaptations of Ibsen, Chekhov, Odets, Miller, and Gorky, and through these texts the probing of slices of life from contemporary Indian reality. The new generation had the passion and idealism to explore the possibilities of an experimental theatre, which opened up a model of theatre quite different from the indigenized Victorian tradition dominated by actors supported by music and spectacle. These new experiments demanded a reverence for the text, a close reading, analysis, understanding, and consistent interpretation of the lines through dramatic action conceived in terms of a "total" theatre, that is to say, theatre as a balance of acting, sound and music, scenic design, and illumination, with the director committed to the text and its inherent values, in perfect control over an ensemble of performers and technicians. This was a new departure and can be seen as the expression of a post-colonial consciousness, reflected in the formation of a new theatrical genre.

The new generations of theatre activists who selected, translated, and adapted the texts of the new repertoire were more educated than their colonial counterparts and also came from far higher socioeconomic strata. Most of them had a wider exposure to intellectual resources, while the new education policy of the post-independence nation had a more open curriculum, compared to its colonial counterpart. The new generation was being exposed for the first time to texts such as Gramsci and Lukacs, as well as the new communist discourses filtering in from China, particularly Lin Piao. Having an in-depth understanding of both language (English and Bengali) and literature, their interventions were rooted in textual nuances and subtlety. In many instances the colonial dramatists have cited how under pressure of finding new texts they would try to get new stories and fit them into the accepted (melodramatic) structures. Chekhov with his anti-melodramatic, static tone would never have been a choice of the preceding theatre. Even in the post-colonial period the appearance of these new texts came thanks to the emergence of the Progressive Amateur Theatre Movement, while the traditional commercial-professional theatre still concentrated on fast-moving emotional narratives within a melodramatic structure. For a long time, until the 1970s, both these genres existed simultaneously in the city of Calcutta, each having its own audience. Crossovers were rare: they were separated by abstract geographical space.[1]

Incorporating Chekhov therefore was a radical departure. Though they were exceptional and rare, Chekhovian adaptations were a very significant phenomenon. Reworking Chekhov for a theatre and performance culture conditioned by and steeped in Victorian melodrama, a nineteenth-century acting tradition, and a plethora of scenographic designs was indeed a courageous act. Its success and impact, however, emphasized the nature of the changing times. The new theatre movement that emerged in the post-colonial period, particularly in Bengal,[2] was named by its own participants as the Progressive Amateur Theatre Movement. These theatre groups emerged in Calcutta in the 1950s and 1960s, setting a pattern of theatre activity that has dominated the theatre scene in India ever since. The pattern may be described as one in which a group of unpaid, semiprofessional actors, actresses, and theatre technicians gather around a director who has virtually dictatorial control over the small organization, the final say in the choice of plays for production and all major decisions. With the members of the group being employed in regular jobs, mostly secretarial work and teaching, their theatrical activity is generally confined to two to three hours in the evening. With no theatre building of their own, the groups have to be content with one-night performances at the theatres available for hire in the city.

In the search for a new repertoire, the movement involved itself in its early phase with productions of Ibsen.[3] *A Doll's House* (1958), adapted and performed by the pioneer group Bohurupee, was regarded as one of the most successful productions and is a testimony to Ibsen's popularity among and acceptance by the Calcutta audience. Ibsen, with his dramatic climaxes and, to use Elin Diamond's term, the hysterical woman tamed and domesticated, played a dual role, being at the same time conformist and a departure. His plays could be interpreted within the norms of conventions and innovations more easily than Chekhov's. Ibsen's women figures could easily be seen as a continuation of the colonial nationalist theatre's central theme of the woman, but gestured at innovations at the same time. Chekhov would mean a more radical departure from established conventions. The late 1960s marked a growing enthusiasm with Brecht and his new texts, which were now available in India in English as well as in Bengali translation. A Brecht Society was formed around a major theatre, which

148 *Bishnupriya Dutt*

was run by one of the leading groups.[4] The director translated *The Days of the Commune (Naya Zamana)*. Brecht's Marxist analysis of historical events was eagerly adopted, reflecting the growing political discontent and radical politics of the 1960s and 1970s, which were challenging the legitimacy of the new nation. Brecht's texts along with his performative norms of gestures, distanciation, and critical moments of breaking communication were appealing for the new theatre activists. Yet one of the major theatre groups of the period, while engaging with Brecht through two successful performances of *The Threepenny Opera* and *The Good Woman of Sechuan*, found a need to include *The Cherry Orchard* (translated into Bengali as *Manjari Amer Manjari*) in its repertoire.

NANDIKAR'S 1964 PRODUCTION OF *MANJARI AMER MANJARI*

As the new theatre movement expanded its repertoire of alternate texts, Chekhov was a natural choice and the adaptation of *The Cherry Orchard* into Benghali as *Manjari Amer Manjari* became its symbol. The text, although originating in prerevolutionary Russia, was popular in the Soviet Union and therefore appealed to the progressive theatre movement, whose predecessor, the Indian People's Theatre Association, had strong ideological ties with the USSR and the Communist Party of India.[5] The 1960s and 1970s witnessed the beginning of a range of leftist and democratic movements. In India it was a time when the euphoria of independence and the first shock of disillusionment was giving way to a new criticality that sought to explore in theatrical terms—more particularly in terms of theatrical abstraction—political, philosophical, and psychological issues left shelved in the years of nationalist struggle to be prioritized only after independence.

The ethos of legitimacy that accompanied the creation of the new nation was replaced by growing criticism and public protests. Spiraling urban unemployment, food shortages, and drought raised fundamental doubts about the Nehru model of planned development and Indira Gandhi's Congress rule. A new level of political engagement became palpable not only because political parties ranged across the ideological spectrum and mobilized support, but also because seemingly apolitical groups were taking to the streets. Young people, students, doctors, scientists, and many others left their urban contexts to join groups and political struggles in rural areas, such as the militant left-wing peasant organizations in Bengal. The theatre thus became a key vehicle of political and ideological thinking and agitation.

Manjari Amer Manjari was adapted and directed by Ajitesh Bandyopadhyay[6] for his group, Nandikar. In context of these new groups, Nandikar, under his direction, more than other groups, specialized in adaptations of Western texts. His style of adaptations was extremely innovative, infusing the text with the essence of local and regional politics and reflecting the turmoil of the period. The use of language, nuances of local events, and interweaving of the larger and smaller narratives reflected his style. Bandyopadhyay played a major role in popularizing a whole new range of Western texts to his Bengali audience. With *Manjari Amer Manjari*, Nandikar moved from the traditional theatre district of Calcutta to a new more modest theatre in the nontraditional area of South Calcutta called the "Muktangan"—literally "open stage." The space of the "Muktangan," more than the actual architectural style, symbolized a protest against the colonial "proscenium" theatre. Muktangan would remain a new space for experimental theatre and would signify a new economic logic, namely, the group theatre's being able to sustain performances through ticket sales and pursue theatre as an amateur activity. The "amateur'" nomenclature came to mean in simple terms a noninstitutional and autonomous space.

THE TEXT AND ITS VARIATIONS

At first glance the text of *Manjari Amer Manjari* seems a close translation with names and locations changed, but the nature of the adaptation becomes clearer in the context of the politics of the 1960s. In 1964 when the play was translated and performed the objective was to expose the problematic of the new state rather than engage in outright antagonism. It was the phase of agonistic politics. The setting of the play in Purulia, which is a nonmetropolis and also the poorest district in West Bengal, is significant, since urban theatre usually depicts the story of its own locus and people. Purulia is a region of unfertile, rough terrain with a large tribal population. Under both colonialism and the post-independence administration the locality was subjected to harsh laws and surveillance. Before independence the local population had been branded as "criminal tribes," a label that the independent government for all intents and purposes retained. Purulia is known for its barren land with very scarce vegetation, and the mango orchard of the play is unusual in this area since mango cultivation is usually concentrated in the more fertile northern Bengal. The juxtaposition of these spaces and localities highlights the contrast between different segments of the population in India and breaks the myth of a new nation progressing and developing as a uniform geographical entity. The setting of the play instantly sets the focus on the nonunitary character of Indian politics and draws attention to the "other domain," which dominant discourses saw as of no importance or even as altogether nonexistent. By the early 1960s a growing regionalism, with the regions demanding more autonomy and asserting their cultural identities, had become an important aspect of the radicalization. Purulia, although a part of Bengal that played an important role in the politics of regionalism, is also an isolated locality even within the larger state. The region's economic, social, and political problems have

150 *Bishnupriya Dutt*

persisted until today and since the 1960s have nurtured a leftist militant politics that resorts to violence and terrorist activities. By the end of the 1960s, the Purulia had given birth to a militant insurgency known as the Naxalbari movement. It was the first tribal revolt against the new state that the city-based middle class joined in large numbers.

In the play text it is very significant that the time—historical or contemporary—and location are left unspecified. They are deliberately kept open, so that it is unclear whether the play is set in colonial or post-colonial times; this creates the illusion of a continuation of historical time. At one level the play appears to be a critique of the new state and nation and its almost continuous policy from a precolonial past to a post-colonial present. Only once does Felaram (Firs), talking of a "death knell," refer to how seventeen years ago the British in "anger" left the country. The word "anger" is key, emphasizing a historical narrative according to which the British were "forced" to leave India. It evokes a series of alternate nationalist movements that played a parallel role to the dominant Congress programs. One of the leading historians of the period sees it as acknowledging "one historic occasion after another and in region after region the initiatives of such campaigns which passed from the elite leaderships to the mass of subaltern participants, who defied high command and headquarters to make these struggles their own by framing them in codes specific to traditions of popular resistance and phrasing them in idioms derived from the communitarian experience of working and living together" (Guha xviii).

The play starts with the trauma of a post-independent nation resulting from the problems of an uneven capitalist development and the apparent lack of choices left to the Indian people. *Manjari Amer Manjari* seeks to capture all these contradictions. The recognition of these tensions is central to the play. It critiques the universalistic pretension of capital and leads logically to a thematization informed not by a primacy attributed to the state, but by an awareness of the unresolved problems of its negotiations with civil society. The setting of Chekhov's work is crucial, as the background itself constitutes the narrative, unlike other texts that unfold in their scenic development. The stagnation of the setting is the dominant narrative itself and implies a critique that goes beyond disillusionment. Against the stagnant scenario, questions are being asked, capturing the clash of doubt and self-doubt, interrogation and response between generations. The critique that is being formulated through the play and the larger political scenario as such is addressed to all incumbents of authority within civil society. Ranajit Guha writes, "However there was something indefinite about that sense of failure. Phrased in interrogation it carried the suggestion that things had not run their full courses yet and a turn for the better could not be ruled out. In other words, the mood characteristic of this disillusionment was one of anxiety suspended between despair and expectation and projected as such into the future" (xi). This political atmosphere reflected what Mouffe would term an antagonistic conception

Theatre and Subaltern Histories   151

of democracy that, according to Mouffe, can "contribute to a revitalization and deepening of democracy" (79). It positions itself against the state-promoted, consensus-based democracy. In these agonistic ideas lay alternative visions of the nation and civil society, which were still being conceptualized and developed at a time when the theatre's illusionistic world opened up a number of such visions.

The nouveau-riche protagonist, Mondol (Lopakhin) is the son of an old, loyal servant in the feudal setup. He stands in contrast to the idle, self-indulgent beneficiaries of the feudal system who are on the verge of impoverishment. This is not a historical struggle between a medieval feudal aristocracy and the bourgeoisie, but between two comprador bourgeois classes who had replaced the older feudal system and its aristocracy with the advent of colonial rule. They were a neo-bourgeois feudal landed class who were allowed to exploit the land for a small profit and send the lion's share of the revenue to the colonial rulers. Thus the degeneration and impoverishment of the feudal class does not follow the grand narrative of the Russian scenario, where the fall of the feudal aristocracy is a tragedy. Mondol, who represents the new nation's bourgeoisie, is not a villain in the conventional sense out to appropriate wealth at all cost. Neither is his enterprising labor eulogized. The fault lies in the system itself and the critique is addressed to the new state. The absence of the note of tragedy present in Chekhov's original is sufficient to emphasize this point. Mondol's rise and economic success is the new story of independent India, where rich peasants were amassing capital and power. Thanks to their economic enterprise this newly emerging middle class would soon be absorbed by the nation's privileged upper-middle class and become the harbingers of the new state. The eradication of cultivated land to make space for upper-middle-class luxury housing was a profitable business for the aspiring new class, while industry shifted from colonial control to a small coterie of Indian bourgeoisie closely nurtured by Gandhi and the Congress program. There was no marked industrial growth in the post-independence phase. The partition of Bengal would actually destroy the last remnant of any industry-based capitalist growth potential. The industrial belt would henceforth spread from Gandhi's homeland of Gujarat to Maharashtra and the western part of India. Since that shift the new capitalist expansion and power in Bengal has rested with a small group of land promoters, small traders, and the strong professional middle class. Even the prolonged left rule in Bengal (1976–2011) could not dislodge this power nexus between the land mafia and the vested interests.

The railways, often equated with colonial expansion, now also became a symbolic marker of the new state and play a prominent role in the text. The characters are waiting for the train from the first line of the play until the last, when they leave by train. Without giving dates, Girin's (Gayev's) comments offer a historical mapping of the formation of the post-colonial capitalist state: "With the new station the importance of the place has increased.

152   *Bishnupriya Dutt*

The railways have also cooked a delicious meat preparation. Ate too much in the afternoon, need to play a game or two of carom" (Bandyopadhyay 34).[7] The context is significant, for the railway is still a coveted institution, bringing "civilization" into the wilderness in the traditional colonial sense and opening it up for capitalism. *Manjari Amer Manjari* is thus not a play about heroes and villains of the nation, but about new class formations and the ruling classes who would dominate it.

The landed class, in this case the family of Lavanyaprabha (Ranevskaya), has no real long-term attachment to the land, only an escapist rural nostalgia that is part of the nationalist imagination. Within the nationalist paradigm this could mean anything from an escape from colonial cities with their chaos and surveillance to the complex ideas underlying Rabindranath Tagore's notion of the rural unit and alternative nationalist visions. Dipesh Chakrabarty perceives in Tagore's rural imagination a marked departure from other national imaginaries in its emphasis on embodiment. This represents a stark contrast to the dominant trend with its stress on the canonization of the body and detachment of body and mind. In that sense Tagore is the most incisive critic of the nationalist cultural project. Examples might be Amina's (Anya's) sense of freedom when she hears the bird sing or Girindra's (Gayev's) very simple description of the gardens: "the entire garden is overcome with mango *mukul*. It's like a picture. Have you forgotten Lavi [Ranevskaya]? That winding narrow land meanders across the orchard right through the middle in the full-moon night, it lights and glistens, it's like a silver ribbon laid out. Do you remember?" (27). The adaptation deliberately retains the simplistic expression of pastoral escapism, thus implying a critique of the romantic nostalgia about nature inherent in the nationalist vision. Independence and the policy of capitalist expansion swept away all such notions. The land, which had inspired so much of the poetry, songs, and music related to nationalist consciousness, was to be the first casualty of capitalism in post-independence India. The word "rural" would become a synonym of "backward." While the rich and the elite could afford such literary escapism, for Ekkari (Yepikhodov), the poor old servant, it is the opium to forget the miseries of reality. This is not just a metaphor to describe the impact of the harsh realities as the dreams of independence faded, but also a direct reference to colonial policies and the opium trade. What remains for the stagnant landed class is a false sense of dignity and self-worth. Lavanya is keener to maintain her reputation as "landed aristocracy" than to let the others know the real state of their economic plight. To become land agents parceling and selling off land is the worst plight that could strike them. Their sacrifice is almost laughable. The crux of post-independence politics is enhanced by the sense of irony that pervades Chekhov's plays. It undermines all the romantic notions and literary culture regarding the land that underpinned the nationalist ideology. The stagnation of narrative in Chekhov's play exposes land politics for what it is worth: a weapon to reinforce class and caste politics. The new

Theatre and Subaltern Histories 153

post-colonial bourgeoisie's increasing control over the land will ultimately, like that of its colonial predecessor, serve to reformulate an anachronistic and oppressive state whose first casualty is the nationalist imagination. Chekhov's anticlimactic scenario with its lack of transformation constitutes a critique of the retrogressive outlook of the new sovereign nation-state. Yet within the critique lies an urge to change the status quo. The static situation revealed in the play begs for a transformative scenario.

Though Chekhov's politics were not directly connected to Soviet socialism, in the 1960s the critique of the Indian state would convey, particularly to a Bengali audience, visions of a socialist ideological alternative. In Bengal, the progressive theatre movement was closely related to the growth of support for the left and the radicalization of the Bengal countryside. The character of Tapas (Trofimov) was a familiar type in this particular genre of plays, and his socialist rhetoric would strike a chord with the politically indoctrinated audience of the 1960s. The irony of his monologue would pass unnoticed and it would be taken at face value:

Three centuries the orchard has been nurtured by the relentless labor of landless men. Yet what have they received as fruits of their labor? . . . At the break of sunset, setting of darkness, don't you see the lurking shadows of these men? In the summer noon, when men do not dare tread out, and the mangoes drop with a thud, we are enclosed and protected in our cool rooms. The choked voices of these men are trying to say something. They have something to say. As owners of the orchard whatever pride you have is related to these men, because collectively they have built the orchard. But as owners what do you have to be proud of? Exploitation of numerous people suffering from scarcity is the history of the orchard. (43)

The belief that those who labor should be given the benefits of their work was a popular idea.

In 1967 the first United Front government under the leadership of the CPI(M) was elected to power.[8] Despite the later critique leveled against the Communist Party as remaining predominantly middle class, the 1960s and 1970s were moments of historical potential. The dominant Congress Party under the leadership of Jawaharlal Nehru and Mahatma Gandhi had already decided that India would adopt unconditionally the capitalist model. I read the popularity of the communists as a reopening of the debate about other possible paths. With the reprioritizing of economic projects in Eastern India and the erosion of the industrial projects themselves, the left was forced to give up its working-class focus and concentrate on peasant programs. The ideas of Marxism so intricately connected to the proletariat in the sense of industrial workers would never henceforth be relevant for the Bengal Marxists. Left mobilization already apparent in the 1960s would gather strength until its landmark victory in 1977 and remain in power at

154 *Bishnupriya Dutt*

the state level for the next thirty-five years. The popularity of the left would be sustained mainly by the land reforms it enacted and its transfer of land to the peasants. The politics of the "landless" and their claim to land would ultimately create a new power network that would create dissidence and weaken the left movement as late as 2010.

Thus Chekhov's play staged forty years ago in a way historically captures a number of anomalies regarding land, labor, and landed capital that gave birth to a new political force in post-colonial India. The backdrop of *Manjari Amer Manjari* is set within regional Bengal politics and cultural identity issues of the 1960s. The translator-adaptor makes certain crucial interventions in terms of the use of dialects and local idioms,[9] hinting at the politics surrounding the linguistic reorganization of the Indian states. Language becomes a key marker of the regional, class, and caste complexities of the time. The nuanced Bengali of the upper class is an urban phenomenon and historically connected with the modernization of the language under the colonial education and cultural system. Amina (Anya) talks about her strict supervision academically in a Calcutta education institution. The local population speaks in the dialect used only by those living in the hinterland between Bengal and Bihar. Beyond class there are subtle nuances of the caste system operating. Mondol speaks in the dialect, but the orientation of the rustic nouveau-riche class is apparent in his speech. Despite their economic prosperity this class has no access to the elitist education system concentrated in the big cities. Geography and class distinction thus make divisions more complex than in any modern capitalist society, where transformation happens uniformly. Bandopadhyay's manipulation of language and dialect thus constitutes a strong critique of new and old class and caste divisions, which in the post-independence phase retain their hegemonic character unchanged. The new nation's ideology refuses to create the mobility necessary for reconstruction between the fundamental segments of civil society. It is significant in this context that *Manjari Amer Manjari* is one of the few plays of the group theatre repertoire whose narrative is set not in Calcutta city, but in a distant region. Middle-class Calcutta theatre is often criticized for its Calcutta orientation and urban-centric themes. The translator is well versed in the local politics and society of rural districts like Purulia, which are usually ignored and marginalized. He also has no qualms about using dialect at the cost of incomprehension by the city audience.

WOMEN'S AND GENDER ISSUES IN THE ADAPTATION

If the new theatre movement was supposed to bring change, then one of the critical signifiers should be the portrayal of women. Both the colonial and nationalist projects were preoccupied with domesticated woman and domestic conjugality as a core theme. Adaptations of Chekhov, Brecht, and even Ibsen were a departure from the genre of melodrama associated with these themes. *Manjari Amer Manjari* centers on Lavanyaprabha (Ranevskaya) and her daughter Amina (Anya); neither of them is domesticated or has a husband to whom she must be subservient. One of the changes Bandyopadhyay makes, which is specified at the outset of the play, is that Lavanyaprabha (Ranevskaya) had left the orchard heartbroken after her son's accident for a religious ashram. The ashram is a protected and insular space for the pious widow to spend her time practicing ascetic living. Amina (Anya) describes the hardship her mother had to bear and the absence of communication between her and the other inmates due to language barriers: "no one spoke Bengali." Lavanyaprabha is not a woman who has led a life of leisure in either Paris or, in this instance, Calcutta. Waywardness in a sense also implies a subsequent narrative of repentance, the possibility of which is erased right at the outset. Yet on her return to the orchard, and in this case back to Chekhov's text, she shows no remnants of her ascetic life or piety. She is full of nostalgic vivacity about the orchard itself, prancing about and full of *joie de vivre*. Amina shares the *joie de vivre* and represents her mother's past, before the experience of a wastrel husband. Exhibiting this *joie de vivre* is not an acting technique that comes automatically to the actresses in the Bengali theatre: the domestication project had imposed conventions regimenting and confining an actress's movements onstage. Focusing on the upper-class woman who personified the moral ideal of passive sexuality, the colonial and nationalist repertoire had almost no other female characters except immoral lower-class ones or the professional dancers with their active sexuality. Chekhov's Bhutu (Varya) and Durga (Dunyasha) represent different lower-class alternatives to the upper-class "model" woman. Bhutu is a *soi*'s daughter. *Soi* in nineteenth-century Bengal parlance meant a female bonding, which was a sharp contrast to the classic heterosexual relationship. Although Durga dresses like a "respectable" lady, both she and Bhutu speak in local dialect, which in itself suggests a characterization different from the goddesslike perfection of the domesticated woman. Such images, language, nuances, and narratives were in sharp contrast to the norms of theatrical portrayal of women in the 1960s.

CHEKHOV IN THE 1980S AND 1990S

Contrasting with this 1960s adaptation are two Chekhov texts dating from after the 1980s. This period differs sharply from the earlier one. By the 1990s the progressive amateur theatre movement had lost much of its radical engagement with the state, although there was a large-scale return to adaptations of foreign masterworks. The reason for the decline was not only the attraction of television for both performers and audiences, but also the fact that democratic debate and negotiation between the forces

156   *Bishnupriya Dutt*

at play in a fast-changing social and political situation no longer provided post-independence Indian theatre with its rationale and inspiration. With the democratic experiment itself reduced to sinister adhockery, the resulting confusion and cynicism seem to have left theatre dry and barren. The post-1980s years have been described as a period of growing hegemonic consolidation on the part of the state, which has abandoned all ideas of the nation as such in what has been broadly called the death of ideology.

In Bengal, a buffer came in the form of a state government controlled by leftist parties; the state had limited powers in terms of economic or industrial policy, but pursued a positive cultural program of nurturing theatre and performance culture. Like all parties when they attain power, the Communist Party went through its own process of negotiation and accommodation in adapting itself to parliamentary democracy. For theatre practitioners, the task of social critique became more complex because their varying loyalties and theatrical engagement with the political and economic forces at work became more simplistic and naive. The incisive political critique and social mobilization that was inherent in adaptations like *Manjari Amer Manjari* would never be repeated.

Bhoma (1989) is a quite straightforward adaptation of *Uncle Vanya*, conveying no apparent leftist critique. It was the product of a new theatre group containing veterans from senior theatre groups who were simply trying to create a competent artistic production. *Three Sisters* (*Ora Teen Bon*, 1998), adapted and directed by Koushik Sen did, however, try to intervene in the text with a critique of the left incumbency. Subsequent vocal critique of the left from former Left Front loyalists is apparent in the work of Sen, who represented the second generation of theatre practitioners, keeping the group theatre genre going, albeit in a far more modest way. In retrospect, the critique centering on left policies and misrule never transcended these to tackle larger issues of state, nation, or civil society. Ultimately such critiques would feed into the statewide anti-left wave that led to the leftist government's defeat in Aril 2011 and a full-scale capitalist expansion in Bengal. I would argue that in its pursuit of a working critique of the left, rather than one based on ideological and political grounds, the group theatres also played a role in valorizing globalization and a renewal of capitalism. The subaltern resistance politics that was so much a part of the group theatre movement is now jeopardized by the onslaught of capitalist and globalized politics that is engulfing Bengal.

HISTORICAL FRAMES

In conclusion, I would like to return the debate to the possibility of a postcolonial theatre contributing to critical and discursive ideas within a globalized world. The potential remained in a subaltern perspective that followed a parallel trajectory to contemporary theatre, with strong connections to

Theatre and Subaltern Histories 157

a number of its ideological and critical ideas and narratives. The 1960s and 1970s saw in the theatre what is today broadly termed the subaltern mentality and a strong historical, even theoretical, perspective that could develop critical moments of historical resistance.

Though the division between academic and theatrical practice remained separate, there was a strong community feeling among the concerned intellectuals about which the founder of subaltern studies, Ranajit Guha, stated:

> with no curriculum, no dogma, no official line to guide it, no professor, prophet, or politburo to watch its every step, it was an outsider only too eager to listen to and participate in the controversies agitating in the space and beyond the temples of learning and the political headquarters. When the noise of the first exchanges was heard in the streets, it did not seek refuge behind intellectual or moral palisades, like some others among its contemporaries, but rushed out and joined. (xiv)

This statement is as apt for the participants and activists of the new theatre movement as it is for the historians of subaltern studies. It would be important in this context to look at the common logic of argument over a broad time frame and dispersed geographical location.

The time period is a very important part of the narration and, for subaltern studies, extends between the Naxal movement of 1967–1972 and the Emergency of 1975. It was a period that Ranajit Guha would describe as follows: "yet with all that was common between old and young into the future-directedness of this mood, it varied significantly between the two instances in its temporal articulations. For the disillusionment that surfaced in that anxiety contemporaneously for both generations within the same decade, that is within a 'now' each could call its own" (xi). The notion of the here and now was further accentuated by the theatrical genre. *Manjari Amer Manjari*, with its constant shift between the colonial and post-colonial perspectives, was in a way getting at the crux of the subaltern studies critique: "What was there in our colonial past and our engagement with nationalism to land us in our current predicament—that is the aggravating and seemingly insoluble difficulties of the nation-state?" or "how are the unbearable difficulties of our current condition compatible with and explained by what happened during colonial rule and our predecessor's engagement with the politics and culture of that period?" (Guha xi). The theatre brought the issues to the surface during the performance as its audience and characters responded to the illusionary yet realistic world of Chekhov. Through the performances the audiences were confronted with the issues with the immediacy inherent in theatre. The production was a critique or challenge to the consensus-based political system and the new state. *Manjari Amer Manjari*, like subaltern studies, was attacking a monistic view of our history and the idea circulated by the state of "the people's consent to the rule of 'their own' bourgeoisie," which was anticipated in

158 *Bishnupriya Dutt*

the anticolonial campaigns (Guha xviii). The play challenged the notion of dominance without hegemony. It encouraged dissent and opposition among the new citizens of a new nation who were for the first time being urged to take a position as citizens of an active civil society. The state, however, had no intention of accepting this mode of agonistic democracy and theatre, regarding it, along with the new intelligentsia, as dangerous. During the Emergency a number of theatre activists as well as leading left intellectuals would be arrested.

The story of the mango orchard is very clear in its political import. It retells the story of the new state as a narrative of victimization, a structure of potential resistance, and a reworking of the logic of capitalism without the consent of civil society. It is not that Mondol does anything illegal to appropriate the land for his capitalist exploitation, but the new forces of the nation are going to give him an advantage denied to the orchard owners. He himself is a tool in the new capitalist state. In contrast, Tapas's visions of labor and a peasantry whose history is entangled in the orchard is almost devoid of any cynicism, serving as a reminder of smaller popular resistances. Chekhov's narrative does not allow one to fall into the trap of depicting a peasant revolution or try to usurp the voice of the subaltern for oneself. Chekhov cannot ever be adapted to be the nonexistent peasant's voice, but his work represents a strong intervention in the historiography of elitist writing of history, "a colonial elitism and bourgeois nationalist elitism" (Guha xiv).

Theatre itself in India and a number of ex-colonial countries was part of a modernist project that confines itself to this day to the spaces of the urban middle class and is set amid an expanding capitalist scenario. Hence, the theatre can only speak from a nonsubaltern space, which invites Spivak's classic critique of how they can then speak in the subaltern voice. What are the modes of negotiation that can gesture the resistance without the hegemony of appropriating voices across the almost insurmountable barriers of the urban and nonurban divide? Here the methodological approaches of subaltern studies' histories and their subsequent critique become relevant for the theatre. Subaltern studies, as expressed by its founder historian Ranajit Guha, aim at two distinct interventions: first, disrupt the dominant historiography by bringing the prospect of the subaltern voices into the picture. In that sense theatre too could intervene in a historiography that excluded subaltern voices. Returning to Chekhov, all those who speak in the play are from the cities, and their text intervenes in the dominant narrative to mark out other spaces. Second, there is the real problem of subaltern histories of expressing those disruptive voices whose existence suggests "resistance," but that are so totally elusive that there is always the danger of misrepresentation. Guha explains such resistance in the following way: "the transformation shaped up essentially as a process of Indianizing the idioms of modernity imported by the Raj" (xx). Yet how are these to be explained in theatrical terms, particularly through a text like

Theatre and Subaltern Histories 159

Chekhov's? Other than gestural interventions in terms of language and certain symbolic references, to comprehend and communicate the indigenization, which is assumed to be Indianization, is almost an impossible task. Adapted and translated theatrical texts in that sense are a classic example of why the process of Indianization, such as embodied resistance, cannot realize its full potential through adaptation. Preoccupation with translations and adaptations exposed the limitations and the contradiction itself, with which post-colonial theatre, emerging out of colonialism, could never reconcile itself.

NOTES

1. Calcutta (or, as it is now called, Kolkata) was the original nodal point of dissemination of colonial culture, the first modern theatre being established in Calcutta in the early nineteenth century. The theatres run by Indians (from 1872 onwards) were concentrated in the northern part of the city, while the new progressive theatre movement would locate itself in the southern part of town. None of the new groups would have a theatre of their own; they performed from time to time in some of the new auditoriums that were springing up in South Calcutta.
2. Bengali or Calcuttan theatre was the model for theatres in other parts of India to follow, at least in this particular phase.
3. Some of the successful Ibsen plays in Bengal at this time were *Ghosts* (1950), *Enemy of the People* (*Dasha-chakra*, 1952), *A Doll's House* (*Putul Sansar*, 1952), *A Doll's House* (*Putul Khela*, 1958), and *Ghosts* (*Bidehi*, 1970).
4. The Brecht Society was formed by Utpal Dutt and the Little Theatre Group; they were still performing at the Minerva theatre in 1965. It was a collaborative project with the GDR. The society's activities centered around Dutt's visit to the GDR and the Berliner Ensemble. Some of the young actors were sent to the GDR for training; regular German lessons were conducted in the theatre; German versions of the plays were imported; translations and adaptations were made; and publication of a theatre journal, *Epic Theatre*, began.
5. The Indian People's Theatre Association was the cultural wing of the Communist Party of India, founded in 1943. The Indian People's Theatre Association in the war years had taken up a project of rediscovering traditional forms of performance and creating an alternative cultural identity. Inspired by the antifascist cultural movements abroad, the Indian People's Theatre Association undertook a number of innovative projects that died premature deaths. Almost all the actors who had founded and established an identity and popular standing in the Indian People's Theatre Association project broke away to join the theatre groups.
6. Ajitesh Bandyopadhyay (1933–1983)—actor-director in theatre, Jatra, and cinema; playwright and translator; lyricist and composer—led the theatre group Nandikar (1960s–late 1970s), acting, writing, directing more than thirty plays ranging from original works to adaptations from Ibsen, Brecht, Chekhov, Pirandello, Priestley, Wesker, and Pinter, and short stories and plays by Rabindranath Tagore. In his pre-Nandikar days he was actively associated with the Indian People's Theatre Association, adapting, directing, and acting in more than fifteen plays. He acted in mainstream Bengali cinema and in award-winning films (both Hindi and Bengali) by Mrinal Sen and

160 *Bishnupriya Dutt*

Tapan Sinha and also acted in the Jatra (1978–1983). He was the recipient of several state and national awards, including the Sangeet Natak Akademi Award for Direction (1973).

7. This and subsequent translations from the Bengali are by the author.
8. The United Front was a political coalition in West Bengal, India, formed after the 1967 legislative assembly election. The United Front dislodged the Indian National Congress for the first time in the state.
9. Far more prolonged and divisive than the controversy over the official language of India was the linguistic reorganization of the states. It raised more fundamental questions of center–state relations. Leaders of language groups launched various movements, especially during the 1950s and the 1960s, for the linguistic reorganization of the Indian states. Only those that were well placed enough succeeded and were able to prevail against rival groups within the former provinces of British India and against the reluctance of central government leaders.

WORKS CITED

Bandyopadhyay, Ajitesh. *Manjari Amer Manjari. Collected Plays (in Bengali)*. 2 vols. Ed. Hiranmoy Karlekar. Kolkata: Pratibhash, 2011. 2: 13–68. Print.

Chakrabarty, Dipesh. "Nation and Imagination: The Training of the Eye in Bengali Modernity." *Topoi* 18 (1999): 29–47. Print.

Diamond, Elin. *Unmaking Mimesis*. New York: Routledge, 1997. Print.

Dutt, Bishnupriya, and Urmimala Sarkar. *Engendering Performance: Indian Women Performers in Search of an Identity*. New Delhi: Sage, 2010. Print.

Guha, Ranajit, ed. *A Subaltern Studies Reader*. Delhi: Oxford UP, 2008. Print.

Ibsen, Henrik. *Putul Khela (A Doll's House). Oedipus and Putul Khela*. Trans. Sombhu Mitra. Kolkata: M.C. Sarkar, 1986. Print

Mouffe, Chantal. "On the Political." *The Applied Theatre Reader*. Ed. Tim Prentki and Sheila Preston. London: Routledge, 2009. 77–85. Print.

9   What Comes "After Chekhov"?

Mustapha Matura and West Indian Reiterations of *Three Sisters*

Victoria Pettersen Lantz

> There's an element of scholarship about [adaptation] because you're observing how another writer has plotted and how his mind works, the different paths he travelled. But there's also an element of looking at the original from a different perspective, showing how it would read in a different culture but with the same essential problems—the universality of a Russian play that can be adapted to the Caribbean.
>
> —Mustapha Matura, 2006 interview

However authoritative he may have been on the conditions of Russian lives at the turn of the twentieth century, Anton Chekhov is not a voice associated with the history or literature of Western colonialism. In the same vein, Trinidad-born playwright Mustapha Matura is not a scholar of any and all things Chekhovian. After immigrating to Britain in 1961, Matura began writing plays, and since 1971, theatres around the UK and around the world have produced his work. He focuses his plays on the language of the Caribbean; the traumas of immigrants; and a direct, harsh critique of both British and Trinidadian societies after colonization. Yet, nearly one hundred years after Chekhov wrote *Three Sisters* in 1901, Matura saw a connection between the lives of Olga, Masha, and Irina and the lives of the colonized Caribbean. That is not to say that Chekhov had no sense of the issues surrounding colonialism; he did, to some extent. In 1890, he traveled to the British colonies of Hong Kong, Singapore, and Sri Lanka (then Ceylon). Chekhov's international travels did not inform his plays directly, however, and *Three Sisters* focuses on the provincial struggles of rural Russians. Matura, for his part, positions Chekhov as part of the classic Eurocentric education foisted on colonized people and as part of the institutional construction of culture and art. At the same time, he sees *Three Sisters* as relatable to the family dynamics of colonial life in Port of Spain, Trinidad.

In 2006, Matura adapted Chekhov's play and created *Three Sisters: After Chekhov*.[1] The play is a more recent work from Matura's extensive corpus of plays, which began in the 1970s and has become a staple of English theatre. In the 1960s and 1970s, as immigrant populations began to

162 *Victoria Pettersen Lantz*

publicly engage with and react to life in the UK, the political and artistic movement of Black British citizens emerged, and Matura was at the heart of Black British theatre. He wrote a number of plays on the tensions between colonial immigrants and white English communities. His first full-length play, *As Time Goes By* (1971), exemplified the trials of being Caribbean in England. Other plays, like *Welcome Home Jacko* (1979) and *Nice* (1973), helped mixed-race audiences understand what it meant to be young, black, and male in England during a time of youth and race riots. In 1979, he cofounded Black Theatre Cooperative (BTC), a company working to promote black artists creating theatre together. Matura is most well known, however, for his Caribbean plays, which relate to his experiences returning to visit post-independence Trinidad. *Play Mas* (1975), *Meetings* (1981), and *The Coup* (1991)—the first play commissioned by London's National Theatre by a West Indian writer—all tackle the trauma of colonialism as Trinidad transitions into a post-colonial society. His most famous play is *Playboy of the West Indies* (1984, adapted from J. M. Synge's *The Playboy of the Western World* [1911]), which reframes Synge's County Mayo into a discussion of life in rural Trinidad's Mayaro. Produced on a regular basis since it premiered, the play is a popular choice for theatre companies in the United States, UK, Canada, and the Caribbean.

After his success with *Playboy of the West Indies*, Matura approached adapting Chekhov's *Three Sisters*. Matura's play both highlights the transportability of Chekhov's themes of isolation and socioeconomic divisions and critiques Western colonialism's impact on West Indian culture. *Three Sisters: After Chekhov* is set in Port of Spain at the beginning of World War II and follows sisters Alma, Helen, and Audrey as they long to go to England, a place that they imagine reflects their high-society standards. As part of the Afro-Caribbean population, however, they, along with most of the men in their lives, are tied up in local concerns of insufficient water supplies, poverty, and Carnival-spurred rebellions. Matura approaches the play with reverence to Chekhov's development of familial relationships and domestic tragedy, but he does not let go of his anticolonial rhetoric. The tension between the aims of Chekhov's *Three Sisters* and the aims of Matura's adaptation is not necessarily negative, but it does lead us to question Chekhov's relevance in the contemporary world outside of Europe. Matura's title itself begs this question. Matura is paying homage to the original playwright, but he is also asking: what comes after Chekhov? Can Chekhov's work find a clear identity and audience in the traumas of race and place inherent in contemporary post-colonial theatre?

Using Matura's play as a case study, we can discuss how Chekhovian adaptations relate to post-colonial adaptations within two general ideas: place and race. Place, a central concern of Chekhov's work in general and *Three Sisters* in particular, is equally important to Matura's writing about the Caribbean, including *Three Sisters: After Chekhov*. Though these men consider different parts of the world in their plays, both explore the

What Comes "After Chekhov"? 163

relationship people have to a specific place and how location can influence major life decisions. The issue of race does not directly relate to Chekhov's *Three Sisters*, but Matura's exploration of the complex socio-racial structures of Trinidad and Britain allows us to relate Chekhovian concerns of family life and domestic strife to politically salient concerns of race relations in the development of the colonized identity. Before examining the nature of place and race in *Three Sisters: After Chekhov*, however, we must consider the nature of post-colonial adaptation and the idea of a counter-canonical discourse.

In essence, *Three Sisters: After Chekhov* is an adaptation about adoption. The various characters transform themselves, willingly or unconsciously, by adopting to various degrees certain histories/characteristics. The sisters adopt England as a homeland, Jean (Matura's Natasha) adopts European traits for social mobility, and Richard Rivers (Vershinin) adopts the persona of sexual colonizer. The repeated moments of adoption in the play serve Matura's dissection of the colonization of land, nationality, language/culture, and the native body. But the idea of using Chekhov for a post-colonial critique of England and the Caribbean does not always necessarily sit well with scholars and critics. Of the first version of the adaptation, *Trinidad Sisters*,[2] Laurence Senelick states, "[the play] sacrificed Chekhov's finer points to an activist message, but in the process, introduced a minority public to a play which has become part of the English collective unconscious" (*Chekhov Theatre* 322). As a way of considering the broader implications of Matura's adaptation, I will consider Senelick's perspective on the play and to what extent remediation helps or hinders *Three Sisters: After Chekhov* as a theatrical experience.

The concern that Matura misses Chekhov's finer points illustrates for Senelick, and many theatre critics, that Matura misses an opportunity. In adapting Chekhov, Matura becomes subject to the supposed rules of adaptation, in which audiences become the arbiters of what can and cannot be done to Chekhov's plays. If *Three Sisters: After Chekhov* contains a political message or if it exchanges Chekhovian characterization for a particular view of Trinidadians or if the play has a quick pace, does it break any unwritten rules? The fact that some critics have lambasted Matura for his changes, though he openly acknowledges that his play is an adaptation, relates to what Linda Hutcheon sees as "the implied assumption that adapters aim simply to reproduce the adapted text" (7). As a long-standing fixture of the British theatre community, Matura has his own concerns that do not reflect a Chekhovian agenda of inertia, time, and (lack of) fulfillment. He uses the template of *Three Sisters* to further explore his favorite themes of Caribbean identities. He does hold to the general structure and character interactions in the play, but in the end, audience/scholar reception unfairly overshadows the interesting intersections between Chekhov and Matura. Pushing past the questions of "fidelity discourse," Matura's play moves Chekhov's work, and his own work for that matter, into a new context. By

164 *Victoria Pettersen Lantz*

offering an altered version of Chekhov, Matura invites the assessment that his play is *not* Chekhov's play.

The general view of critics is that Matura's adaptation is not an improvement over *Three Sisters*. Matura never set out to improve Chekhov nor does he make any claims to be a Chekhovian writer, yet critics continually point to the fact that the play is different, and not better, than the original. Nonetheless, critics hold his play next to Chekhov's and remark that Matura relocates, reworks, translates, assaults, and even amputates Chekhov, but above all else, his play is "not a match for the original" (Grimley 11). The characterization of what Matura's play does to Chekhov's work, and, moreover, what it cannot do in comparison to Chekhov's, overshadows the ultimate purpose of adaptation. Hutcheon reminds us that adaptation is "a derivation that is not derivative—a work that is second without being secondary" (9). Matura's play is its own creative endeavor, as well as an interpretive exploration of Chekhov's *Three Sisters*. In the context of Matura's colonial upbringing and post-colonial writing, adaptation is, for him, also an inherently political act. The adaptation, and producing the adaptation, encourages audiences to consider the complex concern of cultural ownership in a post-colonial society.

The struggle to digest imposed cultural hierarchies and attempt to dismantle them is at the heart of post-colonial adaptation, which is also a means of discussing adoption as much as it is a form of adaptation. At first glance, the process of adapting Western literature is a logical step for artists who have received a Westernized education. After all, as Said explains, "like people and schools of criticism, ideas and theories travel—from person to person, from situation to situation, from one period to another" ("Traveling Theory" 195). Great European writing travels in part because intellectuals translate and transfer to others the powerful ideas, images, and themes they find in such works. As an artistic pursuit, the act of rewriting is a means through which a writer can encourage certain ideas to travel, and there is a wealth of adaptations and parallels that carry canonic works forward.[3] Adaptation promotes the travel of ideas in the sense of intellectual exchange, but the genre also includes overt political co-opting of Western writing, which shifts literary focus onto the nature of how art informs cultural hierarchy. "Counter-discourse" (or "counter-canon" or "oppositional literature") is a term representing a subgenre of post-colonial literature that is subject to a growing area of academic study, as scholars work to discern the combative, creative, and/or collaborative nature of post-colonial adaptation. Such work is combative in the sense that colonized writers seek to challenge the conventional preference for Eurocentric texts, instilled through institutional education. Helen Tiffin, in "Post-Colonial Literatures and Counter-Discourse," illustrates the strategy as the process in which "a post-colonial writer takes up a character or characters, or the basic assumptions of a British canonical text, and unveils those assumptions, subverting the text for post-colonial purposes" (100). She makes a point to highlight the constructive side of the counter-canon, or at least the inevitability of the genre. Colonization is forever imprinted on non-Western colonized cultures, and however much writers and activists wish to reject their colonial past, they cannot realistically move forward without accepting colonization's place in their collective history.

Colonialism, and the promotion of a European education/culture, resulted in a kind of forced adoption of Western culture among the colonies. Colonial subjects face an institutional insistence that European traditions, from language to art to economics, are universally correct and more important, while native traditions are wrong/bad. Artists through the colonies push against their forced cultural adoption with their counter-discursive adaptations. Writers like George Lamming or Samuel Selvon engage with canonic texts in an oppositional way, challenging the assumptions of Western, colonizer culture. Post-colonial artists use adaptation to challenge the discriminatory assumptions embedded in Western texts and the literary and cultural hierarchies the canon upholds. Post-colonial writers undercut the strict adherence to Western hierarchies—based in hegemonic morals—through their re-creations, which champion a plurality of worldviews. Iconic colonial representation of cross-cultural encounters within the English canon, such as Shakespeare's *The Tempest* and Defoe's *Robinson Crusoe*,[4] promote strong colonial idealism, and therefore we find many post-colonial writers frequently recasting pro-colonial, pro-Britain texts. In doing so, these writers are not so much writing back as they are writing forward, and what appears as a hostile literature is actually constructive writing.

Post-colonial adaptations are a means through which citizens negotiate the trauma of institutional colonialism and challenge the widespread acceptance of colonialist literature as a fair or authentic representation of non-white societies. Some of the most influential post-colonial authors and playwrights have engaged in rewriting during their careers. Artists like Wole Soyinka, Femi Osofisan, Aimé Césaire, J. M. Coetzee, Jean Rhys, Derek Walcott, and Matura rework literature from the West to challenge the globalization of Western assumptions. While we may know such artists best for literature that is thematically and stylistically non-Western, their adaptations point to the importance of counter-discursive tactics in post-colonial literature. As a constructive act, counter-canonic literature prioritizes the needs of the post-colonial subject over those of the former colonizer, though it may appear that these artists are focused entirely back on the empire. The process of rewriting is a complex strategy of communal and self-definition that accounts for the "post" in post-colonial. According to Said, "insofar as these [migratory] people exist between the old and new, between the old empire and the new state, their condition articulates the tensions, irresolutions, and contradictions in the overlapping territories shown on the cultural map of imperialism" (*Culture* 332). Post-colonial subjects cannot ignore the colonial experience any more than they can

166 *Victoria Pettersen Lantz*

return to a society built on precolonial traditions, and therefore they construct identities that represent traditions, colonial conflicts, and modern sociopolitical conditions.

Of course, *Three Sisters: After Chekhov* does not fit naturally into the counter-discourse genre, at least when we consider the source material. Even *Playboy of the West Indies* relates Trinidad to colonial source material in terms of pro-Irish, anti-English theatre movements. Chekhov does not come to mind among colonial writers like Defoe and Kipling or anti-imperialists like Yeats, so his work does not lend itself to post-colonial adaptation at first glance. Chekhov, in his personal life and letters, did offer his opinion on British colonization, an opinion that reflected a typical European attitude toward colonialism. In a letter about his brief stops in 1890 in China and Ceylon, he wrote, "I listened to my Russian fellow travellers upbraiding the English for their exploitation of the natives. Yes, thought I, the Englishman exploits Chinese, Sepoys, Hindus, but he gives them roads, aqueducts, museums, Christianity; you too exploit but what do you give?" (qtd. in Borny 44). Here Chekhov implies that any exploitation is a fair trade for what he sees as institutional improvements over native cultures. This personal anecdote contextualizes Chekhov for us into the collective colonial mind-set at the end of the nineteenth century.

Chekhov's reflection on British colonialism is a direct critique of Russia's policies toward its people and regions, which is in part a condemnation of the colonial practices of Imperial Russia. During the nineteenth century, Russian expansion aligned ideologically and practically with the colonial practices of much of Europe. Richard Charques opens *The Twilight of Imperial Russia* with a summation of the geographical power of the country: "From the Arctic circle to the Black Sea, from the Baltic and the Carpathians to the Pacific and the borders of China and India, it covered eight and a half million square miles. It was an empire won for the most part in peace by centuries of migration [. . .] though always in the last resort the advancing frontier had been secured by war" (11). The empire, though comprising more than eighty nationalities and languages and covering a vast geographical space, functioned from central institutions of government and culture. Russia's governmental bodies would move large peasant and criminal populations in order to secure land and political power against the "Yellow Peril." The racist and xenophobic tendency to colonize Asian regions, the forced migration of Russian imperial communities to secure Eastern lands, and the overwhelming sense of cultural ownership over its dominion established Imperial Russia as a colonial stronghold of the East. Perhaps the most disconcerting aspect of Russian imperialism is the aspect that concerns Chekhov the most: the "peasant question" and the complacency of Russian urban citizens. In the face of rising provincial populations detached from metropolises, the extremely poor agrarians of the empire were growing increasingly hostile to the stagnant, better-off populations. Chekhov focuses much of his writing on the static nature of Russian life in

What Comes "After Chekhov"? 167

order to highlight the very real socioeconomic tension sweeping the empire. In this sense, Chekhov uses his personal narratives of his time in Sakhalin and his characterization of social stagnation (both to which I will return) to lambaste Russian imperial policies.

Chekhov, therefore, finds a home, albeit an odd home, in post-colonial theatre. I say odd because when we consider his agenda and aims, Chekhov's writing already fits the anticolonial politics of so many post-colonial plays (though his plays are generally less politically overt than his personal writing). Yet Chekhov's plays were absorbed into the very Western institutions he claims benefit non-European cultures. By the time Matura developed a sense of his own counter-discourse, Chekhov was established alongside playwrights like Shakespeare and Shaw as a definitive example of European art. Regardless of the message of his work, Chekhov fit comfortably into British colonial institutions. Matura's relationship to the original *Three Sisters* is more complex than his claim to "the universality of a Russian play" or the fact that Chekhov's work found a place in colonial education. His counter-discursive efforts relate more to the relationship between Britain and the Caribbean and how Trinidad copes with its colonial/postcolonial identity. One of the fundamental aspects of post-colonial Caribbean culture is the multidimensional, multiracial identities of the people, a central theme in Matura's immigrant theatre. For his part, Matura considers the multicultural narrative of Trinidad—which developed in large part through the influx of African slaves, British landowners and civil servants, Portuguese traders, and South Asian servants—from the perspective of an immigrant. He transplants the multicultural aspects of the Caribbean onto stages in Britain and presents these multiple perspectives to audiences of both British-born and immigrant citizens.

The levels of cultural interplay in his plays, and in the makeup of his audiences, relates to Helen Gilbert and Jacqueline Lo's attempts to chart the movements in cross-cultural theatre. In their article, "Toward a Topography of Cross-Cultural Theatre Praxis," Gilbert and Lo posit a theatre form directly relating to the effort of immigrant artists, such as Matura:

> *Migrant theatre* is centrally concerned with narratives of migration and adaptation, often using a combination of ethno-specific language to denote cultural in-between-ness. Cross-cultural negotiation is more visible in migrant theatre where there is an emerging exploration of cultural hybridity reflected in aesthetic form as well as narrative content. (34)

Caribbean immigrant theatre, of which Matura is a central figure in the UK, relies heavily on the exploration of language and geographical movement. Adaptation, when it occurs in cross-cultural exchanges between Indo-Caribbean, Afro-Caribbean, and Euro-American people, allows for an artistic assessment of the inherent multicultural narrative that immigration

168 *Victoria Pettersen Lantz*

encourages. Gilbert and Lo's insistence that immigrant theatre is an exploration of cultural hybridity reveals the reasons why Matura adapts Chekhov. The ambiguity with which Chekhov imbues his characters offers a point from which Matura can work on his own exploration of nebulous Caribbean identities. Chekhov's work becomes a vehicle through which Matura can attempt to negotiate intersections between cultures.

Though Gilbert and Lo imply a categorization of the subsets of cross-cultural theatre, Matura's adaptation crosses the boundaries the authors set out in the article. The play also falls into what they call the "syncretic" post-colonial theatre, where "performance elements of different cultures [integrate] into a form that aims to retain the cultural integrity of the specific materials used while forging new texts [. . .] syncretic theatre generally involves the incorporation of indigenous materials into a Western dramaturgical framework" (36). Post-colonial syncretic theatre carries with it the political ramifications of post-colonial counter-discourse literature in its aim to dismantle the privilege of Western art over non-Western artistic traditions. As much as Matura's adaptation is an investigation into the cultural intersections of Caribbean immigrants with Europeans, we can also read the play as interplay between Caribbean cultural practices within a Chekhovian structure of European realism. In many of his plays, Matura pushes his work towards the surreal, with the inclusion of ghosts, nonlinear storytelling, and transhistorical narratives. *Three Sisters: After Chekhov* holds to the domestic family drama storyline of the original, but incorporates into the adaptation traditional Trinidadian themes of Carnival, Creole, and traditional racial hierarchies/prejudices. In keeping with the realism of the story, Matura highlights the importance of Chekhovian methods in developing characters, Russian or Trinidadian. In an equally migrant and syncretic move, Matura tries to both assess Caribbean cultural hybridity and disrupt the authority of Western texts, and his adaptation more comfortably resides in a category Gilbert and Lo do not consider, a diasporic cross-cultural theatre.

In the epigraph of this chapter, Matura's statement is in many ways a diasporic approach to the art of adaptation. The diasporic individual is more comfortable (or at least more familiar) with shifting contexts, with transplantations, and so on, from his or her own experiences. For the diasporic author, the idea of transplanting the structure/frame/plot of a particular work into a different context is perfectly natural. We can see Matura's adaptations as an artistic example of the sort of negotiations that the diasporic individual undergoes culturally: the self in constant motion. He considers the work of Chekhov, in this instance, through literal and figurative movement. Following his assertion that adaptation is based in a study of the "travels" undertaken by authors in their writing, the original work functions as a map of multiple experiences, a flexibility that post-colonial or migrant writers find attractive. Matura uses difference, or at least elasticity, to explore the potential for collective understanding among

What Comes "After Chekhov"? 169

seemingly opposed communities. In doing so, he does not transform Chekhovian meaning and themes, but rather adds post-colonial dimensions to the original play.

Matura uses the sisters and the setting in *Three Sisters: After Chekhov* to illustrate Trinidadian concerns, a focus of many of his plays. These concerns are in part born from colonial oppression, but the play is also a reiteration of the multicultural tensions of Trinidad. Chekhov, in his letter about traveling to Asian colonies, uses his assessment of Britain's relationship with colonized subjects to critique the treatment of citizens in Russia. He turns what we could now call a global crisis, the dismantlement of non-Western cultures, into a frame for judging his own community. In its treatment of the mass of poor, or what we might call the mishandling of "the peasant question," Russia stands alongside the imperial powers of nineteenth-century Europe, reflecting similar attitudes of cultural supremacy and "what's yours is mine, but what's mine is not yours," and it is this attitude that Chekhov finds most egregious in his assessment of Russia at the end of the nineteenth century.

Chekhov's travels took him to the Russian penal colony on Sakhalin, an island north of Japan that Russia shared with the Japanese. Having spent three months working with and studying the people of Sakhalin, he wrote prolifically and profoundly on the problems of Russian colonialism, including his account, *The Island: A Journey to Sakhalin.*[5] Specifically, he emphasized that the Russian government neglected and mistreated its penal settlements. He states in no uncertain terms that the colony functions not like a prison, but a hell: "Sakhalin is a place of unbearable suffering, the sort of suffering only man, whether free or subjugated, is capable of" (qtd. in Karlinsky and Heim 159). What is more important about Chekhov's assessment of Sakhalin is where he lays the blame for the horrible lives of the prisoners. He does not blame the prisoners or the wardens, but the Russian people collectively, including himself, for the traumas on Sakhalin. In a letter to Alexey Suvorin, Chekhov illustrates the complacency of Russians as the root cause:

> We have let *millions* of people rot in jails, we have let them rot to no purpose, unthinkingly and barbarously. We have driven people through the cold, in chains [. . .] we have infected them with syphilis, debauched them, bred criminals [. . .] Now all educated Europe knows that all of us, not the wardens, are to blame, but it's still none of our business; it's of no interest to us. (qtd. in Karlinsky and Heim 160)

The repetition of "we" and "us" is an indictment of all Russian people, and represents what Chekhov sees as the need to take responsibility for the poor populations throughout the empire. The most poignant point in Chekhov's lecture is the sardonic comments at the end, in which he clearly indicates that he believes the upper and middle classes lack the capacity to care. His personal

170   *Victoria Pettersen Lantz*

writing, as much as his plays, serves as both a critique of and guidepost for Russian society to reconsider its disconnect from the growing troubles among Russia's peripheral (and poor) populations. In essence, Matura performs a similar ideological relocation in his adaptation through the setting of the play. He turns the global crisis of World War II into an assessment of the racial and political tensions in colonial Trinidad. The idea of a warm Caribbean island working as a U.S. and British naval base in the midst of World War II sounds far afield from provincial Russia, but in his setting, Matura exaggerates many of the tensions at work in Chekhov's play, particularly the tension between the static wealthy and the politically motivated poor.

From the moment his play begins, it seems that Matura has a different agenda than Chekhov, or at least that he is striving for a decidedly un-Chekhovian tone. The stateliness of the Prozorov home in *Three Sisters*, complete with pillars and multiple rooms, becomes a middle-class Caribbean front room, with large windows and Spanish guitar music in the background. Chekhov's oldest sister, twenty-eight-year-old Olga, opens the play with: "It is just a year since Father died, on this very day" (117). Forty-year-old Alma, Matura's oldest sister, offers these opening lines: "Audrey, you don't think I overdid it with the lipstick, do you?" (17). The tenors of the two plays appear not to relate: Chekhov shrouds his play in mourning and thoughts of death from the beginning, while Matura hints at the humorous normalcy of the quotidian, even while the sisters mourn their father. *Three Sisters* spans four years, as compared to the six months of Matura's play. Analogues for nanny or Dr. Chebutykin, along with a few other secondary characters, are absent in *Three Sisters: After Chekhov*. However, Matura, despite the tonal and structural difference of his play, is not playing against Chekhov's aims in his adaptation. If, as many scholars have argued, Chekhov's play at its core addresses delusions about future hopes and the ambiguity of present reality, then Matura uses his changes to highlight overtly the delusions and inertia of the sisters, as well as question the possibility of a happy post-colonial future for Trinidad.

Place plays a vital role in *Three Sisters*. Chekhov locates sisters Olga, Masha, and Irina in a "provincial capital" many miles from Moscow (116). The locale offers up the natural beauty of rivers and forests and is situated away from a train station. But for Chekhov's sisters the serenity of the place is a torment, as the agrarian setting reminds them of their distance from Moscow. Longing to be back in their birth-city, the sisters find provincial life isolating and static. Their romantic idea of living in Moscow heightens as the years unfold with the same monotony. Matura, in setting the sisters in Trinidad's (small) metropolis of Port of Spain, pushes the dreams of relocation into the realm of unattainability. Alma, Helen, and Audrey talk only of returning to Cambridge, England, though this desire comes out of a three-month stay during their youth, whereas Chekhov's sisters have a deep, concrete relationship with Moscow, as it is the place their mother is buried and where they were born and lived for some time.

Matura translates the tangibility of a Moscow connection into a feeble, vague memory of a summer in the university town. Audrey, Irina's counterpart, goes so far as to stake claim to the city, calling it "our Cambridge" (44). Chekhov's use of place as a means of stifling the sisters into stagnation at least hinges on a real association with Moscow. The sisters have a birthright to their relationship to the city, making the fact that they do not go back a constant dull ache in their lives. Matura strips his sisters of the birth connection to England. The fact that they were not born in England, and in fact only visited the country for three months, trivializes and makes ridiculous their ever-present longing to return to Cambridge. Matura recognizes Chekhov's theme of self-delusion over going to Moscow and explodes it to the scale of a completely unrealistic sentiment of finding some sort of home in a distant country. This delusional attachment to a distant place present in the Chekhovian original is the vehicle through which Matura uses adaptation to address his post-colonial, diasporic concerns. The sisters' longing becomes his critique of the attachment that assimilated colonial subjects feel for the imperial "homeland."

Matura amplifies the relationship of the sisters to England to highlight the tenuous relationship between a xenophobic colonizing nation and its nonwhite colonized citizens. The black sisters' longing for Cambridge is, for Matura, born out of a misplaced allegiance to a country that wants to colonize them, not accept them. The tension between homeland and Motherland that Matura outlines in the play comes in part from his experiences as an expatriate writer, but, more important to the issues of adaptation, also comes out of the model Chekhov sets forth. In his discussion of Matura's adaptations, Tobias Döring reminds readers that *Three Sisters* "focus[es] on the backstage rather than the centre" (82). The peripheral space Chekhov creates in the play highlights the tension between the cultural capital and the provinces. Though the sisters are harshly critical of their provincial surroundings, Chekhov is less so, and whereas his sisters see "provincial" as the unsophisticated, the playwright himself views "provincial" as the local or the everyday. He explores the disconnect between living on the periphery and living in a cultural center, and in this exploration, he emphasizes that it is the tension between living provincially while longing for the metropolis that creates inertia (not the provincial life itself). The sisters, who, according to Jovan Hristić, "corrupt everything around them by dint of thinking themselves superior," view their provinciality as vulgar (qtd. in Senelick, "Introduction" 58). However, borrowing from Derek Walcott, there is a "healthy vulgarity of living in a backward [. . .] place" (qtd. in MacDonald-Smythe 89). Walcott continually works to de-vilify provincialism, and for him, writing about local Caribbean concerns iterates the possibility that the (colonial) metropolis is not the cultural center. Chekhov illustrates the provincial to remind Russia that provincial, local, peasant problems must be addressed. Walcott and Matura highlight the provincial not as part of the empire, but as cultural centers in their own right.

172 *Victoria Pettersen Lantz*

The emphasis on Trinidad, or the Caribbean in general, as a locale functions on a practical level in *Three Sisters: After Chekhov* because the actual physical distance between Port of Spain and Cambridge is much further and harder to traverse than a Russian provincial capital's separation from Moscow. Matura places an ocean and a world war between the sisters' reality in Port of Spain and their dreams of going to Cambridge. In terms of post-colonial adaptation, the authorial decision to move the action to the colonial islands emphasizes a dislocation of colonial power, something not necessary at odds with Chekhov's use of the provincial setting. In their extensive discussion of multiple forms of post-colonial rewriting, Helen Gilbert and Joanne Tompkins explain, "there are, as well, many plays that rework texts which are already counter-discursive," and they offer the examples of these plays, which tend to explore "dislocation and placelessness" (47). They use Matura's *Playboy of the West Indies* as an example, but we can draw a line to his adaptation of Chekhov as well. Both *Three Sisters* and *Three Sisters: After Chekhov*, through their settings, deconstruct the center. By highlighting seemingly peripheral worlds, the playwrights indicate through setting that the mood of placelessness is in essence a colonized mind-set. Chekhov's dislocation of the sisters from a cultural center allows the characters to create, however disdainfully, a new center within the provincial to cope with their placelessness. For Matura's part, he extends the idea of the provincial into a doubly peripheral adaptation and works to both explore the themes of placelessness among the colonized characters as well as more broadly dislocate the imperial power of Chekhov's text itself. However, as Döring explains, Matura's adaptations are "amplified and overwritten with colonial meaning," and the playwright's exploration of the sisters' relationship to Cambridge highlights his own colonial concerns outside Chekhov's scope (82).

Matura's sisters, still "thinking themselves superior," struggle to fully realize their placelessness and Englishness (which they long for) because of their internal conflict between their race and their ideal homeland. Matura summarizes their personas into another microcosmic assessment of colonial relations, in this instance, racial assumptions and historical tensions. The sisters are middle-class black Trinidadians who have fallen in love with the idea of England. They are unwilling to accept that part of their experience in Cambridge was based entirely on the spectacle of their skin color. When asked by an Englishman if they caused a stir in Cambridge, Audrey excitedly answers, "Yes we did, the newspaper even took our photograph" (26). The implication of the conversation (which Audrey misses) is that the women were black, a novelty in Cambridge in the 1930s. Whether students were kind or welcoming is irrelevant; the amount of attention they drew from the public, including the newspapers, reflects an exoticization of the sisters by the English population. Cambridge citizens were not interested in three intelligent young ladies; they were fascinated that three black girls were intelligent young ladies. Chekhov's Moscow highlights the tensions

What Comes "After Chekhov"? 173

between a happy past, a hopeful future (for Irina at least), and the monotonous present. Matura alters that more existential tension in his reimagining of Moscow to Cambridge and focuses on a specific friction that colonial race relations invoke.

Early in the play, *Three Sisters: After Chekhov* addresses the issue of interracial relationships and contextualizes miscegenation in the Caribbean experience. Alma, Helen, and Audrey Rivers see themselves as more English than Afro-Caribbean in terms of their upbringing, citing their stay in Cambridge as young women as evidence. When a white English officer, Richard Rivers (Matura's version of Vershinin), enters their social circle the sisters are forced to consider the true nature of any English heritage. The discovery that Richard and the sisters share a surname leads the naive Audrey to question the possibility of a familial connection:

> AUDREY. Do you think we might be related? That would be so exciting.
> RICHARD. Well, I really don't know, when I heard about it, I began thinking of family stories I heard as a boy. There was one rascal who came to the West Indies to make his fortune, but nothing more. I remember coming across a portrait in the attic, of a Ship's Captain, standing against a tropical landscape with a Plantation in the background, and a native female sitting at his feet, never thought of it. (25)

Richard indulges Audrey's enthusiasm over their possible family connections, but he does so in a way that relegates any racial mixing to the most distant, roguish members of his ancestry. The prospect of a family connection would, in Richard's estimation, be the bastardized progeny of a rejected part of his white family. Even then, the painting he describes places his ancestor in a position of power in the colonial socioeconomic dynamic. He is not maliciously racist in his discussion of a possible West Indian family, yet he openly speaks to the Afro-Caribbean sisters from the viewpoint of their ancestral oppressors. As an upper-class Englishman, he sees an exoticism in the colonial history of conquering lands as well as in the possession of foreign women.

This discussion of racial mixing foreshadows the extramarital affair between Richard and Helen. Though the affair is based in a mutual unhappiness in their marriages, it echoes their colonial ancestries. Richard entertains a fantasy of colonial exoticism, with Helen in the role of the subjected black woman, while Helen romanticizes that through love she can raise herself to the level of a proper British woman. Their relationship lacks any likely future outside of the confines of Trinidad, especially in colonial Britain, and is therefore reduced to a modern colonial revision of past interracial relationships. Their love affair grows less out of mutual unhappiness or mutual love and more from Helen's rejection of her racial Caribbean characteristics and a delusion of social whiteness.

174 *Victoria Pettersen Lantz*

Alma, Helen, and Audrey, taught by their father to idealize English-ness, reject the premise of "regular" Trinidadians encroaching on their social stratum. Their relationship with their sister-in-law, Jean (Matura's Natasha), epitomizes their exclusivity and the power that language has to both reflect and shift social status. On the surface, the relationship between Matura's sisters and Jean closely parallels how Chekhov relates his sisters to Natasha. If, as Geoffrey Borny suggests, "the three sisters become syn-onymous with 'culture' and Natasha with 'vulgarity,'" then Matura trans-ports that dichotomy directly into his adaptation (207). Alma, Helen, and Audrey focus their energy on appearing culturally elite, which in essence translates to acting European. Jean, for her part, is subject to the sisters' criticisms of her personality, her dress, and the company she keeps, much like Natasha. While some critics lambaste Natasha as a villain, Chekhov paints his sisters as judgmental and superior in regard to their sister-in-law, illustrating tensions between socioeconomic classes.

No moment more poignantly highlights Natasha's vulgarity, in the eyes of the sisters, than her butchering of the French language. Matura does not create in Jean such an overt, and comic, longing for social betterment. But he does, like Chekhov, use language to craft his own, different critique of society and class. Through Jean's language choices, he maneuvers Chekhov's general confrontations between classes into an examination of how colonial-ism informs social mobility. A master wordsmith, Matura is perhaps most skilled at using language to represent the voices of Black Britain, Indo-Trin-idad, Afro-Trinidad, and at times white-Trinidad. Beginning with *As Time Goes By*, in which he explores the multivoiced soundscape of a transnational Britain, he has emphasized Anglo-Creole as a means of vocalizing post-colo-nial identity. It is his play with language that scholars and critics find most intriguing about his adaptation of Synge, and Gilbert and Tompkins note, "Matura's version takes Synge's interest in the metaphoric richness of the local dialect one step further" (48). I would say that as a Trinidadian, Matura is utilizing his personal colonial narrative to translate more authenticity into Synge's play (as Synge was not a man from Mayo). The question of language is vital to any discussion of post-colonial counter-discourse, as the question of native languages is primary to any study of post-colonial literature.

Gilbert and Tompkins offer a clear explanation of the power language holds in reference to post-colonial power restructuring:

> Post-colonial stages are particularly resonant spaces from which to artic-ulate linguistic resistance to imperialism. [. . .] The mistaken assump-tion that the heightened language of, for instance, Shakespeare's plays was most suitable as a theatrical language frequently prevented colonised subjects, whose facility with the coloniser's language was never "good enough," from being able to theatricalise anything but a "pale" imitation of European classics. [. . .] post-colonial playwrights have concentrated on speaking in voices less inflected by imperialism. (166)

What Comes "After Chekhov"? 175

Matura, with Anglophone languages as his base, follows in the trend of writing to dismantle imperial language assumptions. In many post-colonial adaptations, including *Playboy of the West Indies*, transforming the language, whether through dialect or translation, the post-colonial writer decenters the linguistic power of European classics. This decentering is often vital to emphasize anticolonial sentiment, but in *Three Sisters: After Chekhov*, Matura does not necessarily decenter the language. Rather, he uses the sisters' disdain for Jean's "vulgarity" in her use of Creole to offer a narrative critique of the colonial dismantling of language traditions in the Caribbean (internally and externally).

His language choices are at first glance at odds with the linguistic aims of his writing and with Chekhov's *Three Sisters*, which is, according to Trevor Nunn, "a play of heightened language" (103). Following this line of thinking, the play falls into Gilbert and Tompkins' "unattainable" plays for colonized citizens. However, Chekhov's careful, slow, and muted language offers Matura the opportunity to adopt Chekhovian dialect and create a political point with his language choices. In breaking from his tradition of painting a multivoiced soundscape and relying on his source material for linguistic guidance, Matura shares with audiences the tension of race and class in colonial Trinidad. In the play, the sisters have cultivated a refined level of communication divergent from typical Trinidadian dialect. After Cambridge, the women are determined to represent proper Englishness for Port of Spain society. Their emphasis on accurate use of the English language and appropriate manners places the sisters in a position of both admiration and admonishment among the general black population, a category that Jean represents.

The sisters' idealization of English culture and language is linked to their colonial education but also, more importantly, to their (cultural) wealth. While other characters absorbed, along with their institutional language education, the linguistic Creole most often associated with the speech patterns of Afro-Caribbean culture, the sisters promote an imperial language and cultural hierarchy. They have extracted any sense of Caribbean rhythms, syllables, and tones from their mode of speaking and instead mimic an English patrician lexicon. This act of upholding an imported language repositions the sisters outside the society of Trinidad, though they are stuck on the island. The sisters, not quite Caribbean and not quite English, are left with their rigid standards of colonialism and an inability to connect with their Afro-Caribbean peers. They are left to conversion as a means of coping with their non-English/English identities, and their sister-in-law becomes a candidate for such transformation.

The first time we see Jean, she appears as an obvious contradiction that foils the assumed social respectability of the sisters. To them, her bright dresses emphasize her poor language and manners. In a scene similar to the one between Audrey and her sisters, Jean joins the sisters as she presents Audrey with a birthday gift. She does not sound like Helen or Alma, however. As she enters, she exclaims, "Oh, Audrey, Happy Birthday child, here a brought yer a little some-ting" (34). Jean is the first character we encounter with an overt Trinidadian accent, and her language comes as a stark contrast to that of the sisters. This accent serves as a constant reminder to the sisters that they are not in England, and though they surround themselves in as much Englishness as they can, Jean's entire persona, from her clothing to her Creole, emphasizes the Afro-Caribbean roots the sisters attempt to deny. Matura, in a reflection of Gilbert and Lo's migrant theatre, uses "ethno-specific language" to explore the linguistic markings of cultural inbetweenness—in this instance, between colonial Englishness and Afro-Caribbeanness (Gilbert and Lo 34).

For many scholars and artists, Creole is not just a representation of cultural inbetweenness. Jean speaks in what Edward Kamau Brathwaite classifies as the Caribbean's national language, which is strongly influenced by African traditions. Brathwaite explains how speaking in accented English constitutes a different language when he states, "English it may be in terms of some of its lexical features. But in its contours, its rhythm and timbre, its sound explosions, it is not English, even though the words, as you hear them, might be English to a greater or lesser degree" (282). This Caribbean, Creole language, based in English structures and African characters, is what the Trinidadians in the play grew up hearing and speaking. Jean, more than any other character, promotes a tradition of linguistic post-colonial representation by speaking in a distinctly Trinidadian style. However, in the colonial context of *Three Sisters: After Chekhov*, the power of a national Caribbean language is a disadvantage for Jean's domestic agenda (i.e., marrying their brother, Peter Rivers). The fact that Matura uses language as a hindrance in this instance reinforces the social pressure colonialism places on citizens. If the colonized subject wishes to improve his/her social position, adopting European culture and language becomes fundamental to any "betterment."

In the use of subtle language, and Jean's not-so-subtle linguistic transformation, Matura offers audiences a retelling of muted colonial conflict, and muted conflict is certainly key to Chekhovian theatre. World War II becomes the background, and the minor struggles of everyday cultural supremacy dictate the lives of the characters. In adapting Chekhov's play, Matura found a vehicle for his subtle indictment of colonial cultural hegemonies. Producing *Three Sisters: After Chekhov* offers Matura, along with actors and directors, a way to ask audiences to adopt more critical views about the markers of cultural hierarchies. Senelick offers a reductive and problematic assessment of the benefits of Matura's adaptation by insisting that the playwright takes part of "the English collective unconscious" and "introduced [it to] a minority public" (*Chekhov Theatre* 322). As stated earlier, Chekhov is not only part of English collective culture, but by extension part of the colonial mechanism for establishing cultural hierarchies. The idea that minority audiences, in England in particular, are unfamiliar with Chekhov is presumptive in general and dismissive of Matura's objective. Nonwhite populations in England are primarily first-, second-, and now third-generation immigrants from former colonies, having either a colonial or English education, in which Chekhov is included. Implying that minority communities have no experience with or interest in Chekhov undercuts the cultural intelligence of these communities and ignores the nature of English education. Producing a play like *Three Sisters: After Chekhov* is *not* about introducing black audiences to Chekhov, but rather is a natural outlet for a post-colonial writer interested in counter-discourse.

The racial makeup of the audiences will inevitably affect reception, and, as Hutcheon insists, reception "is just as important as the context of creation when it comes to adaptation" (149). Perhaps a more useful way to discuss reception and levels of understanding is to consider how audiences use "memory in order to experience difference as well as similarity" (Hutcheon 22). With *Three Sisters: After Chekhov*, knowing *Three Sisters* informs the audience's reading of the play, not in terms of how successfully it manages to copy the original, but in terms of how Matura transitions the themes to the Caribbean. The audiences absorb moving from the cold of rural Russia to the oppressive heat of the Caribbean and watch as the sisters still struggle with love and despair. Audiences familiar with Chekhov perhaps cannot help considering how well Matura reproduces Chekhov. At the same time, they also see colonial Trinidad through a Chekhovian frame, something many audiences are unfamiliar with, blending the known with the unknown. In this sense, the adaptation places ideas of race relations and social hierarchies into the lives of the sisters, allowing Chekhovian audiences to experience difference (the unknown) with similarity (the known). Chekhovian and non-Chekhovian audiences alike can still use memory to experience similarity and difference in the play. Returning to Said's assertion that ideas travel, *Three Sisters: After Chekhov* is an investigation into the negotiation of just how "English" colonial subjects are, but it also is a post-colonial export. The play and post-colonial adaptations in general shift the focus of theatrical representation from old colonial ideals to cross-cultural experiences. The appeal of adapting Western works is that the adaptation attracts certain homogeneous communities because of the assumed communal recognition of storylines, characters, and themes. However, in opening themselves up to this form of counter-discourse, these communities expose themselves to moments of cultural hybridity.

NOTES

1. Matura wrote an earlier version of the play, titled *Trinidad Sisters*, in 1988. He was commissioned to rework the play for the Eclipse Theatre in 2006 and gave the play a major rewrite. Given the revisions, and that the latter version is the only one published, I refer to it as *Three Sisters: After Chekhov*.

178   *Victoria Pettersen Lantz*

2. Of this adaptation, Matura says he was too reverential to Chekhov and that he wanted to readapt it with less focus on paying homage to Chekhov.
3. Though we could say that rewriting the canon is a political act, there are many examples of works that are more artistically than politically bent, especially those of Western writers working from the Western canon. Adaptations like the multiple variations of the *Faustus* folktale and the Electra plays, *East of Eden*, and *Pygmalion* all respond to as well as reflect Euro-American cultural literary traditions (especially when we consider the Bible as literature). Parallel writing from contemporary Western artists serves the same "style over politics" aim, as exemplified in work such as the novels of Joan Aiken, Lewis's *Till We Have Faces*, and Stoppard's *Rosencrantz and Guildenstern Are Dead*.
4. Caribbean writers find these texts in particular offensive to their cultural identity, and therefore many contemporary Caribbean artists offer differing versions of *The Tempest* and *Robinson Crusoe*. Other English works that criticize the Caribbean from the safety of an English landscape, such as *Jane Eyre* and *Mansfield Park*, also find alternatives in the counter-canon.
5. In his book, Chekhov provided insight into island life not previously explored, particularly the position of women as prostitutes/concubines. One area of study offers an important relationship with any study of the colonial Caribbean, in that Chekhov discusses the genocide of Sakhalin's native population. In what Simon Karlinsky calls "the most harrowing passages" of the book, Chekhov accounts for the colonial treatment of the indigenous populations, "leading to the extermination of these peoples" (Karlinsky and Heim 154). The widespread destruction of indigenous Caribbean populations by European settlers is well documented, whereas the destruction of Sakhalin's populations is not.

WORKS CITED

Austen, Jane. *Mansfield Park*. Oxford: Oxford UP, 1970. Print.
Borny, Geoffrey. *Interpreting Chekhov*. Canberra: Australian National UP, 2006. Web. 17 Dec. 2011.
Brathwaite, Edward Kamau. "Nation Language." *The Post-Colonial Studies Reader*. 2nd ed. Ed. Bill Ashcroft, Gareth Griffiths, and Helen Tiffin. London: Routledge, 2006. 281–84. Print.
Brontë, Charlotte. *Jane Eyre: Critical Edition*. Ed. Richard J. Dunn. New York: Norton, 2000. Print.
Charques, Richard. *The Twilight of Imperial Russia*. Fair Lawn: Essential Books, 1959. Print.
Chekhov, Anton. *The Island: A Journey to Sakhalin*. Trans. Luba and Michael Terpak. New York: Washington Square Press, 1967. Print.
———. *The Three Sisters. Four Plays*. Trans. David Magarshack. New York: Hill and Wang, 1969. 115–86. Print.
Defoe, Daniel. *Robinson Crusoe: Critical Edition*. Ed. Michael Shinagel. 2nd Ed. New York: Norton, 1994. Print.
Döring, Tobias. "Dislocating Stages: Mustapha Matura's Caribbean Rewriting of Synge and Chekhov." *European Journal of English Studies* 2.1 (1998): 78–93. Print.
Gilbert, Helen, and Jacqueline Lo. "Toward a Topography of Cross-Cultural Theatre Praxis." *TDR* 46.3 (2002): 31–53. Print.

What Comes "After Chekhov"? 179

Gilbert, Helen, and Joanne Tompkins. *Post-Colonial Drama: Theory, Practice, Politics*. London: Routledge, 1996. Print.

Grimley, Terry. "Culture: All Signs of Life Are Lost in Translation." Rev. of *Three Sisters: After Chekhov*, dir. Paulette Randall. *Birmingham Post* 1 March 2006. Print.

Hutcheon, Linda. *A Theory of Adaptation*. New York: Routledge, 2006. Print.

Karlinsky, Simon, and Michael Henry Heim, trans. and eds. *Anton Chekhov's Life and Thought*. Berkeley: U of California P, 1973. Print.

Lewis, C. S. *Till We Have Faces: a Myth Retold*. New York: Harcourt, Brace & Co., 1957. Print.

MacDonald-Smythe, Antonia. "The Privileges of Being Born in . . . A Backward and Underdeveloped Society: Derek Walcott's Prodigal Provincialism." *Callaloo* 28.1 (2005): 88–101. Print.

Matura, Mustapha. *As Time Goes By. Mustapha Matura: Six Plays*. London: Methuen Drama, 1992. 1–66. Print.

———. Interview with Terry Grimley. *Birmingham Post*. 31 Jan 2006, first ed.: 13. Print.

———. *Meetings. Mustapha Matura: Six Plays*. London: Methuen Drama, 1992. 295–374. Print.

———. *Nice. Mustapha Matura: Six Plays*. London: Methuen Drama, 1992. 67–82. Print.

———. *Playboy of the West Indies*. New York: Broadway Play Publishing, 1988. Print.

———. *Play Mas. Mustapha Matura: Six Plays*. London: Methuen Drama, 1992. 83–170. Print.

———. *The Coup: A Play of Revolutionary Dreams*. London: Methuen Drama, 1991. Print.

———. *Three Sisters: After Chekhov*. London: Oberon Classics, 2006. Print.

———. *Welcome Home Jacko. Mustapha Matura: Six Plays*. London: Methuen Drama, 1992. 237–294. Print.

Nunn, Trevor. "Notes from a Director: *Three Sisters*." *The Cambridge Companion to Chekhov*. Ed. Vera Gottlieb and Paul Allain. Cambridge: Cambridge UP, 2000. 101–10. Print.

Said, Edward. *Culture and Imperialism*. New York: Vintage, 1993. Print.

———. "Traveling Theory." *The Edward Said Reader*. Ed. Moustafa Bayoumi and Andrew Rubin. New York: Vintage Books, 2000. 195–217. Print.

Senelick, Laurence. *The Chekhov Theatre: A Century of the Plays in Performance*. Cambridge: Cambridge UP, 1997. Print.

———. Introduction. *The Three Sisters*. By Anton Chekhov. Trans. Laurence Senelick. New York: Norton, 2010. 55–68. Print.

Shakespeare, William. *The Tempest: Critical Edition*. Ed. Peter Hulme and William H. Sherman. New York: Norton, 2004. Print.

Stoppard, Tom. *Rosencrantz & Guildenstern are Dead*. New York: Samuel French, 1967. Print.

Tiffin, Helen. "Post-Colonial Literatures and Counter-Discourse." *The Post-Colonial Studies Reader*. 2nd ed. Ed. Bill Ashcroft, Gareth Griffiths, and Helen Tiffin. London: Routledge, 2006. 99–101. Print.

10 From Moscow to Ballybeg
Brian Friel's Richly Metabiotic Relationship with Anton Chekhov

Martine Pelletier

> No other writer of drama offers us such imaginative space as Chekhov does. We refuse it at great spiritual cost to ourselves. (Friel program notes)

The Irish playwright Brian Friel (1929–) has, on various occasions, been referred to as "the Irish Chekhov," a claim first made convincingly and decisively by Richard Pine in his 1990 book, *Brian Friel and Ireland's Drama*.[1] The critical consensus on the imaginative affinities between the two writers was strengthened as Friel went on to produce no fewer than three adaptations of Chekhov and a fascinating hybrid also related to Chekhov, *Afterplay*, all in the space of the four years between 1998 and 2002. This chapter seeks to discover Friel's Chekhov, to chart the ways in which Brian Friel has drawn on the Russian master. The central concern is to elucidate what aspects of Chekhov's drama and his nineteenth-century Russia have exercised the Irish playwright's imagination. Three different but related and chronologically overlapping modalities in this creative relationship can be identified. A number of Friel plays can be said to contain recognizable "Chekhovian motifs," from *Philadelphia, Here I Come!* (1964) to *The Home Place* (2005), suggesting parallels between the sociopolitical and cultural contexts of Chekhov's Russia and Friel's Ireland as well as dramatic and subjective affinities between the two writers. Secondly, in 1981, Friel wrote what he called a translation of *Three Sisters*[2]—which he also described as "a labour of love"—for the newly founded Field Day Theatre Company. By the time his *Uncle Vanya* was produced in 1998, a subtle shift had taken place as evidenced by the subtitle: "A Version of the Play by Anton Chekhov." In both instances, language issues are very much to the fore as Friel simultaneously acknowledges and distances himself from existing English translations in order to emphasize the need for a Chekhov who would be more in tune with an Irish voice and an Irish ear, echoing recurrent concerns in post-colonial theory. With *Three Plays After* (2001–2002), Friel's engagement with Chekhov reaches a new and exciting stage. *The Yalta Game*, based on Chekhov's short story "The Lady with the Little Dog," and above all *Afterplay*—in which two characters from *Uncle Vanya* and *Three Sisters*, Sonya Serebryakova and Andrey Prozorov, are "reanimated and reimagined" by Friel and allowed to meet in a fictional afterlife—offer conclusive evidence of a fruitful imaginative interaction. Taking one's clue from Friel himself, one may well talk of a "richly metabiotic relationship" (*Living Quarters* 10) between two playwrights separated by time, space, and language but nonetheless united in their subtly ironic yet compassionate rendition of human hopes and weaknesses as well as in their alertness to the deceptive and elusive nature of reality. The term "metabiosis" is borrowed from chemistry, and, as Friel explains in his note to his 1992 adaptation of Turgenev's *A Month in the Country*, it "denotes a mode of living in which one organism is dependent on another for the preparation of an environment in which it can live. The relationship between Turgenev and Chekhov was richly metabiotic" (195). I shall argue that the relationship between Chekhov and Friel can also be seen as "metabiotic" in that most of Friel's *œuvre* stems from and depends on that of Chekhov. This chapter will not draw explicitly on theories of translation or adaptation but will chart Friel's progress as a dramatist engaged, somewhat paradoxically, in an intense artistic conversation with Chekhov, though the Irishman has no knowledge of Russian and therefore finds his access to a work that exercises his imagination and creative energies so powerfully always mediated by others and another language. His own understanding of Chekhov is thus formed in and through representation, translation, and adaptation and none the less remarkable for all that. With time, Friel's engagement with Chekhov testifies to a growing confidence in his own writing, from the echoes and influences discernible at the earliest stages to the adaptations or versions in which the issue of language is foregrounded as Friel gives Chekhov a distinctly Irish and even Northern Irish idiom as part of a typically post-colonial strategy of appropriation of classics. The later stage with *Three Plays After* suggests that as Friel himself now is well on his way to becoming a classic he feels at liberty to borrow from Chekhov to produce yet truly original and deeply personal work.

A LIFELONG COMPANIONSHIP

Brian Friel is not only Ireland's undisputed greatest living playwright; he is also, by any standards, one of the greatest dramatists writing today. Several of his plays have earned him this richly deserved international recognition: *Philadelphia, Here I Come!* (1964), *Faith Healer* (1980), *Translations* (1980), and *Dancing at Lughnasa* (1990). As with Chekhov, what is also truly remarkable is the extent to which Friel's varied and most substantial output adds up to a richly coherent *œuvre*. His career now spans a half-century and comprises two collections of short stories, over twenty original plays as well as several adaptations. A sustained parallel between his

182 *Martine Pelletier*

work and that of Anton Chekhov's first appeared in James Coakley's very perceptive 1973 article, in which he analyzes *Philadelphia, Here I Come!* in the most profitable and useful terms: those we have come to call *Chekhovian* (Coakley 191). Those who knew how *Philadelphia, Here I Come!* had been written could only concur. Tyrone Guthrie, who acted as mentor to the aspiring dramatist, had invited Friel to join him in Minneapolis to see him at work. Friel spent several weeks there in 1963, his first time away from Ireland, and saw Guthrie work on two productions, one being Chekhov's *Three Sisters*. It was immediately upon his return that Friel completed *Philadelphia, Here I Come!*, his first major stage success and a watershed in twentieth-century Irish theatre history. It is also the play in which Friel invented Ballybeg, the archetypal Irish village that was to become the fictional location for most of his subsequent work. Coakley notes how this "memory play set in the country of a young man's mind [. . .] concerns that most Chekhovian of rituals: departure or leave-taking" (192). In Friel's play, Philadelphia replaces Moscow, as Ballybeg replaces the provincial town of *Three Sisters*, but "like [Chekhov] Friel balances familiar truths with the most complex of emotions and mixes banalities with the profoundest of sentiments, while he develops that most truly comic and Chekhovian of attitudes: human understanding" (192). Coakley also stresses Friel's decision to structure the play through "a pattern, or string of incidents that operate only in context," adhering to a Chekhovian rejection of plot:

> Within this organic form, *what* is done is not as important as *how* it is done so that, as in Chekhov, method becomes a servant of manner, tone, or gesture; and action, at once indirect, oblique, and intricate concerns itself not so much with *events* in the characters' lives as with the *effects* of those events upon them. [. . .] Slowly, cautiously, we must infer who they are, were, or might have been. Each is searching for the meaning of life, of love; yet each is tainted, flawed, betrayed not so much by emotional inertia as by present circumstances which, for one reason or another, have denied them some kind of fulfillment, some peace with themselves. Like their Chekhovian counterparts they are hardly aware of what has passed them by. And Friel does not present them as downtrodden souls dwelling in perpetual gloom. On the contrary, as Chekhov does, he mixes humor with pathos, blending irony and compassion with an equal lack of self-pity, or sentimentality. To each of them he gives, in exemplary Chekhovian fashion, a moment when their inner life surfaces to tell us not some great truth, but their truth; it is a realization neither histrionic nor spectacular, but merely and deeply profound: an awareness of what life might have been but is not. (194–95)

Friel's Chekhovian credentials were thus firmly established from the start. With *Aristocrats* (1979), Friel's Big House play, Chekhov's influence came

From Moscow to Ballybeg   183

to the fore again so that Anthony Roche could rightly claim that the play was "Friel's true version of Chekhov, with its own three sisters in Alice, Claire and Judith O'Donnell, on the decaying estate" (*Contemporary Irish Drama* 104–5). With the benefit of hindsight, it became easier to see how in *Living Quarters* (1977), loosely based on Euripides's *Hyppolytus*, Friel had in fact recruited a number of Chekhovian elements, with three sisters as protagonists, a military background and a focus on ensemble playing.[3] It thus came as no surprise when the Field Day Theatre Company, set up by Brian Friel and Stephen Rea in the wake of the huge success of Friel's *Translations* (1980), chose to stage for their second tour Friel's own version of Chekhov's *Three Sisters*. Friel had finally turned his hand at an adaptation and done so in a context that will deserve our full attention. There followed in 1987, at a time when Friel's energy was fully absorbed by the needs of managing the company's varied and demanding activities, an adaptation of Turgenev's novel, *Fathers and Sons* (1987). By then, Chekhov had become a permanent, firmly established reference when looking at a Friel play, so that a journalist could easily comment on "the dreamy, Chekhovian pace" (Kavanagh 220) of Friel's *Dancing at Lughnasa* (1990). This comparison was fleshed out very convincingly by Nicholas Grene, who read the Mundy Sisters as Chekhovian characters. Brian Friel returned to Turgenev with his 1991 adaptation of *A Month in the Country*, finding in the music of John Field (1782–1837), the Irish-born composer whose career took off in early nineteenth-century St. Petersburg and Moscow, the perfect link between his Ireland and his Russia. In the preface to the edition of the text, Friel brings Turgenev and Chekhov together:

> [Turgenev] fashioned a new kind of dramatic situation and a new kind of dramatic character where for the first time psychological and poetic elements create a theatre of moods and where the action resides in internal emotion and secret turmoil and not in external events. We now have a name for that kind of drama: we call it Chekhovian. [. . .] The term metabiosis in chemistry denotes a mode of living in which one organism is dependent on another for the preparation of an environment in which it can live. The relationship between Turgenev and Chekhov was richly metabiotic. *A Month in the Country* was before its time and moved haltingly across unmapped territory. But it established the necessary environment in which Chekhov could blossom. And once Chekhov had achieved his full stature, once Chekhovian drama was confidently established, the environment was again ready for the reclamation and reassessment and full understanding of Turgenev's pioneering work. So they gave life to each other. And between them they changed the face of European drama. (*Month in the Country* 10–11)

After three original works, Friel returned to Chekhov and, in 1998, gave the Gate Theatre a version of *Uncle Vanya*. Looking back at Friel's recent

184   *Martine Pelletier*

work from the vantage point of the 2009 celebrations in honor of the playwright's eightieth birthday, the poet Seamus Heaney, who was awarded the Nobel Prize for Literature in 1995 and is a close friend of Friel, could admire "the glee of his late borrowings and morrowings with Chekhov's displaced loners in chamber works such as *Afterplay* and *The Yalta Game*," while poet, critic and friend Seamus Deane concurred that his late plays testified to a "Chekhovian inflection" and displayed "the tints of an autumnal reflectiveness [that] fleck his language and his settings" (28). Brian Friel's increasingly profound immersion in Chekhovian territory has been both imaginative and actual. Back in November 1992, in an entry in the sporadic diary the writer keeps while working on a new idea, he mused: "I might look at an adaptation. Gogol, maybe? THE INSPECTOR GENERAL? Why does THE LADY WITH THE DOG keep coming back to me?" (Friel qtd. in Murray 153). The Gogol play never materialized, but Chekhov's short story morphed into a one-act play teasingly entitled *The Yalta Game* (2001). The following year it opened at the Gate Theatre in Dublin as a double-bill, featuring *The Bear* and *Afterplay*. Taken together, the three plays—which were then published under the witty and apt title of *Three Plays After*—marked a new subtle and successful stage in this Friel–Chekhov partnership. In real life, too, that relationship was actively pursued: in 2008 Brian and Anne Friel, together with their close friends Thomas and Julie Kilroy, went to Yalta on a pilgrimage of a kind, to visit the two homes of the Russian master. Kilroy, a playwright, is himself no stranger to the work of Chekhov, as he adapted *The Seagull* at the same time Friel was working on *Three Sisters*. He wrote a moving tribute to his friend in which he explains:

> Sometimes there comes into existence a relationship between two writers which defies time, language and geographical distance. This is true of the relationship between Brian Friel and Anton Chekhov. The nexus between them is mysteriously grounded. But it has the same mastery of social detail, the same probing below the surface, the same moral precision, the same comic tolerance before the vagaries of life. They also have a similar interest in portraying the process of time upon the stage, how ageing changes the mind as well as the body, how memory at once deceives as well as consoles. ("In Celebration" 1)

He concludes the piece on their visit to the Crimea thus: "I thought of the great European confluence flowing in and through Brian's work and why it is that he belongs in this company." Friel has indeed kept imaginative company with Chekhov throughout most of his writing career, from Guthrie's Minneapolis production in 1963 to his last full-length original play so far, *The Home Place*, in 2005. The latter marked a much-awaited return to an Irish setting but deliberately cultivated a Chekhovian atmosphere with a late nineteenth-century estate on the brink of violent change complete with "doomed trees" strongly evocative of *The Cherry Orchard*, a social and political order about to collapse as well as a very Frielian, tense father–son relationship. Reviewing *The Home Place*, Michael Billington was quick to point out the Chekhovian echoes: "what Friel has absorbed from Chekhov and *The Cherry Orchard* is a comprehensive compassion for both the victims and the agents of change."

FRIEL'S "CHEKHOVIAN ETHOS"

Through the years, what Scott Boltwood calls "the Chekhovian ethos of Friel's drama" (198) has been brought to light and analyzed with slightly differing emphases since Coakley's inaugural article in 1973. Robert Tracy sees Chekhov as "a presence in certain of Friel's plays, sharing, as he does, Friel's preoccupation with language, communication and memory both as themes and as dramatic devices" (77). Richard York is aware of the two playwrights sharing similar dramatic rhythms and "a dramaturgy of loss, of the wasted opportunity, of a confronting of inertia" (164). For Elmer Andrews, the affinity between Friel and Chekhov proceeds from "a very similar dramatic tension, a tension that stems from the recognition of the disparity between the reality of people's lives and the dreams by which they attempt to live" (182). In *Spelling It Out*, Seamus Heaney saluted "the possible ameliorating effect of theatre such as Chekhov's or his own, a theatre that engages at serious imaginative levels with societies in crisis and transition." In a program note for a revival of Friel's version of *Uncle Vanya* in 2007, Anthony Roche notes how both Friel and Chekhov transformed the theatre they had inherited and singles out the way in which Friel has learned from Chekhov how not to rely on plot for the structure of his plays, relying instead on "an unerring sense of form." In "Playing the Game," Patrick Mason, who has directed several Friel plays elegantly and insightfully, writes: "Both men share a rare capacity for observation and an ability to empathize without sentimentality. Both are masters of stage action—and of the short story." Nicholas Grene takes up this point, viewing the split protagonist, Public and Private Gar in *Philadelphia, Here I Come!* as "the two halves of a single Chekhov character, with Private Gar voicing "the unspoken feelings that we can read between the lines [giving] that subtext a voice" (105). Richard Pine, whose 1990 monograph on Friel first made the decisive claim for a reading of Friel as "the Irish Chekhov," also charts in his more recent essay "Friel's Irish Russia" a number of personal parallels between the two writers: beekeeping, fishing, music, choir-singing. One could add that Chekhov's scientific training as a doctor is to some extent mirrored by Friel's early career as a math teacher, and that the two men display an acute sense of the frustrations of provincial small-town life that stems directly from their personal experience. The mixture of restraint or distance and involvement or passion one finds in Chekhov also applies to Friel. Pine quotes George Moore's pronouncement in 1911 that

186   *Martine Pelletier*

"Ireland [was] a little Russia," a prescient comment at least insofar as both societies were then on the brink of a violent revolution that would annihilate the dominant landowning aristocracy and political elite, leading to the establishment of a new social order and, in the case of Ireland, the birth of the Free State and the emancipation of most of the island from the British Empire. In "Distance and Absence," Richard Pine also stresses how "Friel brings 'Russian' themes into close proximity with those that have preoccupied the modern Irish stage: people who live far away from reality; hopes that are more depressing than inspiring; a lifetime's experience of emptiness, of longing, of deferral; action (the real world) always taking place elsewhere." Perhaps more important still is how Friel himself came to articulate what had drawn him to Chekhov in the program note he wrote for his version of *Three Sisters* in 1981, thus providing a privileged insight into his very personal and idiosyncratic relationship with the Russian playwright:

> Chekhov plays are not addressed to the rationalising mind. They are addressed to the poetic and histrionic sensibility. They are free, as music is free, from the mechanical order of the thesis and the intrigue. I am not suggesting that *Three Sisters* is not susceptible to rational analysis because it clearly is. Nor am I suggesting that events do not evolve with an ascertainable logic, because they clearly do; what I am suggesting is that if one brings to the play a literal mind that demands precise explanation and step-by-step logic and demonstrated reasoning, the true flavour of the play is missed. [. . .] What I am proposing is not a passivity but an alertness, an active attention of a different kind: where one is alive to the word but even more alive to its echoes and resonances; where one recognises that the reverberations of the action are more important than the action itself; where the imagination, getting lift-off from what Chekhov presents to us, allows itself to soar into those uncharted areas where the greater part of our lives is lived. No other writer of drama offers us such imaginative space as Chekhov does. We refuse it at great spiritual cost to ourselves.

This short but dense offering undoubtedly reveals as much about Brian Friel as about Anton Chekhov. The "uncharted areas where the greater part of our lives is lived" echoes Friel's own "dark and private places of individual souls" (Murray 77) that he believes are the proper concern of the playwright. Friel scholars will also relish the phrase "where one is alive to the word but even more alive to its echoes and resonances; where one recognises that the reverberations of the action are more important than the action itself," since it is a version of lines at the end of *The Communication Cord*, Friel's next Field Day play in 1982: "It's the occasion that matters/and the reverberations that the occasion generates" (85). It also anticipates by nearly ten years elements of Michael's beautifully cadenced final monologue in *Dancing at Lughnasa* (1990):

"a dream music that is both heard and imagined; that seems to be both itself and its own echo" (71).

FRIEL'S "ADAPTATION" OF *THREE SISTERS*

In order to probe deeper into this fruitful dialogue, the circumstances in which Friel came to adapt *Three Sisters* must first be fully understood. In the late 1970s, Friel was working on what would become *Translations* and reading George Steiner's *After Babel*, a very influential work on language and translation. His certainty that Chekhov was "best sensed" (note to *Three Sisters* program) convinced him that available English translations of *Three Sisters* did not offer the right music for Irish ears and voices and that this was both an aesthetic and a political issue. Friel was very much aware of how Irish actors and audiences had always been denied access to a Chekhov who would not be filtered through the King's English:

> I think *Three Sisters* is a very important play, but I feel that the translations which we have received and inherited in some way have not much to do with the language which we speak in Ireland. [. . .] Somehow the rhythms of these versions do not match with the rhythms of our own speech patterns, and I think that they ought to, in some way. [. . .] This is something about which I feel strongly—in some way we are constantly overshadowed by the sound of English language, as well as by the printed word. Maybe this does not inhibit us, but it forms us and shapes us in a way that is neither healthy nor valuable for us. ("Talking" 145)

Friel felt that Chekhov was betrayed theatrically as well as linguistically in English productions of his work: "There's the other thing, that the received method of playing Chekhov is just to take up a stance on the downstage right or left, stare into the middle distance and talk desultorily about philosophical questions. Whereas there should be a great reality, about the acting as well as about the words" (Gillespie 156). Friel's mentor, Tyrone Guthrie, had come to much the same conclusion years earlier, when working at the Old Vic in the 1930s:

> Our production [of *The Cherry Orchard*] was the first time that an English version of the play met with a large popular audience. [. . .] We rejected the standard translation by Constance Garnett in favour of a new version by Hubert Butler[4] which was much less "quaint"; the characters emerged as far more human and normal, and the actors were encouraged to regard it as a comedy rather than as a prose poem. It presented Chekhov not as the arch-exponent of Russian gloom but as a charming and easily intelligible humorist. (113)

188 *Martine Pelletier*

Language and acting style conspired to remove Chekhov from the range of audiences; what Guthrie sought to do within an English context, Friel pursued with a slightly different agenda, one in which Northern Ireland featured prominently as he was then setting up his own Derry-based theatre company, Field Day, with Belfast-born actor Stephen Rea. His adaptation of Chekhov in 1981 is the central element in a trio of plays, coming in between *Translations* and *The Communication Cord* (1982), partly based on Erving Goffman's theory of communication. It forms part of a trilogy that addresses, at different levels and from different time frames, issues of language, and communication within an ideological framework informed by then emerging post-colonial theories and by Ireland's history as a British colony. The situation in Northern Ireland worsened as "the Troubles" reached a new crisis point in the early 1980s with the hunger strikes of Republican paramilitary prisoners. *Translations*, Field Day's first play in 1980, addressed those issues from the vantage point of nineteenth-century Ireland at the time when Irish place-names were anglicized as part of the mapmaking exercise of the Ordnance Survey.[5] Great Britain and Ireland are divided by a supposedly shared language but Irish-English is haunted by the ghost of Irish as the theatrical conceit in the play so brilliantly and powerfully demonstrates with English alternatively standing for English and Irish, while Irish only survives in the place-names about to be translated or transliterated. The hegemony of English-English entails, for Irish people, a linguistic loss, an ontological discrepancy, a permanent misunderstanding that only an adaptation that would respect Irish specificities might limit or redress. *The Communication Cord* (1982), placed firmly in contemporary Ireland, shows how shallow and inauthentic the Irish Republic's proclaimed attachment to its Gaelic past and culture actually has become. Part of Field Day's dramatic project can be construed as the transformation of a language imposed from outside into a language that sits easily on the Irish tongue and sounds natural to the Irish ear. This, Friel was convinced, would benefit everybody, but first and foremost the actors too often forced to inhabit an unlikely and ridiculous linguistic space when playing foreign classics like Chekhov: "What has happened up to this is that Irish actors have to assume English accents, so you end up with being an Irishman pretending you're an Englishman, pretending you're a Russian!" (O'Donnell 150–51). Undoubtedly, *Three Sisters*, like the later Field Day adaptations, bridges that gap and offers cadences better suited to an Irish ear. Brian Friel does not speak Russian and worked from existing translations: "What I did was simply to put six texts in front of me and tackle each line at a time, to see first of all what was the meaning of it, then what was the tone and then eventually what was the sound. It took nine months in all" (O'Donnell 150). His friend and fellow playwright Thomas Kilroy was also engaged in adapting a Chekhov play, *The Seagull*, for the Royal Court at the same time. When the play was produced in 1981 in London, Kilroy surprised his English audience by his transposition of

Chekhov's Russian setting to late nineteenth-century Ireland as he felt that "one of the central elements of Chekhov's plays [was] that of the enormous personal and psychological effects of wider social change" (O'Toole, "Kilroy Interview" 13). English audiences were thus encouraged to reimagine Chekhov through the prism of the Anglo-Irish experience shortly before the turmoil of the War of Independence. For his part, Friel chose to retain the original Russian setting and characters but to concentrate on altering the language. Northern Irish actress Eileen Pollock, who played a Masha capable of using words like "pissed" and "bitch," approved of Friel's adaptation: "Brian's translation is much better than others at extracting the humanity of the situation, tragedy and all, with a ripple of humour. It is very hard work and while it is not an Irish play, it brings it into the understanding of the Irish actor" (O'Donnell 152). In keeping with this strategy, Friel asked Irish pianist and composer Micheal Ó Suilleabhain to provide music for the piece, a choice hailed by most critics and audiences. Asked to comment on Friel's *Three Sisters*, Kilroy insisted, "he has done something extraordinary, something which will make it impossible for an Irish company to do Chekhov, or Shakespeare or virtually any non-Irish play in an Anglified way again" (O'Toole, "Kilroy Interview" 13). Joe Dowling, then artistic director of Ireland's Abbey Theatre, concurred enthusiastically in a private letter to the author:

> Dear Brian
>   C'est magnifique—to coin a phrase.
>   The translation has a magnificent sense of language and the natural resonances of speech which distinguishes it from any other translation I know. The skill however is not only in the way it makes the language accessible, it also deepens the relationships and clarifies the characters beautifully. The achievement of this translation is most distinguished indeed and must alter our whole perception of Chekhov and indeed should have reverberations for all our foreign classical productions.[6]

Dowling's opening sentence refers to one of Friel's inventions, giving the Baron a linguistic mannerism. A characteristic of his adaptation generally is a heightened linguistic awareness, as George O'Brien notes:

> The precision of the translation's perception of language delineates with wonderful clarity the characters' dilemmas, particularly in those cases where consciousness and unconsciousness of verbal effect coincide. The coincidence is most obviously seen in the male characters—in Vershinin's mocking and resigned tones, in his gestures of wordless resignation; in Kulygin's pedantry; in what Friel translates as quackquack by Solyony; and Tuzenbakh's repetition of to coin a phrase. The men seem undeceived by their language, whereas the three sisters retain some of their illusions. (12–13)

190   *Martine Pelletier*

The production met with mixed reactions, as several critics felt that moving away from English-English—although only Natasha is consistently given a language that is emphatically Irish in expressions as well as rhythm[7]—somehow diminished the universal appeal of Chekhov's masterpiece, unwittingly confirming the very Anglo-centrism Friel and Field Day were determined to challenge (Richtarik 125–27). Some idiosyncratic alterations usually intended to heighten the comedy also drew criticism as did the length of the piece since, unlike Kilroy, Friel chose not to cut much of Chekhov's text—which might have been wiser given his propensity to expand lines rather than contract them.[8] Thus Kulygin waxes lyrical about his wife as he meets Vershinin: "As for Masha, my wife, Masha I may say is the very personification of kindness and consideration and loyalty and circumspection and . . ." (31), a far less sober and concise version than in most English translations; the English "pie" is replaced by the more exotic "lasagna" while Friel's Chebutykin can say precisely how long he has kept away from the drink—alcohol features quite prominently in both Irish and Russian culture—"I've been dry for five hundred and ninety seven and a half days now" (30) instead of the matter-of-fact "I haven't done any heavy drinking for two years" (Chekhov, *Plays* 266). In the notebook containing the first version of acts 1 and 2, Friel wrote: "Check an important issue: In Chekhov all the characters speak their thoughts aloud,—are not listened to—almost private soliloquy. Has this been respected" (Friel Archive. National Library of Ireland. MS 37,092/1). This is crossed out in green, the color used for later revisions, indicating that Friel was happy he had indeed respected this Chekhovian characteristic, though not all critics would agree, feeling he had made his characters more loquacious and communicative than their originals. This criticism, which is grounded in the fact that Friel's characters do speak more than their Chekhovian originals, may in fact miss the point that talking in the presence of somebody, or even receiving vague, empty encouragements to keep talking, does not indicate that genuine communication and exchanges have been established. While critical reactions to *Three Sisters* differed for ideological as well as artistic reasons, Brian Friel had crossed an important threshold and his engagement with the play was to prove a watershed in terms of his own creative relationship with Chekhov.

FRIEL'S "VERSION" OF *UNCLE VANYA*

In the wake of *Three Sisters*, the Field Day Theatre Company staged a number of adaptations and was partly responsible for the new impetus given to adaptations in Ireland in the 1980s and 1990s. The political implications of such artistic strategies ought not to be underestimated as many of these adaptations could be read as appropriations of classics with an Irish agenda. Poets (Seamus Heaney, Tom Paulin, Brendan Kennelly, Derek Mahon) and playwrights (Frank McGuinness, Thomas Kilroy, Tom Murphy) turned to

From Moscow to Ballybeg   191

ancient Greek drama and European classics to offer their own versions, either fully subscribing to the "de-Anglicization" agenda or promoting a different stance, be it that of contemporary relevance through transposition or recovery of forgotten or neglected valuable dramatic material. Friel himself went on adapting Turgenev before returning to Chekhov in 1998 with *Uncle Vanya*. For this adaptation, as he had for *A Month in the Country*, Friel commissioned a literal translation from the Russian that he used to write his own version. In a postscript to his note to Ben Barnes and Michael Colgan accompanying the finished script, Friel expresses his satisfaction with the literal translation provided:

> Úna Ní Dhubhghaill's literal translation was a model—a real "carrying across" from the original into an English that was totally unadorned and utterly artless. So naked, in fact, that it didn't even read like English. With the result that the characters, denied any linguistic grace or artifice, acquired a bare authenticity. A great tabula rasa to lift off from and return to. (Friel Archive MS 37, 138/7)

In *Uncle Vanya*, which Friel this time calls "a version of the play by Anton Chekhov," the Irish dramatist takes greater liberties with the original than he had in *Three Sisters*. In his letter to Barnes and Colgan, Friel explains at length the "modest license" he has taken:

> I believe I have been faithful to the Gang of four: Vanya, Sonya, Elena, Astrov. Certainly to their personalities and characters. And only in the *way* they express themselves—in their vocabularies and their distinctive idiom—have I tried to fulfil them in my own way.
>
> With some of the other characters I have assumed a modest licence. For example, Maria (mother-in-law) is now a drawing-room revolutionary, passionate and futile. And a bit deaf. I think this reading is justified because throughout the play she is immersed in political pamphlets, and because, as Vanya tells us, she is a women's emancipationist—a fairly extreme position at that time. This would account for the passion. The futile and drawing-room elements are suggested by her political inactivity and by her ill-judged support for the bogus Serebryakov. The deafness is a gesture to her isolation in the house and from outside society. (And offers the possibility for lightness)
>
> I took some liberties with Telegin. His pock-marked face is caused, I suggest, by excessive perspiring. Hence his obsession with climate, clothes, etc. And I felt that his response to his wife walking out on him invited exploration. So the man who cuckolded him is now Hans. Hence Telegin's obsession with Germany and things German and his perverse belief in the superiority of the German race. Of course he appears foolish. But he does reveal a very real and touching core when he tells Marina about the shopkeeper calling after him. And this is becoming an apologia.[9]

192 *Martine Pelletier*

Friel's *Uncle Vanya* actually tilts the subtle balance between comedy and sadness towards the comic by developing the minor characters, Marina to a limited extent and Maria, but mostly Telegin, "who is still, of course, the impoverished hanger-on, the 'sponger' as he is called in the village. But now, I hope, both defeated and *funny*,"[10] which delighted audiences and many critics but also led to reservations on the part of other reviewers who felt this amounted to a betrayal of, or at least a tampering with, Chekhov. In "A Magnificent Vanya," Emer O'Kelly congratulated Friel for giving "an almost flawless version of the play, as Russian in its fuming hopelessness as it is Irish in its pointless, frustrated rage." Paul Arnott, writing for *The Independent*, noted approvingly the differences between this very Irish Chekhov and English productions: "If undercurrents of passion are so often stilled and ironised in English adaptations, Friel's flowing, often amusing dialogue prompted an immediate realisation that these characters, submerged within their impractical lives in a Russian wood, are from the outset, profoundly self-aware." Richard Jones deemed Friel's *Uncle Vanya* much less "Irish" than his *Three Sisters*, which may be a point still open to discussion. More importantly perhaps one could argue that it is more "Frielian" insofar as, in this play, Friel claims his right to deal with Chekhov on his own terms as it were. The central situation of the play enables him to delve deep into what is his own artistic, imaginative territory: illusions; unrequited love; social collapse; and how language colludes or collides with our attempts at concealing our fears, our despair, our frailties, our sense that this cannot be all there is. The celebrations around Friel's seventieth birthday with the "Friel Festival" in 1999, only a few months after the production of *Uncle Vanya*, gave the playwright an opportunity to muse on his own attraction to Chekhov and Turgenev as he turned the spotlight on personal, artistic but also political parallels between prerevolutionary Russia and Ireland at the time of the Good Friday peace agreement and the Celtic Tiger phenomenon:

> I'm not sure why I find the late nineteenth-century Russians so sympathetic. Maybe because the characters in the plays behave as if their old certainties were as sustaining as ever—even though they know in their hearts that their society is in melt-down and the future has neither a welcome nor even an accommodation for them. Maybe a bit like people of my own generation in Ireland today. Or maybe I find the Russians sympathetic because they have no expectations whatever from love but still invest everything in it. Or maybe they attract me because they seem to expect that their problems will disappear if they talk about them—endlessly.[11]

PUSHING AT THE BOUNDARIES OF ADAPTATION

The three short texts published as *Three Plays After* in 2002 were performed, respectively, in 2001 for *The Yalta Game*, and 2002 for *The Bear* and *Afterplay*, and produced in somewhat uneasy tandem. In an interview

From Moscow to Ballybeg 193

given in 1992, as his adaptation of Turgenev, *A Month in the Country* was being staged, the playwright explained one of the advantages he saw in working on an adaptation: "I find the process—the exercise—of translating both interesting and satisfying. Because you are presented with a complete fiction—given characters, given situations, given resolutions. Your 'creative' responsibilities are circumscribed."[12] This may not always be the case. Friel's adaptation of *The Bear* remains very close to the original and therefore is of lesser interest at this point, though in his note to the play Friel is careful to give his assessment of Chekhov's role in theatre history: "Its ambition is to hold our attention briefly, to entertain us, and to make us laugh at people whose over-the-top behaviour barely disguises their terrors and confused hopes. [. . .] But *The Bear* engages for another important reason: it is an early trial piece by the man who reshaped twentieth-century theatre" (*Three Plays After* 37). *Afterplay* was subsequently revived in a happier conjugation with *The Yalta Game*, an adaptation and expansion of the short story "The Lady with the Little Dog" (1899) that had been created at the Gate in 2001. *Afterplay* and *The Yalta Game*—which were once again written starting from a literal translation provided by Úna Ní Dhubhghaill—are particularly worthy of attention because they signal a new stage in Friel's engagement with Chekhov, blurring the borders between adaptation and original creation and demonstrating his determination to take greater liberties and to shape the original Chekhovian material to a fully personal artistic purpose. While it would be inaccurate to say that love has not always been at the heart of Friel's drama, it must be admitted that more political concerns had come to the fore especially in his plays of the 1970s and 1980s. It is largely through his adaptations of Chekhov and Turgenev that the Irish playwright has again inflected the course of his writing and has returned, notably in recent years, to matters of the heart, which are played out in that quintessentially Frielian territory Fintan O'Toole defines as "the borderland between story and history, truth and illusion, memory and invention" (Rev. of *Two Plays After*). Nowhere is this clearer than in *Three Plays After*, thanks to the Chekhov material Friel then reshapes according to his own needs. Thus *The Bear* shows a widow in deep mourning slowly renouncing the fiction that she will be faithful to the death to a husband who was unfaithful to her throughout his life. *The Yalta Game* is a more daring proposition than *The Bear* as far as the interaction between Chekhov's original story and Friel's treatment of it is concerned; it is a clear instance of an intermedial adaptation, moving from fiction to drama and adopting interesting strategies to enable the transition from one medium to another. Friel retains the basic ingredients of the story but proceeds to establish a convention whereby some of the dialogue between the two protagonists, Gurov and Anna, is only addressed to the audience while the rest of the dialogue is between the characters. This clever and highly effective device—partly reminiscent of his subtle game on language in *Translations*—enables Friel to give us access to Gurov's and Anna's inner thoughts, thus taking up at least in part the role played in the story by the

194   *Martine Pelletier*

narrative voice. That Friel intends to make the story his own is evidenced early on, as the title is a pure Friel invention. The script also makes clear that the piece is "based on a theme in 'The Lady with the Lapdog' by Anton Chekhov," not an adaptation. Friel weaves his own pattern and delights his audience with some play around the invisible dog reminiscent of the way he dealt with the invisible child in *Dancing at Lughnasa*. Also typically Frielian is the transformation of Gurov from a "graduate in literature" to an amateur philologist and the addition of military music. As far as characterization is concerned, Gurov, the middle-aged seducer, is more fleshed out and marginally less of a misogynist in Friel than he is in Chekhov. Friel's Anna describes herself as restless and hopes for a form of restoration, typical Friel words and emotions: "I had to keep telling myself that yes, Yalta would restore me, give my life some calm again, show me how much I had to be grateful for. Or at least reconcile me to what I had settled for" (16). She soon falls for Gurov at least partly because he amuses her with his tall tales about other tourists playing his "Yalta game" and inventing stories about the lives of strangers, turning them into heroin addicts, former ballet dancers, or zookeepers so as to shock, entertain, and seduce. The transformation of the affair into an all-consuming passion is faithful to the original story, though the language of the two protagonists is more typical of the Irish playwright. Thus Gurov:

> But back to the peculiar thing, the very peculiar thing. Remember my sly game? Well, it . . . inverted itself. Or else my world did a somersault. Or else all reality turned itself on its head. Because suddenly, for no reason that I was aware of, things that once seemed real now became imagined things. And what was imagined, what I could imagine, what I could recall, that was actual, the only actuality. The bank, colleagues, home, card games, they all subsided into make-believe—they were fictions, weren't they? (29–30)

Anna immediately echoes his remarks: "I began to fill my weeks with small delights, exquisite little treats. Well, expectations really. And I plotted them with great care, indeed with cunning. It wasn't at all a game, a child's make-believe. No, no. It was a rehearsal for what was certainly going to happen" (30). Anton Chekhov gives the narrative voice the final say in an ambiguous ending as the lovers remain trapped in their respective conventional loveless marriages: "And it seemed—given a little more time—a solution would be found and then a new and beautiful life would begin. And both of them clearly realized that the end was far, far away and that the most complicated and difficult part was only just beginning" (Chekhov, *Lady* 240). Friel chooses to give Gurov the last word:

> Yes, a miraculous solution would be offered to us. And that release would make our happiness so complete and so opulent and . . . forever.

From Moscow to Ballybeg   195

But I knew that until that miracle happened, we would have to stumble on together for a very long time; because the end was coming even though it was still a long way off. But the drawing to a close had already begun and we were now embarked on the most complicated and most frightening and the most painful time of all.

Kiss me, Anna. Please. (They kiss. Bring up the exuberant military music in the background.) (35)

The theatrical note on which this adaptation ends (a kiss and music) shows Friel fully in control of his medium.

"*Three Sisters* and *Uncle Vanya* stop. The characters must go on living, but robbed now of hope. [. . .] Friel knows that there is no closure for Chekhov's characters. Their unsatisfied lives will—must—go on," Robert Tracy (75) remarks. *Afterplay* proceeds from that sense that while dramatic action stops, as it must, the characters' lives do continue, offstage, and Friel's short piece boldly and successfully creates both "a sequel" and "a crossover." Friel has written several plays in which the audience come to realize that characters speak from the other side of the grave, notably *Faith Healer, Living Quarters*, and *Dancing at Lughnasa*, but in *Afterplay*, Friel goes further and breathes an afterlife into two Chekhovian characters: Sonya, from *Uncle Vanya*, and Andrey, from *Three Sisters*. In his note to the play, Friel explains how he decided to "revisit" the lives of the two protagonists, reuniting them in one single new play: "Now re-animated and re-imagined they are middle-aged. They cannot escape their origins, of course; those experiences that their creator furnished them with are still determining experiences" (*Three Plays After* 69). Friel also muses on the balance between freedom and constraint that such a situation entails and offers an arresting analogy, suggesting that the two playwrights are indeed related, share a bond of kinship as it were:

Had I created these two characters in the first place I would feel free now to reshape them as I wished. But they are not mine alone. I am something less than a parent[13] but I know I am something more than a foster-parent. Maybe closer to a godparent who takes his responsibilities scrupulously. So when I consider the complex life Anton Chekhov breathed into Sonya and Andrey one hundred years ago I believe that that life can be carried forward into this extended existence provided the two stay true to where and what they came from. That means that the godfather has to stay alert at all times to the intention of their first begetter. (*Three Plays After* 69)

In *Afterplay*, Sonya and Vanya meet in a Moscow café "twenty years after their previous fictional lives ended" (*Three Plays After* 69), and there is a possibility that they might not only confide in each other how lonely they are, but that they might find some comfort and solace together. Yet, as the evening

196 *Martine Pelletier*

unfolds, they come to admit they have not been entirely truthful with each other, in lines that are unmistakable Friel: "I'm afraid I told you a little fable last night. [. . .] No, not a fable; not a fable at all. A small fiction—a trivial little falsehood. Maybe just a tiny fabrication that . . ." (84). Andrey recalls his sisters and wonders why those intelligent women always clung to the illusion that their real lives were elsewhere before concluding: "But I suppose some people live like that—in perpetual . . . expectation" (83). A comment with which Sonya, still madly in love with an aging and married Astrov, can only concur, "Indeed they do" (83), prompting Andrey to question somewhat bluntly: "That's not how you live your life, is it? What stupid dreams are you waiting to be realized? (Suddenly embarrassed) Sorry—forgive me—I beg your pardon—I don't mean to (Rises) I'm going to get some tea" (84). He has unwittingly pierced through Sonya's defenses since that is indeed very much how she lives her life as she finally admits when she asks Andrey not to write to her or expect her to arrange another meeting in Moscow because of her desperate love for Astrov; in those lines, she sounds strikingly like Grace in Friel's *Faith Healer*, though in her fortitude and forthrightness she is equally true to her Chekhovian original:

> But he still comes to me—occasionally. When he remembers me for some reason usually when he's drunk. And when he does remember me, when he does come to me and stands swaying before me and holding my face between his hands, not saying a word, just gazing into me with those quick blue eyes that are now touched with a little uncertainty, at times like that I feel we have never been apart—ever; and I feel—God forgive me—I feel that for that moment I am almost holy, too. Not much of a way to get through your life, is it? (96)

With both *The Yalta Game* and *Afterplay*, Friel keeps in balance emotion and humor, endowing his Chekhovian models with a potent mixture of hope and despair, self-knowledge and self-delusion. He finds in these late works a striking balance between personal creativity and "faithfulness" to the original Chekhov material and personal creativity, bridging the gap as it were between his own well-developed and fully recognizable dramatic style and concerns and those of the Russian playwright.

The aim of this chapter has been to probe the intense and exceptionally fruitful "privileged conversation" Brian Friel has enjoyed with Anton Chekhov over a lifetime of writing for the stage. The Irish playwright is never derivative, and to talk merely of an influence is to miss the point of this truly metabiotic relationship between two exceptionally gifted masters of the word and of the stage. Friel has shown an ability to shift paradigms, to move subtly from his instinctive embrace of a Chekhovian intertext and ethos to adaptations with a strong political agenda—in favor of linguistic and cultural appropriation, claiming the right for Chekhovian characters

From Moscow to Ballybeg 197

to speak in a recognizably Irish-English idiom in his Field Day period notably—to what in recent years has become a powerful desire to fully inhabit and shape Chekhovian imaginative territory, to the point of feeling entitled and being artistically able to breathe a new life into original Chekhovian characters in *Afterplay*. Ultimately, what may prove exceptional and worthy of further investigation is the extent to which, although he has never had any direct access to Chekhov in the original Russian, Brian Friel, through his whole *œuvre*, has developed, shaped, and challenged the understanding of Chekhov of Irish audiences and critics alike.

NOTES

1. See in particular the introduction, in which Pine claims: "Friel becomes the Irish Chekhov because for him the world is not Ireland writ large but Ireland is the world writ small" (3).
2. The published text is presented as "A Translation" though initially, as the notebooks in the Friel archive located in the National Library of Ireland reveal, he had thought of producing "A VERSION (i.e. not a translation)" (Friel Archive. National Library of Ireland. MS 37, 092/1).
3. See, in particular, Tracy.
4. Hubert Butler was from Northern Ireland and became Guthrie's brother-in-law.
5. As in *Three Sisters*, the plot of *Translations* hinges on the arrival of the military into a household, and Friel was quick to underline in his own working notes that Chekhov's Vershinin was not an English officer, a version of his Captain Lancey: "Chekhov writes about officers not strutting about stiffly."
6. Joe Dowling to Brian Friel, no date (Friel Archive. National Library of Ireland. MS 37, 092/3).
7. For example: "Sweet mother of God, I'm late—they're at the dinner already" or "She's a peasant and that's where she belongs—out in the bogs!" As Richard Jones perceptively notes, "Natasha is defined by her class in Friel in a more obvious manner than in other English versions of Chekhov" (35). Jones goes on to stress that Natasha speaks more like members of Friel's audiences while Vershinin would sound more English, like members of the Ascendancy.
8. Richard Jones has provided a thorough and convincing analysis of the changes at work in Friel's version of the play, paying great attention to the additions to the dialogue and Friel's interest in nonverbal expression.
9. Friel Archive. National Library of Ireland. MS 37, 138/7. Letter from Brian Friel to "Michael and Ben" (no date but separate note indicates documents sent to M. Colgan, Ben Barnes, and Anthony Harwood on 4 Aug. 1998).
10. Letter from Brian Friel to Ben Barnes and Michael Colgan, 19 July 1998 (Friel Archive. National Library of Ireland. MS 37,138/7).
11. Friel, "Seven" 18; reprinted in Murray 179.
12. Battersby 2.
13. One may remember that Friel claimed it had taken him nine months to complete the adaptation of *Three Sisters* so that the motif of the writer giving birth and becoming parent to the work goes back at least to 1981.
14. Kilroy, *The Seagull* 13.

198 *Martine Pelletier*

WORKS CITED

Andrews, Elmer. *The Art of Brian Friel*. Basingstoke: Macmillan, 1995. Print.
Arnott, Paul. "Art: Captivated by Irish Confidence Forget Riverdance: The Dublin Theatre Festival Points the Way Forward for Ireland's stage." *Independent* 15 October 1998. Web. 22 Apr. 2012.
Battersby, Eileen. "Drama of Love: From One Great Master to Another." *Irish Times* 1 Aug. 1992. Weekend section: 2. Print.
Billington, Michael. Rev. of *The Home Place*, by Brian Friel. *Guardian* 2 Feb. 2005. Web. 22 Apr. 2012.
Boltwood, Scott. *Brian Friel, Ireland, and The North*. Cambridge: Cambridge UP, 2007. Print.
Chekhov, Anton. *The Lady with the Little Dog and Other Stories*. Trans. Ronald Wilks. Introduction Paul Debreczeny. Harmondsworth: Penguin Classics, 2002. Print.
——. *Plays*. Trans. E. Fen. Harmondsworth: Penguin, 1986. Print.
Coakley, James. "Chekhov in Ireland: Brief Notes on Friel's Philadelphia." *Comparative Drama* 7.3 (Fall 1973): 191–97. Print.
Deane, Seamus. *Friel Festival Brochure*. 1999. Print.
Friel, Brian. *Aristocrats*. Dublin: Gallery Press, 1980. Print.
——. *The Communication Cord*. London: Faber and Faber, 1982. Print.
——. *Dancing at Lughnasa*. London: Faber and Faber, 1990. Print.
——. *Faith Healer*. London: Faber and Faber, 1980. Print.
——. *Fathers and Sons*. After the Novel by Ivan Turgenev. London: Faber and Faber, 1987. Print.
——. *The Home Place*. Oldcastle: Gallery Press, 2005. Print.
——. *Living Quarters*. Oldcastle: Gallery Press, 1992. Print .
——. *A Month in the Country: After Turgenev*. Oldcastle: Gallery Press, 1992. Print.
——. *Philadelphia, Here I Come!* London: Faber and Faber, 1965. Print.
——. Program notes for Field Day's production of Three Sisters. Dublin Theatre Festival, 1981. Print.
——. "Seven Notes for a Festival Programme." 1999. Reprinted in Brian Friel. *Essays, Diaries, Interviews: 1964–1999*. Ed. Christopher Murray. London: Faber and Faber, 1999. 173–80. Print.
——. "Talking to Ourselves. An Interview with Paddy Agnew." *Brian Friel in Conversation*. Ed. Paul Delaney. Ann Arbor: U of Michigan P, 2000. 144–52. Print.
——. *Three Plays After: The Yalta Game, The Bear, Afterplay*. Oldcastle: Gallery Press, 1992. Print.
——. *Three Sisters by Anton Chekhov*. Dublin: Gallery Press, 1981. Print.
——. *Translations*. London: Faber and Faber, 1980. Print.
——. *Uncle Vanya. A Version of the Play by Anton Chekhov*. Oldcastle: Gallery Press, 1998. Print.
Gillespie, Elgy. "The Saturday Interview: Brian Friel." *Irish Times* 5 September 1981. Reprinted in *Brian Friel in Conversation*. Ed. Paul Delaney. Ann Arbor: U of Michigan P, 2000. 153–57. Print.
Grene, Nicholas. "Friel and His 'Sisters.'" *Ilha do Desterro* 58 (Jan.–June 2010): 99–111. Print.
Guthrie, Tyrone. *A Life in the Theatre*. London: Columbus Books, 1987. Print.
Harp, Richard, and Robert C. Evans, eds. *A Companion to Brian Friel*. West Cornwel: Locust Hill, 2002. Print.
Heaney, Seamus. *Spelling It Out. In Honour of Brian Friel on his 80th Birthday*. Oldcastle: Gallery Press, 2009. Print.

Jones, Richard. "Dramatic Interpretation as Theatrical Translation." *A Companion to Brian Friel*. Ed. Richard Harp and Robert C. Evans. West Cornwell, CT: Locust Hill, 2002. 31–52. Print.

Kavanagh, Julie. "Friel at Last." *Brian Friel in Conversation*. Ed. Paul Delaney. Ann Arbor: U of Michigan P, 2000. 218–27. Print.

Kilroy, Thomas. "In Celebration of a Friend." *Irish Times* 10 Jan. 2009. Weekend supplement. Print.

———. *The Seagull. After Chekhov*. Oldcastle: Gallery Press, 1993. Print.

Mason, Patrick. "Playing the Game." Gate/Friel Program Notes, September 2009. Print.

Murray, Christopher, ed. *Brian Friel. Essays, Diaries, Interviews: 1964–1999*. London: Faber and Faber, 1999. Print.

O'Brien, George. *Brian Friel*. Dublin: Gill and MacMillan, 1989. Print.

O'Donnell, Donal. "Friel and a Tale of Three Sisters." *Sunday Press* 30 Aug. 1981. Reprinted in *Brian Friel in Conversation*. Ed. Paul Delaney. Ann Arbor: U of Michigan P, 2000. 149–52. Print.

O'Kelly, Emer. "A Magnificent Vanya." *Sunday Independent* 11 October 1998. Print.

O'Toole, Fintan. "Kilroy Interview." In *Dublin* 17 September 1981: 13. Print.

———. Rev. of *Two Plays After*, by Brian Friel. *Irish Times* 7 March 2002: 14. Print.

Pine, Richard. *Brian Friel and Ireland's Drama*. London: Routledge, 1990. Print.

———. "Distance and Absence." Gate/Friel program notes. September 2009. Print.

———. "Friel's Irish Russia." *The Cambridge Companion to Brian Friel*. Ed. Anthony Roche. Cambridge: Cambridge UP, 2006. 104–16. Print.

Richtarik, Marilynn J. *Acting between the Lines. The Field Day Theatre Company and Irish Cultural Politics 1980–1984*. Oxford: Clarendon Press, 1994. Print.

Roche, Anthony, ed. "Exits and Entrances, Arrivals and Departures." Program for Anton Chekhov's *Uncle Vanya* in a version by Brian Friel. Gate Theatre Dublin, October 2007. Print.

———. *The Cambridge Companion to Brian Friel*. Cambridge: Cambridge UP, 2006. Print.

———. *Contemporary Irish Drama*. Dublin: Gill and MacMillan, 1994. Print.

Tracy, Robert. "The Russian Connection: Friel and Chekhov." *Irish University Review* 29.1 (Spring/Summer 1999; Special Brian Friel Issue): 64–77. Print.

York, Richard. "Friel's Russia." *The Achievement of Brian Friel*. Ed. Alan Peacock. Gerrards Cross: Colin Smythe, 1993. 164–77. Print.

Part III

Performing Chekhov in Radical Mutations

11 Daniel Veronese's "Proyecto Chéjov"
Translation in Performance as Radical Relationality

Jean Graham-Jones

Director-playwright Daniel Veronese is arguably Argentina's most successful theatre artist.[1] A founding member of famed Argentine experimental object-theatre company El Periférico de Objetos and author-director of such plays as *Mujeres soñaron caballos* (*Women Dreamt Horses*),[2] he is also a successful commercial director of Neil LaBute and David Mamet. Nevertheless, Veronese has perhaps had the greatest impact on the international performance scene with what he called his "Proyecto Chéjov" ("Chekhov Project") and its radical versions of the Russian playwright's *Three Sisters* and *Uncle Vanya*.

Rather than regard each production as a revision or free interpretation of its respective individual Chekhovian source, for this chapter I take my cue from Veronese's conjoined titles and approach the productions as a diptych we might entitle "A drowning man spies on a woman killing herself." Each production reenvisions Chekhov's original text: *Un hombre que se ahoga* (*A Drowning Man . . .* , 2004) distills *Three Sisters* to under ninety minutes and inverts gender roles, while *Espía a una mujer que se mata* (*. . . Spies on a Woman Killing Herself*, 2006) condenses *Uncle Vanya* and interpolates fragments of another Chekhov text, *The Seagull*, as well as Jean Genet's *The Maids*.[3] The original productions also overlap in venue, casting, design aesthetics, and performance styles. Taken together they offer a meditation on life in and as theatre or, in Veronese's own words, "God, Stanislavsky, and Genet."[4]

Jonathan E. Abel has asserted, "Translations do share something with the translated, but this sharing is not [. . .] the erasing of one by another, the domineering of one over another [. . .] This sharing is the being-in-common, the standing-in-relation between two texts" (155). Although Veronese's productions share much with the Chekhov source texts, more importantly *A Drowning Man* and *Spies on a Woman Killing Herself* stand in relation to one another as conjoined productions. Such relationality, or being-in-common, is further complicated when we realize that Veronese's own original *Women Dreamt Horses*, which premiered before the two "Chekhovs," shared *Spies on a Woman Killing Herself*'s set and actors. How might we reconsider Walter Benjamin's oft-cited concept of translation's "unavoidable relationality"

204 *Jean Graham-Jones*

in light of such transformative, radical, and multiplied productions of two Chekhovian plays? This chapter constitutes an attempt at precisely such a reconsideration of Chekhov-in-translation.

Chekhov's plays have long been standards of the Buenos Aires theatrical repertoire and, unsurprisingly, are often linked to local interest in Stanislavskyan explorations of acting and directing. By mid-century, Italian companies were touring productions of Chekhov in Italian translation, and the first local productions of Chekhovian texts had been undertaken by the local independent (nonprofessional) theatre troupes working with Stanislavsky-trained émigré practitioners. Chekhov's plays have been translated and published in Argentina, and they continue to be periodically reprised, much like most works of the European theatrical canon.[5] In October 2010, for Chekhov's 150th birthday, Argentinian director and leading Stanislavsky interpreter Raúl Serrano acknowledged the Russian playwright's impact in a month long celebration that included theatrical performances; a photographic exhibit; film screenings; and roundtable conversations with local playwrights, directors, scholars, teachers, and critics.[6] That same year, Veronese's *Vania* was invited to Moscow's Ninth Chekhov International Theatre Festival.[7]

One of the most important artists to emerge after Argentina's return to democracy, Veronese first came to national and international attention through his participation in the haunting and disturbing productions of influential object-theatre troupe El Periférico de Objetos, which he cofounded in 1989 with other puppetry students Ana Alvarado, Emilio García Wehbi, and Paula Nátoli (joined soon thereafter by Román Lamas and, somewhat later, Alejandro Tantanian). Working collaboratively from the self-declared periphery, separating actors theatre and object-theatre, the "Periféricos" radically adapted texts (source-text authors included Alfred Jarry, E. T. A. Hoffmann, Heiner Müller, and Samuel Beckett); created their own (these original texts included Veronese's *Cámara Gesell* and *Circo Negro*); and constructed textual montages. One example would be the 1998 *Zooedipous*, which reworked the Oedipal myth through texts by Franz Kafka, Müller, and Veronese. Periférico productions incorporated various objects—dolls of every shape, size, and material, their heads and eye sockets often emptied; life-size puppets of plastic or foam-rubber; found and constructed objects; and toys—all of which were manipulated in full view of their audiences.[8] Best known abroad for *Máquina Hamlet*, a brilliantly violent version of Heiner Müller's *Hamletmachine*, the company became famous for performances in which words were separated from image and puppets from puppeteers, who in turn split themselves into manipulators and actors. El Periférico de Objetos revolutionized Argentinean object-theatre, which up to that point had promoted the magic of the seemingly independent marionette and its invisible puppeteer. It also provided Veronese with a laboratory for textual revision and adaptation.

Daniel Veronese's "Proyecto Chéjov" 205

Argentinian critic Jorge Dubatti states that a key feature of Veronese's theatre is its "multiplication" (20). As director and playwright, Veronese himself has benefited from multiple training and roles. In addition to an early apprenticeship in carpentry and traditional preparation as a puppeteer (Veronese studied puppetry at Buenos Aires's famed Puppeteers Group, attached to the city's municipal theatre, where he would continue working well into the 1990s), Veronese studied acting and directing with director Ricardo Bartís and playwriting with dramatists Mauricio Kartun and Roberto Mario Cossa. While working in El Periférico de Objetos, he began writing plays for actors, with his first, *Crónica de la caída de uno de los hombres de ella* (*Chronicle of the Fall of One of Her Men*), premiering in 1992 in Buenos Aires's San Martín Municipal Theatre. Like many of his generation's playwrights and their successors, Veronese seems to grant himself complete aesthetic freedom to mix genres, registers, forms, and even political positions in order to create what he terms "bastard theatre." Some of his published plays appear in very conventional form, while others are schematic registers of actions, stimuli, and provocations intended for development in rehearsal and performance.[9] The director frequently recycles sets and set pieces and he often works with the same actors, recasting them in different productions to meet the demands of long-term touring and restaging commitments. Veronese grants equal freedom to others: at times he directs his own plays; other times they've been staged by some of Buenos Aires's best-regarded directors.

Veronese's recent productions reflect the dramatist-director's intensely intimate and interwoven writing, design, and directing style. Audiences are seated closer to the action than might be comfortable (indeed, friends sometimes refuse to join me in the front row); actors perform in the clothes and makeup they wore to the theatre and typically remain onstage or sit with the audience; sets are minimal and often reused from other productions; and there are no apparent light cues (and sometimes not even any artificial lighting). One critic raved about a recent Veronese production, "there is nothing at all" (Koss). Not quite: Veronese's productions are stripped to the most elemental of human interactions with thoughtfully constructed environments and actors bringing their all to the onstage encounter. Today, playwright Veronese says he always writes "thinking about the stage" ("Nueve") with the unsurprising result that he has become not only an accomplished dramatist but also the favorite director of some of Buenos Aires's most talented actors and a director in international demand. All of these elements are present in his "Proyecto Chéjov."

The conceptual departure point for the 2004 *A Drowning Man* was a gender switch. Men played the female roles and women the male roles, with no cross-dressing involved. As so often can happen in the theatre, circumstances inspired invention: Veronese first assembled the actors with whom he wanted to work, and when he realized that the gender distribution did

206 *Jean Graham-Jones*

not correspond to that dictated by Chekhov's play, he decided to invert the casting and reduce the number of actors from fourteen to twelve, omitting the secondary characters Fedotik and Rode and cutting or redistributing their dialogue. Staging was bare-boned, with the actors seated onstage or in the first row of the audience when not performing. Playing at the independent theatre space El Camarín de las Musas (The Muses' Dressing Room), the production had one performance a week, Sundays in the late afternoon, a very strange time of day for the independent theatres but perfect for the production's working actors running to another show that evening.[10] Lighting was provided by sunlight entering through transparent ceiling panels, and the actors wore their own street clothes without any makeup or other theatrical "effects." The performance lasted barely ninety minutes, with Chekhov's text squeezed until all that was left was a distillation of the Russian play and the source of theatre—human relations; or, as Veronese explained it: "I need[ed] to synthesize and illuminate certain zones of reality" (Hernández).

In addition to language changes dictated by the gender inversions (for example, the three brothers refer to Andrey as their sister, the siblings speak of their mother instead of their father, and Natasha wears green pants with a pink shirt), *A Drowning Man* cuts, reorders, and occasionally substitutes Chekhov's text: setting and time changes are left unremarked; longer speeches are condensed to a couple of central lines; parts of scenes are rearranged; and, most interestingly for the text in performance, two-character dialogues are frequently interrupted by interjections from other characters (who often remain onstage longer than indicated in the Chekhovian text), allowing for all present to participate in what might be otherwise considered a private conversation. At times language is added that, to this spectator's mind, seems to speak aloud the source's subtext; at other times, Chekhov's lines are not spoken aloud but whispered by one actor into another's ear. One example of this effective adaptation strategy occurs in act 2, when Vershinin privately tells Masha that her husband has attempted suicide, thus underscoring the intimacy of their relationship and triggering Masha's outburst following Vershinin's exit. Geographic and proper nouns—except for the family names and an idealized Moscow—are often replaced by more generic terms (e.g., Vershinin's act 1 description of the city does not contain references to Nemetskaya Street or the Krasny Barracks; Saratov is inaccurately conflated with the "capital" [Moscow]; and Zasyp is simply referred to as "un pueblito de mierda" [a shitty little town]) or by references more easily identifiable to local audiences (e.g., Dobrolyubov is replaced by Flaubert, an author more likely known to the average Argentine spectator). Other replacements are more overt. For example, in act 4, Veronese exchanges the fragment from Mikhail Yuryevich Lermontov's nineteenth-century poem "The Sail" for two lines from Anna Akhmatova's mid-twentieth-century "Requiem" ("Epilogue 1"—"Aprendí cómo se puede deshojar un rostro / cómo en la seca sonrisa tiembla el miedo" [I

Daniel Veronese's "Proyecto Chéjov"   207

learned how faces fall / And fear trembles in a dry laugh]), an uncredited substitution that is both more contemporary and more despairing. Finally, and very importantly when considering the translation of canonical foreign texts, some of the characters employ the *voseo*, the familiar second-person form that is a feature of the Buenos Aires dialect,[11] but without many of the city's distinctive colloquialisms.

Together, these innovations resulted in a less "foreignizing" (pace Lawrence Venuti) translation that kept actors onstage longer, incorporated nearly all present into the ongoing conversation, created a charged group dynamic not always associated with Chekhov in production, and maintained a focus on the ensemble rather than any individual performer or couple. In *A Drowning Man* Chekhov's ruling-class "tragedy" approached a bitingly ironic celebration of a new modern era, in which women act while men wait and dream.

Though at times critically perceived by the international press as a gimmick, the production's gendered role reversal brought to the foreground issues residing in Chekhov's play that are sometimes overlooked in production: time and aging, divisions of social class, and gender politics. When the Argentine production played at New York's Lincoln Center in 2007, one *New York Times* reviewer chastised Veronese for finding "the grotesque where it doesn't lurk, in an older baron's love of one of the Prozorov sisters. Tuzenbach [. . .] a grandmotherly-looking woman, chases the male Irina as if Chekhov set out to write 'Sunset Boulevard.' The desperation is misplaced" (Bellafante). Ironically, the critic's search for an explicit feminism behind the switched genders blinded her to the production's successes, one being how the would-be lovers' age reversal neatly exposed shared U.S. and Argentinian cultural prejudices about women of a "certain age" (what today's popular culture calls "cougars"). Another New York–based critic ranked the production among her top ten of 2007, writing that the "surface gesture" of exchanging gender roles "paradoxically uncovered Chekhov's deepest, most lacerating intentions" (Shaw 140). The gender inversion also allowed for different types of humor than might be expected of a Chekhovian drama. As one critic put it, "Maybe the unavoidable goofiness that comes with a mustachioed Masha nudges Chekhov closer to the blend of mirth and misery that the playwright famously sought" (Grode). Ultimately, Veronese's cross-cast production did much more than invert gender roles.

With *Spies on a Woman Killing Herself* staged in the same theatre space as its predecessor, Veronese took a different approach to translation and adaptation. While his casting largely followed the gendered lines of Chekhov's *Uncle Vanya*, Veronese radically reworked the text, interpolating it with fragments from Chekhov's own *The Seagull* and Jean Genet's *The Maids*. *Spies on a Woman Killing Herself* opens with a scene between Sonia and her father, Serebryakov. Both are seated at the same table, and Sonia holds a gun in her hand. Their dialogue centers on the theatre, with fragments of text taken from *The Seagull*'s first-act exchange between Sorin and his nephew,

208 *Jean Graham-Jones*

the young playwright Treplyov; only here it is the old and sick theatre critic and scholar Serebryakov who complains about the state of contemporary theatre. The scene ends with Sonia giving her father the revolver, which he promises to save for "the ending." Both the intertextual reference to *The Seagull*'s world of actors and Serebryakov's meditation on the stage overtly place *Spies on a Woman Killing Herself* in the theatre. Once again, the actors dress in their own street clothes, here suggesting a rehearsal more than a performance. Such inferred metatheatricality is reinforced through Veronese's inclusion of Genet's 1947 text. On at least two occasions, Sonia's uncle Vania (suggestively referred to as "Jean" by his Gallicizing mother) rehearses scenes from Genet's play with his acting partner, the doctor Astrov. In those scenes, Vania-Solange performs with Astrov-Claire-as-Madame the opening and closing scenes of *The Maids*. The rehearsals not only serve as metatheatrical reminders; they are also positioned to echo and reinforce Vania's subservient, even trapped (and in some ways feminized), role within his own family. For example, Vania says to Serebryakov during their act 3 confrontation: "¿Yo protagonista de la historia? Pero si siempre fui tu valet" ("Me, history's protagonist? I was always your valet"). The interpolated Genet scenes additionally underscore the consciously constructed nature of the family's daily rituals (when, for example, Teleguin confuses Claire-Madame's request for tea with Astrov's demand for vodka). When the play ends, Sonia and Vania drop their heads onto the table. As the characters resigning themselves to their future? As actors turning off their characters? The metatheatrical strategy, one that we might expect to distance us from Vania and Sonia's shared resigned sorrow, surprisingly pulls us closer, making the ending almost unbearably sad. Indeed, every time I saw the production—both in rehearsal and performance—I found my ironic laughter overtaken by a profound sadness in the final moments.

In *Spies on a Woman Killing Herself*, Veronese returned to several strategies employed in the earlier *A Drowning Man*: a single, unadorned setting was employed (though in this production the actors did not wait with the audience when not onstage); longer speeches were reduced or broken up through dialogue; solitary monologues did not leave an actor alone onstage but were rather observed and even interrupted by others; and minor characters were eliminated or folded into others (for example, the impoverished landowner Teleguin—the only character whose gender is changed—speaks some of the old nurse Marina's lines and carries out many of her duties). Once again, the result was a streamlined mobility often absent from more "respectful" productions of Chekhov.

Despite the individual strengths and peculiarities of each production, it would be difficult for any follower of contemporary Argentinean theatre not to regard them as paired components of a single diptych.[12] First, they are conjoined by their titles, two parts of a single quotation Veronese attributes to Jacques Prévert: "A drowning man spies on a woman killing herself."[13] Veronese has stated in interviews that for him the drowning

Daniel Veronese's "Proyecto Chéjov" 209

man is the provincial universe of landed gentry.[14] And the suicidal woman? Not only does the conjoined title foreground the two genders portrayed (and sometimes inverted) in Veronese's takes on the Chekhov plays; it also suggests a form of fatalistic parity, between the sexes, between classes, between the fading aristocracy and the nascent order(s). A diptychal reading of the plays is also supported by the aforementioned overlaps in translation and adaptation strategies as well as venue, design aesthetics, performance styles, and casting. Both productions premiered at the independent theatre El Camarín de las Musas, in its smaller side theatre space that seats at most some fifty spectators. Veronese worked with many of the same actors, and both productions maintained, as I have described, a scaled-down aesthetic of a single unadorned set, simple furnishings, no period costumes, and minimal light design. The performance style was similarly austere: working centripetally, actors focused in on one another in scenes that had been opened up to provoke exchange (and not internal monologue), with an intensity of emotion and physicality that has become a hallmark of Veronese's productions.

Perhaps the most significant—in terms of extended interpretation— diptychal element was in the original casting. An excellent case in point is Osmar Núñez, an actor of impressive emotional depth and focus. Núñez originated the respective roles of Olga and Vania and received accolades for both performances. Marvin Carlson reminds us that in earlier centuries an actor was often identified by a single stock type (*emploi*) or a particular role ("signature role"),[15] and even today our spectatorial experiences are haunted by earlier theatre outings. Carlson writes, "Almost any theatregoer can doubtless recall situations when the memory of an actor seen in a previous role or roles remained in the mind to haunt a subsequent performance" (10). Veronese's productions draw repeat local audiences, thus many theatregoers watching Núñez's Vania would have remembered his Olga from two years earlier (or even less time, given that these productions enjoyed long runs that themselves occasionally overlapped). Núñez recounts that he was first offered the role of Masha before Veronese decided upon him for Olga: "Olga is very personal to me. I have a lot of siblings and am very family-oriented. We have fewer frustrations than the 'sisters,' but we suffer others, perhaps smaller" (Núñez). After seeing Núñez's performance as Vania, it seems only logical that he would have played Olga: the oldest sister and the aging uncle are both destined to be single, each to be sacrificed on the familial altar. Olga's academic career in a "new" Russia serves as equally unfulfilling counterpoint to Vania's commitment to the old order. Not all casting seemed so ghostly; indeed, the haunting in some cases created a rich contrast. Such was the case of actor María Figueras, who replaced Silvina Bosco as Solioni and originated the role of Sonia. The diminutive Figueras played the mocking Solioni as pathetically crude and obnoxious, a weasel who shoots Baroness Tuzembaj in a duel; it was a performance that strikingly contrasted

210 Jean Graham-Jones

with her devout and devoted Sonia, who begins Veronese's production holding a gun though it is never made clear whether she intends to use it on herself or her father, Serebryakov, played by Fernando Llosa.[16]

The image of a young woman holding a gun on an older man conjures another Veronese-in-performance ghost and further widens our relational analysis of Chekhov-in-translation. Veronese's original 2001 play, *Women Dreamt Horses* ends with Lucera aiming a gun at her husband, Iván, again performed by Fernando Llosa.[17] Not only did the production share some of the two Chekhovs' actors; its set was later recycled for *Spies on a Woman Killing Herself*. Thus, five years later audiences saw the actors playing Serebryakov and his daughter sitting at table near which they had earlier stood as husband and wife. Chekhov was now haunted by Veronese.

It becomes nearly impossible to speak of Veronese's two Chekhovs without considering his own *Women Dreamt Horses*, particularly within the context of Buenos Aires theatre.[18] Thus, in the final section of this chapter, I argue for a radical relationality of Chekhov-in-translation that extends beyond the two source texts to create a theatrical triptych including Veronese's 2001 production. In order to do so, I expand my consideration of translation as relational by taking inspiration from the debates surrounding Nicolas Bourriaud's concept of "relational aesthetics." Arguing for an art of intersubjective, collective (but not necessarily interactive) encounters, Bourriaud presents what Claire Bishop calls a "DIY, microtopian ethos" ("Antagonism" 54). While acknowledging Bourriaud's contribution to reconsidering the role of art and the relationship between the contemporary artist and spectator, Bishop criticizes relational aesthetics' requirement of "a unified subject as a prerequisite for community-as-togetherness" (79) and counterpoises a "relational antagonism" that is "predicated not on social harmony, but on exposing that which is repressed in sustaining the semblance of this harmony" (79).[19] Bishop persuasively argues that we must ask ourselves what kind of relationality is established: "if relational art produces human relations, then the next logical question to ask is what *types* of relations are being produced, for whom, and why?" (65; original emphasis). I propose that we similarly push Abel and Benjamin's relational concept of translation by asking what type of relationality is established in the Veronese productions of Chekhov-in-translation. Opening up Veronese's diptych to include the third production, I suggest that the triptych stands as an example of a relational antagonism that not only exposes the social disharmony Veronese observes in contemporary Argentina, but also demonstrates that while translation is indeed relational, said relationality is a starting, not ending, point.

Women Dreamt Horses takes place during a family reunion of three brothers with their respective spouses. It is a family dinner derailed by what appears to be deeply ingrained familial violence. Roger, the youngest brother, and his much older wife, Bettina, have gathered the family together so the middle brother, Rainer, can inform everyone he has sold

Daniel Veronese's "Proyecto Chéjov" 211

the family business. Roger, a boxer punched too many times and now with a cancerous tumor growing in his head, appears to loathe Bettina. Rainer, the middle brother, is at odds with his own wife, Ulrika. The third brother, Iván, is thirty years older than his wife, Lucera, the outsider removed (or not?) from the sickness surrounding her. They all detest yet seem unable to live without each other. It is a vicious cycle of violence possibly broken by a final act of violence. Veronese himself has said that by the end of the play, he hopes his audience so detests the other characters that it applauds Lucera's assassinations.[20]

By play's end, Lucera will have indeed killed everyone but Iván, at whom she points her gun just after telling him she's pregnant. From the jumbled times reported in the play (is it 8:10, 8:15, 8:50?), the audience is given to understand that it has just witnessed Lucera's narration of these events. Lucera's violent response seems triggered by her own history with this family: according to the brothers, they found her at a campsite, abandoned after her parents were killed when a crazed horse threw itself off a cliff; however, Lucera has a clear counter-memory of her parents leaving her on a building stairway in a desperate escape. And in her final monologue, she recounts that after the "gunshots" (her parents' death? her having killed her in-laws?), an old couple takes her to their hiding place in the basement, where she witnesses a stampede of wild horses, "what should have happened years ago." One way of interpreting this information is generational and historical: Lucera, the youngest, represents a new generation and her unborn child the future. The three brothers' story of how Iván and Rainer "found" Lucera becomes very symbolically loaded when viewed within the context of Argentina's history. What was this horse that plunged Lucera's parents down the mountain? Is Lucera the child of two *desaparecidos* killed by the dictatorship? If so, how did the brothers come to acquire her? Most of the children of the disappeared who have been recovered were adopted by those complicit with the dictatorship. Are Lucera's murders a revenge on the sins of the former regime and its supporters? If so, Lucera returns the violence that has informed her entire young life.

Although Veronese acknowledges that he wrote the play while thinking about the dark period of dictatorship and the tens of thousands of disappearances, he cautions us—in the original production's program notes—not to read the play exclusively in that historical moment, because "it can be applied to any situation. The audience might recognize, not necessarily entirely but at least partially, some aspects of this family." The audience is ultimately drawn into this violent scene. Spectators become witnesses to a ceremony of self-destruction, family members hurling themselves off a cliff and making sure to destroy one another and everyone else as they plummet, a violent cycle potentially ended by an act of violence. Indeed, destructive violence permeates every aspect of human relations in *Women Dreamt Horses*: brothers, couples, families, animals, the environment, and even art.

212 *Jean Graham-Jones*

How might a spectator like myself, who saw all three productions, interpret Veronese's earlier play in relation to his two versions of Chekhov? Three Argentine brothers are replaced by three ostensibly Russian brothers; one Chekhov is bracketed by a Veronese and another Chekhov, both staged on the same set with the latter beginning where the former ended; the same actors appear in different yet at times resonant or contrastive roles, exemplified respectively in the performances of Núñez and Figueras; and, once again, similar design aesthetics and performance styles seek to strip away illusion and in the process offer three different yet not unconnected meditations on art, especially theatre and life. Veronese himself made specific reference to *Women Dreamt Horses* just before the premiere of *Spies on a Woman Killing Herself*: "There won't be any theatrical costumes, nor bucolic rhythms in family salons. Nor pieces of junk denoting a rural period. The action will take place on the old, beaten-up set for *Women Dreamt Horses*" (Hopkins). Thus the audience of *Spies on a Woman Killing Herself* sees the scars left by *Women Dreamt Horses*'s earlier performances and is reminded of the earlier play's violent and ultimately self-destructive family. *Women Dreamt Horses* stages, as one actress notes, "a daily violence that we don't know if it's generated from outside or if we ourselves . . . are creating a violent world" (Torres).[21] The earlier staged daily violence has left its traces on the later play and perhaps leads spectators to wonder about the origins of the tensions experienced in *Spies on a Woman Killing Herself* and their own participation. Are we drowning men? Suicidal women? Or their spying witnesses? As one local critic wrote, implying *Spies on a Woman Killing Herself*'s debt to both *Women Dreamt Horses* and *A Drowning Man*, "[It's] not for nothing that, [caught] between chronic powerlessness and desire with the strength of a thousand horses, women kill themselves while men spy on them. And drown" (Mauro).

Veronese's *Women Dreamt Horses* can in turn be interpreted retrospectively through his two Chekhovian versions. Veronese has spoken of a spirit he sees in all Chekhov's work:

> A search for spiritual or familial well-being and tranquility. In these characters there's an eternal desire to be happy and at the same time everything shows that this is impossible. Perhaps they could have taken a step toward happiness, but since they didn't manage to, they think about the reasons why they didn't. It would appear that no matter what they do they will never be happy. It's a thought that doesn't have anything to do with my daily life but seeing it reflected in the theatre moves and stimulates me a lot. (Hopkins)[22]

"Proyecto Chéjov's" dual portrayal of failed dreams for the theatre and inner personal sorrows married with a biting humor provides a humanizing lens for reconsidering the internalized, devastating violence played out in the earlier *Women Dreamt Horses*.

Indeed, after seeing these three productions, it becomes almost impossible for me to consider any one of them without referring to the other two. *A Drowning Man*'s gender and class politics run through the very violent and Argentinean prehistories that determine the catastrophic outcome of *Women Dreamt Horses*, which in turn triggers *Spies on a Woman Killing Herself*'s opening and its meditation on dreams lost in the theatre and in life. Veronese's three productions emphasize the family over the individual; all three strip expression to its most intense minimalism; and all three insist upon the presence of theatre and art in their considerations of daily life. As a triptych, these three productions from early twenty-first-century Argentina remind us that translation is never unidirectional nor simply relational. Considering Chekhov-in-translation from a larger, radically "relational," and possibly antagonistic perspective can result in more nuanced and enriching understandings of the possibilities for translation in performance.

NOTES

1. Daniel Veronese was born in 1955 in Avellaneda, Province of Buenos Aires. It is not unusual to find multiple Veronese projects running concurrently in Buenos Aires, an occurrence rare even for a national capital with over three hundred theatres. As a playwright and director, Veronese has received some twenty-five awards in his native Argentina. His productions have had extended runs in European and Latin American cities and have traveled to festivals in Belgium, Brazil, Canada, Chile, Colombia, France, Germany, Mexico, the Netherlands, Portugal, Russia, Spain, Sweden, Switzerland, Uruguay, the United States, and Venezuela.
2. Unless otherwise noted, all translations from Spanish are mine.
3. *Un hombre que se ahoga* (*A Drowning Man*) premiered in 2004 at the independent theatre space El Camarín de las Musas, Buenos Aires, Argentina. The original cast included: Claudio Tolcachir (Irina), Luciano Suardi (Masha), Osmar Núñez (Olga), Julieta Vallina (Andrey), Pablo Messiez (Natasha), Osvaldo Bonet (Anfisa), Marta Lubos (Chebutikin), Stella Galazzi (Vershinin), Silvina Sabater (Kuliguin), Elvira Onetto (Tusembaj), Silvina Bosco (Solioni), and Adriana Ferrer (Ferapont). *Espía a una mujer que se mata* (*Spies on a Woman Killing Herself*) premiered in 2006 at El Camarín de las Musas, Buenos Aires, Argentina. The original cast included: María Figueras (Sonia), Fernando Llosa (Serebryakov), Mara Bestelli (Elena Andreevna, replacing Julieta Vallina), Marta Lubos (María Vasilievna), Osmar Núñez (Vania), Silvina Sabater (Teleguin), and Marcelo Subiotto (Astrov).
4. The quotation comes from Veronese's publicity materials. Both productions won awards: *A Drowning Man* received three awards from the Association of Theatre Critics (ACE) for best independent production, best direction, and best actor in an independent production (Luciano Suardi, for his portrayal of Masha). Leading daily newspaper *Clarín* awarded Veronese its annual prize for best author, based on three plays, among them *A Drowning Man*. *Spies on a Woman Killing Herself* received the *Clarín* award for best independent production and best director. Osmar Núñez received the prestigious Trinidad Guevara award for best actor in a leading role for his portrayal of Vania.

214 Jean Graham-Jones

5. As recently as 2005, a collection of Chekhov's complete plays in Spanish translation was reedited. The plays were translated in 1950 by Galina Tolmacheva (1895–1987), a Russian émigrée to Argentina, former Stanislavsky student, and influential acting teacher.
6. 1–31 October 2010 at the Teatro del Artefacto, Buenos Aires, Argentina. See complete program: 150 años con Antón P. Chéjov. 150antonchejov.blogspot. Web. 30 June 2011.
7. IX Chekhov International Theatre Festival, at the Meyerhold Theatre, Moscow, 26–31 May 2010.
8. See Cornago Bernal and Propato for the history and analyses of some of Periférico's key performances. Veronese himself has a provocative essay on the work of the company ("Periférico").
9. Twenty-one of Veronese's plays have been published in two Spanish-language collections: Cuerpo de prueba (Body of Proof, 1997, reedited in two volumes in 2005) and La deriva (Drift, 2000). As recently as 2007, he premiered a new play, Teatro para pájaros (Theatre for Birds), which the author claims will be his last original work.
10. The production went on to add Friday and Saturday midnight performances, with fixed artificial lighting and no cues.
11. This is not always the case with Argentine translation, where sometimes the formal second-person form (usted) may be used or other strategies employed, as playwright-translator Rafael Spregelburd writes, "to find a way to erase the marks of a language that is too fully ours and therefore must be rendered invisible in order to allow the play its normal development" (374).
12. Indeed, they've been referred to as such in the press. See, for example, Santillán.
13. Veronese has never provided the source, but the phrase is very similar to a line of dialogue from Jacques Prévert's screenplay for Marcel Carné's 1938 film, Le Quai des Brumes (Port of Shadows). An artist who will soon commit suicide by drowning (and later impersonated by the film's protagonist), says: "If I see a swimmer, I immediately think he'll drown, so I paint a drowned man." Fatalism or pragmatism?
14. Veronese has made this assertion in many interviews, stating that the phrase strikes him as very "Chekhovian." See, for example, his interview with Argentine critic Cecilia Hopkins: "There's a phrase that's accompanied me for a long time and seems to me very Chekhovian: a man who's drowning spies on a woman who's killing herself."
15. See, especially, Chapter 3, "The Haunted Body."
16. In yet another case of evocative double-casting, Fernando Llosa replaced Osvaldo Bonet as Anfisa in the later performances of A Drowning Man.
17. Mujeres soñaron caballos (Women Dreamt Horses), written in 1999, premiered in September 2001 at Buenos Aires's independent theatre Espacio Callejón. The production, with some periodic changes, has continued to tour internationally and play locally. The original cast included: Fernando Llosa (Iván), Julieta Vallina (Ulrika), Marcelo Subbioto (Roger), Osmar Núñez (Rainer), Lucera Anganuzzi (Lucera, later María Figueras), and Silvina Sabater (Bettina).
18. The potential for such relationality is obviously minimized when we consider these productions within the international festival context, where typically (but not always) the audience sees only one of the productions.
19. The reader might wish to consult also artist Liam Gillick's response to Bishop, as well as Bishop's reply to her critics, "Claire Bishop Responds."
20. Personal conversation with the author, Buenos Aires, 2007.
21. Spanish actress Blanca Portillo, interviewed on the occasion of the 2007 Madrid premiere of a Spanish production directed by Veronese.

22. The original Spanish reads as follows: "Por esa búsqueda del bienestar y la tranquilidad espiritual o familiar. En esos personajes hay un deseo eterno de ser feliz y, a la vez, todo demuestra que esto es imposible. Tal vez ellos pudieron haber dado un paso hacia la felicidad, pero como no lo consiguieron, piensan las razones por las cuales no lo hicieron. Pareciera que hagan lo que hagan nunca serán felices. Es un pensamiento que no tiene que ver con mi acontecer cotidiano pero que, verlo reflejado en el teatro me apasiona y estimula muchísimo."

WORKS CITED

Abel, Jonathan E. "Translation as Community: The Opacity of Modernization in *Genji monogatari*." *Nation, Language, and the Ethics of Translation*. Ed. Sandra Bermann and Michael Wood. Princeton: Princeton UP, 2006. 146–58. Print.

Akhmatova, Anna. "Requiem." *Selected Poems*. Trans. Judith Hemschemeyer. Brookline: Zephyr Press, 2000. 130–51. Print.

Bellafante, Ginia. "Chekhov Compacted, in Spanish." Rev. of *Un hombre que se ahoga*, by Daniel Veronese. *New York Times* 19 July 2007. theater.nytimes.com. Web. 14 Feb. 2011.

Benjamin, Walter. "The Task of the Translator." *Illuminations*. Trans. Harry Zohn. Ed. Hannah Arendt. New York: Harcourt, Brace and World, 1968. 69–82. Print.

Bishop, Claire. "Antagonism and Relational Aesthetics." *October* 110 (Fall 2004): 51–79. Print.

———. "Claire Bishop Responds." *October* 115 (Winter 2006): 107. Print.

Bourriaud, Nicolas. *Relational Aesthetics*. Trans. Simon Pleasance and Fronza Woods. Paris: Les Presses du réel, 2002. Print.

Carlson, Marvin. *The Haunted Stage: The Theatre as Memory Machine*. Ann Arbor: U of Michigan P, 2001. Print.

Chekhov, Anton. *The Seagull, Uncle Vanya*, and *The Three Sisters. Anton Chekhov's Plays*. Trans. and ed. Eugene K. Bristow. New York and London: W.W. Norton, 1977. Print.

———. *Teatro completo*. Trans. Galina Tolmacheva, Mario Kaplún, and Federico Höller. Buenos Aires: Adriana Hidalgo, 2005. (Original publication *Teatro completo*. Trans. Tolmacheva and Kaplún. Buenos Aires: Sudamericana, 1950.) Print.

Cornago Bernal, Oscar. "Los espacios inciertos: entre el actor y el muñeco." *Artes escénicas*. 2006. artesescenicas.uclm.es. Web. 16 Feb. 2011.

Dubatti, Jorge. "Prólogo." *La deriva*. Ed. Daniel Veronese. Buenos Aires: Adriana Hidalgo, 2000. 5–31. Print.

Genet, Jean. *The Maids. The Maids and Deathwatch: Two Plays*. Trans. Bernard Frechtman. New York: Grove Press, 1994. Print.

Gillick, Liam. "Letters and Responses." *October* 115 (Winter 2006): 95–106. Print.

Grode, Eric. "Bending Chekhov's Boundaries." Rev. of *Un hombre que se ahoga*, by Daniel Veronese. *New York Sun* 19 July 2007. nysun.com. Web. 10 Feb. 2011.

Hernández, Margarita. "Unos muñecos rusos." *Radar*. Supplement of *Página / 12* (Buenos Aires) 26 Nov. 2006. pagina23.com.ar. Web. 10 Feb. 2011.

Hopkins, Cecilia. "'Lo profundo puede resultar elitista' (entrevista a Daniel Veronese)." *Página / 12* (Buenos Aires) 11 Sept. 2006. pagina12.com.ar. Web. 10 Feb. 2011.

216   Jean Graham-Jones

Koss, María Natacha. "Pasillo al fondo." Rev. of *La noche canta sus canciones.* *Alternativa teatral.* 20 Sept. 2008. alternativateatral.com. Web. 14 Feb. 2011.

Mauro, Karina. "Mujeres que se matan soñaron hombres que se ahogan." Rev. of *Espía a una mujer que se mata,* by Daniel Veronese. *Alternativa Teatral* 4 Sept. 2006. alternativateatral.com. Web. 14 Feb. 2011.

Núñez, Osmar. Interview. "Como actor sentir que estoy en la cornisa es algo muy interesante." *Crítica teatral.* criticateatral.com.ar. Web. 10 Feb. 2011.

Propato, Cecilia. "El Periférico de Objetos: resignificación político-histórico y distanciación objetual." *El nuevo teatro de Buenos Aires en la postdictadura (1983–2001). Micropoéticas 1.* Ed. Jorge Dubatti. Buenos Aires: Centro Cultural de la Cooperación, 2002. 282–96. Print.

Santillán, Juan José. "Pasaje a Moscú." *Clarín* 7 March 2010. edant.clarin.com. Web. 30 June 2011.

Shaw, Helen. "The Best (and Worst) of 2007." *Time Out New York* 27 Dec. 2007–2 Jan. 2008: 140. Print.

Spregelburd, Rafael. "'Life, Of Course' in 'What's at Stake in Theatrical Translation?: A Forum.'" Trans. Jean Graham-Jones. *Theatre Journal* 59.3 (Oct. 2007): 373–77. Print.

Torres, Rosana. "El teatro tiene que ser un revulsivo, no sólo evasión." *El País* (Madrid) 15 April 2007. elpais.com. Web. 14 Feb. 2011.

Venuti, Lawrence. *The Translator's Invisibility: A History of Translation.* London: Routledge, 1995. Print.

Veronese, Daniel. *Cuerpo de prueba.* Prol. Jorge Dubatti. Buenos Aires: Centro Cultural Ricardo Rojas, Publicaciones del Ciclo Básico Común (Universidad de Buenos Aires), 1997. Print. Reprinted in *Cuerpo de prueba I* and *Cuerpo de prueba II.* Ed. Jorge Dubatti. Buenos Aires: Atuel, 2005. Print.

———. "Espía a una mujer que se mata (Versión de *Tío Vanya*)." Unpublished ms. Personal DVD of performance.

———. *La deriva.* Ed. Jorge Dubatti. Buenos Aires: Adriana Hidalgo, 2000. Print.

———. *Mujeres soñaron caballos. La deriva.* Ed. Jorge Dubatti. Buenos Aires: Adriana Hidalgo, 2000. 87–171. Print.

———. "Nueve nuevos automandamientos." Teatre Lliure program notes. www. teatrelliure.com. Web. 5 April 2012.

———. "Periférico." www.autores.org.ar. 1999–2000. Web. 16 Feb. 2011.

———. Program notes. *Mujeres soñaron caballos,* 2001. Print. Translated in its entirety in *BAiT: Buenos Aires in Translation.* Trans. and ed. Jean Graham-Jones. New York: TCG/Martin E. Segal Theatre, 2009. 4–5. Print.

———. "Un hombre que se ahoga (Versión de *Tres hermanas*)." Unpublished ms. Also available online at laratonera.com.ar. Personal DVD of performance.

———. *Women Dreamt Horses. BAiT: Buenos Aires in Translation.* Trans. and ed. Jean Graham-Jones. New York: TCG/Martin E. Segal Theatre, 2009. 1–53. Print.

12 Canadian Chekhovs
Three Very Different Mutations

James McKinnon

In the 1970s, as Douglas Clayton acknowledges in his 1997 account of Chekhov's assimilation into the Canadian canon, it was an oft-repeated joke that there were two Canadian playwrights: Shakespeare and Chekhov. But at the time of his writing, Clayton laments the passing of the "Chekhov mania" of the 1970s and 1980s ("Touching Solitudes" 151). By the 1990s, Chekhov had been supplanted by a sustained Shakespeare mania.[1] But Clayton's eulogy may have been premature. The twenty-first century has produced numerous Canadian Chekhov mutations, ranging from (ostensibly) faithful productions of Chekhov's major plays at the Shaw and Stratford Festivals, to the widely acclaimed adaptation of *Platonov* produced by Toronto-based Soulpepper in 1999–2000, to Theatre Smith-Gilmour's internationally renowned theatrical embodiments of Chekhov's prose fiction.[2] What is most striking about Chekhov's recent renaissance is its aesthetic and political diversity: contemporary Canadian Chekhov spans a gamut of styles and stances, ranging from reverence to hostility to the source. Some adaptors attempt to resurrect the great author, while others seek not to bring him back to life so much as to scavenge him for parts, *pace* Dr Frankenstein. This variety suggests that, as with their other national playwright, Canadian spectators are receptive to all sorts of creative refashioning of his work—and that what "Chekhov" signifies is increasingly plural.

The range of dramaturgies and adaptive techniques brought to bear on Chekhov in Canada—and the range of responses such appropriations generate—is aptly demonstrated by three very different mutations of Chekhov, which, coincidentally, were all performed in Ottawa in 2005. All three plays share the same basic adaptive strategy of relocating the canonical text in a Canadian landscape in order to activate what Linda Hutcheon defines as the essential experiential pleasure of adaptation: the "conservative comfort of familiarity" combined with "the unpredictable pleasure in difference" (173). In the spring, the National Arts Centre (NAC)[3] welcomed an Albertan adaptation of *Uncle Vanya*; in the summer, a burlesque, grotesque "Black Opera" rendition of *Three Sisters*, also set in the prairies, won an award for Best Production at the Ottawa Fringe Festival; and in

218 *James McKinnon*

September the NAC opened its new season with the premiere of Jason Sherman's *After the Orchard*, which transplants Chekhov's *Orchard* to Ontario cottage country.[4]

Such approximating gestures are a staple of Shakespeare productions in Canada and elsewhere, but while they are relatively popular with spectators, they have received mixed reviews from scholars. Cultural materialists and new historicists have accused such adaptations of erasing historical and cultural specificity in favor of ahistorical, universalist discourse; whereas post-colonial critics view approximation more optimistically, as part of a broader strategy for contesting canonical authority.[5] But rather than attempting to determine the extent to which critical suspicion of this adaptive strategy is well founded, this chapter focuses on how it works, at least in regard to Chekhov in/and Canada. Relocating Chekhov in Canada is a strategy that offers adaptors considerable flexibility in choosing how to position their work in regard to the source. It may imply a claim of fidelity to the original, or a hostile takeover; it may represent an effort to bring the authentic masterpiece closer to the audience, by excising trivial details that merely impede Canadian spectators' easy apprehension of the inherent and universal greatness of the text; or it may imply an attempt to claim the foreign work as "our" own. The plays discussed in the following show the range of possibilities encompassed by putting "Chekhov" in "Canada," an adaptive strategy that may reiterate, challenge, or confound commonplace assumptions about the meanings of both of those terms.

HOW CHEKHOV WAS/IS MADE IN CANADA

But what are those commonplace assumptions, and how did they come to be such? It is easy to understand how Shakespeare became a "Canadian" playwright, but given that Canada was not colonized by Russia or Russian speakers,[6] the cultural processes that made Chekhov a "Canadian" playwright in the first place are obscure even to most Canadians. Yet it is important to illuminate these processes, because they have, consciously or otherwise, shaped contemporary Chekhov adaptation. As Thomas Cartelli points out in *Repositioning Shakespeare*, "what gives an appropriation [. . .] significance is the fact that it is transacted not only in relation to [its source] but to specific constructions [thereof] that are themselves the products of earlier appropriations" (18). A given adaptor may align him or herself with or against those existing constructions, but in either case adaptors seek to exploit the source's cultural capital without triggering fidelity discourse, i.e., the strong tendency of spectators to judge adaptations by the extent to which they are faithful to their vision of the original—a vision that is itself usually a product of earlier appropriations and adaptations. Since both adaptors and audiences work in and through the context of earlier constructions of the source, familiarity with the sources themselves is often less important than what and how they signify to the adaptor and his/her audience. The choices adaptors make in positioning their work in relation to those existing constructions largely determine whether spectators view the adaptation as a faithful representation of the original author's intentions, a bold new spin on a familiar story, or a betrayal of the original.

In Canada, the dominant construction of Chekhov to which contemporary adaptations respond is the notion of Chekhov as the master of realism. Chekhov's reputation in Canada preceded widespread productions of his work by several decades, and since at least the 1920s, that reputation has been associated with realism. In a 1924 review of the Moscow Art Theatre's American tour, in the *Canadian Forum*, Gladys Wookey set a pattern that persists to this day by hailing Chekhov as the progenitor of a revolutionary "new" realism. The association stuck, even though for the next several decades critics felt that Canadian artists rarely if ever achieved "realism" as they imagined it. (Who, after all, could hope to live up to Wookey's description of Chekhov's realism: "It's as if a luminous veil were thrown over life. [. . .] One recognizes Omniscience without being able to point one's fingers and say 'Lo here, lo there,' for it is in the whole texture and fabric" [178]?) Whether or not they were influenced directly by Wookey, later critics echoed her in associating Chekhov with realism, specifically a kind of realism that seemed beyond the abilities of Canadian theatre practitioners (see Clayton, "Touching Solitudes" 154–57). They eagerly awaited a production that would demonstrate that Canadian artists could transcend their amateurish origins and master this subtle, sophisticated aesthetic, and Chekhov came to represent an important symbol of artistic achievement to emerging Canadian theatre artists and their critics.

During the emergence of professional theatre during the 1950s and 1960s, "the integration of Chekhov into a Canadian repertory was seen as [. . .] perhaps the most important [objective] after Shakespeare" (Clayton, "Touching Solitudes" 157). The Stratford Festival, founded in 1953, established Shakespeare at the center of the classical repertory, but the nascent professional theatre needed an equivalent canon of modern plays. Chekhov, like Shakespeare, was highly regarded in Britain, and was not only suitably modern, but suitably *not* American—an important factor, because much of the impetus for founding a Canadian professional theatre came, ironically, from British expatriates and guest artists. Chekhov's plays were also amenable to television adaptations, several of which were produced by CBC beginning in the late 1950s. These broadcasts both raised Chekhov's profile across the country and reinforced his association with realism (Clayton, *Chekhov*). As Chekhov became increasingly familiar and his cultural prestige grew, theatrical productions of his work became increasingly significant. A well-directed, competently acted Chekhov play, such as Stratford's 1965 production of *The Cherry Orchard*, was a bellwether of artistic achievement suggesting that "at last were Canadian actors performing as well as any others and that the Canadian theatre scene was finally

220   *James McKinnon*

coming into its own" (Clayton, "Touching Solitudes" 155). In the 1970s, Chekhov's importance took on an added dimension, as emerging Canadian playwrights, including John Murrell and David French, built nationwide reputations by writing well-received translations in Canadian idioms for the Stratford Festival.[7] Thus, between 1950 and 1980, Chekhov's stature grew to the extent that he became a major benchmark of achievement in Canadian acting; directing; and, rather ironically, even playwriting.

Unlike Shakespeare, however, Chekhov is not typically read in schools, so Canadian audiences are more familiar with his reputation than his plays. In contrast with Canadian constructions of Shakespeare, which are based on language and familiarity with a few of the more famous plots and characters, the word "Chekhov" conjures up a vague constellation of pervasive melancholy, limited action, and samovars, all cloaked in the auratic prestige of high culture. Thus, contemporary Canadian adaptations of Chekhov must grapple not only with Chekhov's text, but with the notions and cultural hierarchies they have come to represent. To cultural connoisseurs, Chekhov represents an aesthetic that was once *avant-garde* but is now commonplace—as Clayton notes, by the 1990s, Chekhov no longer represented an "exciting challenge [. . .] for directors," and had become "a cliché" ("Touching Solitudes" 163). To cultural nationalists, Chekhov steals the spotlight from local authors; for another kind of Canadian, the name invokes all the reasons why they regard theatre as the cultural equivalent of a dental appointment. In other words, Chekhov is a prestigious brand name, but not a popular one. In this context, relocating his plays in Canadian settings represents an attempt to exploit Chekhov's reputation as a timeless genius while compensating for Chekhov's reputation as a tiresome bore, by promising that it will be "accessible" and "relevant," or at the very least that one will be able to keep track of the characters' names. But given that Canada is a notoriously disparate and unruly confederation of distinct and disparate regions, converting Chekhov's global cultural capital into Canadian currency is a complicated and risky exchange. As the case studies show, audiences are not only concerned with fidelity to the original: they also scrutinize representations of "Canada," and it is very difficult to be faithful to all Canadians' ideas about being Canadian.

VANYA

In *Palimpsests*, Gérard Genette illustrates the significance of titles and subtitles in influencing reception, particularly insofar as they alert readers to view one text in relation to another, a function he defines as "architextuality" (1). Architextuality is a useful concept in this context, because each adaptation's title signals, more or less overtly, not only a specific antecedent, but also a particular stance towards it. *Vanya* is a case in point, revealing both its source and, implicitly, its author's conservative approach to adaptation. Coproduced by the NAC and Edmonton's Citadel Theatre, *Vanya* was written by (and starred) Tom Wood, who embraces the notion that there is an original text that can and should be faithfully presented—or "preserve[d]," as the NAC season brochure put it (*English Theatre* 11). Like the other adaptors examined here, Wood adapts Chekhov by relocating his plot in a recognizably Canadian locale and rephrasing the dialogue in a distinctly Canadian idiom.[8] *Vanya* does not claim to be a radical revisioning of Chekhov's play, but rather strives to make the original more accessible to a local audience by making it look and sound more familiar, and thus ostensibly removing the barriers obtaining from historical and cultural difference.[9] Significantly, however, the place and time Wood chose for his adaptation was not present-day Canada, but 1920s Alberta—a world neither Chekhov's nor our own.

Wood reveals his intentions in a variety of public discourses, including newspaper interviews and study guides for student audiences: "*Uncle Vanya* has always been my favorite Chekhov play, and perhaps the most powerful of his works, but every version I've ever read has been adapted in the 30s or 50s. The language was always so stilted" ("What Do Chekhov").[10] In such statements, Wood implies that cultural and historical distance (including the quaint idioms of dated British translations) obstructs access to the authentic text and proposes that by refurbishing the original with a Canadian veneer, he can make its authentic essence more apprehensible to his audience. This is a common vision of fidelity in dramatic adaptation, resting on the relatively safe assumption that playwrights don't intend us to view their plays as historical artifacts. But not all of Wood's assumptions are so unassailable. For example, his definition of Chekhovian comedy states: "There's the smile of recognition. A sort of natural humour. Not slap-your-knees funny, that's for sure. Downright sad. Definitely not a farce. Pants don't fall" (Nicholls, "Wood's *Vanya*" B1). This notion is less congruent with the comic vision of the author of *The Proposal* and *The Bear* than with the exemplar of melancholy and psychological realism popularized by the same dated translations that Wood aspires to surpass.

Moreover, the setting implicitly contradicts Wood's claim that archaic translations create an undesirable distance between Chekhov and the audience. True, there are some interesting equivalences between Chekhov's 1890s and Alberta's 1920s: "The suffragette movement, the ecology-minded doctor . . . 'it all slid in beautifully to the time frame,' [Wood] says. So did the pompous professor's assessment that he's 'fallen off the edge of the world' coming back to Alberta" (Nicholls, "Uncle Tom" G1); however, setting Chekhov's play almost eight decades into the past does not remove that undesirable distance, it simply refigures it, in a way that is at odds both with Chekhov's intentions and with Wood's desire to bridge the gap between Chekhov and the contemporary audience.[11] Wood removes distracting archaic Anglicisms and references to *fin de siècle* Russian society, but he replaces them with an archaic dialect and references to another

222   *James McKinnon*

world that the spectators have neither direct access to nor memories of: few spectators in 2005 could remember 1928. The historical setting and dialect invoke a nostalgic reception—another adaptive strategy often applied to Shakespeare, and extensively analyzed as such in Susan Bennett's *Performing Nostalgia*. Inviting spectators to wax nostalgic is very different from representing characters that are themselves held captive by the past, as Chekhov does. Although *Vanya* appeals to the ideal of fidelity, we might question exactly how it is faithful to Chekhov (or exactly what it is faithful to, if not Chekhov).

In fact, Wood's attempt to use Chekhov's masterpiece to authenticate a moment of Canadian history made him liable to a different kind of fidelity criticism: spectators accused him not only of betraying Chekhov, but also of falsifying Canadian history. Both the positive and negative responses are grounded in the language of fidelity criticism—and justly so, since the production was *trying* to be faithful to Chekhov—but they focus on Wood's fidelity to geography and history as much if not more than his fidelity to Chekhov. In Edmonton, professional critics applauded the authenticity of Wood's adaptation—but they focused on its authentic rendition of the setting, not the play. The *Edmonton Sun*'s Colin MacLean, noting Wood's "fine ear for the way people talk way out here," claimed that his adaptation "takes to its transplant to [. . . 1920s] Alberta [. . .] like a northern scrub pine. [. . .] There is not a false moment or emotion anywhere in this pitch-perfect production" ("Powerful *Vanya*"). MacLean's colleague, Liz Nicholls, praised the suitability of both the setting and Wood's "colloquial, unflashy translation,": "*Vanya* [. . .] brings alienation home, so to speak. Ditto [. . .] the nagging sense of potential wasted and possibility reduced that is the obverse side of frontier can-do zeal" ("Wood's *Vanya*" B1). In both cases, fidelity is defined in relation to the representation of the setting, not the adaptation of the source: a "false" moment would be one that violated the critics' vision of 1928 Alberta.

Negative responses to *Vanya* claim the opposite, attacking the *un*suitability of the language and setting and the abundance of false moments. Bruce Deachman scorned Wood's adaptation as unfaithful *and* anachronistic, distorting both Chekhov and history: "Vera's lengthy diatribe about women's rights (or lack thereof) appears to have been inserted with the sole purpose of announcing that this is, indeed, 1928 Alberta[, and] Astroff['s] . . . overly long dissertation on the vanishing wetlands, flora and fauna, etc., sounds as if Wood had a separate David Suzuki-esque agenda at work" ("*Vanya* Leaves" F4). Deachman's critique exemplifies not only the hostility, but also the fallacy of fidelity criticism: the "diatribes" he refers to as "insert[ions]" are in fact very faithful translations of speeches in Chekhov's play.[12] But since speeches about women's suffrage and environmentalism don't gibe with Deachman's visions of either Chekhov or 1920s Alberta, he excoriates them as unnecessary and unfaithful interpolations.

Kate Taylor also deploys the rhetoric of fidelity criticism to damn *Vanya* with faint praise in the (nationally circulated) *Globe and Mail*, calling the Alberta setting "clever [. . .] but unnecessar[y]" ("NAC's *Vanya*" R3). Although Taylor "delight[ed] in some of the transpositions," such as "references to Rudolf Valentino and Carter's little liver pills," she claimed (not unreasonably) that while "the notion that Albertan farmers would be sending remittances to an Ontario university professor" might "score a few points with any Western separatist, it isn't really a plausible plot line." Although Taylor is not as hostile as Deachman in regard to *Vanya*, she extends her critique beyond the production to challenge the necessity of *all* Chekhov adaptations:

> If Shakespeare is our contemporary, Anton Chekhov is even more so. [. . .] It's so easy to move his plays closer to us—a *Cherry Orchard* set on an Ontario farm; an *Uncle Vanya* in modern dress—but, as long as you have a sound and recent translation, there's no particular need. The plays will do their work just fine in their 19th-century setting. (R3)

Taylor's response highlights the perils of Wood's tactic of inserting Canadian equivalents for Chekhovian referents. Some work well, others are cloying and gratuitous, such as Vanya's lament that he "could have been another [. . .] Robert Service" (43): any Canadian who recognizes this name would be mortified by the implication that Service is the closest thing Canada has to a Dostoyevsky or a Schopenhauer.[13] Ultimately, *Vanya*'s poor reception— the play bombed both critically and commercially in Ottawa[14]—shows how conceptions of both "Chekhov" and "Canada" are as precarious and shifting as they are assumed to be stable and fixed. Wood's authenticating gestures delighted some spectators, but most of the documented responses range from boredom to outright rage.[15] Canadian spectators watching Chekhov's *Vanya* might discover, on their own, surprising parallels between their vision of the past and the lives of Chekhov's characters; but Wood's attempt to lead them by the nose backfired, causing spectators to attribute those parallels to unfaithful interventions by a clueless adaptor.

AFTER THE ORCHARD

Kate Taylor's summary dismissal of Canadianized Chekhov must have been discouraging for the NAC, because the next production on their slate was perilously close to embodying Taylor's hypothetical example of an "unnecessary" adaptation: *After the Orchard*, in essence, is *The Cherry Orchard* set on an Ontario lake. But although Jason Sherman moves Chekhov's plot to Canada, his adaptive strategy is at once much more extensive and yet also much subtler than Wood's. The architextual allusion to Chekhov's orchard

224 *James McKinnon*

is clear only to those who already know it is there,[16] and although the plot may trigger recognition, the given circumstances obscure, rather than reinforce, any link to Chekhov. Early in the summer of 1999, the Levy family reunites at their lakeside cottage to face an ultimatum: the cottage, which has fallen into disrepair since husband/father Sid Levy's death three years earlier, is too close to the water, and the family must decide by Labour Day whether to move it back from the water or tear it down (153). None of the Levys can stomach the thought of losing the cottage, which represents Sid's craftsmanship and forty summers' worth of sentimental significance to the family; yet they possess neither the practical skills nor the capital needed to move or rebuild it (153–54). Local realtor Jack Skepian advises them to clear the forest on their property and build small rental cottages to finance a new cottage of their own, but the Levys, who mistrust Skepian (an old flame of Rose), find this idea appalling (159–62). So, like the Ranevskaya clan, they spend the summer reminiscing about the past, speculating about the future, and evading the present. Ultimately, eldest son Sasha covertly arranges to buy out his brothers' shares of the property, and flip it—for a profit—to Skepian (198), an arrangement (made offstage) that enrages his siblings, who are nevertheless powerless to stop it (197). In the final scene, the family says farewell to the cottage and departs forever—nearly leaving senile Aunt Faye behind.

This synopsis deliberately highlights the similarities between the plots, but Sherman himself, in contrast with Wood, does not delight in pointing out how beautifully the source text works in its new situation. Indeed, rather than calling attention to the cleverness of his equivalencies,[17] Sherman goes to considerable lengths to discourage spectators from reading *After the Orchard* in relation to its source. Aside from Rose (Ranevskaya), Jack (Lopakhin), and Len (Leonid Gayev), Sherman's characters do not obviously resemble their Chekhovian counterparts. Instead of two unmarried daughters, Rose has three married sons, David, Sasha, and Andrew, who each have families of their own, including Sasha's wife (Caroline) and son (Jeremy), Andrew's wife (Donna), and some other offstage in-laws. Sherman's *dramatis personae* reflect the fact that generational differences are more pronounced than class differences within middle-class Canadian families (which typically do not travel with retinues of hereditary servants): Sherman exploits intergenerational conflict by making Rose, Jack, and Len older than their Chekhovian equivalents and adding a third generation in Jeremy (Rose's grandson) and Trish (the granddaughter of the Levys' neighbor, Morris). As in Chekhov's play, great social chasms separate the various characters and inhibit communication between them, but here those chasms are generational, and contemporary spectators will readily identify with the conflict between Caroline, Sasha, and their son Jeremy (who has no aim in life other than to resist his parents' plans for it). The absence of a consistent 1:1 correspondence to Chekhov's characters discourages one from reading Sherman's *Orchard* through Chekhov's.

Orchard's public discourse, too, attempts to discourage such associations. Whereas Tom Wood used public discourse to make his motives perfectly clear, Sherman remained silent, and his director, Marti Maraden, perhaps stung by the recent criticism of *Vanya*, actively downplayed the relationship between the two *Orchards*, claiming that "though Sherman was inspired by *The Cherry Orchard*, 'if you knew nothing about Chekhov, you could see this play and it would not be an issue in any way. It has the same central dilemma [. . .] and a few of the characters have equivalents, but it's entirely Jason's play'" (Mazey E1; see also Ball; McNabb).[18] *After the Orchard* echoes *The Cherry Orchard*, but those echoes are only audible to spectators who know what to listen for. For reasons unknown, both the playwright and the producers avoided this topic in public discourse.

In contrast to *Vanya*, *Orchard* does not invite comparisons with its source. Instead, it reframes Chekhov's plot so that it might affect its contemporary Canadian spectators the same way it affected its original spectators: it confronts its audience with a very real, ordinary, contemporary problem, framed by reflections on a recent period of turbulent change and anxiety over an uncertain future. Chekhov's play has probably never moved Canadians in this way, because history creates distance and a certain metadramatic irony. From a Canadian perspective, Chekhov's setting represents a strange (post-feudal, premodern, Imperial Russian) world that we recognize only, if at all, through history books or program notes that direct us to focus on the "timeless" themes and qualities of the characters rather than on the specific, material causes of (and potential solutions to) their problems. But Sherman reflects on the century both its characters *and* the intended spectators have lived through, looking back on the twentieth century the way Chekhov's play looks back on the nineteenth. Sherman's characters face problems that his spectators can easily recognize,[19] reflect on a past that they can remember living through, and share the same anxieties about the coming century. Thus, by *changing* the original text (i.e., rather than remaining faithful to it) Sherman retains one of its original functions: in order to connect with his audience by engaging with its shared history, as Chekhov did, Sherman must represent the history that his audience remembers living through. Few (if any) contemporary spectators can appreciate the irony of Firs's look back in anger at 1861—the year of Emancipation, which the reluctantly emancipated serf remembers as both a personal and global catastrophe—but Sherman's audience is well positioned to appreciate the irony of Faye's cranky proclamation that "no one knows their place anymore," and "it's all because of that women's liberation" (179).

Sherman also uses space in the same way that Chekhov does in *The Cherry Orchard*: his dramatic space contrasts a relatively limited, fixed onstage space with a vast, detailed imaginary offstage world, which functions the same way that Chekhov's setting did for its Russian audience, i.e., to locate the fictional characters firmly in a world the audience recognizes as its own. This diegetic world includes the nearby village where the Levys

226   *James McKinnon*

go to have lunch and see summer stock plays (159, 175, 145, 154); Toronto, the city where the Levys grew up and most of them still live, and where Rose met Jack and Sid (148–50, 153, 177–79); Montreal, where Sasha and his wealthy in-laws live; Los Angeles, to which David hopes to escape (166); and London, England (153, 157, 160–61, 169), which Sherman uses both as a foreign cultural Mecca roughly equivalent to Chekhov's Paris, and as an ancestral home, where Sid, Lou, and Faye grew up (and where Faye often still seems to be living).

The dramatic space and time also give the story a specifically Jewish-Canadian perspective, creating an idea of "home" that is as temporary and provisional for the Jewish, immigrant Levys, as it is permanently fixed to the orchard for the Ranevskaya family. The Levy family history is embedded not only in the cottage, where they have spent forty summers, but also in offstage spaces they have come from, including London, where Sid battled brownshirts and survived the Blitz (184), and Toronto, specifically the old Jewish enclave where Jewish immigrants like Sid, accustomed to perpetual diaspora, found themselves unexpectedly at home. Early in the play, Jack talks about a walk he and Rose took a half century earlier, "all along Harbord, and down Spadina," reminding David of his late father's experience of suddenly discovering "home" in a foreign city: "he gets to Spadina, he turns the corner, and—what does he see?—He sees shop windows full of Stars of David, and menorahs and tallises . . . he sees delis and he sees men in felt hats and païs . . . and he thinks, 'I'm home'" (149). Both the neighborhood and the street names (Harbord, Spadina, College) to which Jack and David refer are instantly recognizable to anyone who has lived in or visited Toronto, as is the truth of Jack's final observation: one diasporic population has supplanted another, and Spadina is now the heart of Chinatown. So few traces remain of the Jewish community that once dominated the area that Jack now feels as alien there as he once felt at home.

The contemporary Canadian setting endows the central trauma of Chekhov's play—the trauma of losing one's land—with a particularly Jewish historical and cultural significance. As Jews, the Levys are only ever provisionally at home in Canada, or even London. Whereas Mme. Ranevskaya's wandering and exile are self-imposed (and funded by seemingly eternal ties to an ancestral estate), the Levys represent a population that has been symbolically rootless even longer than Ranevskaya's family have been rooted to the orchard. Unlike Russian aristocrats, Jewish families have seldom had the luxury of taking land for granted, even in liberal, democratic Canada.[20] So while both families suffer the pain of losing a home because they are unable to adapt to changing economic circumstances, that trauma in *After the Orchard* is not an unprecedented catastrophe, as in *The Cherry Orchard*, but a repeated one: the loss of the cottage, like the disappearance of the delis, menorahs, and felt hats that once dominated Harbord and Spadina storefronts, represents a trauma that, through its very repetition, has practically defined Jewish culture.

Unfortunately, *After the Orchard* failed to ignite the imagination of its Ottawa spectators (one wonders how the play might have fared in Toronto or Montreal, with their much more prominent Jewish populations), and its most extensive review, in the *Ottawa Citizen*, condemns Sherman's *Orchard* for not being Chekhov's, exemplifying the worst kind of fidelity criticism (Kennedy). The play earned a positive review from *Variety*, but as that reviewer pointed out, the chance of a play with such a large cast getting a second production is very remote (Winston). Moreover, Sherman himself was nonplussed by the production, which he described as "tedious." Sherman cites both the massive, overproduced naturalistic set and the director's attempt to make the play more "somber" than it is as factors in his negative reception of his own play: how remarkable and tragic it would be if Maraden "misread" *After the Orchard* in much the same way that Chekhov accused Stanislavsky of misreading *The Cherry Orchard*, by turning it into a sentimental melodrama and thus blunting its comic aspect and related social critique.

THE THREE SISTERS: A BLACK OPERA IN THREE ACTS

The Three Sisters: A Black Opera in Three Acts is an obscene, grotesque musical parody featuring profanity, graphic and perverse sexual content, gratuitous violence, parodies of sources as diverse as *Lachmae* and Peggy Lee, and other such subtle interpolations as "a transsexual mommy-daddy, a train-induced miscarriage [. . . and] a scene where a dead body is consumed nearly whole, not to mention a psychotic banker who pathologically whispers 'pork'" (Kubik, "Meat" 29)—none of which generally evoke "Chekhov" in the Canadian imagination. Compared to *Vanya*, *Sisters* is explicitly *un*faithful to Chekhov; whereas *Orchard* does not announce its debt to Chekhov, *Sisters*, if anything, claims a debt it does not owe, delivering very little of the Chekhovian content its title seems to promise. The only obvious thing that Nutting's sisters share with Chekhov's is their desperate wish to flee the dismal town of Biggar, Saskatchewan, and find happiness in the great metropolis of Edmonton—and even this is a joke, because Canadians (even many Edmontonians, including Nutting herself) more commonly view Edmonton as a place to escape from. To most Canadians, the sisters' shared dream would suggest both dire straits and pathetic naivety. And yet, in spite of creator Kristine Nutting's blatant infidelity to the original, *Sisters* has enjoyed more productions and a far more positive reception than the other adaptations examined here, so its unique juxtaposition of "Chekhov" and "Canada" is worth a closer look.

As the aforementioned examples suggest, Cowgirl Opera's play does not claim to make Chekhov's timeless masterpiece accessible by transposing it to the Canadian prairies. Rather, it uses the Canadian landscape as the earth down to which its exalted source is mercilessly dragged, in

228 *James McKinnon*

a carnivalesque parody that travesties Canadian constructions of "Chekhov" as a signifier of high art. Whereas Canadians associate Chekhov with restrained action, repressed emotion, and refined diction, Nutting's sisters act without restraint, give in to every emotional impulse, routinely hurl obscenities at each other, and frequently mock—and expose—each other's (often soiled) underwear. The plot, too, defies easy association with Chekhov. Its central crisis is precipitated by a fiendish credit-union banker called Mitch or Mitchell McCracken (Brad Payne), who plots to seize the Cuddy farm and devour Pax's heart. Pax plans an elopement with Billy Hamm, Maggie saves every penny she earns giving twenty-five-cent blow jobs towards a bus ticket to Edmonton (where she dreams of auditioning for the Lawrence Welk dancers), and Olga lures the villain into a trap where she kills and eats him. This is less an adaptation of Chekhov than a cannibalization.

But Nutting's target is not really Chekhov. Instead, as its style, tone, and genre suggest, it is closer to Alfred Jarry's *Ubu Roi* than to anything Chekhovian, and indeed it uses Chekhov in much the same way that Jarry uses Shakespeare. Nutting actually sympathizes with Chekhov, whom she sees as having been falsely appropriated as a champion of psychological realism. As she says in an interview, "Chekhov initially saw himself as a comedian [. . .] he got taken over by realism" (Kubik, "Meat" 29). Although, like her fellow adaptors, Nutting was initially inspired by the parallels between the futile "yearnings" of Chekhov's characters and those of many contemporary Canadians, her play is actually as much a response to this earlier appropriation of Chekhov as to Chekhov himself, exemplifying Cartelli's point that appropriations respond not to their sources but to other appropriations. Nutting's target is not Chekhov, but Canadians' fixation with—and *of*—Chekhov as an icon of realism, an aesthetic Nutting regards as outmoded and boring, and one she blames for the decline of theatre:

> Chekhov, when he was writing, was [. . .] cutting edge, and even realism was [. . .], but we're in *now*. [. . . H]aven't we done anything different since then? [. . .] I really am disappointed in theatre that does realism all the time, because I think for our [culture] it doesn't work anymore, it's not exciting [. . .]. Because the job is to entertain the audience, and somewhere, that got lost. [. . . A]nd that's why people don't go to the theatre anymore. (Personal interview)

Thus, Nutting's play is not a parody of Chekhov's *Three Sisters* so much as an assault on the generic conventions that Canadians have associated with Chekhov (since at least 1924, as Clayton notes). Although the title designates Chekhov's *Three Sisters* as the primary intertext through which we read her play, Nutting appropriates Chekhov not to parody his plot—such a parody would be inaccessible to most spectators, undermining Nutting's populist ideals—but to launch a broad attack on the tired aesthetic

Canadian Chekhovs   229

conventions of mainstream Canadian theatre, an abstract concept for which "Chekhov," by 2005, could readily serve as a convenient signifier.

Nutting uses a framed narrative structure to initiate a metatheatrical parody of theatre: *Sisters* is actually a play within a play, performed by "the travelling freak show players of the North Saskatchewan [River]," a troupe of grotesque, garishly made-up, buffoon clowns. Adopting a presentational performance mode that is more Brechtian than Chekhovian, the freaks call attention to both the theatrical frame and the spectators' perverse voyeurism, reminding the audience that art is a commercial endeavor, and if what they do is offensive and disgusting, they do it because they know that's precisely what the audience pays to see:

> ALL. Welcome to our freak show, we'll give you a good blood bath.
> We know that you'll like it, cuz people like stuff that is sad
> There's violence, Cross-dressing.
> Wheat, canola and corn.
> But ya can't leave til the middle,
> Cuz that's when we show the porn. (2)

From the preshow phase onward, the performers erode the boundary between themselves and the spectators. Furthermore, they also cultivate a deliberately unpolished, improvisational, and amateurish aesthetic, paradoxically exercising considerable skill to appear unskilled. The performance style is not representational "Chekhovian," psychological realism but a carnivalesque travesty thereof. If the freaks make it look as though any fool can "do Chekhov," that is exactly the point: the play de-crowns the idea of theatre as sophisticated high art and reclaims it as a popular entertainment.[21]

Nutting's adaptation cleverly exploits the fact that very few Canadians are actually familiar with Chekhov's plots and characters. The explicit reference to Chekhov in her title causes spectators to assume that her play is a parody of an exalted canonical play, and encourages them "recognize" the elevated, mock-poetic dialogue as a mockery of Chekhov:

> OLGA. Pax. I love you because you are more precious to me than anything in the world. You're better than the blue sky in a canola field, brighter than a shit stain on the back of Maggie's underwear. Your heart will never turn black it is pink and fresh and tender and just like you. And if my heart were a pie it would be a meat pie made of you. (5)

This combination of quasi-poetic diction, obscenity, and stereotypically Canadian landscape imagery is really a general parody of the genteel diction of the stage, and of the widely maligned tendency of Canadian art to belabor its Canadian-ness with gratuitous references to landscape, wilderness, hockey, and so on. But spectators (including supposedly

230 *James McKinnon*

Chekhov-savvy reviewers) assumed that they were not only witnessing, but also *understanding* a sophisticated parody of Chekhovian dialogue. This response contrasts notably with the review of *Vanya*, cited earlier, that criticized Wood's perceived infidelity based on the false assumption that Wood, not Chekhov, must have written the speeches about environmentalism and women's rights. Similarly, the violent, obscene, and revolting imagery in the play—including onstage murder, beatings, disemboweling, scatological imagery, cannibalism, and the aforementioned porn—is a de-crowning of the genteel conventions of theatre in general rather than a parody of any specific Chekhovian moment. The fact that the play is not as clever as it seems is actually the cleverest thing about it: it uses Chekhov's cultural capital to sell the audience a highbrow parody, and then allows them to laugh at lowbrow farce. Spectators are alerted by the title, posters, and reviews to expect a parody of *Three Sisters*, and once this expectation is confirmed by the central "if-only-I-could-get-to-Edmonton" joke, they may continue to assume that the rest of the gags are clever subversions of Chekhov. The play thus allows spectators not only to indulge in lowbrow humor, but to simultaneously congratulate themselves for possessing the cultural sophistication to understand a toilet joke as a toilet joke *about Chekhov*.[22]

The jokes are also about Canada itself. While the title and the dialogue prime the audience for a travesty of Chekhov and all that his name evokes—the exalted diction, lofty themes, and restrained action of the "legitimate" theatre—signifiers of "Canada" also play an important and oddly provisional role in Nutting's carnivalesque debasement of high culture. The single most recognizable (and to Canadians, appreciable) element of *The Three Sisters* is its focus on the sisters' desire to escape a dull provincial existence for the metropolis of Moscow. But while almost any rural Canadian town could serve as the former, there is no city that all Canadians would agree is the equivalent of Moscow. Vancouver is too much on the western edge of the country; Montreal's former eminence has been eclipsed by Toronto over the last four decades; Ottawa is only a political capital; and while Torontonians view themselves as the center of Canada, Toronto is widely resented and loathed by other Canadians (largely for that very reason). With almost a million citizens, Edmonton is no small town, but for most Canadians it is hardly a signifier of cosmopolitan life, urban culture, or political power, but rather something of a hinterland (notwithstanding Edmontonians' pride in their cultural achievements, which include an impressive roster of fine arts companies, countless arts and cultural festivals, and North America's largest fringe festival).[23] Thus, Nutting's substitution of Edmonton for Moscow is a joke appreciated equally, but differently, by spectators everywhere in Canada, depending on whether they identify as Western Canadian, "central" Canadian, etc. In fact, the play allows any Anglo-Canadian audience to convince themselves that *they* are the play's primary audience and that no one else *really* gets the joke. (Nutting herself claims that audiences in

Winnipeg—a city roughly as far southeast of Biggar as Edmonton is north-west of it—enjoyed the play the most, perhaps because they best appreciated the implications of the sisters' choice of destination, i.e., because Winnipeg is even worse than Edmonton.)

Ultimately, Nutting's deliberate betrayal of Chekhov enjoyed much more success than Wood's faithful transposition or Sherman's "homage": it was one of the major hits of the 2005 Canadian fringe festival circuit, and consistently earned sold-out houses and critical acclaim throughout its fringe tour and in its subsequent run at Calgary's High Performance Rodeo in 2006. Even the small, conservative town of Camrose, Alberta (100 kilometers from Edmonton), proved wildly enthusiastic (Nutting, "Bringing"). Although some spectators were sufficiently provoked to walk out, Nutting both planned on this and built it into the show's public discourse, promising spectators the pleasure of watching their less sophisticated peers flee in terror.[24] Nutting's particular juxtaposition of "Chekhov" and "Canada" was accessible and pleasing to a wide range of spectators and, either in spite or because of its promise to provoke Canadian spectators and betray Chekhov, it has never activated the kind of hostile fidelity-oriented criticism (in regard to either Chekhov or Canada) that plagued *Vanya* and *Orchard*—although one spectator in Toronto did express a sense of betrayal when the play turned out not to be, as the title had led him to imagine, a full operatic version of *The Three Sisters*.

CONCLUSION

Kate Taylor's claim, that it is "easy to move [Chekhov's] plays closer to us [. . .] but there's no particular need," is wrong on both counts: reciting the Chekhovian canon in Canada is neither as simple nor as useless as she claims. These three plays indicate both the staggering variety of dramatic and dramaturgical possibilities implied in putting Chekhov in Canada and the range of "particular needs" such adaptations address. Chekhov can be appropriated to serve nostalgic desire through an idealized vision of Canadian history; to explore a particular and particularly Canadian experience of traumatic loss; and to joyfully lampoon the tired, stale aesthetic conventions and pretentiousness that have driven all but a few Canadians away from the theatre.

In all three cases, both "Chekhov" and "Canada" are provisional constructions that attempt to appeal to, subvert, or challenge the spectator's existing definitions of those concepts, and while fidelity discourse is a significant factor in reception, it is activated more strongly by the adaptor's representation of "Canada" than by his or her representation of Chekhov. Spectators in both Edmonton and Ottawa rejected Wood's nostalgic vision of northern Alberta as inauthentic, and *After the Orchard*'s representation of a particularly Jewish experience of Canada may have missed the mark in

232 *James McKinnon*

Ottawa audiences (Ottawa's Jewish population is tiny compared to those of Toronto and Montreal, and none of the few documented responses comment on that aspect of the play). Nutting's adaptation, by contrast, allows a wide range of spectators to view her adaptation through a provisional and personal construction of "Canada."

These divergent responses to Canadian Chekhov challenge the idea that contemporary settings help audiences appreciate the universal genius of canonical classics; instead, they suggest that Chekhov's cultural and historical difference is less problematic than adaptors' assumption that a particular vision of Canada (or Chekhov) can or should mean the same thing to all Canadians regardless of regional differences. In addition, the success of Nutting's flagrantly *un*faithful adaptation of Chekhov bears out Nutting's belief that theatre has lost its audience by ceasing to offer them compelling theatrical spectacles—or at least by overestimating the extent to which the demand for "theatrical spectacle" is met by expensive sets and period costumes. *Sisters* succeeded, in part, simply because it offers more pleasures to the spectator: its objective is not to familiarize Chekhov, as *Vanya* tries to do, but to *de*-familiarize habitual perceptions of both Chekhov and theatre, which turns out to be more fun and less predictable.

Notwithstanding their mixed results, the recent proliferation of Chekhov mutations indicates that Chekhov has achieved a rare level of prestige and familiarity in the Canadian theatrical consciousness. For decades, culturally sensitive Canadians have awaited the prophet of Canada's long-awaited cultural maturity, wondering when Canada's Shakespeare or Chekhov will emerge. But until relatively recently, great artists—including Shakespeare and Chekhov—did not simply "emerge" out of thin air: they developed their skills and learned their crafts by adapting, emulating, and appropriating familiar masterpieces. Perhaps cultural maturity is not announced by the arrival of the mythical creative genius—the Dostoyevsky or Schopenhauer Uncle Vanya thinks he could have been—but by the emergence of an audience that can appreciate how well its artists make use of the diverse range of familiar cultural material already circulating around them, without worrying about whether it is sufficiently Canadian. Just as we point to the diversity of Canadian Shakespeares as a sign of cultural achievement, it is promising that Canadian audiences prefer the subversive originality of a "Chekhovian freak show" to a faithfully dull reproduction of the original.

NOTES

1. The proliferation of Canadian adaptations of Shakespeare, extensively documented by the *Canadian Adaptations of Shakespeare Project* (Fischlin 2007) is rivaled by an explosion of scholarship on the same, as Canadian theatre scholars have rushed to document this cultural activity and put it in the context of similar trends worldwide. Some notable recent Canadian Shakespeares include Anne-Marie MacDonald's *Goodnight Desdemona*

Canadian Chekhovs   233

(Good Morning Juliet) (1989), Djanet Sears's *Harlem Duet* (1997), Michael O'Brien's *Mad Boy Chronicle* (1995), Vern Thiessen's *Shakespeare's Will* (2005), and Robert Lepage's *Elsinore* (1996). Notable scholarship on the topic includes Brydon and Makaryk; Knowles; Fischlin and Fortier; Knutson; and the twinned anthologies Knowles, *The Shakespeare's Mine*, and Lieblein, *A Certain William*—the former of Anglo-Canadian adaptations, the latter of French-Canadian plays in translation.

2. The Shaw and Stratford festivals are large-scale professional festivals loosely centered on the repertories of their eponymous authors; very loosely in the case of Stratford, which is now North America's largest theatre festival and produces musicals, modern drama, and new plays as well as "the classics." Soulpepper is a relatively new (formed in the 1990s) but highly regarded professional company dedicated to modern classics. Theatre-Smith Gilmour uses a Jacques Lecoq-style, physically based dramaturgy to create their acclaimed, highly theatrical adaptations of Chekhov's prose fiction ("Russia Consumed").

3. The NAC, created by an act of Parliament in 1969, produces French and English theatre, dance, and classical music. In spite of the grand intentions implicit in its name, it is not widely regarded by Canadians outside Ottawa as Canada's "national" theatre and is in most ways equivalent to other large Canadian regional theatre companies.

4. Jason Sherman is a widely acclaimed and highly regarded playwright, screenwriter, and journalist; Kristine Nutting is an Edmonton-based performance artist, musician, and theatre professor; and *Vanya* adaptor Tom Wood, currently an artistic associate at the Citadel Theatre, has enjoyed a lengthy career across Canada as an actor, director, and playwright.

5. Denis Salter, for example, argues that such "canonical re-sitings," "instead of radically reconstituting Shakespearean [or perhaps Chekhovian?] textuality, [. . .] merely seek to extend its authority in seemingly 'natural' ways"— especially when re-siting becomes a "normative practice" (Salter 127, 128; also see Ric Knowles' critique of Stratford in *Reading the Material Theatre*). On the other hand, Joanne Tompkins and Sonia Massai are more optimistic about the possibilities of "re-citing" the canon, although Tompkins' examples are all radical adaptations, not simply temporal/geographical transpositions of an ostensibly stable, fixed original text. Refurbishing old plays with new scenery is also, of course, a way to sell a familiar play as a new product, and as such this strategy is used extensively by companies whose mandates limit them to repeating historical repertories.

6. Ukrainian and East European immigration is, however, an important factor in both general Canadian history and, as Clayton points out, in the assimilation of Chekhov into the Canadian repertory ("Touching Solitudes" 158–59).

7. This is not to suggest that a singular or monolithic Chekhov aesthetic prevailed in Canada throughout the twentieth century. As Clayton notes, the Canadian Chekhov was significantly reinvigorated in the 1960s and 1970s by the interventions of several directors of Eastern European descent, including John Hirsch and Urjo Kareda, as well as by the aforementioned Canadian adaptations.

8. To the best of my knowledge, all three adaptors worked from extant English translations rather than the original Russian, which, from the perspective of translation theory, complicates any pretense to fidelity.

9. The implication that such differences are merely incidental details obscuring the essential sameness and universality of human experience is, of course, exactly what critics like Salter object to, and *Vanya* illustrates why they find this strategy appalling: Wood's decision to turn Marina into an aboriginal

234 *James McKinnon*

woman named Nana implies an equivalence between the conditions of serfdom and of aboriginality. (A senseless one at that, given that aboriginal women did *not* typically work as domestic servants, indentured or otherwise, in white homes in Alberta.)

10. As Hutcheon notes, such public declarations problematize the critical orthodoxy that, since Wimsatt and Beardsley's "The Intentional Fallacy," has disputed the validity of textual interpretations based on claims about the author's intentions. When spectators read authors' claims about why they have adapted an existing text, it clearly influences their reception, regardless of the proscriptions of literary critics (106–8).

11. Chekhov set his plays in his audience's present, not its distant past, and his characters' seemingly sentimental references to the past are generally ironized in the present context (as when the former serf in *The Cherry Orchard* describes Emancipation as a catastrophe).

12. Whether or not the allegedly "Suzuki-esque" agenda reflects Chekhov's own beliefs, its presence in the play clearly originates with him. The following passage from Wood's version is very similar to Marian Fell's 1916 translation, which safely predates both Wood and David Suzuki:

    Alright, I admit we need to use some wood, but why wipe out everything? Clear some land for our crops, but in harmony with nature. In the name of breaking the land, we level, we decimate the woods. Our axes lay waste to the homes of wild animals and birds. The creeks and rivers are dwindling and [. . .] drying up. [. . .] The climate is being ruined and the earth is getting poorer and uglier day by day [. . . .] But when I walk in the woods and pass a stand of fir or poplar that I've saved from the axe or when I hear the rustling of leaves of young trees I've planted with my own hands, I feel that I've done something. That the climate, to some little extent [is] in my control. And if people are happy a hundred years from now, I'll be a small part of that. (13)

13. Robert Service's folksy ballads about life on the northern frontier, such as "The Cremation of Sam McGee," are well known, but in addition to falling well short of Dostoyevsky in terms of literary merit, his representations of the Canadian frontier are clichéd and notoriously inauthentic. Wood's other substitution, Robert Banting, is more likely to be a source of national pride to Canadians, but it still seems gratuitous—even Chekhov, after all, did not feel the need to patronize his audience by giving Vanya exclusively Russian role models.

14. See Babiak and Gessell; the play's failure was significant enough that it was still being written about a year later.

15. Few Edmonton spectators shared the opinions of their newspaper critics, and one was sufficiently enraged to write a letter to the *Journal* protesting *Vanya*'s selection as a representative of Alberta theatre in Ottawa—a very unusual response to a play with no obscenity or sexual content. See Prodor.

16. Since no orchard is referred to in Sherman's play, a reader or spectator who was totally ignorant of Chekhov's *The Cherry Orchard* might find Sherman's title utterly baffling.

17. Limited space prohibits an extensive demonstration of how painstakingly Sherman's dramatic action matches Chekhov's—almost line for line, beat for beat—a remarkable feat that is, however, invisible to spectators (unless they bring a copy of Chekhov's play to the theatre).

18. Maraden was the NAC's outgoing artistic director, and as such she presided over the failure of *Vanya* only a few months earlier. In addition, she had commissioned Sherman to write the play and directed it as her farewell production. Her anxiety about going out with a thud may explain her otherwise

Canadian Chekhovs 235

puzzling insistence that *After the Orchard* was not an adaptation of Chekhov, a tactic similar to and about as effective as commanding someone *not* to think of a pink elephant.

19. The Levys' problem is a familiar one to many contemporary Canadian families whose ancestors bought cheap land and built recreational properties on it in the early to mid-twentieth century. The family cottage, which once facilitated family bonding, ironically becomes a catalyst for conflict and resentment when the family multiplies and can neither decide how to divide the property nor afford to maintain it.

20. Within the lifetimes of most of the characters in *After the Orchard*, and thus of many of its spectators, there were still Jewish quotas on property ownership in Montreal's Town of Mount Royal (and on admission to McGill University). Mordecai Richler, of course, has written about Jewish Canadians' struggles between an inherited culture that defines itself as landless and an adopted culture that distinguishes people by how much land or property they own.

21. These tactics were more or less potent in different cities: in Vancouver the audience participated vigorously, calling back to the performance à la *Rocky Horror Show* (perhaps they recognized Mommy-Daddy as a descendent of Frank-n-furter); in Victoria, on the other hand, audiences utterly resisted attempts to break the fourth wall, and sat grimly and silently in their seats for the duration of the performance—which they nevertheless gave a standing ovation.

22. As Ric Knowles has pointed out, allowing spectators to "have their cultural authority and eat it too"—by mocking the authority of the source while simultaneously allowing spectators to congratulate themselves for possessing the cultural literacy to get the joke—is also a distinctive feature of several successful Canadian Shakespeare adaptations ("Othello" 144).

23. Perhaps Chekhov intended his heroine's longing for Moscow to be interpreted ironically by an audience of Muscovites who themselves longed, like Mme. Ranevskaya, for sophisticated, urbane, Paris—but if so, this irony is lost on Canadian spectators.

24. In an interview with Liz Nicholls of the *Edmonton Journal*, Nutting describes the reactions of spectators on earlier stops in the tour: "Half the audience cheers and stands up. The other half looks like they've been run over by a truck" ("Love It or Hate It" G2). Of course, readers prepared to be shocked by such paratexts are thus encouraged to identify with the former half and will hasten to the theatre in the hope of watching the other half get hit by the proverbial truck (and the show's opening song accuses the audience of indulging in precisely this sort of perverse voyeurism: "You know you stare at a car accident even though you might see a decapitated head" [3]).

WORKS CITED

Babiak, Todd. "Alberta Scene a \$3.5M Loser in Ottawa." *Edmonton Journal* 6 June 2006: A5. Print.

Ball, Jennifer. "The Uneasy Burden of the Past." Rev. of *After the Orchard*, by Jason Sherman. *Ottawa Xpress* 15 Sept. 2005. Web. 7 April 2008.

Bennett, Susan. *Performing Nostalgia: Shifting Shakespeare and the Contemporary Past*. London: Routledge, 1996. Print.

Brydon, Diana, and Irena R. Makaryk. *Shakespeare in Canada: "A World Elsewhere"?* Toronto: U of Toronto P, 2002. Print.

236　*James McKinnon*

Canadian Theatre Review. Special edition on Shakespeare in Canada 111 (2000). Print.

Cartelli, Thomas. *Repositioning Shakespeare: National Formations, Post-colonial Appropriations.* London: Routledge, 1999. Print.

Clayton, J. Douglas, ed. *Chekhov Then and Now: The Reception of Chekhov in World Culture.* New York: Peter Lang, 1997. Print.

———. "Touching Solitudes: Chekhov in Canada 1926–1980." *Chekhov Then and Now.* Ed. J. Douglas Clayton. New York: Peter Lang, 1997. 151–72. Print.

Deachman, Bruce. "*Vanya* Leaves Audience Crying 'Uncle!'" Rev. of *Vanya*, by Tom Wood. *Ottawa Citizen* 23 April 2005: F4. Print.

English Theatre 2004–05. National Arts Centre Season Brochure. nac-cna.ca. Web. 6 April 2012.

Fischlin, Daniel. *Canadian Adaptations of Shakespeare Project.* University of Guelph, 2007. Web. 6 April 2012.

Fischlin, Daniel, and Mark Fortier, eds. *Adaptations of Shakespeare: A Critical Anthology of Plays from the Seventeenth Century to the Present.* London: Routledge, 2000. Print.

Genette, Gérard. *Palimpsests: Literature in the Second Degree.* 1982. Trans. Channa Newman and Claude Doubinski. Lincoln: U of Nebraska P, 1997. Print.

Gessell, Paul. "America Has Eye on Our Scene's Success." *Edmonton Journal* 11 May 2005: C1. Web. 6 April 2012.

Hutcheon, Linda. *A Theory of Adaptation.* London: Routledge, 2006. Print.

Kennedy, Janice. "*After the Orchard* Goes Sour." Rev. of *After the Orchard*, by Jason Sherman. *Ottawa Citizen* 17 Sept. 2005: F6. Web. 12 July 2007.

Knowles, Richard. "Othello in Three Times." *Shakespeare and Canada: Essays on Production, Translation, and Adaptation.* Ed. Richard Knowles. Bruxelles: P.I.E.-Peter Lang, 2004: 137–64. Print.

———. *Reading the Material Theatre.* Cambridge: Cambridge UP, 2004. Print.

———, ed. *The Shakespeare's Mine: Adapting Shakespeare in Anglophone Canada.* Toronto: Playwrights Canada Press, 2009. Print.

Knutson, Susan, ed. *Canadian Shakespeare.* Toronto: Playwrights Canada Press, 2010. Print.

Kroetsch, Robert. *Seed Catalogue: A Poem.* Calgary: Red Deer Press, 2004. Print.

Kubik, Jeff. "Meat, Murder and Accordions: Grotesque-Loving Cowgirl Opera Sticks It to Chekhov on the Prairies." *FFWD Weekly* [Calgary] 29 Dec. 2005. Web. 4 Aug. 2009.

Lepage, Robert. "*Elsinore.* 1996." *Canadian Theatre Review* 111. (Summer 2002): 89–99. Print.

Lieblein, Leanore, ed. *A Certain William: Adapting Shakespeare in Francophone Canada.* Toronto: Playwrights Canada Press, 2009. Print.

MacDonald, Ann-Marie. *Goodnight Desdemona (Good Morning Juliet).* Toronto: Coach House Press, 1990. Print.

MacLean, Colin. "Powerful *Vanya* Draws You Right In." Rev. of *Vanya*, by Tom Wood. *Edmonton Sun* 29 March 2005. jam.canoe.ca. Web. 7 April 2008.

Massai, Sonia, ed. *World-Wide Shakespeares: Local Appropriations in Film and Performance.* London: Routledge, 2005. Print.

Mazey, Steven. "Maraden Takes Her Curtain Call." *Ottawa Citizen* 15 Sept. 2005: E1. Print.

McNabb, Jim. "*After the Orchard* Study Guide." National Arts Centre, July 2005. Web. 7 April 2008.

Nicholls, Liz. "Love It or Hate It, But Don't Ignore It: Has Edmonton's Cowgirl Opera Created the Ultimate Fringe Freak Show?" *Edmonton Journal* 19 Aug. 2005: G2–3. Print.

———. "Uncle Tom." *Edmonton Journal* 27 March 2005: G1. Print.

———. "Wood's *Vanya* Brings Alienation Home." Rev. of *Vanya*, by Tom Wood. *Edmonton Journal* 27 March 2005: B1. Print.

Nutting, Kristine. "Bringing Cross-Dressing to Camrose." *See Magazine* [Edmonton] 12 March 2009. Web. 4 Aug. 2009.

———. Personal interview. 9 May 2007.

———. *The Three Sisters: A Black Opera in Three Acts*. Unpublished play. 2004–2009. TS.

O'Brien, Michael. *Mad Boy Chronicle: From* Gesta Danorum *by Saxo Grammaticus, c. 1200 A.D. and* Hamlet, Prince of Denmark *by William Shakespeare, c. 1600 A.D.* Toronto: Playwrights Canada Press, 1996.

Prodor, Peggy. "Is This the Best Alberta Can Do?" Letter. *Edmonton Journal* 15 May 2005: A15. Print.

"Russia Consumed by Canadian Culture at Chekhov Theatre Festival." *Government of Canada*. 17 Jan. 2008. Web. 7 April 2008.

Salter, Denis. "Acting Shakespeare in Post-Colonial Space." *Shakespeare, Theory and Performance*. Ed. James C. Bulman. London: Routledge, 1996. 113–32. Print.

Sears, Djanet. *Harlem Duet*. Winnipeg: Scirocco Drama, 1997. Print.

Sherman, Jason. *After the Orchard. Adapt or Die: Plays New and Used*. Toronto: Playwrights Canada Press, 2006: 145–211. Print.

———. Personal interview. 13 Feb. 2008.

Taylor, Kate. "NAC's *Vanya* Not at Home on the Range." Rev. of *Vanya*, by Tom Wood. *Globe and Mail* 26 April 2005: R3. Print.

Thiessen, Vern. *Shakespeare's Will*. Toronto: Playwrights Canada Press, 2005.

Tompkins, Joanne. "Re-Citing Shakespeare in Post-Colonial Drama." *Essays in Theatre/Etudes Théâtrales* 15.1 (1996): 15–22. Print.

"What Do Chekhov, Alberta, and Ottawa Have in Common? *Vanya* by Anton Chekhov—In a New Version by Tom Wood—Directed by Bob Baker." *Ottawa Start*. 15 April 2005. Web. 6 April 2012.

Wimsatt, William K., Jr. and Monroe C. Beardsley."The Intentional Fallacy." *Sewanee Review* 54 (1946): 468–88. Print.

Winston, Iris. Rev. of *After the Orchard*, by Jason Sherman. *Variety* 15 Sept. 2005. Web. 7 April 2008.

Wood, Tom. *Vanya*. Unpublished MS. March 2004. TS.

Wookey, Gladys. "What We Owe the Russian Theatre." *Canadian Forum* 4.42 (March 1924): 177–80. Print.

13 The Work of the Theatre
The Wooster Group Adapts Chekhov's *Three Sisters* in *Fish Story*

Sheila Rabillard

> IRINA. Someday everyone will know what this was all about, all this suffering—it won't be a mystery any more—but until then we have to go on living . . . and working, just keep on working. I'll go away tomorrow, by myself. I'll teach school and devote my whole life to people who need it . . . who may need it. It's autumn; winter will come, the snow will fall, and I will go on working and working. (Act 4, *Three Sisters*, Chekhov 318)

> The charming personal variations on Chekhov's *Three Sisters*—*Brace Up!* and *Fish Story*—told me more about The Wooster Group, and their thoughts about themselves as they entered middle age, than about Chekhov. (Brantley)

The Wooster Group "indigenizes" Chekhov's *Three Sisters*, to use Linda Hutcheon's term for a localizing and very free adaptation, transposing to their late twentieth-century American context the play's pervasive concern with the nature and meaning of work in modern life. Hutcheon comments: "When stories travel—as they do when they are adapted [. . .] across media, time, and place—they end up bringing together what Edward Said called 'different processes of representation and institutionalization'" (150; Said 226). Drawing an analogy with Said's analysis of the ways in which ideas or theories travel, Hutcheon observes: "adaptations too constitute transformations of previous works in new contexts. Local particularities become transplanted to new ground, and something new and hybrid results" (150). Hutcheon's formulation suggests several aspects of the Woosters' adaptation of *Three Sisters*: their free treatment of the play—Hutcheon notes that the concept of "indigenization" implies agency and people's power to pick and choose what they will use (150); their thematization of transactions across time, space, and media; and their use of the adaptive encounter (in a fashion that recalls Said's comment on the interplay of different processes of representation and institutionalization) as a means of exploring the framing institutions of their art—the history of their own American theatre and the nature of their creative work.

The Work of the Theatre   239

In *Brace Up!* (1990), which engages with the first three acts of Chekhov's play, and *Fish Story* (1993),[1] which samples and riffs on the last act of *Three Sisters*, the Woosters use their characteristic blend of live and recorded performance, choreographed movement, and dislocating layering of disparate cultural references. As in other Wooster Group pieces, mannered performance styles, references to diverse theatrical traditions, and the marriage of live and recorded draw attention to the various ways in which reality is mediated in a postindustrial world. Particularly in *Fish Story* The Wooster Group uses this performative and theatrical self-consciousness to explore—with and through Chekhov—acting as work, theatre as a life's work, even theatre as the characteristic work of the current age. This chapter will unfold some of the implications of the Group's reworking in *Fish Story*[2] of a film about a Japanese traveling theatre troupe entertaining tourists and small local audiences; their incorporation of a farewell to the terminally ill member of their company, Ron Vawter, who plays Vershinin; and their implicit allusion to a Stanislavskyan acting tradition in America, a tradition associated with Chekhov and rejected by the alternative American theatre from which The Wooster Group itself springs (Savran, *Breaking the Rules* 2). These disparate elements, put into play with the ending of *Three Sisters*, generate a theatre piece not only "charmingly personal," but also profoundly responsive to Chekhov's drama of longing, loss, and the role of work. My argument here owes much to Johan Callens's study of *Fish Story*'s "intercultural take on time and work"; but where Callens discusses autobiographical elements (many of them related to the passing of time) alongside the play's shifting perspectives on work ethics—the "listlessness . . . of Russia's gentry," "the Calvinist moral duty to work hard, with which Americans are indoctrinated," "Japanese workaholism" (Callens, "FinISHed" 151)—I propose to look at *Fish Story* as a meditation on theatre work: a meditation at once personal, historical, and in a different sense ethical as it suggests Negri's "creation beyond measure" (Hardt xv).

I focus on *Fish Story* rather than *Brace Up!* for several reasons, although I will allude frequently to the earlier, allied piece.[3] The two plays are closely associated in the company's history as well as sharing the same source text and essentially the same set: *Fish Story* "began preparation almost immediately after *Brace Up!* was completed" (Quick 13);[4] Elizabeth LeCompte, The Wooster Group's director, recalled in an interview that *Fish Story* was originally intended to be attached to *Brace Up!* and the two plays were performed together "in a couple of places in Europe" (qtd. in Quick 112). As mentioned, *Fish Story* uses Chekhov's play much more selectively: The Wooster Group's website describes *Three Sisters* as a "jumping off point" for *Fish Story*, whereas in *Brace Up!* "the play as a whole is re-imagined through the prism of our developing aesthetic" (*The Wooster Group*). Kate Valk recalls that The Wooster Group began *Fish Story* because "when we finished *Brace Up!* there were still eight pages left of Chekhov's *Three Sisters*. We did do the beginning of Act IV and we summed up what happened to all the characters but we didn't actually do the last eight pages"

240 *Sheila Rabillard*

(Quick 161). Its more marked departure from source text makes *Fish Story* an interestingly extreme version of adaptation, testing my use of the term and prompting reflection on the nature of adaptation. Such extremity also serves as a characteristic instance of The Wooster Group's usual freedom with its source texts.[5] I argue in the following for the benefits of emphasizing continuity in the Group's history and the handling of *Three Sisters* in *Fish Story* (while in many respects peculiar to the piece itself) lends itself to this project. *Fish Story* presents prominently the story of a Japanese touring theatre company that had merely "ghosted" in *Brace Up!*, where references to a variety of Japanese theatre traditions and films abound.[6] In *Fish Story*, The Wooster Group takes up the story of the Japanese theatre troupe[7] and engages playfully with its life as documented on film, a life that Valk remarks "seemed such a good vehicle for our story—you know, a thinly veiled tale of a theater troupe that was forced to reinvent itself in a modern world" (qtd. in Quick 161). Combining elements from the documentary *Geinin* (1977) with passages from act 4 of *Three Sisters* not only allows The Wooster Group to juxtapose disparate texts in characteristic fashion, but also, via resonances between the Japanese troupe and the Woosters themselves, to develop a kind of subtextual conversation among various performance traditions and Chekhov's drama. While *Brace Up!* makes dramaturgical engagement with Chekhov's text the matter of the performance and the basis of the structure of the piece, as Quick perceptively comments (13), and Kate Valk's presence as onstage dramaturg and Narrator allows stage and page to remain in some respects distinct (LeCompte told Quick that "the two things—the stage and the page—never meshed in that piece" [110]), in contrast in *Fish Story* the essential matter of the piece is not so much an encounter of text and performance as a self-reflexive engagement with performance traditions and the work of the theatre. As a sequel or pendant to *Brace Up!*, it focuses on elements of the prior work and develops them more fully. That is, *Fish Story* presents the work of the theatre as understood through act 4 of Chekhov's work-haunted play: through the Woosters' present performance layered with an imagined Japanese performance of Chekhov's text, both layers incorporating attention to theatrical life on- and offstage, and through an implied history of modern American theatre (including the Woosters' own story), a history marked in many ways by engagement with Chekhov.

DECONSTRUCTION, REFRAMING, ADAPTATION

It may be slightly unusual to refer to *Fish Story* as an adaptation, even in Hutcheon's most expansive variation of the term; however, it is the usual practice of the Woosters to create from preexisting texts. In the words of Johan Callens:

The Work of the Theatre   241

> Ever since its development out of Richard Schechner's Performance Group (in 1975) and the assumption of its current name (in 1980), The Wooster Group, under the direction of Elizabeth LeCompte, have appropriated and incorporated a number of canonical writings in their productions. These are combined with other "texts," considered of a lower or non-artistic status, which they happen to have come across and linked up associatively. LeCompte's scavengings . . . include interviews, historical documents, letters, autobiographical material, film, video, recordings, original dialogue, improvisations, dances, paintings, photographs, even the performance space and props from former productions. ("FinISHed" 143–44)

The pre-text or source text of Frank Dell's *The Temptation of Saint Antony* (1989) is Flaubert's *La Tentation de saint Antoine*; most productions, however, play off canonical dramas. Thus, work prior to *Brace Up!* and *Fish Story* used Eliot's *The Cocktail Party*, O'Neill's *Long Day's Journey into Night*, Wilder's *Our Town*, Miller's *The Crucible*; subsequent to the Chekhov variations, the Woosters have borrowed from O'Neill's *Emperor Jones* and *The Hairy Ape*, as well as Stein's *Dr. Faustus Lights the Lights* and Racine's *Phèdre*.

Before I make the more abstract case for considering *Fish Story* under the general rubric of adaptation, I should explain at some length exactly how the Chekhov text appears in The Wooster Group's piece. The print version of *Fish Story* is quite properly labeled a "Score." Passages from Chekhov's fourth act, along with text taken from the *Geinin* documentary narration, provide merely the textual element of the Score's four parallel columns: spoken words (some live and some on tape); stage actions; sound effects and music; and video images. I mention the orchestral structure of the Score here in order to underline the fact that The Wooster Group adapt *Three Sisters* in several ways at once: they interpret Chekhov's play; they generate text around it (drawing largely on the *Geinin* film, but also including dialogue of their own such as Vawter's comments on the process of putting glycerin in his eyes); they transmute dramatic fragments and related themes into other performance genres and other media—dance, taped sound, video imagery. These different kinds of adaptation interact. For instance, when Natasha (on video) speaks her lines chastising the unseen servant for a misplaced fork, a downstage monitor shows Jeff tapping a fork in sync with her words (the audience can see him, as the character "Sensaburo," in the process of being filmed at a live camera station) while an upstage monitor shows "Natasha, in bubble, with blossoms, add fork" (*Fish Story* 135). Just moments before Natasha speaks, "Sentaro" places a fork on a table as the downstage monitor shows a "fork with blood" (*Fish Story* 135). The interactions here produce an interpretive emphasis on both Natasha's beauty (her face appearing on the monitor as if in a circular portrait frame,

242   *Sheila Rabillard*

with blossoming boughs superimposed) and her forcefulness (the blood, the repeated appearance of forks, plus Jeff reproducing the emphatic rhythm of her words). Via the video image of blossoms, the performance evokes Natasha's (omitted) assertion that she intends to alter the family garden radically, cutting down all the trees and planting "lots and lots of flowers, all over the place" (Chekhov 317) as well as calling to mind softer, nostalgic stagings of Chekhov (perhaps *The Cherry Orchard*) that the present adaptation challenges. In addition, the fork so prominent here (and foreshadowed in an earlier scene where Yukio drops forks and kneels to pick them up; *Fish Story* 133) alludes to the history of The Wooster Group and thus to the interests and biases inherent in their adaptation of Chekhov. For the Woosters are deeply identified with the Performing Garage—it has been their permanent home since the group's inception, providing a place for the extended development and rehearsal necessary to their theatre work and serving as their most important performance venue, a setting always left visible to the audience by their stage designs—and the Performing Garage was once a flatware factory.[8]

It would be difficult to enumerate every aspect of the fourth act of *Three Sisters* adapted into *Fish Story* or to catalogue all of the subtle allusions and analogues to Chekhov's play in the superficially unrelated, juxtaposed materials that contribute to the Woosters' multilayered adaptation. The most readily recognizable passages from *Three Sisters* include: Vershinin's farewell speech to Olga, as he waits to say good-bye to Masha; snippets of Andrei's confession to Ferapont; Irina's speech about going away to work alone; Olga's "If only we knew" speech; Kulygin fooling with the false moustache; Masha weeping; Masha and Vershinin's kiss.

Tusenbakh's touching request to Irina for coffee to be ready when he returns (from his duel with Solyony, of which she is unaware at this point in Chekhov's play) presents a particularly interesting instance of the effects the Woosters produce through their mode of adaptation. Tusenbach's pretended confidence about the outcome of the duel, his avoidance of a farewell to Irina or any troubling indication to her of something serious afoot, acquires added import and emphasis in its adapted form because it resonates with the coffee-drinking of the *Geinin* troupe facing artistic extinction. Both Tusenbach and the Japanese troupe, it seems, are doomed and carry on as if all is well for as long as they can; a comic ordinariness and gallantry infuse both. The Woosters' ordering of scenes contributes to this effect: the Japanese troupe takes coffee (140) before Tusenbach's request (143), which thus seems a kind of echo, and more notably Irina receives the news of Tusenbach's death (137) well before the scene in which he takes his leave for the fatal duel. Irina and Tusenbach's final conversation about the coffee is played without reference to the preceding news of his death or the duel, thus creating layers of almost comic pretended normalcy for actors and characters. (Though the reordering of Chekhov's scenes could be explained by reference to the fiction of the *Geinin* troupe rehearsing, the

The Work of the Theatre   243

sequencing of the *Three Sisters* material in *Fish Story* nevertheless has its own interpretive force. Like the anticipation of Tusenbach's death, an effect of ending postponed but inevitable is created by the way in which the first and final dances of the piece, "Dance 0" and "Dance 0 Reverse," present respectively the opening and the conclusion of the scene in which Vershinin comes to say good-bye so that this scene's action hangs suspended for much of *Fish Story*.) Given that "Masha," too, takes coffee from Sensha in an "offstage" moment, marking a parallel between a Wooster performer and a *Geinin* character, and given the location of the coffeepot in the uncertain territory between the raised stage and the audience,[9] Tusenbach's request for coffee also becomes a moment reflective of The Wooster Group's theatrical career. Is their future threatened? the Woosters seem to be asking. Has the audience for their theatre begun to fade? Interestingly, LeCompte comments that they lost money touring *Fish Story*, perhaps, she speculates, because in Europe audiences were disconcerted by a play of theirs that for the first time did not include "a person standing at the front of the table speaking to the audience, letting them in" (Quick 112). At the same time, the comedy and dryness of this sampled fragment of *Three Sisters* also allows for an implicit comment on The Wooster Group's devotion to nonillusionistic performance, playing that does not depend upon psychological identification and its attendant manipulation of emotion in actor or audience (such as Elin Diamond has analyzed). Meditating on Tusenbach's request for coffee because it is a fragment isolated and framed by means of the Woosters' curious adaptational practices, and distanced by their layering of performances, one can notice that players and character alike do not ask for easy emotion from their audiences. Tusenbach is unwilling or unable to use the impending duel in order to warm Irina's cool acceptance of him into concern and caring. The self-defeating, if possibly gallant, quality of Tusenbach's reticence reads as belonging also to The Wooster Group's persistence in its characteristic nonnaturalistic performance mode.

As this brief discussion of the passages taken from *Three Sisters* may suggest, any attempt to describe the matter adapted in *Fish Story* entails analysis of the manner of adaptation and the complex effects The Wooster Group creates in its "indigenizing" of Chekhov. One of their most important adaptive moves, weaving *Three Sisters* with the story of a Japanese theatre troupe, deserves extended consideration. In *Fish Story*, The Wooster Group frames selected passages from the last act of *Three Sisters* within another fiction, that of a Japanese acting troupe who are touring the provinces and performing memorable scenes from the Chekhov play—"arias," so to speak (a selectivity reminiscent of the Woosters' own earlier *LSD . . . Just the High Points . . .*). In the late 1980s, during the rehearsal of *Brace Up!*, the Group had encountered a documentary film, *Geinin*, about the daily life of a troupe in Japan, whose brand of popular and traditional performance no longer appealed to audiences with a wide range of media entertainment and who were reduced to performing for tourists and provincials.[10] Although

244 *Sheila Rabillard*

the documentary about the life of the Sentaro Ichikawa Troupe was never used directly in *Brace Up!* it was an important element of the rehearsal of that play. Furthermore, during the rehearsal process, it went through "a very sophisticated and lengthy process of appropriation" (Arratia 138). Assistant director Marianne Weems[11] reported that LeCompte imagined the *Geinin* troupe in New York at a point in the future when Chekhov's play has survived in some imperfect fashion "and they are performing this Western classic that may or may not be *Three Sisters*." (qtd. in Arratia 139). Appropriation included recreating parts of the documentary in a film shot by Leslie Thorton in 1990 and 1991 with members of The Wooster Group playing the Japanese performers and autobiographical details from the Woosters' lives interwoven with fragments from the original film (Arratia 139). Although the setting seems to be rural Japan rather than New York,[12] and there are no indications of text borrowed from the Woosters' recreated documentary in the Score of *Fish Story*, this history of appropriation lies behind the piece and its complex layering of performance. In a conversation with Quick, LeCompte does not contradict his recollection that in rehearsals she discussed "how the piece is set in the future where there are traces of a theater tradition that have, in the main, been forgotten" (Quick 113) and on another occasion tells him "I wasn't even thinking so much of the Japanese; I was just thinking and imagining us in the future" (108).

In *Fish Story*, we see onstage a good deal of the Japanese troupe supposedly "behind the scenes"—waiting for a tour bus to deliver an audience, drinking coffee, fishing, eating, and so forth.[13] A narrator's voice from the film *Geinin*[14] tells us about the performers' personal lives (Sentaro is a bachelor and an avid fisherman; "Asako, the maid, wanted very much to express her feelings about the troupe" [*Fish Story* 123]) and comments throughout on the composition and activities of the Japanese troupe. Interwoven with these "backstage" elements are scenes from Chekhov's fourth act, for the most part as performed by the *Geinin* actors. Although one layer of fiction frames the other conceptually, it doesn't do so structurally (with a prologue and epilogue or a clear alternation of fictive scenarios). Instead, there is a continual oscillation and interpenetration of the fictions. When Chekhov's scenes are presented there is in effect a treble focus for one is aware of The Wooster Group members taking on the roles of Japanese performers, who are taking on the roles of Kulygin, Irina, Andrei, Rohde, Olga, and Tusenbach. Each of the Chekhov characters just named is doubled in the cast list with a member of the Japanese troupe (Peyton Smith, for example, plays "Sensha/Olga"). However, several of The Wooster Group actors play only a Chekhov character, and one effect of this inconsistency is to keep the audience aware of the juxtaposed layers of fiction and of performance—aware, in other words, of the work of theatre. Ron Vawter, Karen Lashinsky, Anna Kohler, and Elion Sacker play, respectively, "Vershinin," "Masha," "Natasha," and "Ferapont." All of these Chekhov-only performances, perhaps not coincidentally,

The Work of the Theatre   245

are presented on video (Vawter's, Kohler's, and Sacker's performances entirely so, with Lashinsky's "Masha" appearing onstage as well as via video monitor) and the technological mediation, which creates a contrast between video head-shots and bodily presence onstage, likewise solicits attention to performance conventions and the actor's work.

Further strategies maintain *Three Sisters* and *Geinin* as juxtaposed and/ or nested fictive premises—rules for games, almost, rather than absorbing (or mutually exclusive) fictional worlds. (I compare the fictions to "games" because of the extensive use of games in Wooster Group rehearsals: Arratia reports that during the preparation of *Brace Up!*, gamelike rules were proposed by LeCompte when "the rehearsal appeared to be stuck and performers seemed to be falling into what she defined as 'a kind of naturalism'" [128], and Kate Valk comments that "the performance has the feeling of a board game" and "the linoleum on the floor we used [which was reused for *Fish Story*] actually has the same grid pattern as a *Go* board" [qtd. in Quick 159].) Masha, a character as just noted not played by a *Geinin* actor, has what seems like a backstage moment eating potato chips at the rear table located behind the raised main playing space (*Fish Story* 135), an action that resembles the later popcorn-eating of Sensha (153) as well as the coffee-drinking of the off-duty *Geinin* troupe (140), which Masha herself shares (143). These paralleled actions of eating and drinking simultaneously question and assert the boundaries between *Three Sisters* and *Geinin* fictions as well as between the fictions of "onstage" and "offstage." Another such technique is to use sound effects from the *Geinin* film or tapes of other Japanese material as background to lines from Chekhov's play. LeCompte explains: "all the sound in *Fish Story* is from Japanese tapes." One sound in particular "from one of the Noh tapes—a kind of 'keee'" was used a lot for punctuation "to put an end to something, to say 'hahah,' to be like a door slamming shut" (Quick 109). For example, the "Sound" column of the score indicates "Geinin soundtrack" as Olga (in conversation with Vershinin who has come to say good-bye to Masha) says, "Why doesn't that Masha hurry up . . ." (124). The "Text" column of the score supplies the following title for this segment of the action: "Dance 0 in which Olga has a conversation with Vershinin who has come to say goodbye to Masha." However, despite the title, Vershinin does not speak in this scene, and the "Video" segment of the score during "Dance 0" indicates no video performance of Vershinin but instead "Olga tape." Where Vershinin might be expected to say something, Olga's script indicates "(pause)" and when Olga resumes speaking she seems to respond to the contents of Vershinin's missing lines: "Do you think we'll ever see each other again? (pause) Yes, yes. Of course. Don't worry" (124). This odd association contributes to the complexity of what I've called, for want of a better term, oscillation between fictions and perhaps also alludes playfully to Stanislavsky's affection for elaborate naturalistic soundscapes in his productions of Chekhov, suggesting a teasing relationship with theatre traditions I will explore in

246 *Sheila Rabillard*

more detail in the following. A further device involves the shadowing of one character by another in such a way as to draw attention to parallels between the work of the Japanese troupe and that of The Wooster Group, and perhaps also call attention to the rules of the juxtaposed games, the boundaries between performing the role of a Chekhov character, a Japanese actor, or one's persona as a Wooster Group member. Auslander comments; "the baseline of the Group's work is a set of performance personae adopted by its members, roughly comparable to the 'lines' in a Renaissance theatre troupe" (305). LeCompte, in published notes for the performance of *Fish Story* at the Vienna festival in 1993, describes the operation of such personae or masks: "Actors are searching for masks of themselves—not of character. Who they are onstage is who they are onstage—period. They must be more 'themselves' than in life" ("*Brace Up!* Notes on Form"). One complex instance has "Assistant" shadow "Asako" in the Dance 6 Finale (*Fish Story* 150). "Assistant" is a named character in the cast list who for most of the play is seated with the *Geinin* character "Taro" at the video table beside the raised playing area, and is dressed in contemporary clothes, rather than in the eccentric, vaguely Japanese manner of the performers playing members of the *Geinin* troupe. Thus "Assistant" reads simply as a Wooster, and there are intriguing parallels between the tasks performed by this "Assistant" (managing some of the video and also putting a skirt on Eiji [137]); similar tasks and prop handling by the *Geinin* character "Taro"; the elaborate stage management conducted by the Japanese maid "Asako" (played by Kate Valk, who brings with her the history of her comparable assistive function as dramaturg and Narrator in *Brace Up!*); and the servants in *Three Sisters*: Anfisa and the unseen maid whose carelessness with a fork is a small but significant element in both Chekhov's act 4 and *Fish Story*. Such parallels insist upon the task of assisting, and invite attention to the valuation of theatre work and of the servants in Chekhov's plays. While this insistence doesn't rise to the level of a political critique, as in the Woosters' controversial deployment of the Tituba role in *LSD*, it nevertheless pushes against tendencies to romanticize the fading gentry in productions of Chekhov's plays.

I've emphasized in the foregoing analysis the ways in which oscillation between fictive premises and layers of performance draws attention to performance as such, and in particular The Wooster Group's own methods, history, and concerns about the future. I don't want to suggest, however, that the audience loses sight of the fictions of *Geinin* or *Three Sisters*. Instead, I have attempted to respond to what John Rouse calls The Wooster Group's "intertextual ostension," which "shares the space of interpretation with the spectator" (148, 151)—a space where none of the elements of the piece is merely "supportive or secondary" (LeCompte qtd. in Rouse 151) and the actors are not hidden behind the characters. The various texts-as-performed, and the performance itself, are interwoven strands creating a developing intertextual intercourse in which the audience participates. As

The Work of the Theatre   247

I turn to another way in which the Chekhov material is adapted—via the inclusion of choreographed movement—I will attempt to sustain this conversation among the Woosters' presentation of themselves as performers, the lives of the Japanese actors, and Chekhov's play.

The scenes from *Three Sisters* are interspersed with dances—the subtitle of the Score is "A Documentary about Theatre Life in Eight Dances"— dances that seem, in the American modernist tradition (cf. the Judson Dance Theatre), to be based on movement *per se* rather than story and emotion but that nonetheless comment on the Chekhovian comedy. For example, in one dance, Sentaro counts out loud, timing the movement (*Fish Story* 127). This counting finds an analogy in the heightened awareness of last moments and time passing in the final act of *Three Sisters* and thus suggests that the idea of impending loss might extend, by further analogy, to include the Japanese players, whose theatre is dying, and The Wooster Group confronting the departure of members and perhaps waning support (Callens, "FinISHed" 149–50). In another movement sequence, Sensha whacks Asako, who does pain gestures while Dave (the actor's real name, so not a character in the usual sense but rather his persona as a member of The Wooster Group) moans into an upstage right microphone, providing the sound of physical suffering (*Fish Story* 124). Dividing the task of performing draws attention to performance as work, as well as demonstrating The Wooster Group's refusal of the techniques of naturalistic acting and the psychological structures of identification. At the same time, separation between suffering the blow and vocally expressing the pain comments on Chekhov's depiction of displaced and repressed emotion, as when Chebutykin (in an act 4 scene not staged by the Woosters) claims that he can't recall if the girls' mother returned his affections. (When Masha asks "Did you love my mother?" Chebutykin replies "Very much" but when she then asks: "Did she love you?" he says, after a pause, "That I can't remember" [Chekhov 309].) Chebutykin's evasive response comes in answer to a question from Masha, which itself seems an indirect expression of anguish at the end of her extramarital affair with Vershinin, and perhaps displaced concern about Irina's loveless betrothal and Andrey's crumbling marriage.

SELF-CONSCIOUS ADAPTATION

In the preceding discussion I've outlined elements The Wooster Group adapts from Chekhov's drama and implied some of what they omit (there's no Chebutykin, for example); and I have attempted to analyze the ways in which the Woosters "indigenize" his play by bringing it into a contemporary conversation with other texts, their present performance, their place in theatrical history. Now I'd like to address in more general terms the usefulness of adaptation as a critical framework for discussing *Fish Story*. Admittedly, LeCompte herself might reject the term; she told Susie Mee: "I don't

248 *Sheila Rabillard*

think of *Brace Up!* as an adaptation of Chekhov. I think of it as a double portrait of Chekhov and The Wooster Group. We're not interpreting him. We're putting him on. We're inhabiting him" (Mee 147).

Callens, Quick, Knowles, Savran, and Vanden Heuvel all notice that the relationship of The Wooster Group to their canonical source texts has changed since the deconstructive period brilliantly analyzed by Savran in *Breaking the Rules*. Quick begins his book where Savran left off, acknowledging a turn in the Woosters' career; Savran titles a discussion of the Woosters' later work "Obeying the Rules." Knowles argues that when in more recent projects the Woosters find their source in a text from the American avant-garde tradition, Stein's *Dr. Faustus Lights the Lights*, rather than in the establishment canon of Miller, O'Neill, and Wilder, nostalgia not iconoclasm results. Callens refers to this more recent use of preexisting texts as reframing ("Of Rough Cuts" 47); given the richness of Hutcheon's terminology and the changes rung by the Woosters on their pre-texts, I prefer "adaptation." Indeed, the breadth of possibility in the adaptive gesture (which includes an element of antagonism) may allow us to avoid erecting too rigid a barrier between earlier and later Wooster Group. By suggesting continuity it may avoid the rather unproductive critical conclusion that if the early work is seen as deconstructive, the later work is merely *not* deconstructive. The divisive approach runs the risk of implying that The Wooster Group has just gotten old: along with the politics of 1970s theatre, it has lost energy; as if affected by ebbing academic enthusiasm for French theory since the 1980s, it has been stranded by a low tide. But Vanden Heuvel perhaps says it best:

> [The Wooster Group's] current treatment of texts as (relatively) stable entities need not indicate a more conservative agenda, but could instead signal that the work has reached a state of such advanced robustness that the complexity lies, not solely in the deconstruction of an existing text or pattern of meaning, but rather in the new structures of densely patterned order that emerge in the interactions between textual order and performative chaos. (82)

The Woosters' encyclopedic approach to adaptation in *Fish Story* is, crucially, self-conscious. Savran calls some of their work "historiographic" (*Breaking the Rules* 6), and *Fish Story* is indeed theatre that comments consciously on the adaptive process in the creation of the piece, in the career of The Wooster Group, and in the history of the modern theatre. In one respect at least, *Fish Story* is not an outlier but an exemplary adaptation insofar as it exposes a definitive process of reception. For *Fish Story* depends crucially upon the audience's prior knowledge of *Three Sisters*, upon what Julie Sanders in her overview of adaptation calls "the intellectual juxtaposition of (at least) one text against another that [. . .] is central to the reading and spectating experience of adaptations" (26). What the

Woosters offer is extraordinary, however, in that they anatomize and display this adaptational relationship. Because it adapts act 4 only, the Woosters' piece acknowledges within its basic structure the role played by evoked memory of the precursor text. An audience responding to Tusenbach's request for coffee in *Fish Story*, I suggest, recalls the story of his relationship with Irina from the three preceding acts of *Three Sisters* that *Fish Story* does not adapt and recognizes a changed sequence of scenes relating to his death, a prolepsis that comments on the audience's anticipation of events resulting from the adaptation's reworking of known material. This ostension of the role of memory in the reception of an adaptation (which hints at the pervasiveness of some degree of adaptation in every production of a well-known text) chimes with a scenario LeCompte proposed during rehearsal—that a Japanese troupe is performing at a point in the future when Chekhov's text and its surrounding traditions are imperfectly understood. According to this scenario, the present spectator watching a "future" performance is prompted by lacunae to compare what he or she recollects. As Kate Valk comments, with *Fish Story* "there's an empty centre, where there isn't really a play, but just its signs, the props, costumes, articles" (qtd. in Quick 161). A letter LeCompte wrote to Arthur Miller about her treatment of *The Crucible* is relevant here because it shows that even in this earlier, deconstructive, performance piece she is deeply interested in provoking an audience response where past experience with a familiar text is a vital part of reception:

> I want to put the audience in a position of examining their own relation to this material as "witnesses"—witnesses to the play itself, as well as to the "story" of the play. Our own experience has been that many, many of our audience have strong associations with the play, having either studied it in school, performed it in a community theatre production, or seen it as a college play. And the associations with the play are important to my *mise en scène*. (Savran, *Breaking the Rules* 181)

The found materials associatively added to Chekhov's text constitute an implicit commentary on the adaptational "discourse" of *Three Sisters*, in Hutcheon's definition of the term: the century-long tradition of adapting (translating, transforming) this work, a tradition in which the Woosters participate. The triangulation between America, Japan, and Russia draws attention to adaptation in a slightly different sense—the inevitable adaptation in even the most faithful transmission of a canonical work due to differences in time, place, language, and culture, a process that is here emphasized rather than elided. The title of the piece, I suggest, alludes to such adaptation via translation and cross-cultural transmission and implies, as well, that The Wooster Group invites attention to their own adaptational practices. A fish story, after all, is a tall tale, usually self-aggrandizing. Often one describes in exaggerated scale a fish that got away—so perhaps the Woosters refer to the

250   *Sheila Rabillard*

elusiveness of Chekhov filtered through so many layers of history and culture as well as to their own theatrical history, recalled with inevitable regrets and inevitable self-flattery. The *Geinin* troupe have fallen out of fashion and consequently have a lot of time on their hands, including time to fish; thus the title may allude to the effects of shifting taste on Japanese performers, the Woosters, and the versions of Chekhov that get staged in various times and places. The published title could also be an anticipation of "FinISHed Story." If so, the title—like the work itself—alludes to the Woosters' history in yet another way: their practice of staging works described as "in progress," and LeCompte's devotion to continually changing pieces even after they have premiered so that successive performances are seldom the same (as Kate Valk reports in conversation in Quick 158).[15]

LeCompte's "*Brace Up!* Notes on Form" suggests that the title relates to the Woosters' practice as performers: "Be as ignorant of what you are going to catch as is a fisherman of what is at the end of his fishing rod." Perhaps, as well, there's an allusion to Alan Sekula's *Fish Story*, an extended photographic project on the global shipping trade. The theme of this art project suits *Fish Story*'s triangulation of America, Japan, and Russia: Sekula explained that he photographed harbors around the world because "the harbour is the site in which material goods appear in bulk, in the very flux of exchange" (qtd. in Bhabha 8). Sekula's *Fish Story* opened in Rotterdam in 1995, with a number of prior exhibitions and publications as a work in progress, and it seems entirely possible that the Woosters encountered the seven-year cumulative project (1988–1994) at some point in the development of their own *Fish Story*, on which work began in January 1992 (Quick 278).

The use of Japan as an indicator of the widespread translation and cultural adaptation of Chekhov is very apt. Since 1910, when his work was first performed there, Chekhov has been second only to Shakespeare among foreign playwrights for number of stagings in Japan (Tanaka 1–2).[16]

The Woosters may or may not have been aware of a number of Japanese directors and playwrights who have devoted considerable attention to interpreting Chekhov—such as Hisashi Inoue, Iwamatsu Ryo, and Tadashi Suzuki—but they were highly likely to have known about Romanian director Andrey Şerban and his work with Chekhov in New York and Japan. In 1977 Şerban produced *The Cherry Orchard* at Lincoln Center and in Japan. During the summer of 1980, Şerban directed *The Sea Gull* for the Shiki Theater Company in Japan, and in the fall directed a second, quite different production for Joseph Papp's Public Theatre. The Japanese production, according to Şerban, was "more Western, it had a heavy kind of Russian feeling, a heavy realism" and a very naturalistic lake; in contrast the New York production was cool and formal, with "this very austere, polished Japanese floor" (Shyer 61). The Woosters' very different *japonisme*, then, may allude to recent theatre history and the amusing cultural negotiations that resulted in the same director creating a realistic "Russian" Chekhov in Japan and a stylized "Japanese" Chekhov in New York; LeCompte perhaps has this association in

The Work of the Theatre 251

mind when she comments that the Japanese films she watched resonated with an idea of Russia because of "repression and a certain kind of Victorianism" (qtd. in Quick 107). Also, with characteristic wit, the Japanese elements allude to The Wooster Group's own inevitable localizing of Chekhov: the "Japanese" costumes come in part from nearby. "At the time I remember there were several designers around who were also interested in Japanese culture and we would go and look at their things and then we would recreate our own version of what we saw, or we would buy second-hand pieces" (LeCompte qtd. in Quick 107). The costuming thus tacitly recognizes both the fading of the avant-garde edginess of the Performing Garage's location, as designer shops become common in SoHo, and the complexities of trans-global cultural exchanges, perhaps matching the exchange of goods tracked in Sekula's identically named photographic project.

Adaptation, then, is consciously bound to autobiography because one sees the Chekhov one sees through the filters of one's place, time, and theatrical traditions. *Fish Story* develops a series of analogies between the themes of loss and aging in Chekhov's play; the loss or change wrought by the inadvertent adaptation involved in the history of transmitting a canonical text; personal farewells because Wooster Group member Ron Vawter is dying of AIDs; and the Woosters' collective concern with the fate of their specific American theatre tradition. Kate Valk says in an interview:

> We had thought of *Fish Story* as a sort of flash forward and Liz [Elizabeth LeCompte, director] always imagined what would happen if a troupe in the future, after the great days of theatre were long gone, found the last eight pages of Chekhov's *Three Sisters* and recreated a performance of the play from video tapes.
>   Interviewer: Remnants of video tapes of The Wooster Group's performance of the play?
>   Valk: Yes, The Wooster Group's. (Quick 161)

It was Vawter who originally suggested that the Group work on *Three Sisters*; "in his way," LeCompte says, "he was preparing the group" for his death (Quick 106). According to LeCompte, he was still able to perform when *Fish Story* was first staged, but the Woosters decided that he should play Vershinin entirely on videotape, implying departure via his physical absence.

> Ron could have performed in *Fish Story*. But, I wanted it to be like *Point Judith* (1979)—that was a goodbye piece as well. I knew during *Point Judith* that Spalding wasn't going to be in the work in the same way again and it was the same with Ron in *Fish Story*. This was a similar goodbye to Ron. (Quick 112)

The extraordinary taped sequence of Vawter doing Vershinin's good-bye that plays at the end of *Fish Story* becomes, in Valk's words, "a kind of fetishization of Ron's goodbye" (Quick 161). Concern for the fate of an

252   Sheila Rabillard

American theatrical avant-garde is figured in the tenderness with which the outmoded *Geinin* troupe is treated, and bound closely to the hopes of Chekhov's Tusenbach, Irina, Vershinin, even Olga, that present effort will somehow be validated, given meaning, by the future.

At the same time as *Fish Story*'s adaptation of *Three Sisters* invites attention to the personal and particular, it also implicitly comments on the role Chekhov has played in American theatre history, both directly as his plays have become part of the standard repertoire and indirectly via the influence of Stanislavsky's teachings, however understood, on American performance. Aware of linguistic and cultural distance, of the inevitable torsions of adaptation, the Woosters present an Americanized Chekhov. This is offered, I propose, as a counterbalance to the influential English Chekhov—the nostalgic Chekhov of gently fading, aimless gentry and lost estates. I use "English" here both literally and figuratively. Following Senelick, I distinguish the conservatism in English-speaking productions of Chekhov from more experimental, oppositional, European approaches. Surveying reactions in the English-speaking world from the late 1960s through the 1990s to approaches critical of the Prozorov sisters, Senelick contends that "British and American audiences want to identify with the Prozorovs and are loath to accept productions which do not favor them" ("Directors' Chekhov" 186). Aronson notes that in American scenography, the general trend of the late 1980s and 1990s was, with some notable exceptions, "a return to Romanticism" ("Scenography" 146). Mindful of the Woosters' broad interest in film and popular culture, I use "English" figuratively as well to suggest that a taste for Romanticized Chekhov is cognate with an appetite for nostalgic, often English, *Masterpiece Theatre*–style costume drama.[17] LeCompte comments that the translation of *Three Sisters* they first read, "the standard one," was "kind of icky." "It had an awkward tone. . . . But the Chekhov also felt very English, very afternoon tea" (qtd. in Quick 106). The Wooster Group created instead an American nostalgia. I borrow here from Knowles, who argues that the Woosters' adaptation of Stein expresses nostalgia for an American modernist avant-garde and for the aesthetic of Manhattan's SoHo when it was dangerous, experimental territory for theatre. In radically adapting Chekhov, the Woosters allude semi-ironically to the anti-naturalistic American experimental theatre tradition, a tradition opposed to the famed Method, which of course derived (with a deal of adaptation) from Stanislavsky, director of Chekhov. Even the translator they use reinforces this allusion. Paul Schmidt provided them with a new, unpublished translation of *Three Sisters* and played the role of Chebutykin in *Brace Up!*; in the early 1960s Schmidt (with Randall Jarrell) had previously translated the play for the Method actors of the Actors' Studio, a translation used on Broadway by Lee Strasberg. Laurence Senelick offers a cautionary tale of this landmark in the history of American theatre, much anticipated at the time: "If Strasberg was Stanislavsky's American heir (a title vigorously disputed by Stella Adler), then his production of a Chekhov

The Work of the Theatre   253

masterpiece was bound to be authoritative and definitive" (*Chekhov Theatre* 288). In the event, New York audiences and reviewers praised the production, but more discerning viewers considered the actors' highly emotional performances uncoordinated, crude, and exaggerated. London critics and audiences alike rejected it. Senelick writes: "The emotional onanism of the Strasberg version was bound to conflict with the more genteel approach of the English school" (*Chekhov Theatre* 290). As a result of the failure of the Actor's Studio *Three Sisters* outside Manhattan, Senelick concludes, Strasberg never again attempted to direct a play "but *en revanche* he became the most famous acting teacher in the world" (290). If Paul Schmidt's contributions call to mind a specific 1963 Method production of *Three Sisters* (with its emphasis on internalization and the re-creation of the actor's personal feelings) evidence from the rehearsals shows that LeCompte was concerned to counteract a more general naturalism. Marianne Weems, serving as assistant director during the preparation of *Brace Up!*, records in her notebook that "Liz [LeCompte] has always used 'naturalism' as a formal, decorative device, incorporating it convincingly into a mélange of many styles which comment upon themselves through their juxtaposition. The error of almost all critical writing in rel. [*sic*] to t/work [*sic*] is the *identification* of the bearer of the narrative (i.e., Spalding in the first trilogy, Ann Rower, Ron, etc.) with the 'story'" (Quick 69). It's in this context that we might understand her self-aware opposition to naturalism. In one of the early tapes of rehearsals for *Fish Story*, Quick recalls in conversation with LeCompte, "you say to the performers that you don't want them to fall back on an easy form of naturalism" (Quick 111). And Arratia observed that in rehearsing *Brace Up!* LeCompte told performers "I want physical actions, not emotions" (133). This nuanced opposition is condensed and simplified in Weems's statement that, in *Brace Up!*, "The Wooster Group is challenging the Stanislavsky interpretation" (Mee 152). Senelick comments that "it was amazing that she should think they needed to" given the long tradition of anti-Stanislavskyanism in American theatre (*Chekhov Theatre* 341). But I think it's possible to understand her challenge to Stanislavsky as shorthand for her opposition to his historical influence, and acknowledgment of the power of what Senelick himself terms "naturalistic 'acting' or re-acting, the bread-and-butter of the American stage" (*Chekhov Theatre* 340) rather than as evidence of ignorance of decades of experiment.

Articulating a stance against Stanislavsky suggests as well the consistently historical thrust of the Woosters' collective enterprise. To return briefly to the argument for seeing their career as a whole, one could argue that earlier work was chiefly concerned with a deconstructive approach to canonical dramas, and the later perhaps more concerned to interrogate the performance traditions of American (especially New York) theatre. Just as one can list canonical American dramatists whose work the Woosters have addressed, one can see their career in terms of investigations of historically significant American performers and American performance traditions:

254 *Sheila Rabillard*

among these Pigmeat Markham; Lenny Bruce (in his persona Frank Dell); the "Poor Theatre" of Grotowski (whose work was introduced to America by Richard Schechner, himself so important to the beginning of the Woosters); and—via Chekhov—Method acting and the disputed heritage of Stanislavsky's teachings in America. Concerning her use of Grotowski in *Poor Theatre*, LeCompte told Maria Shevtsova, "It probably had to do with my thinking about why I was working, what I was doing in the theatre, and one of the main things still very present in my mind was Grotowski, when he came to New York in 1968" (Shevtsova and Innes 97).[18] Even the Japanese elements, as mentioned, allude to recent New York theatre history. Comparison with the field of visual art may help to clarify the continuity I see in the Woosters' body of work between the deconstruction of drama texts and the display of performance tradition and theatre history via a variety of self-reflexive strategies. LeCompte has a visual art background, and Rosalind Kraus, a critic and theorist with a deconstructivist approach to contemporary art, sees a way forward for artists in something like the modernist focus on the medium, yet distinct from modernism in not subscribing to the artwork's independence from the conditions of its frame. Instead, she proposes that the medium provide "a source of rules that prompts production but also limits it, and returns the work to a consideration of the rules themselves" (45, 674). In interrogating the American canon and performance history from Stanislavskyan Chekhov to minstrelsy and stand-up comedy, the Woosters consider the rules of their game.

In emphasizing the work of the theatre—the process of adapting, acting as doing, theatre as craft and tradition, the question of the impact of a life's work—the Woosters direct attention to the importance of the theme of work in *Three Sisters* and give us, in another sense, an Americanized Chekhov (rather than an English Chekhov, melancholic prophet of the disappearance of a leisured, cultured class). Many elements emphasize the work going forward onstage: Valk wore bungee cords on her legs, providing resistance for every step; her role was devoted to facilitating the others' actions and moving props; Vawter's multiple attempts at inserting glycerin drops in his eyes showed the effort involved in performing the farewell; we are told that a member of the *Geinin* troupe carries on despite a grave illness. Callens suggests that they bring to bear a characteristically Calvinist American view of work; without subscribing to that notion, I must admit that the Woosters made me think again about the variety of perspectives on work presented in Chekhov's *Three Sisters* (from Irina's idealization to Chebutykin's shirking). I recalled Chekhov himself, who did not come from landed gentry—contributing to his family's finances at an early age, writing comic short pieces to fund his medical studies, traveling overland to Sakhalin (another Japanese resonance). The Score of *Fish Story* gives us Irina's disillusioned fourth act comment on work, which she no longer sees romantically as a source of meaning but rather as what one does in the absence of meaning: "Someday everyone will know what this was all

The Work of the Theatre   255

about, all this suffering, it won't be a mystery any more [. . .] . . . but until then we have to go on living . . . and working, just keep on working" (137). Vershinin's lines, "We must find a way to join love of work to love of higher things, mustn't we? Well, now I must go . . . I came to say goodbye," which occur some three pages from the end of Schmidt's *Three Sisters*, become the final words of *Fish Story* (156). Because much of the Chekhov text has been cut, lines such as these invite meditation. For me, they resonate powerfully with Antonio Negri's view of work as no longer having measurable value, and I'd like to use his *The Labor of Job* to try to capture something of the contemporary, Americanized Chekhov The Wooster Group gives us. Admittedly, the association between *Fish Story* and Negri's poetic, leftist philosophy may seem unexpected (especially given that The Wooster Group's politicized aesthetic is hard to pin down), but I juxtapose in a very modest imitation of the Woosters' own methods.

Since the 1970s, Hardt explains, "Negri has argued, against most streams of Marxism, that the labor theory of value is in crisis" (Hardt xi). In the context of immaterial production, and as production moves outside the factory walls and schemes of cooperation are no longer furnished by the capitalist, "capital can no longer measure and quantify value in relation to labor" (Hardt xi). Developing a parallel between the injustice Job suffers and the position of labor in contemporary capitalist production, Negri reads Job's suffering not as a violation of measure, which could be restored, but rather as a symptom of the impossibility of measure and the exhaustion of the mechanisms of equivalence (Hardt x, xi). Even Marxism, he seems to suggest, subscribes to these exhausted mechanisms. In place of calls for justice, for measure, Negri presents Job's rebellious expression of pain: "Whereas fear establishes the vertical relation between subject and sovereign, pain is the foundation for horizontal relations among humans" (Hardt xiv); "Pain is a key that opens the door to community" (Negri 90). In *Fish Story*, this is the democratizing, American version of suffering that links Chekhov's characters "horizontally" to one another, to the *Geinin* troupe, and to pain and loss among the Woosters. The second and more significant connection Negri makes between Job and workers rests on the human powers of creativity. "The only system of value that can be legitimate [. . .] is one that is based on human power and creativity," creativity beyond the system of measure (Hardt xv). This catches something of the Woosters' countertheme of theatre work as doing for its own sake—a nostalgic view perhaps, a memory of the days before success found them. Yet setting aside nostalgia, the theme of theatrical labor is developed in each iteration of the piece by the choreographed, almost lunatic precision of the Woosters' work onstage. LeCompte recalls: "In *St. Anthony* Katie had some leeway before she went to touch the bed—she had three or four seconds of free time to do whatever she wanted there. Whereas with *Fish Story*, because of what was being negotiated, no one moved without knowing exactly what they were doing" (Quick 112). It's in this sense, perhaps,

256   *Sheila Rabillard*

that we might understand *Fish Story*'s theatrical work as characteristic of work in our present age, work beyond measure. In Negri's words, "The product of labor is no longer simply surplus labor and surplus value but the collective creation of a new world" (14). Beside this assertion, one can place Marianne Weems's description of the Woosters at work onstage: "The main idea is that they're in a room with an audience, not in a 19th-century Russian salon. And they're making a world, but it's not a Chekhovian world" (Mee 150).

NOTES

1. The dates are those of first performances according to Quick's chronology (277–80).
2. I encountered *Fish Story* in Brussels in May 1993, where it was performed as a double bill with the Group's *The Emperor Jones*. It is this performance I will discuss here, supplemented by the multicolumn (text/stage/sound/video) illustrated "Score" published by Andrew Quick, subtitled "A Documentary about Theatre Life in Eight Dances" (115) and based upon a notation by Clay Hapaz, Wooster Group assistant director 1994–1996. Quick describes *Fish Story* as having reached its "final form" in 1994 (13) so the "Score" presumably reflects the state of the piece at this date. This basis for analysis, of course, provides a limited approach to a performance piece, which, like all of the Woosters' projects, was altered by director LeCompte many times in the course of its performances.
3. Few essays or articles, aside from Callens's admirable piece, have been devoted to *Fish Story*, while *Brace Up!* was the focus of a cluster of articles by Schmidt, Mee, and Arratia in the *Drama Review* 36.4 (Winter 1992), and chapters in Senelick's *The Chekhov Theatre*; Allen's *Performing Chekhov*; and Aronson's *American Avant-Garde Theatre: A History*.
4. Paul Schmidt records in 1992 that "LeCompte says she intends to use Act IV as part of the next Wooster group piece, which will return to the Japanese material that was gradually abandoned in the work on *Brace Up!*" (156).
5. Jim Clayburgh, commenting on the treatment of Chekhov's text, said in an interview with Euridice Arratia that *Brace Up!* was "the most accurate rendition of a script we've ever done" (Arratia 125).
6. The scenic elements of *Brace Up!* are modeled on the Noh stage; the Narrator role alludes to the figure of the *benshi* who used to accompany silent movies with live narration; live-feed video images of the performance are mixed with visual material from Godzilla films and the cinema of Yasujiro Ozu (Quick 13, 82, 83, 89, 91, 110).
7. According to the notebooks of assistant director Marianne Weems, the idea of a Japanese theatre troupe staging Chekhov's play in New York at a time in the distant future had occurred to the Group early in the process of rehearsing *Brace Up!* (Quick 65). The Group's engagement with the documentary film that inspired this idea is complex but might be summarized as follows. LeCompte recalls that "at the end of the eighties" she saw a documentary film (*Geinin* 1977) about the daily life of the Sentaro Ichikawa Troupe, a traveling Japanese theatre troupe. At this point, however, she "was thinking of making a film like the *Geinin* documentary instead of making a theater piece" (LeCompte qtd. in Quick 107). Although Weems and LeCompte don't agree entirely about the ways in which The Group first responded to the documentary, they accord in dating the initial encounter with it, as Quick's

The Work of the Theatre 257

chronology places the first rehearsals of what would become *Brace Up!* in February and March of 1989 (277). In the event, the concept of a Japanese theatre troupe performing Chekhov faded out of *Brace Up!* but was used directly in the structure of *Fish Story*. To make matters more complicated, the Woosters did carry out the plan of making a film "like the *Geinin* documentary" in which members of the Group played a Japanese theatre troupe going about its daily routines. Andrew Quick refers to this fictive documentary, called *Geinin (Today I Must Sincerely Congratulate You)*, as an "unfinished video" (58) and his chronology records preproduction in June 1990, and a film shoot at the Performing Garage in July 1990 and again in April 1991. The period of work on the fictive documentary thus overlaps with rehearsals for *Brace Up!* (the last of these in November and December 1990) and precedes the beginning of work on *Fish Story* (January–March 1992) by approximately a year (Quick 278). Quick reports viewing both the original 1977 *Geinin* documentary film, and The Wooster Group's video version of it (58); I depend upon his accounts, as I have not been able to view either, and use Quick's spelling for the name of the Japanese troupe.

8. Presumably not an insignificant fact, as The Wooster Group website includes this detail of architectural history.

9. The coffeepot is "set off S. L." according to the "set and props preset drawing" (Quick 121).

10. The opening narration in the *Geinin* documentary (a passage not included in the text of *Fish Story*) is quoted by Arratia. She notes that she saw not the original, but a videotape with clips from the BBC documentary intercut with other material (142). The narration begins as follows:

> Kabuki plays and noh dramas are famous throughout the world for their refinement and delicately rendered sophistication. Kabuki and especially noh, are the apex of Japanese theatre. Ranking somewhat below these sophisticated theatrical art forms but no less ageless lies the gypsylike world of the traveling Geinin. For centuries, these troupes of entertainers have been touring Japan, performing for the working classes and country peasants in cramped and often dirty theatres. With the advent of television and the closure of many of these theatres, a lot of these troupes have died out, and only the best of them have survived to entertain at modern hot springs, at hotels in Japan resort areas. Ichikawa Santuro troupe are such survivors. (Arratia 138)

11. Weems served as assistant director in 1993 (Quick 282).

12. The Japanese troupe seem to be in a rural setting: there is mention of villagers and opportunity for fishing.

13. I distinguish these "backstage" actions belonging to the daily life of the *Geinin* troupe, many of them accompanied by documentary film narration, from elements such as visible preparations for entrances, entrances, or exits via a long ramp (stage left), rearrangements of props, microphones, stage furnishings, and the like. Stage activity of this latter kind (which one might call visible staging), unlike actions associated with the personal lives of the Japanese players, characterizes both *Fish Story* and *Brace Up!* and reflects The Wooster Group's experimentation with a variety of Japanese theatrical conventions, including the use in both pieces of a stage design based on Noh staging. Of course, it is also in keeping with the Group's history of self-reflexive, anti-illusionistic theatre: "in all former pieces," for example, "no attempt is made to conceal the walls of the Performing Garage with flats or wings; performance space and theatre space have no delimiting borders" (Arratia 124).

258   *Sheila Rabillard*

14. See Quick's "Production Credits" for *Fish Story* where "Texts" are credited to act 4 of Chekhov's *Three Sisters* translated by Schmidt and to "*Geinin*, a documentary film, 1977" (282).
15. Callens gives these successive titles: *Fish Story*; *Fish Story II*; *A Work-in-Progress (Today I Must Sincerely Congratulate You)*; *UnFinISHed Story*; and, finally, in 1996, *FinISHed Story* (Callens, "FinISHed" 144).
16. See also Evgeny Steiner's "The Reception of Chekhov in Japan."
17. Senelick notes that by the mid-1960s, surveys showed that the most respectable and dependable classics for local resident theatres in America were Shakespeare, Moliere, and Chekhov, and that nonchallenging productions of Chekhov tended to be bland, or played in what was believed by American actors to be the English tradition, namely, to play "trippingly and to focus on the boredom" (*Chekhov Theatre* 291).
18. Marvin Carlson, surveying the evolution of the *Drama Review* under Richard Schechner's editorship, notes that he shifted the periodical's emphasis from dramatic literature to contemporary production. "The pivot of the change" was the two-issue (Fall–Winter 1964) reassessment of the influence of Stanislavsky in America "rightly called one of the magazine's finest achievements"; the next issue (Spring 1965) "almost prophetically" contained Barba's two articles introducing the work of Grotowski (Carlson 455). LeCompte and Spalding Gray worked with Schechner's Performance Group from 1970, gradually developing their own distinctive approach and attracting a number of people who would eventually become The Wooster Group when Schechner left in 1980 and turned over the Performing Garage to the Woosters. These close early ties with Schechner suggest why the Woosters, like the editor of the *Drama Review*, see Stanislavsky and Grotowski as important influences on American performance.

WORKS CITED

Allen, David. *Performing Chekhov*. London: Routledge, 2000. Print.
Aronson, Arnold. *American Avant-garde Theatre: A History*. London: Routledge, 2000. Print.
———. "The Scenography of Chekhov." *The Cambridge Companion to Chekhov*. Ed. Vera Gottlieb and Paul Allain. Cambridge, Cambridge UP, 2000. 134–48. Print.
Arratia, Euridice. "Island Hopping Rehearsing The Wooster Group's *Brace Up!*" *Drama Review* 36.4 (Winter 1992): 121–42. Print.
Auslander, Philip. "Task and Vision: Willem Defoe in *LSD*." *Acting (Re)considered: A Theoretical and Practical Guide*. 2nd ed. Ed. Phillip B. Zarrilli. London: Routledge, 2002. 305–10. Print.
Bhabha, Homi. *The Location of Culture*. London: Routledge, 1994. Print.
Brantley, Ben. "The Wooster Group: An Ensemble Tailor-Made for an Age of Anxiety." Critic's Notebook. *New York Times* 28 Feb. 2005. Web. 6 Aug. 2011.
Callens, Johan. "FinISHed Story: Elisabeth LeCompte's Intercultural Take on Time and Work." *Contemporary Drama in English Vol. 5: Anthropological Perspectives*. Ed. Werner Huber and Martin Middeke. Trier: WVT Wissenschaftlicher Verlag Trier, 1998. 143–58. Print.
———. "Of Rough Cuts, Voice Masks, and Fugacious Bodies: The Wooster Group in Progress." *The Wooster Group and Its Traditions*. Ed. Johan Callens. Brussels: Peter Lang, 2004. 45–59. Print.

The Work of the Theatre 259

Carlson, Marvin. *Theories of the Theatre: A Historical and Critical Survey, from the Greeks to the Present.* Exp. ed. Ithaca: Cornell UP, 1993. Print.

Chekhov, Anton. *The Plays of Anton Chekhov.* Trans. Paul Schmidt. New York: HarperCollins, 1997. Print.

Diamond, Elin. "The Violence of 'We': Politicizing Identification." *Critical Theory and Performance.* Eds. Janelle Reinelt and Joseph Roach. Ann Arbor, MI: U of Michigan P, 1992. 390–398. Print.

Hardt, Michael. Foreword. "Creation beyond Measure." *The Labor of Job.* By Antonio Negri. Trans. Matteo Mandarini. Durham: Duke UP, 2009. ix–xv. Print.

Hutcheon, Linda. *A Theory of Adaptation.* London: Routledge, 2006. Print.

Knowles, Ric. "The Wooster Group's *House/Lights.*" *The Wooster Group and Its Traditions.* Ed. Johan Callens. Brussels: Peter Lang, 2004. 189–202. Print.

Kraus, Rosalind. "Poststructuralism and Deconstruction" and "Roundtable: The Predicament of Contemporary Art." *Art Since 1900: Modernism, Antimodernism, Postmodernism.* Ed. Hal Foster, Rosalind Krauss, Yve-Alain Bois, and Benjamin H. D. Buchloh. New York: Thames and Hudson, 2004. 40–48 and 670–679. Print.

LeCompte, Elizabeth. "*Brace Up!* Notes on Form." *Felix: A Journal of Media Arts and Communication* 1.3 (1993). Web. 8 Aug. 2011.

Mee, Susie. "*Three Sisters* and The Wooster Group's *Brace Up!*" *Drama Review* 36.4 (Winter 1992): 143–53. Print.

Negri, Antonio. *The Labor of Job.* Trans. Matteo Mandarini. Durham: Duke UP, 2009. Print.

Quick, Andrew. *The Wooster Group Work Book.* New York: Routledge, 2007. Print.

Rouse, John. "Textuality and Authority in Theater and Drama: Some Contemporary Possibilities." *Critical Theory and Performance.* Ed. Janelle G. Reinelt and Joseph R. Roach. Ann Arbor: U of Michigan P, 1992. 146–58. Print.

Said, Edward. "Traveling Theory." *The World, the Text, and the Critic.* Cambridge: Harvard UP, 1983. 226–47. Print.

Sanders, Julie. *Adaptation and Appropriation.* London: Routledge, 2006. Print.

Savran, David. *Breaking the Rules: The Wooster Group.* New York: Theatre Communications Group, 1988. Print.

———. "Obeying the Rules." *The Wooster Group and Its Traditions.* Ed. Johan Callens. Brussels: Peter Lang, 2004. 63–70. Print.

Schmidt, Paul. "The Sounds of *Brace Up!* Translating the Music of Chekhov." *The Drama Review* 36.4 (Winter 1992): 154–157. Print.

Senelick, Laurence. *The Chekhov Theatre: A Century of the Plays in Performance.* Cambridge: Cambridge UP, 1997. Print.

———. "Directors' Chekhov." *The Cambridge Companion to Chekhov.* Ed. Vera Gottlieb and Paul Allain. Cambridge: Cambridge UP, 2000. 176–200. Print.

Shevtsova, Maria, and Christopher Innes. *Directors/Directing: Conversations on Theatre.* Cambridge: Cambridge UP, 2009. Print.

Shyer, Laurence. "Andrey Şerban Directs Chekhov: *The Sea Gull* in New York and Japan." *Theater* 13.1 (1981): 56–66. Print.

Steiner, Evgeny. "The Reception of Chekhov in Japan." *Chekhov Then and Now: The Reception of Chekhov in World Culture.* Ed. J. Douglas Clayton. New York: Peter Lang, 1997. 191–200. Print.

Tanaka, Nobuko. "Reflections of Chekhov's Russia in Modern-Day Japan." *Japan Times Online.* 23 July 2010. Web. 20 June 2011.

Vanden Heuvel, Michael. "L.S.D. (Let's Say Deconstruction!): Narrating Emergence in American Alternative Theatre History." *The Wooster Group and Its Traditions.* Ed. Johan Callens. Brussels: Peter Lang, 2004. 71–82. Print.

260 *Sheila Rabillard*

Wooster Group. *Brace Up! The Wooster Group Work Book*. By Andrew Quick. New York: Routledge, 2007. 62–105. Print.

———. *Fish Story: A Documentary about Theatre Life in Eight Dances. The Wooster Group Work Book*. By Andrew Quick. New York and London: Routledge, 2007. 114–57. Print.

———. *Frank Dell's The Temptation of St. Anthony. The Wooster Group Work Book*. By Andrew Quick. New York: Routledge, 2007. 16–55. Print.

———. *The Wooster Group*. Web. 6 Aug. 2011.

14 The Japanization of Chekhov
Contemporary Japanese Adaptations of *Three Sisters*

Yasushi Nagata

Anton Chekhov played an important role in the evolution of modern Japanese theatre. The translation of Chekhov's works started with Kayo Senuma's 1903 rendition of *The Moon and People*, followed by the translations of his full-length plays, including *Uncle Vanya* in 1912, and *The Cherry Orchard* and *Ivanov* in 1913. These were followed by translations by Rokuro Ito and Masao Kusuyama. The assimilation of Chekhov's works continued during the 1910s, culminating in 1919, when a complete collection of his works began to appear. By then, translations into Japanese of all his important works had already been published. Famous novelists such as Hakucho Masamune and Kazuo Hirotsu referred to Chekhov, but Japanese dramatists had yet to reflect Chekhov's works in their plays. His plays first began to be introduced in Japan in 1909, when the Free Theatre, which is now regarded as the starting point of modern Japanese theatre, presented *The Proposal* as its second production. Before the absorption of Chekhov by Japanese dramatists was to occur, however, they had to experience productions of his major plays on the Japanese stage. Such productions started later at the Tsukiji Little Theatre, which was established in 1924.

The Tsukiji Little Theatre played a decisive role in promoting Japanese modern theatre. Kaoru Osanai, the director and one of the founders of the theatre, loved Chekhov's works so much that he directed productions of his plays intensively from 1924 until his death in 1928. These productions included *Swan Song* in 1924; *The Cherry Orchard* in 1925 and 1927; *Three Sisters* in 1925 and 1926; and *Uncle Vanya* in 1925, 1927, and 1928. He thus presented full-length plays almost every year, as well as such one-acters as *Jubilee*, *The Bear*, and *The Proposal*. Undoubtedly, it was these productions, which took place intensively over a span of four years, that promoted the full-scale introduction of Chekhov's plays into Japanese theatre. Moreover, these productions determined how Chekhov's plays would be accepted in this country. Osanai's understanding of Chekhov's plays was mainly fostered by his experience of having seen them presented by the Moscow Art Theatre from 1912 to 1913.[1] He took meticulous notes on Stanislavsky's direction and brought them back to Japan. Osanai's direction, based on these notes, determined the presentation style of

262   *Yasushi Nagata*

Chekhov's works in Japan almost single-handedly. As Sugai pointed out (58), Hakucho Masamune, who had already understood Chekhov's talent as a short story writer, commented on the first production of a Chekhov play at the Tsukiji Little Theatre: "This is the way a play should be. Even simple language can delve into the depth of life." He added that he felt a renewed respect for Chekhov. Osanai believed that simple language could reveal deep truths, and therefore he avoided excessively dramatic direction. He thought that nothing was more dramatic than speaking lines in simple language. However, he also believed that you needed to look and behave like a Russian in order to approach Chekhov. In other words, he thought that, in presenting a Chekhov play, you needed to put aside your Japanese identity and become Russian (Nagata 277). After Osanai passed away in 1928, the Tsukiji Little Theatre lost its centripetal force and split into two. At the same time, the appearance of proletarian theatre in the 1930s meant a decline in the presentation of Chekhov's plays, especially during the war.

Osanai's approach to Chekhov's plays did not contribute much to their adaptation in Japan. However, their influence was indeed felt. Chekhov's plays stimulated many Japanese dramatists in terms of their own work. His dramaturgy was different from that of Ibsen, whose works were introduced to Japan almost at the same time as Chekhov's. Chekhov's dramaturgy, which was influenced by Turgenev's stories, does not focus very much on incidents or explain characters' feelings. It simply depicts scenes. Events are generally not dramatic. Feelings are not well explained. Things largely depend on lingering tones and subtexts. On the other hand, the unspoken atmosphere and feelings reveal themselves, which suited the spiritual climate of the Japanese people. This is most likely the reason why Chekhov's plays influenced Japanese playwrights, who began to use Chekhov-like techniques in creating modern plays. Composed mainly of dialogues with few dramatic events, these functioned through implications and connotations and emphasized atmosphere. Characters often reflected on their pasts and fell into melancholic depression. Although they hoped to solve the problems they faced, they could not take the necessary action. Among the dramatists who acquired the skills to handle these techniques was Kunio Kishida. A perfect example is his play *Hotel Ushiyama* (1929), which depicts a Japanese woman who is running a hotel in Vietnam, and the people around her. One of the principal themes in Chekhov's works is lack of identity or uneasiness about identity. *Hotel Ushiyama* reflects this theme, depicting Japanese who live far away from Japan and seek their identity among the local population and other foreigners.

Numerous Japanese plays written after the Second World War were clearly based on Chekhov's dramaturgy. These include plays about returning soldiers, such as *Copsewood* (1948) written by Naoya Uchimura, or *The Daughter of the Lake* (1946) by Ryuichiro Yagi, which depicted tragedies arising from

The disintegration of postwar society, which had an entirely different mentality and attitude to that of the repatriated soldiers; this theme aroused interest of a rather vulgar nature among the audience. Other plays that reflected the influence of Chekhov's dramaturgy were *A Ball for Only the Two of Us* (1956) by Yushi Koyama and Sakae Kubo's *A Dairy of Apple Fields* (1947) particularly. They focused on the gaps between ideals and reality in Japanese civil consciousness during the postwar reconstruction period. It was in the 1970s, when avant-garde or underground theatre became popular, that Japanese modern theatre began to actively adapt Chekhov's plays. Actors in these new approaches to theatre tried to incorporate elements of traditional theatre, and a trend of "Japanizing" the methods and content of European theatre emerged; this included adapting Chekhov's plays in the Japanese manner. In the following sections of this chapter, I will examine three major characteristics of the contemporary adaptation of Chekhov's plays.

RECONSTRUCTING FAMILIES

Many of the plays written in Japan from the 1970s through the 1980s dealt with family breakdown. They included Shuji Terayama's *Lemming* (1979), Koharu Kisaragi's *Moral* (1982), and Masataka Matsuda's *On the Summer Sand* (1991). These plays not only are representative works of each decade, but each also deals with the theme of family breakdown in its own way. *Lemming* includes an episode of a son trying to become independent from his mother, who tries to force him to have a deep relationship with her, a relationship that could be viewed as pseudo-incestuous, within the feudalistic family system. Terayama develops this plotline in an illusionary framework of storytelling. He constructs the story around the familiar theme of the old paternalistic family system and independence from it through his own surrealistic techniques. *Moral* depicts family breakdown in urban life, a symbol of Japan's rapid economic growth in the 1980s. The work, which repeatedly uses the Brechtian technique of alienation, poignantly demonstrates how completely modern families are destroyed. *On the Summer Sand* depicts a man who failed in marriage. He and his niece happen to live together. The realistic portrayal of the interaction of their minds serves to reveal the situation of Japan in the 1990s, when it suffered from a long-term economic recession and unemployment. These works are based not on Chekhov's plays but on the themes that the Japanese theatre tackled in and after the 1970s. It may be argued that the breakdown of old communal families as a community achieves economic growth and becomes urbanized is a universal phenomenon. However, they are unique in that each of them depicts the disruption of the patriarchal family, the cruelty of the process of families becoming nuclear, and the difficulty of reconstructing families, all themes strongly connected to the reality of Japanese society.

264 *Yasushi Nagata*

Since 2000, however, family dramas about modern Japan have not depicted family breakdown itself, but rather dealt with more specific issues, using family breakdown as a mere premise. For example, Nozomi Makino's *Supreme Existence* (2000), and Miri Yu's *Fish Festival* (1993) deal with family affairs, but do not use family breakdown as their theme. They focus more on some problems that Japanese society has deeply experienced more recently, such as homosexuality and women's issues. It was the framework of Chekhov's works that was used in these types of plots, the most successful work being Ai Nagai's *Three Sisters of the Hagi Family* (2000). Nagai leads her own theatre company, Nitosha, and is arguably one of the female Japanese playwrights who is most energetically involved in theatre activities. Nagai and Shizuka Oishi founded Nitosha in 1981. Since Oishi left the company in 1991, Nagai has been directing her own plays by herself. Nagai has focused in a comical way on ordinary Japanese people who have experienced some social changes in contemporary Japan. *Daddy's Democracy* (1995), *Brother Comes Home* (1999), and *The Men Who Want to Force People to Sing* (2005) depict contemporary Japanese lives satirically and are highly evaluated. The plot of *Three Sisters of the Hagi Family* depicts an old, established family with three main characters: Takako, the oldest daughter, who is an associate professor at a university and teaches feminism; Nakako, the second oldest, who is a stay-at-home mother with a happy-go-lucky husband; and Wakako, the youngest, who lives with two men and is thinking of moving to Tokyo. Needless to say, these sisters are based on the main characters of Chekhov's *Three Sisters*. Takako, who is modeled on Olga, continues her relationship with her colleague Takeo, a professor, though she knows it is an extramarital affair, but she breaks up with him when she finds out that his wife is pregnant. The professor, however, cannot give her up and suggests that they study their love relationship together as a research topic. Through this joint study, the professor modifies his views and his prejudice against his own sexual identity. In the end, he discovers his identity in his femininity and decides to live as a woman. Nakako, the second oldest sister, is modeled on Masha. She is fed up with her husband, who resembles Kulygin. She meets her childhood friend, a Vershinin-like character who is a farmer, and falls in love with him. Unlike Vershinin, the farmer does not like philosophy, but his wife is mentally ill as in Chekhov's original. In Chekhov she is only referred to but never appears onstage, whereas the fact that she does appear in Makino's play adds color to the work. Wakako, the youngest sister, is, of course, modeled on Irina; like Irina, she is desired by two men, in this case two furniture workers. These two men do not, however, get into a duel like Tuzenbakh and Solyony. Wakako ends up having sexual relationships with both of them and in the end the three of them leave for Tokyo to live together.

There is no counterpart to Andrey in *Three Sisters of the Hagi Family*; the absence of Andrey makes the play seem less solitary and desolate than

The Japanization of Chekhov   265

Chekhov's original. On the other hand, there is a character who is a counterpart to Anfisa and who serves as a second fiddle. After all, *Three Sisters of the Hagi Family* does not conjure up much of the atmosphere particular to Chekhov's original. Instead, the play presents farce-like elements and aspects of comedy of manners, so in sum it is more like a comedy. Moreover, there is no character similar to Chebutykin, who sprinkles Chekhov's play with nonsense remarks full of deep implications, and in this sense the story of *Three Sisters of the Hagi Family* is not as profound as Chekhov's *Three Sisters*. Nonetheless, *Three Sisters of the Hagi Family* does include a sense of humor like that in Chekhov's plays. Chekhov's characters say one thing and do quite another; such inconsistency is humorous and beautifully describes human nature. Trofimov in *The Cherry Orchard*, who enthusiastically talks about the future of human beings, is actually so immature that in fact he cannot do anything by himself, and Olga is promoted as school principal though she never wanted a promotion. Similarly, in *Three Sisters of the Hagi Family*, Takako, who argues for feminism at the university, faces the reality of being a feminist in her private life and cannot find happiness. In Chekhov's plays, humor relativizes every value. There is no such thing as a firm belief or ideal upon which the world should be based. This is Chekhov's view of the world. In this regard, *Three Sisters of the Hagi Family* deals with women's status through gender-based arguments. The more enthusiastically Takako discusses feminism, the more humorous she appears, and the more relative and less absolute feminism seems. These scenes imply that the future of feminism is not as bright as it seems. Naturally, *Three Sisters of the Hagi Family* does not admire the outdated male-centered idea and the paternalistic view of families, but, on the other hand, it regards feminism with humor and thereby relativizes it, which is similar to Chekhov's attitude. Towards the end, Takeo, who used to be Takako's lover, realizes that his identity lies in his femininity, appears in woman's clothes, and declares that he will live as a woman. This scene beautifully connects the comedic element of cross-dressing with the theme of the play, effectively symbolizing the essence of this work.

It is often pointed out that Chekhov's plays lack a father figure. The fact that a father figure is absent in a paternalistic family brings about confusion and tragedy as well as comedy. *Three Sisters* starts on the first anniversary of the father's death, as does *Three Sisters of the Hagi Family*. In *Three Sisters*, this is the day when the sisters finally escape the spell of their late strict father and start to become independent, as he had been, as it were, the norm for the family. Then, ironically, when they finally try to become independent, each of them goes through agony as they discover that they are not able to do so. In a way, however, in *Three Sisters of the Hagi Family*, the oldest sister, Takako, plays a father-like role. Takako forces feminist ideals or ways of thinking onto her sisters whenever she deems it necessary. Her sound feminist arguments drive her younger sister, Nakako, to an extramarital affair and her youngest sister, Wakako, to run away to Tokyo

266   *Yasushi Nagata*

with two men. Takako is the norm for the family. In this sense, *Three Sisters of the Hagi Family* has a fundamentally different internal structure from Chekhov's *Three Sisters*. Ai Nagai freely borrows motifs from *Three Sisters* and the lives of the sisters in a comedic way. Unlike other Japanese modern family dramas in and after the 1970s, which dramatically depict family breakdown, the family of *Three Sisters of the Hagi Family* does not break down so much on the surface. Instead, the play comically portrays the breakdown of the internal world of the sisters. It may be said that Nagai succeeded in this because she borrowed the framework of Chekhov's play.

"JAPANIZING" CHEKHOV

Another characteristic of the adaptation of Chekhov's plays is the tendency for them to be "Japanized." The plots and characters of Chekhov's plays are not changed much, but the setting is simply transferred to Japan. Examples of this characteristic include adaptations of *Three Sisters* (2000) by Tomomi Tsutsui. This work was set in Asashikawa, Hokkaido, before the Second World War and takes place in typical rural districts, far from the central capital city, Tokyo. The plot of Tsutsui's *Three Sisters* remains the same as that of Chekhov's original, but it is set at the end of the Meiji Era. In this way, the militaristic motifs exhibited by the sisters overlap those of Japanese imperialism, thus connoting the history of Japan's past wars. At first, the idea of transferring the setting of Chekhov's plays to Japan was not so popular. Japan's modern theatre emphasized the value of presenting European plays as they were and did not accept the idea of changing them to suit Japanese climate and backdrops. This was because they thought modern Europe should first be adopted in Japan as it was; this was how Japan's modernization was supposed to take place. Simply transferring the setting to Japan seemed an easy compromise. These days, the adaptation of European plays to Japanese settings is not unusual. This trend should not be taken as negative, but rather as proof that Japanese theatre is now more tolerant. Before the war, those in Japanese theatre, in a way, tried to be European (or, rather, Russian). Nowadays, Japanese theatre is finally becoming Japanese.

One of the most experimental examples of recent "Japanized" adaptations is *Three Sisters in a Thousand Years* (2004) by Minoru Betsuyaku. He uses many plots from Chekhov's original and modifies them to suit his world. Betsuyaku began in the 1950s by writing absurdist plays, influenced by Beckett's work. He has written well over a hundred works, which form his very unique world. The stage setting of most of his plays is very simple and abstract: only a utility pole and a bench. Ordinary dialogue gradually becomes eccentric, implying the comedic and tragic dark side of humans, who have to live through absurdity. *Three Sisters in a Thousand Years* is experimental because, while it presents all the important characters of Chekhov's *Three Sisters*, it sets the story in Japan, from the first act to the final fourth one, which covers almost one thousand years. The first act is set in the tenth century, the era of Japanese aristocracy. It is in March, when people in Japan traditionally celebrate Girls' Day. The play starts with a line saying that their father passed away one year before, just like Olga's line in the original. However, the story gradually reveals that the main character makes a living as a prostitute for aristocrats. The owner of her brothel is Andrey and his wife, Natasha, runs the business. Vershinin also appears. Masha, as in Chekhov's original, falls in love with him, despite the fact that she is married to Kulygin. Irina lives a carefree life with Tuzenbakh and Solyony. Chebutykin is poisoned by Vershinin and dies. The second act is set in a red-light district in the Edo Period (the eighteenth century). The three women live as prostitutes. Vershinin deceives Andrey into gambling and seizes his fortune and his brothel where the three sisters work. Andrey hangs himself over this incident. The third act is set on a harbor in the 1920s. The three sisters still live on prostitution. Still, Vershinin loves Masha. Masha falls into a river, and Vershinin tries to rescue her but drowns. However, it turns out that it was not Masha who fell into the river, but Vershinin's wife. The fourth act is set in a slum area in modern times. Irina decides to live with Tuzenbakh, but Solyony kills him out of jealousy. Solyony is arrested and kills himself by swallowing a razor in a prison cell. Kulygin tries to save the child of Andrey and Natasha, but is hit by a train and dies. At the end of the play, all the characters are dead, except the three sisters, who remain alive. They lose hope for the future and attempt suicide by taking cyanide, but somehow the cyanide does not work and they cannot die. The play ends as they say they might find out something if they live a little longer. The story in each act is complete and at the end of each act, one character dies. However, this dead character is somehow revived in the next act. The only thing that is consistent from the first act to the fourth is that the three sisters work as prostitutes. They become extremely old as each act proceeds. At the end they look like ghosts.

This play is an adaptation of Chekhov's text against the backdrop of the one-thousand-year history of Japan, starting from the era of aristocracy in the tenth century, through the era of samurai in the eighteenth century, to the 1920s, and the modern era. The play completely excludes any Russian atmosphere, incorporating Japanese seasonal motifs, including early spring Girls' Day in the first act, the Tanabata Star Festival in the second, and the autumn viewing of the moon in the third. The story thus represents a sort of dialogue between Chekhov and traditional Japanese seasonal motifs. However, Betsuyaku does not simply transfer the location of Chekhov's *Three Sisters* into Japan. He "Japanizes" the theme of *Three Sisters*. As mentioned previously, *Three Sisters* starts with an episode one year after the death of the father of the main characters, when the four children finally start searching for their identities, agonize, and fail. Each of the children is urged to find education-related jobs and forced to receive foreign language education; at the same time, they are pushed to become good wives in the future. They are strictly educated at home and live to meet their father's

268 *Yasushi Nagata*

expectations. His death liberates them from these constraints. They finally have an opportunity to lead their lives as they wish. However, each of them encounters difficulties, suffers, and eventually loses her way.

On the other hand, the three sisters in Betsuyaku's *Three Sisters in a Thousand Years* live for a thousand years. All of the people they ever knew have passed away in the present time, but the sisters can't even die. They seem to search for their identities, but in a different way than in Chekhov's *Three Sisters*. It is important that Betsuyaku popularized Beckett's worldview. In his plays, characters usually exchange nonsense dialogue in a simple square, an empty space with only a utility pole for decoration in most cases, which suggests the absurdity of human relationships. Betsuyaku gazes coldly at the absurd nature of humans, who cannot help but deviate from their ordinary values while living ordinary lives. The main characters of Betsuyaku's plays do not feel uneasy about their identities: they have firm identities, so they do not bother to question them. However, as the play proceeds, their relationships with those around them gradually become unstable and cracks appear, not in the identities of the main characters as such, but in these relationships. Thus, Betsuyaku's plays do not concern characters' identities, but rather the fissures between them and those around them. *Three Sisters in a Thousand Years* is a typical example of this characteristic. The three sisters continue to live in the same place, doing the same job, but people around them change, causing problems or incidents that take place one after another. This is similar to Chekhov's *Three Sisters*: the three sisters remain in the same local city, and only those around them change. In the case of the Betsuyaku's play, however, they are not seeking to establish their identities. Rather, they are troubled by the fissures that separate them from the people around them.

The thousand-year range of the lives of the sisters almost coincides with the thousand-year history of Japan so that they come to represent that history. Betsuyaku chooses to present the millennium of Japan, or rather how the country has continued to exist, in his unique way, based on the formula of Chekhov's *Three Sisters*. The sisters in the Betsuyaku's play, at a loss in an apocalyptic world where the meaning of life is completely lost, connote how empty it is to search for identity. The characters in Chekhov's *Three Sisters* feel uneasy about their identities, a notion that gained much sympathy from Japanese intellectuals. By contrast, the characters in Betsuyaku's play go through the emptiness of identity, and this emptiness, along with the cruelty of the irreversible nature of time, implies a vague uneasiness about the future of Japan.

JAPANESE TRADITIONAL THEATRE AND CHEKHOV

Basically, modern Japanese theatre has developed completely separately from the country's traditional theatre. At the beginning of the twentieth century, Kabuki attempted to modernize itself by absorbing modern theatre. This

The Japanization of Chekhov   269

attempted fusion included an innovative production by Sadanji Ichikawa, Kabuki plays written by Kido Okamoto and Seika Mayama, among others, and the establishment of leftist Kabuki theatres such as the Zenshin-za Theatre or the Kokoro-za Theatre. These attempts succeeded in fusing modern theatre with its traditional counterpart to some extent; however, a number of Kabuki groups later united at Shochiku and the trend of Kabuki shifted to its classical form. Traditional theatre became conservative and stopped building and maintaining an active relationship with modern theatre. As a result, both traditional theatre and modern European theatre took different paths of development. In the 1970s, the avant-garde theatre trend gained momentum around the world and many pieces of experimental theatre appeared in Japan as well, where they actively attempted to fuse those experimental pieces with traditional theatre, including Kabuki and Noh. *Gekitekinarumonowo-Megutte II* (*On the Dramatic Passions*, 1970), the experimental early works by Tadashi Suzuki presented at the Waseda Little Theatre, succeeded in establishing a very unique world through a pastiche of elements of Kabuki and those of European theatre. At the Tenkei Theatre, Shogo Ota borrowed the story structure and actors' physical presentation from Noh and recreated them in the form of modern theatre. His *Komachi Fuden* (*A Biography of Komachi*, 1977) and *Mizuno-Eki* (*A Water Station*, 1981) revealed the potential of this novel new theatre. Based on these attempts, the fusion of modern theatre with traditional theatre has finally become common in recent years.

This fusion of traditional theatre with modern theatre follows two patterns: either the adaptation of a work of traditional theatre into a modern piece or the presentation of a European play within the framework of traditional Japanese theatre. Although there are interesting examples of adapting traditional theatre in modern ways, there are also many examples, these days, of adapting European plays to the style of Japanese traditional theatre. In particular, there are countless examples of adapting the plays of Shakespeare, Brecht, and Maeterlinck in the Bunraku style. There are also an increasingly large number of examples of adapting the plays of Tennessee Williams and Shakespeare in the style of Nihon-Buyo or classical Japanese dance. There are also examples of adaptation in the Noh style. For example, *Tsukimachi*, or *Waiting for the Moon*, by Masataka Matsuda is an adaptation of Kafka's "In the Penal Colony," performed by Noh actors on the Noh stage in traditional Noh style, accompanied by songs and music.

Within the framework of Japanese traditional theatre, the adaptation of Chekhov's plays is significant. One of the active dramatists in this approach is Yoji Sakate. He leads the theatre group Rinkogun, which actively raises questions on the nature of politics and society in modern Japan and the modern world. Sakate adapted modern plays by Ibsen and Chekhov in the Noh style and put them together in a book entitled *Gendai Nohgakushu* (*The Contemporary Noh Collection*, 2010). In this way, he seems to be comparing his work with that of Yukio Mishima, who wrote *Kindai Nohgakushu* (*The Modern Noh Collection*, 1950–1960). Mishima had

270 Yasushi Nagata

translated existing Noh plays into a modern idiom by using contemporary Japanese. Sakate, on the other hand, translates the works of Ibsen and Chekhov, which have no prior relationship to Noh, into the Noh style in a way he finds appropriate. If Mishima seems to have intended to revive Noh plays in modern times, Sakate, by rewriting European plays in the Noh idiom, demonstrates the depth of the European plays and at the same time reveals the universality of the Noh style.

In *Gendai Nohgakushu-Chekhov* Sakate translated four of Chekhov's plays in the Noh style: *The Seagull, Uncle Vanya, The Cherry Orchard,* and *Three Sisters.* However, his adaptations did not adhere strictly to the authentic Noh style, unlike *Tsukimachi* by Masataka Matsuda. For example, Sakate's adaptation does not clarify the difference between *shite,* or the leading character, and *waki,* or supporting characters. There are no songs or musical accompaniment. The stage is not arranged in the Noh style, but only has a minimal amount of furniture. Actors do not wear Noh costumes, but modern clothes. Nevertheless, his adaptation is based on the style and spirit of the Fukushiki-Mugen-Noh, or the Dream-Noh-in-Two-Parts. Thus, the *Gendai Nohgakushu* is a collection of Japanese European traditional theatre, particularly of Chekhov's plays, perceived through the Noh worldview.

Sakate's plays are based on social or political themes. In his adapted *Three Sisters,* the sisters appear in the setting of the ruins of a theatre. They are ghosts, an idea that obviously comes from *nochi-jite,* or *shite* in the second act, which is a Mugen-Noh style. While these ghosts are rehearsing the lines of *Three Sisters,* Japanese soldiers storm in. At first, these retreating soldiers do not notice that they are in a theatre because of the darkness. Thinking that the place is a perfect site for their camp, they decide to stay. Then they notice the presence of the actors on the stage and start a conversation with them. Masha talks about her past. She says that her husband ruined their life together because of gambling, abandoned her, and eventually enrolled in the army. She picks up one of the soldiers present and talks to him as if he were her husband. The soldier, remembering that he was forced to forget about his past life due to the execution of his military missions, starts to think that Masha, who is right in front of him, is his former wife. Then the soldiers find out that all the sold-out theatre audience is dead and that flags draped in black are hung outside. They also discover that in the place where they are numerous civilians were surrounded by enemies, attacked, and killed. The three sisters ask the soldiers to come up onto the stage. The soldiers find out that the sisters have been holding a continuous memorial service to honor the dead at the theatre.

Another play by Sakate can be regarded as a precursor of this one: *"Three Sisters" That Was Not Performed* (2005). This play uses the same story-framework as the other one, but the soldiers are not from the same country as the sisters. They are armed terrorists who are plotting guerrilla activities against their government. They occupy the theatre, take the actors and the audience as hostages, and hole themselves up. Despite the presence of the terrorists, the actors start the rehearsal of *Three Sisters*. The exchanges between the sisters and the terrorists are incorporated into the structure of *Three Sisters*. In the end, the government army storms in and all the terrorists are killed. Needless to say, this play uses as a motif the 2002 incident in Moscow, in which an armed group of Chechens occupied a theatre. In this incident, all the members of the group were killed by the government forces as a result of the exchange of gunfire and more than 120 civilians who were taken hostage were also killed. Compared with *Gendai Nohgakushu-Chekhov*, *The "Three Sisters" That Was Not Performed* (2005), played by the actors who are taken hostage, presents almost all of the characters of Chekhov's original *Three Sisters*, upon which, of course, Sakate's adaptation is based. Furthermore, *The "Three Sisters" That Was Not Performed* is filled with the tension between those in the theatre and the government forces, as well as with the feeling of political oppression. The play is also a great metatheatrical piece in that the fictional nature of the story and the reality of the theatre-occupation incident, on the one hand, and the fictional nature of *Three Sisters* (rehearsed on the stage) and the pseudo-realism of the terrorists surrounding the actors, on the other, are beautifully interwoven.

In contrast, *Gendai Nohgakushu-Chekhov* presents only the three sisters from Chekhov's original and the rest of the cast are soldiers. These soldiers do not occupy the theatre, but only use the place to stay temporarily. There is no imminent danger of the theatre being involved in a battle. Nonetheless, *Gendai Nohgakushu-Chekhov* still causes the same mixed feelings of strong reality and illusion. This is most probably because of the use of the Mugen-Noh form. During the dialogue with the soldiers, the sisters say "the stage is the bridge between the life here and the life over there." As this line implies, the theme of this drama lies in the gap between the world of the living and that of the dead: it seems to try to connect us with the dead. Here, "the dead" seems to imply, at first, those killed in the war, but it gradually becomes clear that the dead in general are referred to. When a soldier mentions a flag draped in black outside the theatre, the theme of the play becomes perfectly clear. Through the adaptation of *Three Sisters*, it reproduces the theme of mourning and honoring the dead, a theme that frequently appears in Noh. Furthermore, this is done in purely Noh style.

CONCLUSION

It is often said that Japan has accepted Chekhov more than any other country in the world. However, the trends of such acceptance are different between prewar Japan and contemporary Japan. The Chekhovian themes and motifs that prewar Japan mainly accepted include the Russian sense of

272 *Yasushi Nagata*

depression, or *toska*, the powerlessness of the intellectual, and the lack of identity. The patterns of adaptation of Chekhov's plays in contemporary Japanese theatre are diverse, but each of them is "Japanized" in its own way, unlike those in the prewar period, when his plays were first transposed into Japan. These patterns cover almost the entirety of Japanese modern theatre, including family plays, absurdist plays, traditional theatre, and plays with political messages. The Chekhovian themes and motifs to be found in contemporary Japanese theatre include family breakdown, the irreversibility of time, the nature of politics, and traditional theatre, none of which was seen before the war. These themes and motifs are parallel to the path that postwar Japanese theatre has taken. Modern Japanese theatre practices are an unprecedented theatrical attempt both to incorporate the identities of Japan and the Japanese into Chekhov's plays and, in the process, to closely analyze these identities.

NOTES

1. Osanai attended the Moscow Art Theatre thirteen times over twenty-three days during his stay in Moscow, seeing the following performances: *The Lower Depths, The Cherry Orchard, Three Sisters, Uncle Vanya, Hamlet, The Living Corpse, Monna Vanna, L'Oiseau bleu, Enough Stupidity in Every Wise Man, A Month in the Country, A Provincial Lady,* and *Breakfast at the Chief's.*

WORKS CITED

Betsuyaku, Minoru. *Three Sisters in a Thousand Years.* Tokyo: 12th Tokyo Opinion's Festival, 2004. Print.
Chekhov, Anton. *Ivanov.* Trans. Kayo Senuma. Seito 6, Tokyo: Toun-Do, 1913. Print.
———. *The Moon and People.* Trans. Kayo Senuma. Shinshosetsu 8. Tokyo: Shunyodo. 1903. Print.
———. *Oji Vanya.* Trans, Kayo Senuma. Seito 3~8. Tokyo: Toun-Do, 1912. Print.
———. *Sakura no Sono.* Trans, Kayo Senuma. Seito 3~5, Tokyo: Toun-Do, 1913. Print.
———. *Zenshu.* 10 vols. Tokyo: Shincho-sha, 1919–1928. Print.Kisaragi, Koharu. Moral. Tokyo: Shinjuku-Shobo, 1987. Print.
Kishda, Kunio. *Hotel Ushiyama, Chuo-Koron* 1. Tokyo: Chuo-Koron-Sha, 1929. Print.
Makino, Nozomi. *Supreme Existence, Serifu no Jidai* 17. Tokyo: Shogakukan, 2000. Print.
Masamune, Hakucho. "Attending the Tsukiji Little Theatre." *Engeki Shincho.* July 1924. 65. Print.
Matsuda, Masataka. *On the Summer Sand. Kirarazaka.* Tokyo: Shinya-Sosho, 2002. Print.
———. *Tukimachi.* Kyoto International Performing Arts Festival. Nov. 2010, Performance.

The Japanization of Chekhov   273

Mishima, Yukio. *Kindai Nohgakushu*. Tokyo: Shincho-Sha, 1990. Print.
Nagai, Ai. *Brother Comes Home*. Tokyo: Jiritsu-Shobo, 2000. Print.
———. *Daddy's Democracy*. Tokyo: Jiritsu-Shono, 1997. Print.
———. *The Men who Want to Force People to Sing*. Tokyo: Jiritsu-Shobo, 2008. Print.
———. *Three Sisters of the Hagi Family*. Tokyo: Hakusuisha, 2000. Print.
Nagata, Yasushi. "Russia as Mise-en-Scene: An Interculturalism of Osanai Kaoru." *Theories of Japanese Arts*. Ed. Akira Usami. Kyoto: Minerva, 2000. Print.
Ota, Shogo. *Komachi Fuden*. Tokyo: Hakusui-Sha, 1978. Print.
———. *Mizuno-Eki. Complete Works of Ota Shogo*. Tokyo: Sougetu-Do, 2007. Print.
Sakate, Yoji. *Gendai Nohgakushu-Chekhov*. Rinko-Gun, Sep. 2010. Performance.
———. *"Three Sisters" That Was Not Performed*. Rinko-Gun, Jul. 2005. Performance.
Sugai, Yukio. *Chekhov: A Journey to Japan*. Tokyo: Toyoshoten, 2004. Print.
Suzuki, Tadashi. *Gekitekinarumonowo-megutte*. Kosaku-Sha, 1977. Performance.
Terayma, Shuji. *Lemming, Chikaengeki 14*. Tenjosajiki, 1979. Print.
Tsutsui, Tomomi. *Three Sisters*. Setagaya Public Theatre & Hokkaido Theatre Foundation. Jan. 2000. Performance.
Uchimura, Naoya. *Copsewood. Gekisaku 9*. Sekaibungaku-Sha, 1948. Print.
Yagi, Ryuichiro. *The Daughter of the Lake*. Miraisha, 1957. Print.
Yu, Miri. *Fish Festival*. Hakusisha, 1996. Print.

15 Interrogating the Real

Chekhov's Cinema of Verbatim. "Ward Number Six" in Karen Shakhnazarov's 2009 Film Adaptation

Yana Meerzon

When asked to define the genre of his 2009 film *Ward No. 6* (*Palata N 6*) based on Anton Chekhov's 1892 enigmatic novella, the director Karen Shakhnazarov says that he created "a drama or even a tragedy," aimed to convey Chekhov's "truth of life that we choose not to notice. [. . .] In this novella Chekhov came to the edge of an abyss and looked down in it. He reveals what we already know but would rather not think about" ("Shakhnazarov perelozhil"). Set in the Russia of 2007 and unfolding on the premises of the Nikolo-Poshekhonsky monastery (now an asylum) of the Dmitrovsky region near Moscow,[1] Shakhnazarov's *Ward No. 6* retells the story of Chekhov's Doctor Ragin, who becomes the patient of his own hospital, namely, its ward for the insane. In its complex style of storytelling the film seeks to find a cinematic analogue to the eclectic manner of Chekhov's own writing. It becomes an interesting case of mutation, when the means of one medium (film) are creatively used to evoke the stylistic and compositional particulars of another (short story).

At the core of Chekhov's story is a philosophical debate on the nature of human suffering. Doctor Ragin believes that in order to comprehend suffering one does not need to live through the experience; whereas Gromov, one of the asylum's inmates, is convinced that only one's personally embodied knowledge of misery can teach us the moral values of tolerance and forbearance. Hence, the Ragin–Gromov debate must be recognized both as "a signal of Chekhov's disenchantment with Tolstoyan notions, particularly nonresistance to evil," "a sociological document," and the author's "exercise in philosophical polemic" (Durkin 50). Most importantly, Durkin suggests, the story manifests its clear connection with Dostoyevsky's philosophical preoccupations and his writing style:

> [In "Ward Number Six"] for eight chapters out of nineteen, the diffuse yet perceptible voice of the narrator chronicles events in a provincial town. This opaque narrative persona, somewhat self-conscious and

ineptly literary in manner, differs sharply from the transparent, objective narrator typical of the mature Chekhov [. . .]. This obtrusive, traditional narrator "dissolves" in the later chapters [. . .] but while on stage he displays many of the attributes of a Dostoevskian chronicler-narrator, taking the reader by the hand in the opening paragraph, openly guiding the reader's attention and, even more uncharacteristically for Chekhov, his responses. The narrator freely reveals and seeks to impose his own, already formed attitudes toward the characters, with whom he is obviously long familiar. He provides biographies of the central characters, selecting significant incidents from their lives up to the start of the action. Such definition of character through retrospection is rare in Chekhov, who more typically demands that the reader infer the character's past and personality from the unordered information provided in the here and now. (51)

In other words, written as an elaborate fusion of dramatic (present tense) and epic (past tense) modes of narration, with the noticeably traceable narrator, the novella allows Chekhov to create the effect of the real, i.e., make the characters and the environment of "Ward Number Six" vivid, almost physically palpable, in the readers' imagination.

The 2009 film by Karen Shakhnazarov is remarkable for its efforts to seek means of cinematic narration to evoke the Chekhovian effect of the real on-screen and so to bring the story of Chekhov's characters as close as possible to today's audiences. For example, it becomes emblematic that Shakhnazarov chooses the 1960s literary and cultural icons of the Soviet intelligentsia to set what used to be Dr. Ragin's moral, intellectual, and spiritual values: "The film characters are all our contemporaries, including Dr. Ragin. It is no coincidence that he has photos of Hemingway and Vladimir Vysotsky on the wall of his tiny apartment" (Pruzhanskaya). Set in the Russia of the 2000s, Shakhnazarov's film suggests that the fictional Ragin belongs to the Thaw generation of the Soviet intellectuals, to whom Vladimir Vysotsky, the leading actor of Taganka Theatre in Moscow, was at that time and remains today the symbol of intellectual resistance and free-thinking. The film also argues that these values have become inconvenient today:

When Dr. Ragin sets out on a trip to Moscow with Mikhail Averyanych [the postmaster, Ragin's only friend in the story], the Moscow of the time (the 2000s) is depicted as a modern, noisy metropolis with traffic jams and glitzy casinos. Ragin is fired by today's "modernized" bureaucrats clad in expensive suits and sitting at a well-polished solid-wood table. With their blank faces they remind one of those one can find in today's Duma. (Pruzhanskaya)

However, in looking for the Chekhovian effect of the real, Shakhnazarov not only shifts the story of Dr. Ragin in time; he also presents it as a

276 *Yana Meerzon*

cinematic potpourri. The film combines the devices of cinematic dramatization with those of journalistic reportage and home video. It includes
interviews with the patients of Nikolo-Poshekhonsky asylum, mockumentary footage of the fictional characters made with a handheld camera
(the Dogma 95 technique),[2] and paradoxically but very effectively stylized
scenes à la silent movies. Shakhnazarov turns Chekhov's story into a cinematic paratext: *Ward No. 6* employs a variety of today's cutting-edge cinematic devices to convey the atmosphere of Chekhov's *inbetweenness*, "a
permanent dynamic vacillation between opposite textual poles (semantic,
thematic, and metaphysical)" (Lapushin 3), and the qualities of *stylistic
liminality* that allow Chekhov's text to freely oscillate between the representational tendencies of nineteenth-century naturalism and the presentational aesthetics of the period's symbolism and impressionism. Thus,
Shakhnazarov evokes the atmosphere and the environment of Chekhov's
story on-screen by creating an *analogy* of the original not its *transposition* or *commentary*.

According to Geoffrey Wagner's taxonomy of adaptation techniques in
film, there are three types of film adaptation. They are: (a) transposition, "in
which a novel is directly given on the screen, with the minimum of apparent interference" (222); (b) commentary, "where an original is taken and
either purposely or inadvertently altered in some respect," so the adaptation becomes either "re-emphasis or re-structure" (223); and (c) analogy—
when an original serves the adaptor only as a point of departure to create
a new work of art (226).[3] To Wagner, transposition and commentary function as forms of transformation of the original, whereas analogy does not
alternate or violate the original work. Adaptation as analogy can be seen as
the adaptor's attempt to create a new work of art independent in its artistic
and ethical objectives from the original that has inspired it. In the work
of art created by analogy with/to the original, the adaptor would never
propose as his/her artistic objective to reproduce the source text in a new
cultural, temporal, or any other environment (Wagner 227). Accordingly,
adaptation as analogy should not be considered within the moral discourse
of fidelity, a discourse that proves fruitless for the study of adaptation strategies in film or literature (Hutcheon 7). "Analogy films may [. . .] take but
the merest hints from their sources," or even further they may only offer
its viewers "analogous rhetorical techniques" to those found in the original
(Wagner 230). Shakhnazarov's *Ward No. 6* serves here, therefore, as an
example of the analogy technique of adaptation, because it employs in its
narrative modes a mixture of cinematic devices analogous in their eclectic
complexity to Chekhov's own style of writing. It manages to reinstate the
sense of "inbetweenness" on-screen the way Chekhov creates it in his story.
In this way, the film reveals the filmmaker's subjective take on the original.
It stages Shakhnazarov's social, religious, and artistic position, which is
marked by the artist's own time and preoccupations; these are somewhat
different than those of Chekhov.

Interrogating the Real   277

ON AUTHENTICITY OF THE REAL: CHEKHOV'S "WARD NUMBER SIX" VERSUS SHAKHNAZAROV'S FILM

As the *New York Times* once wrote, Shakhnazarov's cinematic style is diverse; he is "a prolific and under-recognized Russian filmmaker with a surrealist touch" (Holden). He started his career as film director, screenwriter, and producer in the early 1980s,[4] and the idea of adapting Chekhov's "Ward Number Six" came to Shakhnazarov in the early 1990s. Together with the writer Aleksandr Borodyansky, he envisioned a script that would serve as a point of departure for a Russian-Italian cinematic coproduction with Marcello Mastroianni as Dr. Ragin. However, the project did not go through. Although the coauthors used Chekhov's dialogues verbatim in their script, they moved the action into the contemporary realities of Russia in the 1990s. The Italians were expecting a traditional costume drama similar to Nikita Mikhalkov's 1987 Russian-Italian film *Dark Eyes*, also inspired by Chekhov's short stories, in which Mastroianni played a wealthy nineteenth-century Italian who falls in love with a married Russian woman. As Shakhnazarov explains, the Italian producers could not accept this new, experimental version of a feature film that would tell Chekhov's story by mixing many modes of cinematic narration, including elements of documentary film and silent movies (qtd. in Dolin). For twenty years, Shakhnazarov had been contemplating whether he had made the right choice when he rejected making changes to his script, and so lost the opportunity to work with the famous Italian actor. For twenty years, he searched for another actor to play Ragin, someone who could replace in his mind's eye the image of Mastroianni as the philosophizing provincial physician, bound to become the victim of his own indifference and indecisiveness. When Shakhnazarov met Vladimir Il'in and asked him to read the script, he felt that "it was so current [. . .] that it seemed to me that it had not only not lost its edge in the past 20 years, it was ahead of its time back in the 1990s" (qtd. in Dolin). The choice of the leading actor convinced not only the director Shakhnazarov; Il'in's Doctor Ragin won him the prize for the best male actor at the 2009 Moscow Film Festival.[5]

Back in 1991, Shakhnazarov had worked on another film *Assassin of the Tsar*, an Anglo-Russian coproduction between Courier Studios, Mosfilm, and Spectator Entertainment.[6] This work allowed him to start experimenting with documentary and feature-film modes of narration. *Assassin of the Tsar* tells the story of a mental patient Timofeyev (Malcolm McDowell) who believes that he assassinated Tsar Alexander II in 1881 and that he also organized the execution of another Russian tsar, Nicholas II, in 1918. In this film (written by Aleksandr Borodyansky in collaboration with Shakhnazarov), Dr. Smirnov (played by Oleg Yankovsky), the cinematic predecessor of Dr. Ragin, concludes that the only way to treat Timofeyev is to play along with his delusions and thus enter them. Dr. Smirnov takes on the persona of Tsar Nicholas II, whereas Timofeyev becomes Yurovsky,

278 *Yana Meerzon*

the tsar's assassin. Before long, the film's present and past, the imaginary and the real blur together, so that 1918 and its gloomy events come true. Interview/interrogation as a form of documentary film technique lies at the basis of this work's narrative mode, which allows Shakhnazarov to blur the imaginary and the real on-screen, to illustrate how the method of dramatic dialogue can be used in order to treat a mental disorder. The 1991 *Assassin of the Tsar* served Shakhnazarov as a testing ground for his stylistic experiments and gave him an opportunity to treat the themes of unstable identities and Russian history.

In 2009, in his *Ward No. 6*, Shakhnazarov turned to the theme of madness and to the technique of interview once again. This time, he engaged with existential issues of "the truth of life that we choose not to notice" and with social problems in today's Russia. When asked to explain how he conceived the idea of inviting the Nikolo-Poshekhonsky monastery's patients to become part of his film, Shakhnazarov states: "unlike us sane people, mental patients have natural reflexes. They are like children. And in that sense they are always above us. They do certain things consciously and some things unconsciously, a phenomenon that Chekhov explores too" (qtd. in Korneeva). At the same time Shakhnazarov insists that the presence of real patients on-screen adds to the film's social and political appeal: "Schizophrenia, sick people—this is a philosophical question, of course . . . But the thing is that their living conditions [in today's Russia–YM] are horrible. When you find yourself around them you see that these people are by and large left to their own devices" (qtd. in Korneeva). Hence, in his film Shakhnazarov uses the artistic and political premises of *documentary film* and *verbatim theatre* to reveal his critical position on the subject and so to remind his audiences that "the government must create some semblance of decent living conditions for these unfortunates" (qtd. in Sakharnova).[7] Thematically and stylistically, therefore, *Ward No. 6* is in line with those theatrical experiments in Russia today that widely employ documentary and verbatim techniques of storytelling. As Mark Lipovetsky and Birgit Beumers write:

> In the early 1990s artists, freed from the fetters of ideology, trying to re-engage with reality, produced a wide range of neo-realist or neo-naturalist discourses [. . .] that represented those aspects of social reality previously hidden under the cover of Socialist Realism. The chernukha naturalism [a style similar to the British in-yer-face theatre—YM], especially important for cinema, relayed the surrounding chaos whilst refraining from glossing over reality and abstaining from any indications of concise meaning or hope. Its appeal to audiences was therefore limited, and neo-realism was marginalized as a cultural phenomenon. In this cultural and political context the documentary style re-entered the stage. The new theatrical documentarism represents a return to social reality and to those social problems that the

Interrogating the Real   279

Yeltsin era generated and that the cultural establishment of the Putin era refuses to notice. This escape from the glamorous hyper-reality of glossy magazines therefore positions documentary theatre in the margin of cultural developments, in those spheres of culture that have traditionally pushed the limits of conventions in their search for new forms, styles and means of cultural production. (294)

By mixing the elements of TV-reportage, documentary film, and surrealist cinema in his *Ward No. 6*, Shakhnazarov continues this search for neo-naturalism and new cinematic authenticity. He investigates "the potential of the real" as it is practiced in the docu-film and verbatim theatre, artistic forms that are equally depend on the authenticity of the everyday word and the materiality of the performer's body, be it onstage or on-screen. The expressivity of verbatim theatre (or documentary film, one may suggest) is, in Paget's view, "firmly predicated upon the taping and subsequent transcription of interviews with 'ordinary' people, done in the context of research into a particular region, subject area, issue, event, or combination of these things" ("Verbatim Theatre" 317). This style is based on "an essentially non-theatrical tradition of social observation and oral documentation" ("Verbatim Theatre" 318), a technique that relies on the trustworthiness of recording devices. The tape recorder or camera can be "operating in and seeking to extend the space left by the 'official' recording and reporting media" ("Verbatim Theatre" 326). This way verbatim is always characterized by the political position of its makers, and it "seems particularly well suited to the demystification of history, given its ability to foreground its sources while simultaneously utilizing them for entertainment." ("Verbatim Theatre" 326).

Furthermore, by emphasizing the difference between the narration found in a documentary film and that of a feature film, *Ward No. 6* reminds its audience of the origins of cinematic art, the time period in which Chekhov's story was written. As Yury Lotman explains, "historically, cinema art was created at the intersection of two traditions. One derived from the tradition of non-artistic film documentary, and the other from the theatre" (84). Each art form presents its viewers with the live human being in action, the fundamental difference being that "theatre presents us with an ordinary person, our contemporary," whereas "film documentaries show us a series of black and white spots on the flat surface of a screen. But we must forget about this and perceive the screen images as living people" (Lotman 84). Watching a feature film, therefore, triggers a dual mechanism of perception: on the one hand, we identify cinematic signs with reality, taking the black-and-white spots on the screen for real people and objects; on the other hand, we recognize the constructed nature of cinematic narrative. Film, which is defined by its visual "overspecification" (the dominance of the visual sign), shares this property with visual arts. Hence, any given film operates with cinematic signs characterized by their "high iconicity

280   *Yana Meerzon*

and uncertain symbolic function." These cinematic signs work "directly, sensuously, [and] perceptually" on the filmgoer's receptive mechanisms (McFarlene 27). Accordingly, unlike in prose, which evokes the characters' physicality and landscape through words, in film "the frame instantly, and at any given moment, provides information of [. . .] visual complexity" (27). This information concretizes and contextualizes "any given word," because it is conveyed to the audience through "the spatial impact of the frame" (27). The film's iconicity and its spatial/temporal concreteness afford the on-screen story its "physical presence" (29), so that any film, be it a documentary or a feature film, is rooted in the verisimilitude of the visual sign. Accordingly, when Shakhnazarov employs both the elements of feature film and documentary film in his *Ward No. 6*, he challenges "the emotional confidence of the [film] audience" (Lotman 12). He makes the viewer question the notion of cinematic authenticity and embark on a process of interrogating the real. Thus Shakhnazarov brings his audiences closer to Chekhov's own stylistic inquiry. He forces the film's viewers to question the concept of the real in today's cinema, just as Chekhov's own practice interrogated the real as it had been practiced in literature and theatre of his time. By collapsing the naturalism of televised reportage with the surrealist poetics of dream and fantasy, Shakhnazarov's *Ward No. 6* not only celebrates Chekhov's particular style of writing; it also presents the story's philosophical dilemmas in a rejuvenated fashion, accessible for today's audience. In his film, Shakhnazarov demonstrates how dangerous the practice of digital communication can be when it is used as a device of personal archive and collective memory. He reminds his audiences that mediated communication invites Benjamin's mechanical reproduction and Lyotard's automatization or simulacra, if not in the production of goods then as a marker of people's relationships. By employing contemporary audiences' favorite means of techno-communication (from home video devices to digital sound recording), the film positions Chekhov's story in the present-day context of digital culture. Paradoxically, although the setting of the asylum and the context of digital communication make the moral and philosophical dilemmas of the story even more remote from today's filmgoers, the same setting and the same communication devices enable today's viewer to discover something new about Chekhov's writing style and to understand better his characters' moral and ethical positions.

In its search for a documentary style of cinematic storytelling, Shakhnazarov's *Ward No. 6* emerges from the dramatic mode of narration that dominates Chekhov's short stories, often written entirely in the present tense. Turner traces this quality of Chekhov's prose back to the author's journalistic practices (between 1882 and 1887), when as the writer of humorist vignettes he regularly published his *little scenes/stsenki* in the weekly journal *Fragments* edited by N. A. Leikin. Writing humoristic scenes obliged Chekhov to create a complete but minimal setting, evoked in the story through the

Interrogating the Real 281

descriptive mode in the present tense. This narrative device resembles the opening stage directions found in a theatre play. As Turner suggests, the style of this literary/journalistic genre, though not necessary unique to Chekhov, significantly changed when the writer added to it the realistic depth of psychological depiction of the characters (3–5). The absence of an omnipresent narrator, rapid dialogue based on colloquialisms, and a simple but complete plotline with a minimum number of peripeteias characterize the dramatic structure and the writing style of these scenes. Chekhov employs similar narrative devices in "Ward Number Six," but also enriches them with his knowledge of the period's popular theatre. Chekhov despised the practice of melodrama and romantic tragedy: "today's theatre is the rash, the disease of the city [. . .] today's theatre is not above the mob; on the contrary, life, the mob are higher and more intelligent than the theatre" (*Chekhov i teatr* 41); but his acquaintance with these theatrical practices and his own artistic intuition made Chekhov adapt the composition of his short stories, and even "Ward Number Six," to that of the little scene, on the one hand, and to that of the vaudeville, on the other. Turner specifies the lopsided use of present and past tense of narration characteristic of this novella, a feature that adds to its stylistic enigma:

> The temporal structure of "Ward 6" is such that the whole gamut of grammatical tenses and aspects is used. Approximately half of the first half of the story [. . .] is narrated in the present tense; [. . .] the rest of the first half represents one-time events that temporally precede this present and are narrated in the past tense. The present-tense passages depict the regular, day-to-day life of the ward and of Dr. Ragin [. . .]. [Their] effect is to bring the setting and the protagonist more closely and vividly before the mental eye of the reader, the same effect promoted by the direct address to the reader in the story's second paragraph; which speaks of "you" and "us." In this way the reader is prepared for being plunged into the main philosophical debate of the story, which is conducted in the form of a dialogue and which commences at the point where the past tense decisively takes over the narration. (9)

Following Lapushin's logic of "inbetweenness" as the norm rather than the exception in Chekhov's writing, one can argue that in their poetics Chekhov's stories create:

> a special verbal environment, in which his word reveals its hidden potentials and begins to fluctuate between possible connotations, and between literal and figurative meanings. The word becomes not only multilayered but also multi-vectored, leading the reader in several directions simultaneously and acquiring features generally associated with poetry rather than prose. (Lapushin 6)

282 *Yana Meerzon*

"Inbetweenness," in other words, becomes "a manifestation of the intrinsically poetic nature of Chekhov's word" (6). The "prosaisms" found in Chekhov's writing become the basis of its particular poeticity. The word, which is characterized by its multi-vectored stylistic tendency, functions as the basis of Chekhov's stylistic and philosophical enigma, something that makes Chekhov's work especially challenging for translators and adaptors. As Lapushin explains, Chekhov's short stories are often capable of evoking both the sense of truth found in the great realist novels of the nineteenth century and the sense of lyrical poeticity, pertinent to a poem:

> Chekhov's short story—and his mature art in general—transcends this opposition. Nurtured by the tradition of nineteenth-century realist prose, Chekhov does not deny, but rather transforms, the concepts of a hero, plot, and conflict characteristic of this prose. Simultaneously, in its treatment of the word, Chekhov's verbal art anticipates Russian modernist poetry with its poetics of allusions, omitted links, and fluctuating meanings and its penchant for bringing ostensibly disparate and categorically diverse elements into association. (14)

In other words, Chekhov's prose creates the sense of the real on two separate planes: "the illusion of verisimilitude is scrupulously preserved along with the borders between the autonomous world" and "the isolated and not apparently compatible elements [that] are intertwined in a capricious and almost like dreamlike way" (Lapushin 15). This technique, therefore, allows Chekhov to escalate an ordinary person's life-story, the fall and redemption of the provincial physician Dr. Ragin, to some mystical dimensions. Thus the novella "Ward Number Six" forces its reader to reconsider the existential questions of human mortality, responsibility and forgiveness.

Shakhnazarov's film accentuates the value of a single human experience, true faith, and each person's responsibility for the consequences of his/her actions, the Dostoevskian theme heavily echoed and paraphrased in Chekhov's story. As Shakhnazarov explains, *Ward No. 6* is a

> special movie in my life. The most important thing is that I understood Chekhov in a new way. I rediscovered him as a religious writer, no less so than Dostoyevsky. But while Dostoyevsky has pages and pages on faith, in "Ward Number Six" these ideas are scattered through the text. [. . .] The religious messages seem to be hidden, but not random, including Gromov's remark on immortality, and the fact that Ragin had wanted to study in a seminary [before becoming a physician]. These religious references create hope in the morbid atmosphere of the story. (qtd. in Parsegova)

Thus, it is the ability of Chekhov to depict in a seemingly anecdotal story the universal undertones of human suffering that brought Shakhnazarov to

Interrogating the Real 283

"Ward Number Six." As he explains, Chekhov described "the nature of the human experience, which is unchangeable. What changes is the scenery: automobiles replace horses and carriages, the fashion and the hairstyles change but the essence of the human being remains. [. . .] As far as the world itself goes, I don't foresee any global changes. There is always a piece of "Ward Number Six" in this world" (qtd. in Arefiev). By shifting the moral dilemmas that mark Chekhov's story toward the discourse of faith and religious beliefs, Shakhnazarov proposes to rethink the genre of the story itself and the function of its major character.

THE PLOT OF "WARD NUMBER SIX"

Chekhov published his "uncharacteristic and in some ways unappealing" (Knapp 145) novella "Ward Number Six" in 1892, two years after his famous trip to the penal colony of Sakhalin. It represented the writer's reaction to this journey, being "a response more indirect, in form, than *The Island of Sakhalin*, but, in essence, perhaps just as immediate" (Knapp 145). The setting of the asylum with its windows covered by metal bars and the likeness of the inmates to convicts in a jail make the story's space and atmosphere reminiscent of Russian nineteenth-century prisons and twentieth-century labor camps, which, much like those hospitals or asylums, stand abandoned and forgotten by human justice and empathy. Hence, as Knapp sees it, "Ward Number Six" functions as Chekhov's social protest. It illustrates his belief that society, individually and collectively, bears a responsibility for "eliminating, alleviating, or at the very least acknowledging the suffering that takes place, with an exceptionally high concentration, in these two locales, penal institution and hospitals, places that nobody wants to visit, much less, of course, to inhabit" (146). At the same time, the story can be read as an example of modern tragedy that suggests that human suffering "cannot be understood in the abstract. One needs to have it made as immediate as possible" (Knapp 146). Moreover, as Knapp states, "by evoking in the reader a response to the suffering that is witnessed in *Ward 6,* Chekhov aims at evoking pity and fear, the same emotions that, according to Aristotle, a good tragedy will evoke in its audience" (147).

Dr. Ragin, however, is not your classical tragic character. He lacks the strong will, clear mind, and determination that often characterize the protagonist of classical tragedy. Although "Ward Number Six" ends with Dr. Ragin's realization that in the suffering of a human being there is someone's personal guilt, this character is weak and unsettled in his moral and philosophical opinions. Now the inmate of his own ward for the insane, taken there against his will, and kept among those people for whom he did nothing in the twenty years of his career as the hospital administrator, Ragin recognizes his tragic fault. His personal fault is in his erroneous judgment:

284 *Yana Meerzon*

a self-centered individual and a hard-hearted doctor, such as Ragin, possesses no faith either in God or humanity:

> Suddenly a fearful thought past all bearing flashed through the chaos of his mind: that just such a pain must be the daily lot, year in year out, of these men, who loomed before him like black shadows in the moonlight. How came it that for twenty years and more he had ignored that—and ignored it wilfully? He had not known pain, he had no conception of it, so this wasn't his fault. And yet his conscience proved as tough and obdurate as Nikita, flooding him from head to heels with an icy chill. (Chekhov, "Ward Number Six" 166)

After he recognizes his fault, however, Ragin does not experience a reversal. He does not become the "scapegoat" of humanity, someone whose death or rather sacrifice can bring a better life to others. Ragin's death—as happens very often in Chekhov's literary and dramatic world—has neither a moral nor an educational meaning. It has no meaning at all and it is one of many. Chekhov writes this story with the emotional detachment of a family physician, someone who daily observes human sickness and mortality. In his text, Chekhov only registers human transience and testifies to the fact that no individual or collective death (or life for that matter) can explain in any logical way the meaning of human mortality. It is not surprising that, when describing Ragin's last seconds, Chekhov insists that the doctor "did not want any immortality, he only thought of it for a moment. A herd of deer, extraordinary handsome and graceful, of which he had been reading on the previous day, darted past him. A peasant woman held out a registered letter, Michael Averyanovich said something. Then it all vanished. Dr. Andrew Yefimovich Ragin plunged into eternal oblivion" ("Ward Number Six" 167). "Ward Number Six" finishes with one more image of human indifference: the image previously evoked during one of Ragin's philosophical encounters with Gromov. After Ragin's death, "the peasant orderlies came, seized his hands and feet, and hauled him off to the chapel. [. . .] A day later Ragin was buried. Only Michael Averyanovich and Daryushka went to the funeral" ("Ward Number Six" 167). The ending of "Ward Number Six" seems not only to reinforce Chekhov's atheistic views on life and death, but also to illustrate his statement on how the writer should choose the plots for his/her literary works. As he once observed, "one does not need plots [for stories], for in reality, such things do not exist. Everything is mixed up in life, the profound and the trifling, the great and the insignificant, the tragic and the comic. You, ladies and gentlemen, are simply robots and slaves to routines from which you cannot part" (qtd. in Bunin 126).

In his own version of "Ward Number Six," Shakhnazarov radically changes the fate of Chekhov's Dr. Ragin. In the film, as in the original, the character is put into the asylum against his will, beaten up, and suffers a stroke. But

Interrogating the Real   285

he does not die. Now an internee of the monastery/asylum himself, Doctor Ragin joins his co-inmates for the Christmas dance. A young woman, a patient from another ward, approaches him. The evening star shines over the party. As Shakhnazarov explains, in his film Ragin stays alive thanks to one of his actors/patients of the asylum, who asked the filmmaker to change the ending of Chekhov's story, to let Ragin live so as "to give your audience some sort of hope" (qtd. in "Shakhnazarov perelozhil"). Perhaps in this phrase and thus in the modified ending of Chekhov's story one can find the director's attempt to convey to today's audiences Chekhov's view of human tragedy as the inevitability and indifference of death. As Chekhov once observed: "to empathize with tragedy, one does not have to create tragic characters in the spirit of Shakespeare, since human life, in and of itself, is a tragedy. The loneliness of the human soul is especially calamitous" (qtd. in Bunin 67). "Ward Number Six," written by a practicing doctor, reminds its reader that the only truth one can experience in life is one's loneliness. As Chekhov said, "tragic is the life of anyone who has not drowned in vulgar self-contentment," and "it is enough merely to look into any soul to respond with overwhelming pity for it" (qtd. in Bunin 67).

Shakhnazarov's film stresses its tragic overtones in a different way to Chekhov's story. Here the figure of a young woman from the asylum's Christmas party acquires a special significance. This woman appears on the screen for the first time in one of its prologues. Using the devices of cinematic dramatization, Shakhnazarov stages the legendary history of the Nikolo-Poshekhonsky monastery. As we hear the voice of the child-narrator, the camera depicts the monk Varlaam (later cast as the soldier/gatekeeper Nikita) and two sisters who came to the region in 1606 to found the monastery. In the epilogue, the same woman, cast as a mystical reincarnation of the nun who founded the monastery, invites Dr. Ragin to a Christmas dance. As many critics wrote, the Christian symbolism of Shakhnazarov's film goes beyond Chekhov's story. It reaches even beyond the writer's own very complex relationship with Christian doctrine, but it speaks eloquently to the filmmaker's audiences. As Perunov writes, with this new ending Shakhnazarov suggests that Ragin himself does not need faith; it is today's audience who needs it. Perunov takes his cue from the director, who believes that "high-brow literature is always stronger then cinema," that a good movie can "survive only for twenty or thirty years," and that film is only "a half-art," an industry, coming alive as a result of people's collective effort, always determined by the needs of its own time (qtd. in "Shakhnazarov perelozhil"). Consequently, Perunov suggests that in his own *Ward No. 6* Shakhnazarov wanted only "to remind the audience that the sole purpose of the intelligentsia is to bring about [. . .] faith no matter how absurd it may be." Accordingly, one can say that the filmmaker's personal philosophy justifies the choice of the film's location and his insistence on the authenticity of the real that it can create. By making this dramatic gesture, Shakhnazarov suggests "the disbelieving Dr. Ragin

286   *Yana Meerzon*

is granted mercy for his suffering. [So] through its visual imagery the film emphasizes the religious discourse even more than in the original" (Giniatulina and Timasheva).

ON THE CHARACTERS AND THE ACTORS OF *WARD NO. 6*

The success of Shakhnazarov's film, as this study argues, paradoxically and perhaps contrary to its intentions, does not lie in the sphere of religious or philosophical debates. It is rooted in the film's ability to evoke on-screen the very special style of Chekhovian writing, to remind today's viewer that "Ward Number Six" originates at the intersection of (a) the naturalistic or representational mode of verbal expression; (b) the dramatic mode of narration; and (c) the emerging language of cinema and its own mode of storytelling. By no means am I trying to suggest that Chekhov was influenced or mimicked the mode of narration that originated in the moving pictures of his time. At the time "Ward Number Six" (1892) was written and published, the Lumière brothers had only started their cinematic experiments and had not yet even shown their famous moving train to Parisian audiences. Still I argue that the multiplicity of narrative modes found in this novella anticipates the particulars of narration that moving pictures, the moving photographs of Chekhov's time, were about to develop. An example of adaptation as analogy, Shakhnazarov's *Ward No. 6* succeeds in evoking Chekhov's mode of storytelling and makes the viewer turn his/her gaze back to the original. For instance, as Shakhnazarov explains, the choices both in the cinematic environment and the casting helped him to re-create Chekhovian authenticity: "we were trying to incorporate the entire action of Chekhov's story into the real atmosphere of a monastery. [. . .] If we had kept the original time setting of the story, the turn of the twentieth century, the impression would have been artificial, cinematic. On the contrary, here we tried to immerse Chekhov's plot in today's reality" (qtd. in "Shakhnazarov perelozhil"). The action of the film unfolds in the "found spaces" of the Nikolo-Poshekhonsky monastery's courtyard, the inmates' bedrooms, their workshops, and a restaurant. The director cast professional actors only in the key roles of the story (Vladimir Il'in as Dr. Ragin; Aleksey Vertkov as Gromov; Yevgeny Stychkin as Dr. Khobotov; and Aleksandr Pankratov-Chorny as the postmaster Mikhail Averyanovich) and invited the inmates of the asylum as well as other nonprofessional actors to play the additional roles. In its dialogue, however, the film preserves Chekhov's original language, including some archaic phrases like "if you please." When asked why he decided to keep the original dialogue, Shakhnazarov responded: "Chekhov is much deeper than any of our attempts to 'tack' him onto today's reality" (qtd. in Sakharnova). Still, as the critic Sakharnova observes, "there are a few exceptions to that in the film. In one of the scenes the head physician Khobotov [. . .] suggests that Ragin take a vacation in Antalya instead of

Chekhov's Kislovodsk. The name of the Turkish resort area [quite popular in Russia today] instantly brings the audience back into today's world, thus depriving the film of its extratemporal atmosphere." Hence, by mixing the codes of cinematic narration and through separation of the visual (on-screen) information from the supporting (off-screen) dialogue, Shakhnazarov's *Ward No. 6* achieves not only the effect of the real, but truly brings Chekhov's story closer to today's audiences.

Ward No. 6 opens with a prologue that features the patients of the Nikolo-Poshekhonsky asylum. The unseen narrator/journalist, or perhaps Shakhnazarov himself, asks the inmates questions about their life in the monastery, their dreams, and their religious beliefs. The patients recall unhappy stories of their childhood, blaming their alcoholic parents for their fate. When asked what they wish for in life, they all provide strikingly simple answers. These people wish to start their own families, have children, and get jobs; or they do not want to dream at all, because "dreams never come through." Some of them are profoundly religious; some stoically believe in the power of their own free will; and some, much like little children, believe in goodness and magic. Accordingly, as Shakhnazarov explains, in his film *Ward No. 6*, as in the theatre of verbatim, the presence of asylum patients on-screen adds to the film's sense of the real, its authenticity: "First of all, the patients enjoy being filmed. Second, they have great work ethics, they do what they are told to do. [. . .] The difficult part is that you never know what to expect from them. [. . .] They become part of the dramaturgy, they always take part in it" (qtd. in "Shakhnazarov perelozhil"). The opening sequence places the action within the world of disorder, which the director Shakhnazarov interprets as Hamlet's "time out of joint." This world appears in the form of multiple modalities, as a juxtaposition of the everyday reality of the Nikolo-Poshekhonsky monastery with the several fictional worlds created by Shakhnazarov.

Michael Kirby's *acting/not-acting continuum* (3–21) can be used to theorize the cinematic function of the patients used by Shakhnazarov as *cinematic objects* or *models/naturschiks*[8] on-screen, a device found in today's theatre of verbatim and in documentary films as well. To Kirby the not-acting phenomenon is defined by the presence of a human being onstage, a performer, who "does nothing to feign, simulate, impersonate" (3) and who does not wear a costume specially designed for the role (5). This non-matrixed performance in theatre can be seen as equal to the use of people as objects on-screen:

Kirby's acting/not-acting continuum (10)

NOT-ACTING				ACTING
Nonmatrixed Performing	Symbolized Matrix	Received Acting	Simple Acting	Complex Acting

288 *Yana Meerzon*

Shakhnazarov's inmates/characters appear at the farthest end of the continuum, serving as examples of not-acting or non-matrixed performance, and functioning as objects not characters (*film figures*) on-screen.[9] Lotman identifies three semiotic codes used in the creation of a film figure: "1) directorial; 2) everyday behavior; 3) actor's acting" (85), thus recognizing in the film figure a mixture of documentary and artistic representation. This mixture equalizes actors and objects on-screen, making directing, shooting, and editing compete for the dominant position in the hierarchy of the film aesthetics. This way, as Lotman argues, the film figure becomes a complex cultural sign. It embraces the materiality and the symbolism of the human body on-screen, as well as the actor's work as such (86–88). The creation of a film figure is objectified, therefore, by the cinematic mise-en-scène, the actor's everyday behavior, and his/her craft, embracing a mixture of documentary and artistic representation. In film the individuality of an actor—his/her physique or type of voice—is either equal or superior to that of a character. Character types determine the acting style of a performer and influence the viewer's evaluation of it: "If the actor looks and behaves in a manner *appropriate* to his or her character's *function* in the context of the film, the actor has given a good performance—*whether or not* he or she behaved as a real person" (Bordwell and Thompson 132).

Although the construction of a cinematic character/film figure relies on the identification between the actor's physical presence and his/her character, Shakhnazarov takes into consideration the significant difference between the inmate's personality and the implied character. While he claims it necessary to escape any forms of directorial presence in film, to let the reality speak for itself, in *Ward No. 6* the two levels of cinematic representation—physical portrayal and nominal portrayal—are accentuated at the same time. This junction of levels of presentation brings more levels of semiotization to the shot material and points to theatre as the place of origin for the film. In *Ward No. 6* the asylum's patients demonstrate how the individuality of the actor (the patient's psychophysical presence on-screen) can be either equal or superior to that of a character. By gradually increasing the surrealistic feel of his movie, Shakhnazarov forces his audience to constantly wonder whether what we see on-screen is real or fictional. As Aleksey Vertkov (who plays Gromov) recollects, right on the first day of their work, Shakhnazarov asked him to carefully observe the inmates who will appear in the shot, because as an actor he would never be able to be more truthful than either of them on-screen: "'Watch them carefully. You'll never be able to compete with them, they will always steal the show.' This is exactly how it turned out: the real mental patients in the film look like real mental patients" (qtd. in Ershov); whereas:

> Vertkov performs with his voice, intonation, facial expressions, gestures; his Gromov, a long-time inhabitant of Ward No 6, is edgy, emotional, disdainful. [. . .] Unlike his partner, Il'in is heavy with Weltschmerz.

Interrogating the Real   289

You look at him and you don't understand—what does he act with? He is slow, unexcited, glassy-eyed for the most part, almost no facial expressions, let alone significant gestures. But this is exactly what great acting is all about—to act the absence and at the same time to create a vivid figure. (Barabash)

Thus, when juxtaposing the inmates of the asylum with the actors on-screen, Shakhnazarov goes beyond Chekhov's stylistic liminality or "inbetweenness." He insists on the impossible: to melt the two poles of Kirby's continuum—the complex acting and the nonmatrix acting—together, within the territory of a single performance, be it by Vertkov or Il'in. The super-objective that Shakhnazarov imposes on his professional actors is "not to act," and thus to seek the documentary or "the real" appeal of the film. "The authors demonstrated such a skillful mastery of the craft of the nonfiction film that had it not been for the recognizable faces of the actors [. . .] the audience would have thought they were watching a documentary. [. . .] Thus [Shakhnazarov's] new film confirms the common trend to mix fiction and documentary in today's cinema" (Sakharnova).

Moreover, Shakhnazarov keeps the discrepancy between the authenticity of the opening interviews and the rest of the film at the level of dialogue: he puts next to each other the everyday speech of the interviews and Chekhov's constructed dialogue. This discrepancy serves as another marker of the verbatim quality of the film. As Paget explains:

The writer's ability to 'be an editor' is dependent upon a restraint and humility in the face of the verbatim material which parallels similar qualities in the work of the actors. Writers must recognize that, however good their ear for ordinary speech, it is unlikely that they would ever be able to introduce into a conventional play the variety of speech patterns and rhythms emanating from the verbatim technique. ("Verbatim Theatre" 330)

In Shakhnazarov's case, the discrepancy between the interviews and Chekhov's text is a given. However, when juxtaposing the speech of the inmates with Chekhov's text the filmmaker tricks the audience, who expect Chekhov's text to sound archaic. This way, Shakhnazarov collapses the fictional Gromov-Ragin world with the reality of an actual monastery. By juxtaposing professional actors and inmates of an asylum as cinematic objects on-screen, and by putting Chekhov's unedited text next to the interviews of the inmates, Shakhnazarov seeks new artistic devices to deal with the issues of cinematic realism today. As he explains:

You can talk about the most painful of topics—in fact, you must—but through artistic means. This is the essence of film. [. . .] You don't need to pour buckets of cranberry juice to show the death of

290   *Yana Meerzon*

> a person—this does not constitute art. You must be able to cause an audience to respond. [. . .] Unfortunately today's film often chooses the path of naturalism. [. . .] This is a simplification. [. . .] You have to be able to solve an artistic task by creating an artistic image. (qtd. in Aref'ev)

In order to seek this cinematic metaphor, Shakhnazarov reaches even further in his eclectic manner of storytelling. In addition to exploring the stylistic particulars of documentary film, he also experiments with the cinematic devices of silent film. For example, he films the scenes in Ragin's apartment (both at the beginning of the movie, when the audience is invited to visit Ragin's home after he has been hospitalized, and later, the scene when Doctor Khobotov visits his sickly superior in his house) as if they were episodes in a silent film. In the first example, the camera browses across Ragin's study, while Ragin's housekeeper (played by Albina Yevtushevskaya, another nonprofessional actor in the film) recites Chekhov's text off-screen. In the second episode, Shakhnazarov employs the metacinematic technique. The argument between Ragin and Khobotov took place before the film's opening, but it is inserted into its narrative as a flashback. The scene is shot by the postmaster, but his camera does not record sound. Hence, the audience can see Ragin's outburst, but cannot hear his voice. It is Mikhail Averyanovich himself who recites Ragin's monologue. In this way the film insists on the dominance of a cinematic rather than dramatic mode of narration. The story of Dr. Ragin is retold by his former colleagues and friends, who act now not as participants in the events but as witnesses. This way, the film recasts the philosophical and moral issues raised in Chekhov's short story in terms of today's ethical problems. As it argues, our technologically advanced practices of mediated being lead (much like in the nineteenth century) to human indifference, personal corruption, and finally madness. In our society today, much as in Chekhov's time, the only person who is capable of independent thinking and producing an original idea is indeed the patient of the asylum.

* * *

The enigma of any textual mutation or performative adaptation, whether it keeps its fidelity to the original or not, lies, in my opinion, in how it reveals the subjectivity of the adaptor and his/her cultural, political, and existential position, and what sort of new information it brings out about the source text. Made with a wide spectrum of cinematic devices, the film *Ward No. 6* testifies to Shakhnazarov's personal belief that the use of digital technologies in filmmaking today will significantly change if not revolutionize the cinematic industry and its language of expression (qtd. in Dolin). It also reveals something new about Chekhov's own style of writing and about the writer's attitude to the emerging types of artistic mimicry, as found in photography and even cinema of his time. The artistic value of adaptation as analogy is in its ability to discover in the work of the canon—the work that long ago entered our collective memory and became our cultural myth—the stylistic, ideological, and philosophical potential previously unknown or hidden from us.

This chapter discusses Wagner's adaptation as analogy, the way Shakhnazarov creates equivalents or sometimes goes further to investigate the cinematic potential that seems to be marking Chekhov's text. By setting his film within the territory of the Nikolo-Poshekhonsky monastery and by giving voice to its inmates as the film's framing device, Karen Shakhnazarov continues this theme of social injustice as tragedy and our responsibility for this injustice found in many of Chekhov's works. By exploring the richness of today's digital culture—the narrator uses the fragments of home video to evoke Dr. Ragin's past and the characters listen to Ragin's voice on the digital voice recorder—Shakhnazarov warns his audience that our practices of mediated being, when we constantly and repeatedly create life as mediated reality, using technology as the only device of interpersonal communication, personal memory, and national history, are dangerous. In the film's final episodes, the camera returns the viewer to the "real world" of the Nikolo-Poshekhonsky's inmates. The closing scene features the patients from the prologue meeting the actors playing Chekhov's characters. The two worlds collapse into each other for the New Year's dance: an episode that melts all possible modalities and realities of the film. The added scene of the epilogue features a young woman with her two daughters in a mockumentary of a constructed interview. The film ends with one sister laughing: the sound gradually moves from the intradiegetic space of the last shot into the extradiegetic space of the film's credits, leaving the audience to decide what sort of Chekhovian modality—a variation on the theme of the world's madness—we live in today.

NOTES

1. The monastery was founded in 1606. In 1934 it became a hospital for tuberculosis patients; in 1962 it was converted into an infirmary for the mentally challenged people.
2. In his manifesto Dogma 95, following Goddard's experiments with the "neorealist" film aesthetics, Lars von Trier, the creator of the technique, fights against the framed nature of cinema and demands that his supporters loosen up the directorial presence on the film set by giving their actors a leading role in the shooting period. The naked truth, pure anthropological mimesis without a touch of any artistic means, as the manifesto suggests, will make films less artificially scripted and executed. In cinema, both actor and object function as various parts of the film set used by the director to narrate the story. The ideas of alienation and the practice of creating self-reflecting signs in film dominate Lars von Trier's cinematic narratives, which makes them an expression of the classic Dogma 95 rules.

292 *Yana Meerzon*

3. For further development of Wagner's taxonomy see Cartmell and Whelehan; Sanders; and Hutcheon. I have decided to use the original schema proposed by Wagner, since it seems to me that Wagner's categories of film adaptation are much more flexible and inclusive than those developed in the subsequent studies. I specifically disagree with Hutcheon when she places transposition-commentary-analogy within the fidelity discourse. It seems to me that in his definition of analogy as one of the adaptation techniques, Wagner invites the reader to avoid the compare-contrast strategy when looking at the gap between the source and the target texts.

4. During his thirty years' career in the Russian film industry, Shakhnazarov made a number of commercial and noncommercial films in various genres, from musical comedies to historical dramas. His early film/musical *Jazz men* (1984) presented the filmmaker's look at the dramatic history of jazz in the Soviet Russia, the story of its short glory in the early 1920s, and the history of its banishment. Shakhnazarov continued with this theme in his next work, the lyrical comedy *Winter Evening in Gagry* (1985) and much later in *Vanished Empire* (2008). Shakhnazarov, who is interested in surrealist aesthetics, made the important film *Zero City* (1990), a social satire of the absurd that depicted the rotting environment of late Soviet times. In 1998 he became director general of Mosfilm studios, the major filmmaking Russian company since the Soviet era.

5. *Ward No. 6* was also Russia's official submission to the Best Foreign Language Film Category of the 82nd Annual Academy Awards in 2010.

6. This film was selected as an official entrant in the main contest of the Cannes Film Festival, France (1991); it received the Grand Prize at the International Film Festival, Belgrade (1991), among others.

7. Following the objectives of these theatrical and cinematic forms to investigate contentious events and issues in local, national, and international contexts (Paget, "Broken Tradition") and to reopen trials in order to critique justice (Martin), the cinematographer Alexander Garnovsky made his own documentary film *Checkers and Dominoes Contests* (2009), which features uncut interviews with the inmates of the monastery, material that did not make it into Shakhnazarov's own feature.

8. Back in 1927, Boris Kazansky, one of the first Russian film critics, wrote of the privileged position of the human being on-screen. He denied the film actor's professional skills, seeing an actor in front of a cine-camera as equal to a *naturshchik* (model) standing in front of a painter. Tracing film's direct dependency on the art of photography, Kazansky stated that since photography "cannot tolerate any falseness," film, photography's next of kin, "demands only nature as its filmed object" (114). This way, in film, the actor—the person—always "serves as 'nature' for reproduction," and "to that extent he exists for the viewer only in the sense of "a natural type," "a model." The fact that this person is also an actor has no significance in principle: "If cinema is a shadow painting, i.e., a graphic art, then the actor reproduced as a representation on the screen must in principle be only a model" (113). Hence, film assumes a conventional verisimilitude or correspondence between peoples' behaviors in life and on-screen.

9. A *film figure* is a construction both on the part of an actor and on the part of a spectator, which signifies the viewer's image of the actor's creativity on-screen. Film figures represent "a system of components aesthetically deautomatized and organized into a complex hierarchy, which is unified by the prevalence of one component over the others" (Mukařovský 170). The film figure acquires a number of substructures meant to express the character's emotions. All of

them carry the dynamics of a character "by the interference [. . .] of two types of gestures: gesture-signs and gesture expressions" (Mukařovský 174). In its functions, the film figure is equivalent to cinematic lighting, sound, time, and space. In fact, it constitutes the film's mise-en-scène as any other object does (furniture, makeup, costumes, and props), the significance of which is to express the artistic will of the narrator/film director staging the event for the camera. As an aesthetic object, the film figure corresponds to the character, which is an agent of cause and effect in a continuous narration. It is a collection of traits that involve "attitudes, skills, preferences, psychological drives, details of dress and appearance" (Bordwell 86).

WORKS CITED

Aref'ev, Egor. "Shakhnazarov: V mire vsegda est' element *Palaty N 6.*" *UTRO.RU.* 3 Sept. 2009. Web. 15 Oct. 2011.

Barabash, Ekaterina. "Kto-to potoptalsia v gnezde kukushki." *Nezavisimaia gazeta* 3 Sept. 2009. Web. 12 Oct. 2011.

Bordwell, David, and Kristin Thompson. *Film Art.* New York: Knopf, 1986. Print.

Bunin, Ivan. *About Chekhov. The Unfinished Symphony.* Ed. and trans. Thomas Gaiton Marullo. Evanston: Northwestern UP, 2007. Print.

Cartmell, Deborah, and Imelda Whelehan, eds. *Adaptations: From Text to Screen, Screen to Text.* London: Routledge, 1999. Print.

Chekhov, Anton. *Chekhov i teatr: pis'ma, fel'etony, sovremenniki o Chekhove dramaturge.* Ed. E. D. Surkov. Moscow: Iskusstvo, 1961. Print.

———. "Ward Number Six." *Stories 1892–1893. The Oxford Chekhov.* 9 vols. Ed. and trans. Ronald Hingley. London: Oxford UP, 1971. 6: 121–67. Print.

Dolin, Anton. "Interview with Karen Shakhnazarov." *VESTI.FM.* 4 Oct. 2009. Web. 15 Oct. 2011.

Durkin, Andrew R. "Response to Dostoevskii: The Case of 'Ward Six.'" *Slavic Review* 40.1 (1981): 49–59. Print.

Ershov, Evgenij. "Mertvaia ruka Chekhova." *GZT.RU.* 24 June 2009. Web. 10 Oct. 2011.

Giniatulina, Lejla, and Marina Timasheva. "Na MMKF pokazali film Karena Shakhnazarova 'Palata n6.'" *Radio Liberty.* 26 June 2009. Web. 11 Oct. 2011.

Holden, Stephen. "Rites of Passage through the Rolling Stones and Fallen Civilizations." *New York Times* 10 July 2009. Web. 20 Oct. 2011.

Hutcheon, Linda. *A Theory of Adaptation.* New York: Routledge, 2006. Print.

Kazanskii, Boris. "The Nature of Cinema." *Russian Formalist Film Theory.* Ed. and trans. Herbert Eagle. Ann Arbor: U of Michigan P, 1981. 101–31. Print.

Kirby, Michael. *A Formalist Theatre.* Philadelphia: U of Pennsylvania P, 1987. Print.

Knapp, Liza. "Fear and Pity in 'Ward Six': Chekhovian Catharsis." *Reading Chekhov's Text.* Ed. Robert Louis Jackson. Evanston: Northwestern UP, 1993. 145–54. Print.

Korneeva, Irina. "Kak Doktor Chekhov propisal." *Rossiiskaia Gazeta.* N4940. 26 June 2009. Web. 15 Oct. 2011.

Lapushin, Radislav. *"Dew on the Grass". The Poetics of Inbetweenness in Chekhov.* New York: Peter Lang, 2010. Print.

Lipovetsky, Mark, and Birgit Beumers. "Reality Performance: Documentary Trends in Post-Soviet Russian Theatre." *Contemporary Theatre Review* 18.3 (2008): 293–306. Print.

294 *Yana Meerzon*

Lotman, Jurij. *Semiotics of Cinema*. Trans. Mark E. Suino. Ann Arbor: U of Michigan P, 1976. Print.

Martin, Carol. "Bodies of Evidence." *Drama Review* 50.3 (2006): 8–15. Print.

McFarlene, Brian. *Novel to Film: An Introduction to the Theory of Adaptation*. Oxford: Clarendon Press; New York: Oxford UP, 1996. Print.

Mukařovský, Jan. "An Attempt at a Structural Analysis of a Dramatic Figure." *Structure, Sign and Function. Selected Essays by J. Mukařovský*. Ed. and trans. John Burbank and Peter Steiner. New Haven: Yale UP, 1978. 170–77. Print.

Paget, Derek. "The 'Broken Tradition' of Documentary Theatre and Its Continued Powers of Endurance." *Get Real: Documentary Theatre Past and Present*. Ed. Alison Forsyth and Chris Megson. New York: Palgrave MacMillan, 2009. 224–39. Print.

———. "Verbatim Theatre: Oral History and Documentary Techniques." *New Theatre Quarterly* 12.3 (1987): 317–36. Print.

Parsegova, Galina. "Karen Shakhnazarov snial fil'm o vere i shizofrenii." *Vecherniaia Moskva*. 29 June 2009. Web. 18 Oct. 2011.

Perunov, Igor. "31 MMKF, den' shestoi: smert'iu smert' poprav'." *ProfiCinema. Ru*. 25 June 2009. Web. 10 Oct. 2011.

Pruzhanskaia, Ludmila. "Vot takoe kino." *Russian Canadian Media*. Russians. Ca. 8 Sept. 2009. Web. 12 Oct. 2011.

Sakharnova, Kseniia. "Karen Shakhnazarov. 'Moia tsel'- vyzyvat' emotsii u ludei'." *PROFICINEMA*. 25 June 2009. Web. 20 Oct. 2011.

Sanders, Julie. *Adaptation and Appropriation*. London: Routledge, 2006. Print.

"Shakhnazarov perelozhil Chekhova v Palate n 6." *TV LENTA RU*. N. 70047. 26 Jan. 2009. Web. 15 Oct. 2011.

Turner, C. J. G. *Time and Temporal Structure in Chekhov*. Birmingham: Department of Russian Language and Literature, U of Birmingham, 1994. Print.

Wagner, Geoffrey. *The Novel and the Cinema*. Rutherford: Fairleigh Dickinson UP, 1975. Print.

Afterword
On Chekhov, Adaptation, and Wonders of Writing Plays: Dialogue with Patrice Pavis, J. Douglas Clayton, and Yana Meerzon

Question 1: Patrice Pavis is the author of numerous books on theatre and performance theory and one of the major theoreticians of theatre semiotics and intercultural performance theory. What makes a theatre academic, a specialist in performance, turn his gaze to the art of translation, then to the art of dramatic adaptation, and even more to the world of Anton Chekhov?

My first response to your question is that I don't think of myself as doing "dramatic adaptations." My field today is not so much semiology or intercultural studies, but rather contemporary theatre stagings and writing for the theatre. I will try to answer your questions or parts of them, adding may be a final question, if you agree.

Question 2: What do we mean by "Chekhovian": a lack of resolution; the absence of a definitive conclusion, event, or catharsis; a realization that events progress but do not resolve; or the presence of a continuum of human endeavor over which fate hovers infinitely? How do we position Chekhov's drama in the history of dramatic literature and theatre: can we say it is anti-Aristotelian but not Brechtian?

I'd prefer to leave out the second part of the question, which I answer later on. I don't use the term "Chekhovian" any more than I do "Shakespearean" or "Beckettian," because that would mean that there is an essence of this author that one can extract and which would provide the key to his writing. This is precisely what I have tried to get beyond in my Livre de Poche edition of the four great "Chekhovian" plays (here I think it's permissible to use the term). In my view the only possible approach to this writer would be to describe and interpret the forms and the structure of his dramas, the main rhetorical devices, and the nature of the writing. Chekhov has been both beneficiary and victim of this tautological manner of describing his dramaturgy and his writing in terms of the vagueness and the imprecision of the actions, statements, and "philosophy" of his characters. As a result, the formal study of his dramatic writing has often been neglected. The characteristics you mention are not wrong, but they are very general and moreover neither relevant nor limited to this writer. In my own comments I have on the contrary always focused on the specifics of acting and staging in his lifetime and in our own present-day theatre.

296 Afterword

I don't want to respond to the rest of your question, except to say that in my view Chekhov remains Aristotelian in his use of mimesis and an easily understood plot. There is obviously nothing Brechtian about him even if, like Brecht, he really doesn't believe in fate, in destiny.

Question 3: Does Chekhov look "universal" to you? Why? Do you find some unchangeable or immutable elements in Chekhov's writing, elements that survive any interpretation, adaptation, or translation?

The term "universal" is also problematic. It is true that Chekhov is staged all over the world and appreciated whatever the country. His language is sufficiently vague to allow translations that are themselves vague and imprecise and therefore permit stagings in the most diverse cultural contexts. In that sense he is definitely universal. But what is even more universal about his work is the subconscious structures inherent in his characters and perhaps in the author too, especially the Oedipus complex, the presence of which has often been traced through the reference to Hamlet and hence to the Greek tragedians. This universality of the subconscious, along with the falsely naturalistic and profoundly symbolist character of his work, explains why every culture, society, and individual manages to identify with the characters and situations in his plays. Who would not be seduced and "comforted" by seeing onstage the failure of our lives and the loss of our ideals? This sense of failure, of the attrition of time, of the impenetrability of one's fellow beings, is particularly appreciated by readers and audiences of all kinds of backgrounds. One only has to compare this closeness with the difficulty of identifying, and identifying with, the conflicts in the plays of Shakespeare, Corneille, or Gogol, to understand how Chekhov, the classic of all classics, adapts to new societies and audiences, thus giving the impression of universality. Moreover, productions throughout the world help to facilitate Chekhov's reception and adaptation to ever-changing circumstances. This indeterminacy of meaning, the absence of a message on the part of the author or of any implied certainty, is what confirms his universality and transcends different translations (unless they take it upon themselves to adapt Chekhov by rewriting him while pretending that it is the original text—that is bound to be fatal!). Thus, what is universal and unshakeable in Chekhov is the meaning, which is never sure, fixed, definitive, but on the contrary changing and irresolvable.

Question 4: What in your opinion makes Chekhov's enigma? His universe is not built on recognizable archetypes of Western literature and does not operate with mythological plots and characters, unlike the world of Shakespeare. Yet many playwrights of the twentieth century, mostly after World War II, turned to Chekhov in order to use his stories and say something else, something very personal to them. So, what do you think makes Chekhov's drama and prose attractive for interpretation?

The enigma of Chekhov lies precisely in the fact that there is no real undecipherable enigma that is hidden there, only the illusion of an enigma, at least when one looks for a solution like Oedipus searching for the truth. The only way to approach his universe is through archetypes of the unconscious and an Oedipus-like search for the origin. Isn't that precisely one of the main "recognizable archetypes of Western literature"? So Chekhov does have recourse to Western archetypes, both on the level of the writing and on the thematic level. It's just that they are cunningly masked by a false naturalism that creates the illusion of a complete and diverse world, and because the plays are a part of Russian fin de siècle culture, which is basically immediately transferable to any other family or sociocultural context. What makes these works attractive for present-day playwrights is the impression that anyone could write this play (though less well, to be sure), because they find in it their own existential preoccupations and believe they can try to shape and adapt Chekhov's dramaturgy while at the same time finding or keeping their own voice.

Question 5: You have been living in South Korea for a couple of years now and been working on your own adaptations of Chekhov's plays. Does the change in geographical location and in your cultural context have an impact on your relationship with Chekhov? Does it change your vision of this writer's universe? How in general, do you think, does one's point in time and space influence one's reading of Chekhov's texts? Are they more "reader specific" or "culture specific"?

My relationship to Chekhov changes constantly over time anyway. I prepared the edition of the main plays quite a few years ago; I translated The Cherry Orchard *in collaboration with Elena Pavis-Zahradnikova, but I don't keep up with the scholarly literature, especially since I do not consider myself a "Chekhov scholar." I'm not a Slavist, I'm a theatre specialist. I go and see productions of his plays either because of the expectations aroused by the name of the director or because they are in cultural contexts very different from my own, such as, currently, South Korea, and because I want to see how the director is going to "bring it off." The few productions I have seen in Seoul lead me to believe that they are not so much "culture specific" as they are "reader specific," especially since they seem to be inspired by the theatrical canon and by Western productions as regards the psychological interpretation and by a belief in the play's universality as far as the problematics are concerned. Koreans are fascinated by Chekhov, almost as much as by Shakespeare, and more than by the other classical European playwrights. This is certainly because of the universality you mentioned. I find Koreans' occasional claims about the affinity of Korean and Russian culture highly arguable and unconvincing. The emotionality, the extreme sentiments, and melancholy of the Koreans seem very different. What surprises me even more, but is, by the way, not confined just to Chekhov, is the feeling that one can "chop and change" the play however one wants, adding material to the*

298   *Afterword*

text or making heavy cuts to it and using elements of scenery or costumes or gestures believed to be Korean and thus supposedly making it accessible for a Korean audience (a grave delusion, in my opinion). I have my doubts about the notion of cultural appropriation. This category, which appeared in the 1980s and 1990s, is implicitly normative and even fundamentalist: so appropriation is expropriation? But how can that be avoided when one translates, adapts, or puts on a play? I would prefer another vaguer and more neutral notion: that of cultural transfer, of the use of stereotypes or of supposed local identities to "dress up," embody, and "perform" a foreign text so that readers or audiences might feel themselves on more familiar ground (although that is not always, by the way, what the audience wants, nor is it in itself progress). As for the term "post-colonial," the use of which has been spreading with the growth of "post-colonial studies," it should be reserved for a literature or an artistic practice that truly belong to a context where the country has been culturally or administratively colonized and not just in the sense of economic control. A production may of course situate a play by Chekhov in a post-colonial context and send a critical message by relocating the play in this way, but the play must lend itself to this transfer. I recently (in December 2011) saw a production in Seoul of Three Sisters *situated in Korea during the Japanese colonization (1910–1945). It was difficult to see how this historical configuration corresponded with the problematics of the play which does not, to my knowledge, have anything to do with Japanese colonialism.*

Question 6: Is it Chekhov's dramatic craft or rather the ambiguity of his philosophical position that constitutes Chekhov's enigma?

In my opinion it is better not to frame the question the way Esslin does, in terms of a mutually exclusive opposition between "dramatic craft" and "philosophical position." Chekhov's philosophical position cannot be deduced from the plays: it's ambiguous. It is and remains so thanks to the form of the theatrical text. One should absolutely avoid dividing form and content. In my commentaries on the plays, I tried to focus on the mechanics of writing and dramaturgy and examine how these techniques are skillfully and intentionally adapted to produce ambiguity, inscrutability, atmosphere, melancholy, etc. All these vague concepts can only be elucidated by technically unraveling the stylistic and dramaturgical devices. As soon as one gives up trying to interpret the atmosphere and confusion and focuses on the dramaturgy and stylistics, that is, on the nature of the text, then one can hope to be more precise in the elucidation of the play as a textual, semiotic system, a literary and theatrical work with its rules of the game but also its drawstrings and its tricks.

I agree with the idea that "this adaptation pioneers the creation of new dramatic and performative traditions and expectations" (Esslin 5). I would even go so far as to say that adaptation is part and parcel of the history of drama of the nineteenth and twentieth centuries and of the study of formal inventions in theatrical practice. In fact, one can only understand the changes in the nature of the text by comparison and juxtaposition with scenic practice, whether or not the authors in question were concerned or interested in the staging of their plays. The various rewrites have to take into account this evolution of the stage and the aesthetics of stage production at least as much as, if not more than just the dramaturgical innovations and thematic changes that Chekhov's plays supposedly contain, according to their "rewriters" (I am here drawing on Barthes's distinction between the écrivant, the transitive form of the one who writes in order to act on the world and the écrivain, the intransitive form, meaning the one who writes out of an internal need and without intention and thus creates an artistic work of literary fiction).

Question 7: What particular qualities are there in Chekhov's dramaturgy (themes, dramatic structures, theatrical devices) that allow and invite other writers, including such great playwrights as Tennessee Williams or Brian Friel, to write their own versions of his stories? What role do Chekhov rewrites play in the development of individual dramatists or national dramaturgy? How should we categorize those "rewrites": as translations, adaptations, or in fact "mutations," as the title of this volume proposes?

I do not think that those who "rewrite" Chekhov do so because of the particular qualities of his dramaturgy or his writing, but rather because they desire to explore, imitate, or exploit the themes, images, and possibilities of his plays. It is certainly not in order to write "their own version of his stories." Why would they be interested in retelling the same story in their own words, i.e., making a summary or an adaptation the way a scenarist would adopt a novel for the stage or the cinema. They are more likely attracted by the question or hypothesis of this "enigma" of Chekhov, one might even say that they are fascinated by the enigma and driven by the desire to respond to it in a personal way. This might actually help them to form their identity, although most of the time that identity is already very solid: by "coming up close" to a master like Chekhov they pick up the challenge, give homage, recognize their debt and their admiration. They all take care not to imitate the stylistic devices of their idol: they don't, in general create a pastiche or a travesty or an imitation "in the manner of . . ." and obviously even less a parody. For a contemporary playwright the danger is much greater of being influenced by or becoming a parasite of Chekhov's offspring, for example, in France, of Vinaver, Lagarce, or Minyana, who refer back to Chekhov, sometimes explicitly.

As for knowing whether and how these rewrites influence a country's drama, that would have to be examined on a case-by-case basis. I doubt that the influence would turn out to be decisive. On the other hand, there is no doubt that the style and theatricality of Chekhov have influenced the development of theatre in non-European countries, even to the detriment of local traditions that are just as important, but are driven out.

300 *Afterword*

You ask how one can characterize these "rewrites." They are obviously not translations, even though every translation, even those that claim to be the most "faithful" to the original, cannot help being an adaptation to the target culture. The term "adaptation" seems to be rather unfortunate, for in most cases it is not a question of transforming the original work into another text while keeping the plot, the meaning, or the style. Quite the contrary.

For me the question of adaptation is a false question and the subject is a nonsubject. Adaptation or "rewriting" is not an individual phenomenon, but the general rule: something is always rewritten, as we know from Bakhtin's theory of intertextuality, which was popularized and one might say "adapted" by Kristeva in the 1970s. No writer, and indeed no speaker, can help rewriting or resaying something that came before. Every text adapts and is itself adapted.

Whatever term we choose—adaptation or mutation—I would insist on one point: the staging of a play or of any textual material is by no means an adaptation of the text by the stage. It is the creation of the text, at least of one possible interpretation of the text, a more or less coherent or contradictory, productive, or banal interpretation, one possibility among others and by no means an embodiment or mutation of what existed before that would mutate into a new form. A staging is not a mutation of the dramatic text (or whatever else it might be): it is a qualitative change, not an intratextual or intracultural one; an autonomous new work (independent of the preceding text that is available to be read); a creation that can be approached, appreciated, described, and interpreted in and of itself. In no case is it a "remediation," a term invented by Grusin and Bolton to designate the capture, absorption, and rejection of one medium by another in the historical evolution of technologies and media.

I perceive adaptation as part of a continuum moving gradually from one state to another along a continuous cycle: reading/translation/adaptation/ mutation/supposedly original rewriting/almost original writing/rereading, then back to the beginning: reading, etc.

Between translation and adaptation it is difficult to see which formal criteria, whether textual, dramaturgical, or stylistic one might use to distinguish one from the other. So the only difference might lie in the intention, in the attitude of the translator or adaptor towards the text. One can easily feel intuitively the different intentions: the translator strives to get as close as possible to the source text (while being aware that this goal is an illusory one, since the two can never coincide); the adaptor, by contrast, does not hesitate to stray from it, since his objective is to create a new work that will not feel bound to the source text (although it must be admitted that the two works will remain linked by an intertextual relationship).

Question 8: Why, after publishing your editions of the four plays, did you decide to "rewrite" (or what term should we use?) Chekhov by writing four plays the titles of which borrow at least one word from Chekhov's?

Afterword 301

I couldn't say exactly. Perhaps it was to celebrate the end of the painful ordeal of editing his plays! To amuse myself somewhat and test all that I had learned from the master and in the theatrical milieu. To use the dramatic tricks that I thought I had perceived in his work, to use his material as a trampoline to do and say something else, to receive his blessing before starting off. To mutate, you would no doubt say! There is indeed something of the mutant about me!

Question 9: But how did you get to that point? How did you make the transition from writing a commentary on Chekhov's plays to writing works that were a distant echo of the author?

All over the world apprentice actors have always wanted to "make it" in a scene from Chekhov—usually The Seagull. *In entrance competitions to every drama school from Seoul to New York all one can hear is Chekhov's plays. The results are often fairly academic; the young actors use the scenes to convince others and themselves that they have talent and are able to identify with the characters they feel close to. This fascination with the great scenes is touching and understandable, but sometimes it forces the young actors into stereotypes that block their vision against quite different types of interpretation. It leads them to limit their acting to several tricks borrowed from Stanislavsky, sometimes, alas, via the Actors' Studio, without considering the scene in its entirety and even less the staging. But an isolated scene cannot help being reductive and gives rise to misunderstandings regarding the psychology of reliving and motivation, which is precisely what I want to avoid.*

Despite the dangers, Anton Pavlovich's theatre is a laboratory for the actor and director. My most memorable experience of a workshop was an internship with Sergey Isayev (the former president of the Russian Academy of Theatre Arts, Moscow) and Nikolay Karpov (Russian Academy of Theatre Arts, Moscow). The former analyzed and made us act a scene from Three Sisters *in the Stanislavsky manner, while the second ran a very technical and physical workshop on Meyerhold's biomechanics. Sergey let me run the Michael Chekhov workshop—I had always admired Michael Chekhov's clarity and subtlety, especially concerning the "psychological gesture." I have to say that by contrast the books by Stanislavsky and the mannerisms of his followers had always annoyed and bored me. I did not have the ability to experience the very physical exercises of Meyerhold, but Michael Chekhov seemed to me an unhoped for synthesis of these two trends (let's call them naturalistic and symbolist for short) and moreover allowed me to combine acting technique with an attention to the staging.*

More recently, though not daring to risk working with a scene in the Stanislavsky style the way my late lamented friend Sergey used to do, I have had actors prepare studies of scenes using the study technique as theorized and practiced by Stanislavsky and his follower Anatoly Vasilyev. My "method," if there is one, is to waste as little time as possible reading and analyzing

302   *Afterword*

the text (the way one would with a class of students) and to immediately move to action. First of all, the assignment is to identify and mark out, by acting, the "tochki" or orientation points and the turning points in the scene we are working on, so that the latter will become readable and then visible for both actor and audience, and so that it will embody the interpretation that we are all collectively working to establish, by trying physical actions, images, pauses, and attitudes. This analysis gives a holistic sense of the text, then movement by movement. This analysis of the text as action deploys improvisations based on situations: the actors use their own words, images, and impulsions in the studies. A study reveals and establishes the dramatic composition and the construction of the text as read by the actors and manifested in the directed improvisation. In my own program as a teacher the next stage, for the same group or for a completely different one, is a drifting exercise starting with a theme or an image from the play: each member of the group writes a short scene. Beginning with the material thus obtained, usually a page of text, each in his turn directs the other participants all together or in parallel groups, and they produce a sketch of the staging. The results are compared; one version is chosen or, more often, an assemblage is constructed out of the different proposals.

My own artistic work, come to think of it, consisted, several years later, in inventing (I wouldn't say adapting) a completely different play that retained only some formal elements of Chekhov's original (the name and age of several characters and the initial situation). I am obliged to admit that, like in the series of translation/adaptation/rewrite mentioned above, the transition that takes place is smooth and continual. There is an endless circular drift that ends up by bringing us back to our point of departure: how does one act a short scene from Chekhov?

In the National Conservatory of Dramatic Art in Seoul I have currently (2011–2012) the opportunity of collaborating in my workshop with actors, playwrights, authors, directors, and specialists in children's theatre. I suggested to my group that they either begin their drift using The Cherry Orchard *as point of departure or create their own scenario. I was greatly relieved when they all chose a personal drift and suggested then to stage their own scenario. So, slowly but surely, I have managed to rid myself of the great scene from* The Seagull, *which was as fascinating for my actors and it was frightening for me. I believe that for actors (from Korea or elsewhere) it is always good to separate oneself from one's idol and model to drift to a place where one will end up by rediscovering oneself.*

Question 10: In this collective and personal drift, what do you think you were looking for and what did you find?

When an author is motivated to use another's text as point of departure, to begin drifting from an existing play, it is very often for personal considerations: the need to solve the existential problem of the moment. Chekhov's work is simply an enlarging mirror, a symptom that points the author to his/her own interests and obsessions. Is the exercise helpful in getting to know Chekhov's techniques of writing? Sometimes, to become aware of some properties of his dramaturgy, but more so for observing how other dramaturgies develop in relation to the phenomena of rewriting and intertextuality.

For my play M(o)uettes (Seagulls/Silent Women), *which I wrote and staged in 1997 with a group of students under the European Erasmus exchange program, I wanted to bring out the role of the park and enclosure of a group or a family in a natural setting. I explained this at length in* Degrés.

In the play Mes trois sœurs (My Three Sisters) *I amused myself by imagining how had or could have met three seductive sisters in a country that itself is seductive: Korea. Manuel, the protagonist, had been sent to a sort of prison or penitentiary: a school for mannequins, where he was tasked to teach French using some rather original pedagogical methods . . . What I borrowed from Chekhov was the constellation of the three sisters, their differences in age, vision, and femininity. This observation had formerly seemed to me to be central in his play, and I simply wanted to try it out in my own way in a story of love and confusion from which Manuel could extricate himself only with great difficulty.*

Vania et elle (Him and Her) *allowed me to imagine what had taken place, or could have taken place, between a woman and a man who had missed their chance together as a result of a misunderstanding in their youth and who throughout their entire life from when she was seventeen and he thirty-seven, until she was fifty-seven and he seventy-seven had loved each other and tried in vain to come back together again.*

For Embrassons-nous dans la Cerisaie (Let's Kiss in the Cherry Orchard) *I used the metaphor and the gesture of the* embrassade, *which means both "hug" and "kiss" in French, to illustrate the relations between four characters in the Russian play, in which arrivals and departures, meetings and farewells take place to the rhythm of such embraces. I test the difference between a fraternal, compassionate embrace and an erotic one. This distinction illustrates the difficulty of differentiating the two attitudes, and I use it to show the evolution in human and social relationships between 1968 and the present day by using this practice as a metaphor. In this* Cherry Orchard *I wanted to mark the end result of an experience, the sum of a lifetime at its end: Chekhov's life, his characters', and my own.*

I took these four "rewrites" rather as permission to try my hand at writing by hiding, like a child or a beginner, behind externalities: the form, themes, and identity of another author, whereupon I rejected all these elements in an act of renunciation. Very quickly the inevitable drift of the writing gave me the illusory sensation of flying with my own wings rather than robbing a defenseless author.

(December 2011)
Translated from French by J. Douglas Clayton

304 *Afterword*

WORKS CITED

Esslin, Martin. *The Theatre of the Absurd.* New York: Anchor Books, 1969. Print.

Pavis, Patrice. *Mis tres Hermanas, Mes trois sœurs, My Three Sisters.* Ed. Angel Berenguer. Coleccion Textos/Teatro: Obras 10. Madrid: Ateneo de Madrid, 2007. Print.

———. "M(o)uettes. *La dramaturgie de l'actrice.»* *Degrés : Revue de synthèse à orientation sémiologique* 97–98–99 (1999): 1–55. Print.

———. *Vania y Ella, Vanya et elle, Him and Her.* Ed. Carlos Alba Peinado. Coleccion Textos/Teatro: Obras 12. Madrid: Ateneo de Madrid, 2007. Print.

Contributors

Veronika Ambros is Associate Professor in the Department of Slavic Languages and Literatures and Centre of Comparative literatures, University of Toronto. She is co-editor of *Structuralism(s) Today. Paris, Prague, Tartu* (New York; Ottawa; Toronto: Legas, 2009). Among her numerous articles are studies on semiotics of drama and theatre, Czech cinema and literature, and Czech Surrealism, as well as articles dedicated to the work of Josef and Karel Čapek, and Václav Havel.

Marie-Christine Autant-Mathieu is director of research at CNRS and teaches at Paris III Sorbonne Nouvelle University. She is a theatre historian specializing in Russian and Soviet theatre. Her current research encompasses acting theory (Stanislavsky, Michael Chekhov), artistic communities (the theatre of Lev Dodin), and new dramatic writing in Russia. She has published three monographs: *Le Théâtre soviétique durant le degel* (CNRS Editions, 1993); *Le Théâtre de Boulgakov* (L'Age d'Homme, 2000); and *Stanislavski: La Ligne des actions physiques* (L'Entretemps, 2007). She has also edited several collections and published numerous articles on Russian theatre.

J. Douglas Clayton is Professor Emeritus of Russian at the University of Ottawa, Canada. His research interests include the poetry of Aleksandr Pushkin, Russian modernist theatre, the plays and prose of Anton Chekhov and Franco-Russian cultural relations. His publications include *Ice and Flame: Aleksandr Pushkin's Eugene Onegin* (Toronto U P, 1985); *Pierrot in Petrograd: Commedia dell'arte/Balagan in Twentieth-Century Russian Theatre and Drama* (McGill-Queen's U P, 1994); and *Dimitry's Shade: A Reading of Alexander Pushkin's Boris Godunov* (Northwestern U P, 2004).

Bishnupriya Dutt is a practitioner-researcher and Associate Professor in the School of Arts and Aesthetics, Jawaharlal Nehru University, Delhi, India. She has acted in forty plays and directed five. Her research focuses on colonial and post-colonial theatre in India, feminist readings of Indian theatre, and performative practices and popular culture. Her

306 *Contributors*

recent publications include *Engendering Performance: Indian Performer's Journey in Search of an Identity* (coauthored with Urmimala Sarkar, Sage, 2010) and articles on female actors in India.

Jean Graham-Jones is Professor of Theatre at the City University of New York's Graduate Center, where she currently serves as the executive officer of the PhD Program in Theatre. She is the author of *Exorcising History: Argentine Theater under Dictatorship* (2000) and the translator/editor of *Reason Obscured: Nine Plays by Ricardo Monti* (2004) and *BAiT: Buenos Aires in Translation* (2007). She has published numerous essays in *Theatre Survey, Theatre Journal, Theatre Research International,* and *Latin American Theatre Review,* among others. Graham-Jones's current research focuses on theatrical and extra-theatrical responses to the ongoing socioeconomic crisis in Argentina.

Maria Ignatieva is Associate Professor in the Department of Theatre, Ohio State University in Lima and specializes in Russian theatre history and drama. Previously Ignatieva was Assistant Professor at the Moscow Art Theatre School-Studio in Moscow, Russia. She has over fifty publications on theatre, including her book *Stanislavsky and Female Actors: Women in Stanislavsky's Life and Art* (U P of America, 2008).

Charles Lamb is the former Head of Performing Arts at Bournemouth and Poole College and an Associate Lecturer at the University of Winchester. Of the fifty productions he has directed, many have been by contemporary writers. His association with Howard Barker extends back over twenty years to his production of *Fair Slaughter* at the Quay Theatre in Suffolk. He subsequently directed the premiere production of *Crimes in Hot Countries* and has also staged *The Possibilities and Wounds to the Face* by the same author. He has written a number of articles on contemporary theatre, and is the author of *Howard Barker's Theatre of Seduction* (Harwood Academic, 1997) and *The Theatre of Howard Barker* (Routledge, 2005).

Victoria Pettersen Lantz teaches in the English Department at Gettysburg College. Her research focuses on post-colonial representations in popular culture, in comic books, and on television. In her doctoral work, she studied Mustapha Matura's writing and the nature of post-colonial theatre among diaspora communities. She has contributed essays to *Border-Crossings: Narrative and Demarcation in Postcolonial Literatures* (2012) and *The Literary Angel: Essays on Influences and Traditions Reflected in the Joss Whedon Series* (2010).

Diana Manole is a scholar, writer, and theatre director. Her research focuses on post-colonial and post-communist representations of national identity in English Canadian and Romanian theatre. In her published articles and manuscript in progress, she studies the expression of national identity in post-colonial and post-communist theatre. She has also contributed to several literary anthologies and magazines in Romanian, English, Polish, and German; has published eight books (poems and plays); and has been awarded fourteen literary prizes.

James McKinnon teaches at Victoria University of Wellington, New Zealand. His research focuses on dramatic adaptation and appropriation, particularly contemporary Canadian appropriations of Chekhov and Shakespeare, and on the pedagogical implications of adaptive dramaturgy. He is the coordinator of the Honours Theatre program at Victoria University, and teaches various courses on dramaturgy, modern and classic drama, and performance-based research.

Yana Meerzon is Associate Professor in the Department of Theatre, University of Ottawa. Her research interests are in theatre and drama theory, theatre of exile, and Russian theatre and drama. Her book publications include: *The Path of a Character: Michael Chekhov's Inspired Acting and Theatre Semiotics* (Peter Lang, 2005); *Performance, Exile and "America,"* co-edited with Dr. Silvija Jestrovic, Warwick University (Palgrave, 2009); and *Performing Exile—Performing Self: Drama, Theatre, Film* (Studies in International Performance, Palgrave, 2012).

Yasushi Nagata is Professor of Theatre Studies in the Section of Theatre Studies and Course of Art & Media, Osaka University. He is editor of the *Journal of the Japanese Society for Theatre Studies, International Studies of the Modern Image*, and other Japanese academic journals. He is the author of *The Birth of Modern Theatre and Historiography* (2005), and *Practice and Theory of Modern Acting Method* (2003), and a co-author of *The Age of Avant-Garde* (2001), *The Theory of Japanese Art* (1999), and *The Transformation of European Theatre* (1994). He has published widely in English and Japanese on contemporary Japanese, Russian, and Asian theatres and plays.

Patrice Pavis was previously Professor of Theatre Studies at the University of Paris (1976–2007). He is currently a Professor in the School of Arts at the University of Kent in Canterbury, England. Since 2011 he has been Visiting Professor in the Department of Theatre Studies of the Korea National University of the Arts in Seoul. He published a *Dictionary of Theatre* (translated into thirty languages), and books on performance analysis, contemporary drama and theatre. His most recent book is: *La Mise en scène contemporaine* (Armand Colin, 2007; English translation: *Contemporary Mise en Scene: Staging Theatre Today,* translated by Joel Anderson, forthcoming with Routledge, 2012). His

308   *Contributors*

current research areas include: performance theory; theory and practice of mise–en-scene; intercultural and globalized theatre; contemporary dramatic writing; creative writing and staging; theory of contemporary theatre and performance.

Martine Pelletier, Ph.D. lectures in English and Irish studies at the University of Tours, France. She has published widely on Brian Friel, Field Day, and on contemporary Irish and Northern Irish theatre. She is currently prefacing the French translations of Brian Friel's plays by Alain Delahaye, published by L'avant-scène théâtre, Paris.

Sheila Rabillard is Associate Professor of English, University of Victoria, Canada. She has published numerous articles on modern and contemporary drama and edited the collection *Essays on Caryl Churchill: Contemporary Representations* (1999). She is currently co-editor of a special issue of *Canadian Theatre Review* devoted to ecological drama and is also editing with K. Bamford a collection of essays on performing motherhood in contemporary theatre.

Magda Romanska is an Assistant Professor of Theatre Studies at Emerson College and Head of Theatre Studies and Dramaturgy. From 2001 to 2002, Romanska was an exchange scholar at the Yale School of Drama's Department of Dramaturgy. Her research interests are in Polish drama and theatre. A recipient of Huret Grant and Mellon fellowships, she is the winner of the 2010 Gerald Kahan Scholar's Prize (ASTR). Her forthcoming books include *Theatre and Meaning: The Strange Case of Kantor and Grotowski* (Anthem Press, 2012) and the Palgrave anthology *Comedy: Theory and Criticism* (2012).

Index

A

Abbey Theatre, 189

Abel, Jonathan E., 203, 210

adaptation: as analogy 7, 11, 276, 286, 291, 292; as appropriation, 7, 9, 52, 101, 181, 190, 196, 217, 218, 228, 231, 232, 241, 244, 298; as borrowing, 113–16, 120, 184; as collage, 37, 41, 43, 75, 117, 121; as commentary, 115, 249, 276, 292; as deconstruction, 34, 40, 43, 46, 52, 116, 240, 248, 254; as hybrid, 111, 113, 117, 118–19, 168, 177, 180, 238; as indigenization, 10, 117, 159, 238; as mutation, 5, 7, 8–10, 57, 61, 67, 68–69, 73–74; as palimpsest, 5, 9, 33, 38, 47, 52, 141, 220; as parody, xv, 7, 22, 39, 41, 42, 44, 52, 53n1, 58, 114–115, 117–118, 121–122, 124, 227–30; as pastiche, 7, 52, 82–83, 115, 129–130, 139, 269, 299; as recycling, 19, 41, 115, 117; as reframing, 240, 248; as transformation, 2, 5, 7, 33, 42–43, 46, 52, 63, 68, 92, 104, 111, 113, 116–117, 123, 138, 153, 175, 176, 188, 194, 238, 276; transcultural, 109, 117, 121, 123, 124; as transplantation, 168; as travesty, 7, 9, 52, 115, 129, 130, 229–30, 299; as variation, 5, 7, 39–41, 47, 49, 52, 54n10, 70, 71, 78, 129, 149, 178n3, 238, 240, 241, 291

Actors Studio, 252, 301

Adler, Stella, 252

aesthetics, 2, 72, 203, 210, 212, 276, 288, 291, 292, 299

Akhmatova, Anna, 206

Akunin, Boris, 24, 48, 54n23; *Seagull, The,* 48

Aksenov, Vasily, 54n10

Alexa, Felix, 112

Alexandru Davila Theatre, 113

Allen, Graham, 114

Appia, Adolphe, 9

Auslander, Philip, 246

avant-garde movement, 2, 8, 28, 32, 41, 43, 45, 76, 78, 220, 248, 251, 252, 263, 269

B

Bach, Richard, 63; *Jonathan Livingston Seagull,* 28

balagan, 28–29, 30n10

Bandyopadhyay, Ajitesh, 148–152, 155, 159n6; *Manjari Amer Manjari,* 148–150, 152, 154–155, 157

Barker, Howard, 3, 9, 87–105; *Bite of the Night, The,* 88; *Death, The One and the Art of Theatre,* 102; "Disputing Vanya," 89; *Gertrude—The Cry,* 88; *He Stumbled,* 95; *Knowledge and a Girl: The Snow White Case,* 95; *Seven Lears,* 88, 95; *(Uncle) Vanya,* 87–105

Barbu, Daniel, 121–23

Baudrillard, Jean, 101, 103

Beckett, Samuel, 3, 4, 71, 73, 75, 80, 133, 204, 266, 268, 295; *Waiting for Godot,* 75

Benjamin, Walter, 10, 32, 43, 52, 203, 210, 280

310 *Index*

Bennett, Susan, 222

Betsuyaku, Minoru, 19, 266–68; *Three Sisters in a Thousand Years*, 266, 268

Black Theatre Cooperative (BTC), 162

Bogaev, Oleg, 34, 44; *Dead Ears or a Completely New History of Toilet Paper, The*, 44

Borodyansky, Aleksandr, 277

Bosch, Hieronymus, 113; *Temptation of St. Anthony, The*, 113

Botticelli, Alessandro, 83; *Birth of Venus*, 83

Brathwaite, Edward Kamau, 176

Bratu, Horia, 109, 110

Brecht, Bertolt, 87, 147–148, 154, 159n4, 229, 263, 269, 295–96; *Days of the Commune, The*, 148; *Good Woman of Sechuan, The*, 148; "Short Organum for the Theatre, A," 87; *Threepenny Opera, The*, 148

bricolage, 115–116

Brook, Peter, 30n7, 74

Bruce, Lenny, 254

Bucharest National Theatre (BNT), 109, 125n3

Bulandra Theatre, 110, 111

Bulatov, Erik, 41

Bulgakov, Mikhail, 28, 49, 54n20

bunraku, 269

burlesque, 52, 146, 217

Buzoianu, Cătălina, 110, 111, 112

C

Camarín de las Musas, 206, 209, 213n3

Caragiale, I.L.,113, 116–117, 120, 122–123, 125n7; *Lost Letter, The*, 122, 123, 125n7; *Mr. Leonidas and the Reactionaries*, 121; *Stormy Night, A*, 120, 125n7

carnivalesque, 34, 37, 38, 228, 229, 230

Carlson, Marvin, 114–116, 209, 258

Carnicke, Sharon, 7

Ceauşescu, Nicolae, 109, 110, 112, 125n2; *July Theses*, 110

Césaire, Aimé, 165

Chekhov, Anton, *Bear, The*, 27, 184, 192, 193, 221; "Dreary Story, A", 24; *Cherry Orchard, The*, xiii, 1, 17, 19, 20, 22, 26, 27, 28, 32, 36, 37, 38, 39, 40, 41, 42, 45, 47, 49, 50, 51, 52, 53n8, 66, 72, 75, 80, 81, 82, 83, 84n2, 110–124, 148, 185, 187, 223, 225, 226, 227, 234n11, 242, 250, 261, 265, 270, 297, 302, 303; *Island: A Journey to Sakhalin, The*, 169, 283; *Ivanov*, 32, 40, 42, 46, 66, 74, 76–77, 80, 81, 111, 261; *Jubilee*, 261; "Lady With the Little Dog," 17, 180, 184, 193–194; *Marriage Proposal, The*, 27, 125n3, 221, 261; "On the Road," 17; *Platonov*, 217; *Seagull, The*, xviii, 20, 22–25, 33, 39, 40, 42, 43–44, 45, 46, 48, 52, 54n10, 58–67, 74, 76, 91, 110, 111, 119, 184; *Swansong, The*, 19; *Three Sisters*, 20, 22, 34–36, 38, 40, 42, 49, 50, 51, 52, 53n8, 66, 73, 75, 77, 78, 79, 80, 109, 110, 111, 112, 119, 129–133, 136, 156, 161–167, 173–177, 180–184, 186, 187–190, 191, 192, 195, 203, 217, 227–231, 238–256, 261, 264, 268–270, 298, 301, 303; *Uncle Vanya*, 18, 20, 22, 30n6, 32, 40, 42, 36, 49, 50–51, 53n8, 87–105, 111, 118–121, 118–119, 120–121, 124, 132, 156, 180–181, 183, 185, 190–195, 203, 217, 221, 223, 232, 261, 270; "Unsuccessful Visit, An," 17; "Ward Number Six," 28, 277, 281–286; *Wedding, The*, 22, 27, 29; *Wood Demon, The*, 20, 89, 92

Chekhov International Theatre Festival, 29, 32, 204

chernukha, 34, 278

Chudakov, Aleksandr, 17, 53n9

Citadel Theatre, Edmonton, Canada, 221

Clayton, J. Douglas, 217, 219–220, 228, 233n7

Cluj Hungarian Theatre, 110, 111

Coetzee, J.M., 165

Comedy of Manners, 40, 90, 265

Communism, 2, 40, 41, 109, 110, 114, 122, 123, 124, 128, 135, 136, 138, 140

Communist Party of India, 148, 159n5

Congreve, William, 90

Index 311

Corneille, Pierre, 296
Cossa, Roberta Mario, 205
counter-canon, 163–165, 178
counter-discourse, 9, 164, 166,
167–168, 174, 177,
Cowgirl Opera, 227
Craig, Gordon, 9, 37

D

Dali, Salvador, 113
Darie, Alexandru, 111
deconstruction, 34, 40, 43, 46, 52,
116, 240, 248, 254
defamiliarization, 41
Defoe, Daniel, 165, 166; *Robinson
Crusoe*, 165, 178n4
Dell, Frank, 241, 254; *Temptation of
Saint Antony, The*, 241
Diamond, Elin, 147, 243
documentary film, 41, 132, 133,
135, 140, 240, 241, 243, 244,
256–257n7, 277–280, 287–290,
292
documentary theatre, 46, 279
Dogma 95, 291n2
Doležel, Lubomir, 5
Dostoyevsky, Fyodor, 41, 46, 89,
125n1, 223, 232, 234n13, 274,
275, 282
Dvořák, Antonín, 83; *Rusalka*, 83

E

Eco, Umberto, 1, 9
Eliot, T.S., 241; *Cocktail Party, The*,
241
Elam, Keir, 69
Esslin, Martin, 4, 25–26, 84n10, 298
estrangement, 15
Euripides, 183; *Hyppolytus*, 183

F

Field Day Theatre Company, 180, 183,
186, 190
Flaubert, Gustave, 80–81, 224, 241;
Tentation de saint Antoine, La,
241
Free Theatre, 261
French, David, 220
Frič, Martin, 72; *Bear,The*, 72; *Tears
the World Can't See*, 72
Friel, Brian, 3, 4, 9, 125n6, 180–199,
299; *Afterplay*, 125n6, 180, 181,
192–196; *Aristocrats*, 182; *Communication Cord, The*, 186, 188;

Dancing at Lughnasa, 181, 183,
186, 194, 195; *Faith Healer*, 181,
195, 196; *Home Place, The*, 180,
184–185; *Living Quarters*, 181,
183, 195; *Philadelphia, Here
I Come!* 180, 181–182, 185;
Three Plays After, 180, 181, 184,
192–193, 195; *Translations*, 181,
183, 187–188, 193, 197n5; *Yalta
Game, The*, 180, 184, 192–193,
196
Frye, Northrop, 20–23
Fuchs, Elinor, xvii, 4, 19, 116
Fuchs, Georg, 19

G

Gabor, Tompa, 111
Gandhi, Indira, 148, 151, 153
Gandhi, Mahatma, 153
Gârbea, Horia, 1, 111–124; *Cleopa-
tra the Seventh*, 112; *Madame
Bovary Are the Others*, 112;
*Seagull from the Cherry
Orchard, The*, xi, xii, 112–124;
Who Killed Marx? 112
Gavrilova, Marina, 40; *Three Sisters
and Uncle Vanya*, 40
Gay, John, 40; *Beggar's Opera, The*,
40
Geinin, 240–246, 250, 252, 254, 255,
256n7, 257n10, 257n13
Genet, Jean, 203; *Maids, The*, 203,
208
Genette, Gérard, 8, 10, 33, 38, 47, 52,
53, 114, 115, 220
Ghelerter, Moni, 109
Gilbert, Helen, 167–168, 172, 174,
175, 176
Gilman, Richard, 23
Ginkas, Kama, 52
Gogol, Nikolay, 38, 41, 45, 83, 119,
125n1, 184, 296
Gorky, Maxim, 146
Glińska, Agnieszka, 130, 137, 141
Glowacki, Janusz, xi, 1, 128–142;
Antigone in New York, 128,
129–130; *Cinders*, 133; *Fort-
inbras Gets Drunk*, 128, 130;
Fourth Sister, The, xi, 128–142;
Hunting Cockroaches, 128, 133
Gramsci, Antonio, 146
Gremina, Elena, 32, 33, 34, 64–47;
Ch. Brothers: Scenes, The, 46;
Sakhalin Wife, The, 46

312 *Index*

grotesque, 27, 28, 38, 44, 82, 132, 133,136,141, 207, 217, 227, 229
Grotowski, Jerzy, 254, 258n18
Guha, Ranajit, 150, 157–158
Guthrie, Tyrone, 182, 184, 187

H

Harag, György, 110
Hare, David, 3
Hauptmann, Gerhart, 32, 64; *Lonely Lives*, 64
Havel, Vacláv, 3, 9, 68, 71, 78, 80–83; *Garden Party, The*, 71; *Leaving*, 71; *Mountain Hotel, The*, 71, 81, 83
Heaney, Seamus, 184, 185, 190
Hemingway, Ernest, 275
Hen, Józef, 136; *Lovers' Afternoon*, 136
Hirotsu, Kazuo, 261
Hitchcock, Alfred, 63; *Birds, The*, 63
Hoffmann, E.T.A., 204
Houth, Eduardo, 87
Hrubín, František, 68, 72, 73, 74; *Sunday in August, A/The*, 68, 72, 73
Hugo, Victor, 38; *Misérables, Les*, 38
Hutcheon, Linda, xv, 2, 4, 5, 8, 9, 10, 113, 114, 117, 128, 129, 141, 142, 163, 164, 177, 217, 234n10, 238, 240, 248, 249, 276, 292
hypertext, 33, 115, 116, 117, 124

I

Ibsen, Henrik, 3, 32, 80, 90, 113, 116, 119, 121, 145, 146, 147, 155, 159n3, 262, 269, 270; *Doll's House, A*, 3, 119, 147; *Enemy of the People, An*, 159n3; *Ghosts*, 159n3
imperialism, 2, 165, 166, 174, 266
Impressionism, 19, 276
Indian People's Theatre Association, 148, 159n5
Ingarden, Roman, 69, 83
Inoue, Hisashi, 250
intertextuality, 6, 7, 33, 41, 114, 300, 303
intermedial transposition, 10
intramedial transposition, 8, 9
Institute of Theatrical and Cinematographic Arts (IATC), 111
Ionesco, Eugène, 73
in-yer-face theatre, 9, 278

Iskrenko, Nina, 33, 34, 44–45, 52; *Has the Cherry Orchard been sold?* 45
Ito, Rokuro, 261

J

Jakobson, Roman, 82
Jarry, Alfred, 204, 228; *Ubu Roi*, 137, 228

K

Kabuki theatre, 257n10, 268, 269
Kafka, Franz, 204, 269; "In the Penal Colony," 269
Kantor, Tadeusz, 140
Kartun, Maurico, 205
Kennelly, Brendan, 190
Kharms, Daniil, 29; *Yelizaveta Bam*, 29
Kheifits, Iosif, 17
Kilroy, Thomas, 184, 188, 189, 190
Kisaragi, Koharu, 263; *Moral*, 263
Kishida, Kunio, 262; *Hotel Ushiyama*, 262
Knowles, Ric, 233n5, 235, 248, 252
Kohler, Anna, 244, 245
Kokoro-za Theatre, 269
Kolyada, Nikolay, 33, 34, 37–40, 52; *Oginski's Polonaise*, 38, 52
Komissarzhevskaya, Vera, 23
Krejča, Otomar, 70, 71, 73, 74, 75, 76, 78, 81, 82, 83
Kristeva, Julia, 2, 8, 10, 83, 300
Kohout, Pavel, 72, 73; *Third Sister, The*, 72
Kostenko, Konstantin, 33, 34, 43–44; *Seagull by A.P. Chekhov, The*, 43
Koyama, Yushi, 263; *Ball for Only the Two of Us, A*, 263
Krymov, Dmitry, 32; *Ta-ra-ra-boom-de-ay*, 32
Kubo, Sakae, 263; *Dairy of Apple Fields, A*, 263
Kundera, Milan, 71, 78, 79; *Owner of the Keys, The*, 71, 79
Kusuyama, Masao, 261

L

Lamming, George, 165
Lapushin, Radislav, 11, 276, 281, 282
Lashinsky, Karen, 244, 245
LeCompte, Elizabeth, 239–241, 244–247, 249–255, 256n2, 258n18

Index 313

Lepage, Robert, 233n1; *Elsinore*, 233n1
Lermontov, Mikhail, 41, 206
Levanov, Vadim, 47; *Apocalypse of Firs, The*, 47; *Death of Firs, The*, 47
Lévi-Strauss, Claude, 115, 116
Levý, Jiří, 5, 6
Lewis, C.S., 178n3; *Till We Have Faces*, 17n3
Lo, Jacqueline, 167
Lotman, Yury, 57, 58, 59, 61, 62, 279, 280, 288
Lukacs, Georg, 146
Lyotard, Jean-François, 91, 92, 280

M

MacDonald, Anne-Marie, 232n1; *Goodnight Desdemona (Good Morning Juliet)*, 232–233n1
Machiavelli, Niccolo, 120
Maeterlinck, Maurice, 30, 269
Magarshack, David, 23, 58
Mahon, Derek, 190
Makino, Nozo, 264; *Supreme Existence*, 264
Malevich, Kazimir, 53n2
Mamet, David, 3, 203
Manhattan Theatre Club, 133
Mastroianni, Marcello, 277
Maraden, Marti, 225, 227, 234n18
Markham, Pigmeat, 254
marxism, 87, 153, 255
Masamune, Hakucho 261, 262
Matsuda, Masataka 263, 269, 270; *On the Summer Sand* 263; *Waiting for the Moon* 269
Matura, Mustapha, 1, 161–178; *As Time Goes By*, 162, 174; *Coup, The*, 162; *Meetings*, 162; *Playboy of the West Indies*, 162,166, 172, 175; *Play Mas*, 162; *Three Sisters: After Chekhov*, 161, 162–163, 166, 168–177; *Welcome Home Jacko*, 162
Mayakovsky, Vladimir, 28, 29; *Bathhouse, The*, 28; *Bedbug, The*, 29; "Two Chekhovs, The," 29
Mayama, Seika, 269
McGuinness, Frank, 190
Meiji, Era, 266
melodrama, 8, 90, 133, 141, 146, 147, 155, 227, 281
Merezhko, Viktor, 54n25

metadrama, 33, 225
metatextuality, 33
metatheatre, 28
method acting, 90, 252, 253, 254
Meyerhold, Vsevolod, 28, 29, 52, 54n19, 301; "Balagan, The," 28
Middleton, Thomas, 87; *Women Beware Women*, 87
migrant theatre, 167, 176
Mikhalkov, Nikita, 277; *Dark Eyes*, 277
Miller, Arthur, 3, 72, 146, 241, 248, 249; *Crucible, The*, 241, 249
Mishima, Yukio, 269, 270; *Modern Noh Collection, The*, 269
Molière, Jean-Baptiste, 113,118, 258; *School for Wives, The*, 118
Moscow Art Theatre, 219, 261, 262, 272n1
Moscow Film Festival, 277
Mrożek, Sławomir, 84n10, 136; *Love in the Crimea*, 136
Mugur, Vlad, 110
Mukařovský, Jan, 6, 39, 73, 81, 292–293
Müller, Heiner, 204; *Hamletmachine*, 204
Murphy, Tom, 190
Murrell, John, 220

N

Nagai, Ai, 264, 266; *Brother Comes Home*, 264; *Daddy's Democracy*, 264; *Men Who Want to Force People to Sing, The*, 264; *Three Sisters of the Hagi Family*, 264–266
Nandikar, 148–149, 159n6
National Arts Centre (NAC), Ottawa, Canada, 217
National Theatre: Athens, 131; Bratislava, 131; Bucharest, 110, 125n3; Canada's "national" theatre, 233n3; Craiova, Romania, 111; Iaşi, Romania, 110; London, 132; Novi Sad, Serbia, 131; Prague, 76; "Radu Stanca" Sibiu, Romania, 111
naturalism, 8, 18, 36, 90, 91,104, 132, 146, 245, 253, 276, 278, 279
naxalbari movement, 150
Negri, Antonio, 239, 255, 256; *Labor of Job, The*, 255
Nehru, Jawaharlal, 148, 153
neo-avant-garde movement, 41

314 Index

New Comedy, 22–23, 27
New Economic Policy, (NEP) 29
"New Wave," Russia, 34, 36, 54n12
Nihon-Buyo, 269
Nitosha, 264
Noh Theatre, 245, 256n6, 257n10, 269–271
Nutting, Kristine, 227–232; *Three Sisters: A Black Opera in Three Acts* 227–231

O

Oberiuty, 41
O'Brien, George, 189
O'Brien, Michael, 233n1; *Mad Boy Chronicle*, 233n1
Odets, Clifford, 146
Offenbach, Jacques, 19; *Belle Hélène, La*, 19
Oishi, Shizuka, 264
Okamoto, Kido, 269
Old Vic, 187
Olivier, Claude, 74
Olivier, Laurence, 77
O'Neill, Eugene, 241, 248; *Emperor Jones*, 241, 256n2; *Hairy Ape, The*, 241; *Long Day's Journey into Night*, 241
Osanai, Kaoru, 261–262
Osofisan, Femi, 165
Ostrovsky, Alexander, 45
Ota, Shogo, 269; *Biography of Komachi, A*, 269; *Water Station, A*, 269
Ottawa Fringe Festival, 217

P

Pankov, Vladimir, 32; *Marriage, The*, 32
Papp, Joseph, 250
paratext, 11, 33, 235, 276
Pavis, Patrice, xvii, 6, 11, 295–303
Paulin, Tom, 190
Penn, Arthur, 133
perestroika, 23, 33
Performing Garage, 242, 251, 257n13, 258
Periférico de Objetos, 203–205
Petrushevskaya, Ludmila, 9, 34–36, 52; *Three Girls in Blue*, 34–35, 52
Piao, Lin, 146
Pinte, Gavriil, 113
Pinter, Harold, 3, 73

Pirandello, Luigi, 4, 116, 159n6; *Six Characters in Search of an Author*, 116
Pogrebnichko, Yury, 52
Polish Television Theatre, xi, 130
Positivism, 18
Post-colonial(ism), 3, 7, 9, 117, 146, 147, 150, 152, 154, 156, 157, 159, 162–165, 167–172, 174, 175, 177, 180, 181, 188, 218, 298
Postmodern(ism), 2, 7, 33, 34, 40–43, 52, 54n13, 58, 111, 112, 114–117, 118, 123, 124
Prague School (Prague Linguistic Circle), 68, 69, 84n11
Priestley, J.B., 159n6
Prigov, Dmitry, 33, 41
Progressive Amateur Theatre Movement, 147
Public Theatre, 250
Pushkin, Aleksandr, 41, 51, 120, 125n1

Q

Quick, Andrew, 239, 240, 243–245, 248, 250–253, 255, 256n2, 257n3

R

Racine, Jean, 241; *Phèdre*, 241
Radio Romania, 113
Razumovskaya, Lyudmila, 34, 40, 54n12; *French Passions in a Dacha near Moscow*, 40
Realism, 3, 8, 10, 18, 28, 29, 115, 132, 168, 219, 228, 250, 271, 289; Critical, 18, 28; neo-, 278; Psychological, 18, 28, 145, 221, 228, 229; Socialist, 29, 34, 71, 72–73, 78, 109, 110, 125n4, 278
relational aesthetics, 210
relationality, 10, 203, 204, 210, 214n18
Regina Maria Theatre, 125n3
re-mediation, 9, 10
Revista Teatrul, 110
Rhys, Jean, 165
Rinkogun Theatre Group, 269
River Arts Repertory Company, 133
Romanian Communist Party, 125n2
Romanticism, 28, 115, 252
Ryan, Marie-Laure, 5
Ryo, Iwamatsu, 250

Index 315

S

Sadova, Marietta, 110
Said, Edward, 164, 165, 195, 238
Sakate, Yoji, 269; *The Contemporary Noh Collection*, 269; *"Three Sisters" That Was Not Performed*, 270
Sacker, Elion, 244, 245
San Martín Municipal Theatre, 205
Sanders, Julie, 3, 4, 7, 8, 248
Savran, David, 239, 248, 249
Scena Kameralna, Wroclaw, 130
Schechner, Richard, 241, 254, 258n18
Schmidt, Paul, 252, 253, 255
Sears, Djanet 233n1; *Harlem Duet*, 233n1
Selvon, Samuel, 165
Sen, Koushik, 1, 156
Senelick, Laurence, 3, 4, 7, 163, 171, 176, 252, 253, 258n17
Senuma, Kayo, 261; *Moon and People, The*, 261
Şerban, Andrei, 111, 250
Serebrennikov, Kirill, 33
Shakespeare, William, 1, 3, 83, 88, 109, 111, 116, 118, 130, 146, 165, 167, 174, 189, 217, 218, 219, 220, 222, 223, 228, 232, 235, 258, 269, 285, 295, 296, 287; *Hamlet*, 19, 88, 118, 128, 131, 204, 287, 296; *King Lear*, 82, 83, 88; *Othello*, 19, 235; *Romeo and Juliet*, 74; *Tempest, The*, 165, 178n4
Shakhnazarov, Karen, 274–292; *Assassin of the Tsar*, 277–278; *Vanished Empire*,292; *Ward No.6*, 10, 274–292; *Jazzmen*, 292; *Winter Evening in Gagry*, 292; *Zero City*, 292
Shaw, Bernard, 3, 167, 217
Shaw, Helen, 207
Shaw Festival, 233n2
Sherman, Jason, 223–227, 231, 233n4; *After the Orchard*, 218, 223–227, 231
shestidesiatniki, 34
Shevtsova, Maria, 254
Shiki Theatre Company, 250
Slapovsky, Aleksey, 34, 40; *My Little Cherry Orchard*, 39
Slavkin, Viktor, 33, 34, 36–37, 52, 53n8; *The Hoop*, 36–37, 52
Smith, Peyton, 244

Sophocles, 128, 130
Sorokin, Vladimir, 33, 34, 41–44, 52; *The Jubilee*, 41–43
Soulpepper, 217, 233n2
Soviet Union (USSR), 32, 34, 38, 39, 41, 51, 121, 125n4, 148
post-Soviet(ism), 33, 38, 48, 52, 54n13
Soviet repertoire, 33
Soyinka, Wole, 165
Šrámek, Fráňa, 70; *Summer, The*, 70
Stalin, Josef, 34, 117
Stalin Prize, 50
Stam, Robert, 5
Stanislavsky, Konstantin (Stanislavskian), 61, 71, 89, 90, 91, 112, 146, 203, 204, 227, 239, 245, 252, 253, 254, 258n18, 261, 262, 301
Stein, Gertrude, 241, 252; *Dr. Faustus Lights the Lights*, 241
Steiner, George, 187
Stoppard, Tom, 3, 19, 178n3; *Rosencrantz and Guildenstern are Dead*, 19, 178n3
Strasberg, Lee, 252, 253
Stratford Festival, 217, 219, 220, 233n2
Strehler, Georgio, 26
Strindberg, August, 32
subtext, 36, 53n2, 64, 65, 67, 185, 206, 240
surrealism, surrealist(ic), 132, 141, 263, 277, 279, 280, 288, 292
Suzuki, David, 222, 234n12
Suzuki, Tadashi, 250, 269; *On the Dramatic Passions*, 269
Svoboda, Josef, 75–79, 81, 82
symbolism, 8, 18, 62, 276, 285, 288
Synge, J.M., 162, 174; *Playboy of the Western World, The*, 162
Szondi, Peter, 71, 73, 77, 79, 81, 88, 102

T

Tagore, Rabindranath, 152, 159
Tanabata Star Festival, 267
Târgu-Mureş State Theatre, 110
Teatr Powszechny, 130
Teatr.Doc., 33
Teatro del Artefacto, 214n6
Tenkei Theatre, 269
Terayama, Shuji, 263; *Lemming*, 263
Théâtre des Nations International Festival, 74
Théâtre Silvia Montfort, Le, 131

316 *Index*

theatre of the absurd, 8, 49, 72, 84
Theatre Smith-Gilmour, 217, 233n2
Thiessen, Vern, 233n1; *Shakespeare's Will*, 233n1
Tiffin, Helen, 9, 109, 164, 166, 168, 177
Tolstoy, Aleksey, 55
Tolstoy, Leo, 9, 18, 41, 58, 125, 274
Tompkins, Joanne, 172, 174, 175, 233n5
Topol, Josef, 68, 71–74, 78, 79; *Their Day*, 4, 72; *End of the Carnival, The*, 71, 78, 79
transcoding, 10, 128, 129
Trier, Lars von, 291n1

U

Uchimura, Naoya, 262; *Copsewood*, 262
Ugarov, Mikhail, 33, 53n2,
Ulitskaya, Lyudmila, 34, 50, 52; *Russian Jam*, 50
Ulmu, Bodgan, 113
USSR. *See* Soviet Union.

V

Valk, Kate, 239, 240, 245, 246, 249–251, 254
Vanden Heuvel, Michael, 248
Varodi, Matei, 113
Vawter, Ron, 239, 241, 244, 245, 251, 254
velvet revolution, 83
verbatim, 10, 26, 68, 274, 277, 278, 279, 287, 289
Veronese, Daniel, 1, 203–212, 213n1; *Cámara Gesell*, 204, *Circo Negro*, 204; *Crónica de la caída de uno de los hombres de ella*, 205; *Espia a una mujer que se mata (Spies on a Woman Killing Herself)*, 203, 207, 208, 210, 212, 213nn3–4; *Mujeres soñaron caballos (Women Dreamt Horses)*, 203, 210–212; "Proyecto Chéjov," 203, 205, 212; *Un hombre que se ahoga (A Drowning Man)*, 203, 205–208, 212–212, 213nn3–4
Victor Ion Popa Theatre, 113
Vineyard Theatre, 131, 133
Visarion, Alexa, 111
Vişniec, Matei, 111, 112; *Chekhov Machinery, The*, 111, *Nina or The Fragility of Stuffed Seagulls*, 112

Vodička, Felix, 5, 6, 68–70, 72, 84n4; actualization, 68–70, 74, 79, 83, 84nn4–5; concretization, 2, 5–7, 68–74, 78, 82, 83; literary history, 68–70
Vysotsky, Vladimir, 275
Vyrypayev, Ivan, 32

W

Wagner, Geoffrey, 7, 11, 276, 291, 292
Wajda, Andrzej, 128; *Hunting Flies*, 128
Walcott, Derek, 165, 171,
Waseda Little Theatre, 269
Weems, Marianne,
Wilde, Oscar, 65, 90
Wilder, Thornton, 241, 248; *Our Town*, 241
Williams, Tennessee, 3, 4, 9, 57–61, 63–67, 269, 299; *Cat on a Hot Tin Roof*, 59; *Glass Menagerie, The*, 59, 60; *Notebook of Trigorin, The*, 57–61, 65–67; *Streetcar Named Desire, A*, 59
Witkowski, Andrzej, 130
Wojtyszko, Maciej, 136; *Semiramida*, 136
Wood, Tom, 221–225, 230, 231, 233n4, 234n12
Wooster Group, The, 238–256; *Brace Up!* 238–256; *Fish Story*, 238–256; *LSD . . . Just the High Points . . .*, 243
Wrestling School, The, 88

Y

Yagi, Ryuichiro, 262; *Daughter of the Lake, The*, 262
Yu, Miri, 264; *Fish Festival*, 264
Yukhananov, Boris, 52; MIR group, 52, 264; *Cherry Orchard Sketches, The*, 52

Z

Zabaluyev, Vladimir, 34, 48, 52; *Cherries Have Ripened in Uncle Vanya's Garden, The*, 48, 52, 54n24
Zakharov, Mark, 34
Zenshin-za Theatre, 269
Zenzinov, Aleksei, 34, 48, 52
Zholdak, Andrei, 52
Zooedipous, 204